The Creative Generalist

The Creative Generalist:
A Guide to Social Work Practice

Michael Heus & Allen Pincus

Micamar Publishing
Barneveld, Wisconsin

Library of Congress Catalog Card No. 86-61308.

ISBN: 0-937373-00-1

Printing: 9 8 7 6 5 4 3 2 1 Year: 93 92 91 90 89 88 87 86

Printed in the United States of America.

Acknowledgments

Our sincere thanks to those who helped in the preparation of this book. John and Karen Stremikis played a key role in its design and production. They are indeed creative generalists in the world of computers and publishing. Anne Minahan, John O'Neill and Al Feist helped by reviewing our manuscript. Harvey Dahl served as technical advisor on printing.

As expected, we thank our families for moral support throughout the long and, at times, tedious process of writing. They contributed in other important ways which deserve recognition. Marilyn Heus helped with typing and correspondence. Greg and Jeff Heus designed many of the graphics. Judy Pincus did technical editing. Ellie and Mike Pincus gave useful feedback on the chapters.

Many other colleagues, students and friends, though not directly involved with the book, contributed to our ideas along the way. Especially notable in this regard are Judy Borree, Bob Hatmaker, Lorraine Davis, Ann Lynaugh, Eileen Riley and Bruce Pamperin.

Contents

Part I
mindset

When we use the term "generalist" we are referring to a *way of thinking* and a *way of doing*. This is why you'll typically hear references to the generalist *perspective* (way of thinking) or the generalist *approach* (way of doing).

Allen and I believe this essential thinking-doing relationship is captured in the term *"mindset"* with an additional and important emphasis.

We have learned much about "mind" in the past decade. We have new understandings that enrich our capacity to solve problems. We need these new understandings because our society is currently undergoing some very fundamental changes. We are in an important period of transition and will have many opportunities in our daily work to guide the drift of our culture in a direction we value. It is critical, then, that we heighten our readiness to *make things happen*. The "set" of "mindset" reminds us that with strong conviction, creativity, optimism and skill we could, individually and collectively, direct our problem-solving efforts toward a vision of a better world.

Join us in the following chapters as we explore this mindset of the *creative generalist*.

CHAPTER ONE: HOW WE GOT WHERE WE ARE

With an eye to the journey ahead, Allen and I team up in this chapter to get our bearings. We take a brief look back to highlight the historical period in which generalist social work emerged and trace its development to the challenges that now confront us. We also explain why we are writing this book and why we believe it is time for generalist practice to take another step in its development, time for the generalist to become a *creative generalist*.

CHAPTER TWO: THE NATURE OF SOCIAL WORK PRACTICE

Here Allen helps develop the meaning of the creative generalist mindset by clarifying important choices in how we view a diverse social work practice and how our actions reflect the view we hold. He also presents a way to understand the nature of social work and emphasizes the importance of our own personalized, individual definitions.

CHAPTER THREE: SOCIAL WORK VALUES

In this chapter I invite you to explore the beliefs our profession considers important. I sort out several of the key differences between values and ethics and with the creative generalist mindset begin to sketch an important but missing element in social work values, *vision*.

CHAPTER FOUR: VOCATIONAL STYLE

For creative generalists there is more to practice than thinking and doing like a social worker. They are professionals with a sense of *vocation*. In this chapter I show you some of the differences between profession and vocation and encourage you to express your values, vision and vocation in something I call *vocational style*.

CHAPTER FIVE: CREATIVITY AND THE CREATIVE GENERALIST

Here I explore the *creative* side of the creative generalist. I highlight key aspects of the phenomenon we call creativity and develop a basis for understanding the *tools* of a creative generalist presented in Part II of this book.

How we got where we are

1

The trail that led to the writing of this book began in the late Sixties when societal needs and conditions gave rise to the generalist perspective in social work. Through a brief retracing of that trail we will be able to show you how we can adapt the generalist perspective to be more responsive to a current and very different society.

THE EMERGENCE OF THE GENERALIST PERSPECTIVE

Our memories of the 1960s are filled with images of erupting energies and sharp contrasts: civil rights, turmoil, assassination, flower children, demonstrations, Vietnam, LSD, Kent State, communes, "Great Society," Woodstock, "War on Poverty." Values were challenged in passion and violence. Our beliefs about family, race, class, education, welfare and the "good life" were questioned in a press for relevance and human rights. Bob Dylan sang, *"The Times They Are a Changin'."*

The "War on Poverty" and "Great Society" renewed the spirit of advocacy and commitment to social reform in the profession. To use a popular phrase of the day, people were asking whether social work was "part of the solution or part of the problem." There was mounting pressure for the profession to reexamine its methods and mission and become more relevant and responsive to social problems such as poverty and racism. Criticisms of social work practice centered on two key points:

— Practitioners were making problems and clients fit their methods and techniques rather than the other way around.

— Practice models were too narrowly focused on the treatment of the individual, neglecting the broader environmental factors contributing to the problem.

The struggle over the question of relevance was compounded by another issue. Stemming from different roots (Settlement Houses and Charity Organization Societies) and developing in diverse settings, social work lacked a coherent sense of professional identity. Prior to 1955, when the National Association of Social Workers was formed, seven separate organizations represented the interests of different groups of social workers. In spite of the existence of a single professional association, social work remained fragmented by method (casework, group work, and community organization), fields of practice (e.g., medical social work, child welfare, corrections) and divided purposes (e.g., individual change versus environmental change, service versus reform).

With mounting pressures social work was ready for change, open to new perceptions. In searching for ways to approach the problems of the profession, social workers were attracted to general systems theory and models of planned change. Drawing from this body of knowledge, a new direction was set in the development of social work practice:

— Systems theory and the concept of interdependence helped bridge the person vs. environment dichotomy. Social work now emphasized its focus on the interaction of people *and* their environment. It reaffirmed its commitment to cause *and* service.

— Social work practice was conceptualized as planned change, a rational, goal-directed process of problem solving. Terms describing the process, such as assessment, planning, implementation and evaluation, replaced the more clinical sounding "study, diagnosis and treatment."

— Certain tasks (e.g., data collection, contracting, forming action systems) were identified as central to the practice of social work, regardless of the setting or system size (individual, family, group, organization, community).

— Practitioners began adopting a variety of roles (e.g., enabler, teacher, broker, advocate) and working with different system sizes to make their methods more responsive to problems.

— A broad systems view of the client's situation led to recognizing the many factors that interact to maintain a problem (multicausality). The client was no longer automatically assumed to be the appropriate "target" of change.

During this period, Allen and his colleague Anne Minahan were developing these ideas through an "integrated methods" course they were co-teaching at the University of Wisconsin. Class handouts evolved into papers presented at meetings, culminating in 1973 with the publication of their book, *Social Work Practice: Model and Method.*[1]

This book consolidated the various ideas and developments growing out of the Sixties and set a pattern for teaching introductory methods courses over the following decade. The approach taken by the book became known as the "generalist approach" or "generalist perspective." A concern with broad perspectives, connecting and integrating parts to achieve a new sense of the whole, flexibility and diversity seemed to fit the notion of a generalist.

LINGERING QUESTIONS

Throughout the next decade the generalist perspective remained a dominant and debated idea. Systems theory had helped the profession conceptualize a perspective on the overall nature of social work. The contributions of this perspective to unifying a disparate profession were widely recognized, but answers always have a way of leading to more questions.

While a broad systems perspective encompassed the diversities of the profession, it was difficult to apply this perspective in the activities of day-to-day practice. What are the boundaries of a given problem circumstance? If everything is connected to everything else, how do we sort out and justify what needs doing in what situations? How can broad understandings be converted to practical interventions?

The generalist perspective increased the breadth of our understanding of people and problems but fell short of offering specific ways to deal with the complexities involved. How do practitioners cope with the increased complexity, the uncertainties and frustrations? How do they develop alternative strategies and solutions responsive to the unique patterns of interconnected relationships revealed with systems thinking?

Some of the questions raised were more concerned with career development. Is a generalist practitioner a jack-of-all-trades and master-of-none or a BA-level worker? Can a generalist specialize?

Mike was already beginning to address these questions while Allen and Anne were completing their book. When he left a teaching position in California to join the Wisconsin faculty in 1971, he brought a different path of study to contribute to a developing generalist perspective.

He believed that, while the generalist perspective helped social work comprehend and map out a diverse profession, the full potentials of this perspective would not be realized until we sharpened our focus on *problems* and *problem solving*. Systems theory bridged major divisions in the profession but we would next need to turn our attention to the place where perspective converts to action, where practitioners face the complexities of their daily work. It was here that we needed to work through another kind of division, one found in our struggles with the art and science of social work practice.

Unquestionably, the scientific method had contributed much to making our services more effective and efficient. It also increased the credibility of social work as a profession. But effective, imaginative and resourceful problem solving requires more than science. We needed to further understand the *art* side of practice.

Mike was convinced that we could integrate our science and art with the help of an extensive and growing body of knowledge in the interdisciplinary field of *creativity*. Research and conceptual development in this field had, like social work, incorporated systems theory. But it also had a strong emphasis on applying systems thinking to the problem-solving process.

Because of his convictions, Mike aligned his research, coursework and the development of a school social work field placement in the direction of creativity and creative problem solving. Over the next several years he pulled together a variety of concepts and procedures for developing the problem-solving capacities of generalist practitioners.

EMERGENCE OF THE CREATIVE GENERALIST

During this time we (Mike and Allen) became close friends and teamed up to explore and experiment with what we are now calling the *creative generalist.*

For more than a decade we have put our ideas to the test in classrooms, agencies, field projects and research studies. We applied, adapted and reframed the various principles and techniques of creative problem solving to fortify a generalist perspective for the realities of day-to-day practice. Other faculty, many students and a variety of practitioners contributed along the way. And now we are writing this book to report our conclusions:

— A focus on problems and problem solving does serve to guide a generalist through a complex range of activity in practice.

— An emphasis on creativity does unite art and science for social work practice.

— Perceiving ourselves as creative problem solvers does help answer many of the questions raised about the generalist perspective.

— The creative generalist is better prepared to confront the challenges now facing social work.

Problem-focus

Some social workers shy away from the term "problem-focus" because to them it implies an emphasis on the negative rather than positive aspects of a situation. We are using the term here in a very different sense. To explain what we mean, let's briefly consider the following ways of viewing problems:

Problem as undesirable condition

Few people like problems. Social problems like poverty, racism, child abuse and crime are conditions we want to eliminate. Personal problems like a major illness in the family or the breakup of a long standing relationship cause great distress. Even small things like losing your car keys are irksome. From this viewpoint, a problem is an undesirable condition we aim to get rid of.

Problem as life task

When people say that problems are part of living, they don't mean that bad social conditions are inevitable. Rather, they are speaking of "problem" in another way. We all face life tasks and pressures (e.g., getting through school, leaving home, deciding on careers, raising families). Learning to adapt, cope and develop resilience is part of growing and learning. From this viewpoint, problems are a necessary and normal part of life.

Problem as interacting elements

From yet another viewpoint, problems don't reside in a situation itself but in our perceptions of the situation. A problem is a situation that someone is evaluating as undesirable. A problem is an unsuccessful solution. Problems and solutions are different patterns of the same set of variables.

This way of regarding problems does not deny feelings or suffering. Rather, it enables us to get on with the job of problem solving by providing a handle on the problem and offering a way to understand its various aspects. By viewing a problem as a set of interacting elements within and between particular systems (an individual, a family, a group, a neighborhood, a community) we are able to temporarily separate problem from person, avoiding the perception that the problem is something a person is, has, causes or falls victim to.

Problem as challenge

Do you enjoy puzzles? Do you get satisfaction from figuring something out, whether a car repair or getting job training funds for a client? Are you continually curious, excited when you turn a difficulty into an opportunity? Here we are relating to "problem" as challenge, puzzle or question posed for resolution. From this viewpoint, problems are the raw material to which we apply our craft as problem solvers.

The first two ways of looking at the term "problem" (undesirable condition and life task) are useful in thinking about the goals of social work. The profession is committed to eliminating social problems and helping people gain access to resources and opportunities necessary for accomplishing life tasks and learning. Our use of the term "problem-focus" reflects the last two viewpoints on "problem" (interacting elements and challenge). With a problem-focus, creative generalists *view* problems as interacting elements and *relate* to them as challenges.

The generalist perspective popularized the notion that a problem consists of interacting elements. To handle the complexity resulting from an expanded view of "problem," we have added specific tools and techniques from the field of creativity. We emphasize viewing problems as challenges because successful solutions often depend upon the attitudes with which we engage the problem-solving process.

"Problem-focus" has another important meaning for us. It emphasizes key elements common to research and learning as well as the problem-solving process. In this sense when we are problem solving, we are also increasing our skills and wisdom (learning) and contributing to the knowledge base of the profession (research). A problem-focus helps us realize this multiple purpose of the problem-solving process.

Creativity Emphasis

Understanding creativity helps us integrate the art and science of practice. Creative problem solving requires the use of both rational (scientific) thinking and intuitive (artistic) thinking. Research has documented the contribution each mode of thinking makes to the problem-solving process. Specific procedures have been developed to tap our neglected intuitive powers and use them in concert with rational thinking. When we apply this integrated form of thinking to practice we cast a new light on the meaning of our work; we find a better fit between values and actions. The use of rational and intuitive thinking in problem solving is a major concern of this book.

Creative Problem Solvers

Having a certain degree, training, profession or job does not make a person a creative generalist. Creative generalists are found in all walks of life. What they have in common is a way of thinking and a way of engaging the problem-solving process. Some are attracted to *technical* problems and make career choices in that direction. Others are challenged by the world of *social* problems and attracted to fields having diverse activity, interdisciplinary approaches and opportunities to problem solve in a variety of cultural contexts. Obviously many such individuals find themselves in a profession called social work.

As we come to understand the creative problem solver, many of our questions about the nature of a generalist practitioner are answered.

Is a generalist a jack-of-all-trades and master-of-none?

The implication in this question is that a generalist is just an *eclectic*, someone who knows bits and pieces about a lot of different areas. A specialist on the other hand, supposedly knows a lot about, is *expert* in, one particular area...and since expertise is the hallmark of professionalism, an eclectic is, of course, less than professional. The message conveyed is that "a little knowledge is a dangerous thing."

What a creative generalist knows a lot about, is master of and expert in, is simply different from what the specialist knows a lot about. The creative generalist pays attention to, understands and develops expertness in the *problem-solving process*; discovering, utilizing and making connections to arrive at unique, responsive solutions. A broad background and ability to transfer learning from one problem-solving experience to another equips him or her with an enriched capacity for confronting succeeding problems.

Eclecticism is born of pragmatism. Whatever works is kept, what doesn't work is excluded. The variability in human nature and life predicaments often eludes elaborate and standardized practice procedures. Therefore, a creative generalist *is* eclectic in drawing upon, improvising and adapting different practice theories. But the creative generalist also has a knowledge and value framework necessary to the thoughtful use of eclecticism in a coherent problem-solving process. A generalist is eclectic, but an eclectic is not necessarily a generalist.

Does generalist mean BA-level social work?

The mission of undergraduate social work education is to teach a "professional foundation," a core of practice knowledge and skills which prepares students for entry level practice positions and provides a base for various concentrations in graduate school.

For this reason it is understandable that many undergraduate programs have a generalist orientation. Unfortunately the phrases *entry level* and *base for concentration* encourage a misconception of the meaning of generalist...that it refers to the rank of "buck private" in an army of professional social workers.

Developing problem-solving talents is a lifelong process for a creative generalist. Treating generalist and specialist as separate categories of rank and competence may satisfy a desire for clarity in professional organization but severely constrains the resourcefulness of our profession in attending to social problems.

Can a generalist specialize?

Some view generalist social work as suited only for practice in settings where specialized resources are not available (e.g., in small towns and rural areas), or in settings of special diversity (e.g., a multipurpose neighborhood center).

It is true that such settings would benefit from the attention of a creative generalist. It is true that a generalist would be attracted to the openness and variety of such settings. However, the view that generalists *belong* primarily in areas lacking specialists is short-sighted.

With the current stress on accountability, licensing and regulation, it is perhaps tempting to see generalists and specialists in social work as analogous to those in the medical profession. In medicine the general practitioner and specialist coexist within reasonably clear boundaries. But a foot, heart and hemorrhoid do not translate easily to the world of social problems.

Can a creative generalist specialize?...Yes, but it does not require giving up one for the other. A creative generalist may develop a specialization or area of concentration without forfeiting a generalist identity. For example, a school social worker will know more about the complex world of public education than social workers from other settings. A creative generalist may, in this sense, specialize by field-of-practice. Specialities may also be developed in problem areas or population groups. Here special training, coursework and experience are related to problems (e.g., chemical abuse, delinquency) or populations (elderly, rural).

In the field-of-practice, problem or population area specializations a creative generalist is claiming to have special knowledge and experience for *problem solving* in those particular areas.

Some specializations are incompatible with a creative generalist view. You'll recognize them when you consider them in terms of the problem-solving process.

A creative generalist first identifies the unique problem pattern in a situation and *then* rearranges it into a solution pattern. The best solution in a given problem situation *may* involve working with an individual and/or a small group and/or a series of "town meetings." A behavioral management program *may* be part of the solution.

But specializations that emphasize treatment approaches (e.g., behavior modification) or system sizes (e.g., family group, organization) are, in effect, specializations by *solution*. They are thus incompatible with a creative problem-solving orientation of the generalist.

The Creative Generalist and Society's Challenge

We live in a time very different from that when the generalist perspective emerged. The words, phrases and images of the Seventies and Eighties reflect the changing pattern of our problem priorities, understandings, potentials: Watergate, energy crisis, inflation, recession, "small is beautiful," "Black is beautiful," "back to basics," "Live Aid," yuppies, computers, cocaine, "Star Wars," networking.

The ending of the Vietnam war, scandals in government and sharply escalating energy costs, shifted the mood of our country. Relevance was converted to accountability. The language of activism changed to the language of cost effectiveness. "Small" became the *modus operandi*, whether in automobiles, homes or social programs. Retrench, restrain, constrain, seemed the dominant strategies of survival in a world of shrinking resources. We pulled in our belts and turned inward to mend, to conserve, to regain our strength.

The Eighties are characterized by push-and-pull contrasts. We are experiencing what some refer to as the "recovery," and at the same time hear warnings that our massive federal deficit will again bring our economy to its knees. We hear of plans to put weaponry in orbit and at the same time watch worldwide, satellite-beamed, rock concerts raising funds to feed starving nations. We struggle against our steady decline as an industrial nation while at the same time try to gain superiority in the "information age" of high technology.

We are in a period of transition and ambivalence. Social work is challenged to be both cost effective and imaginative in the face of shrinking resources. Meeting this challenge requires more than developing new techniques or models of practice, more than placing social work on a scientific footing. Once again we have to build new bridges, develop a new sense of the whole and a vision of the future.

Creative generalists in all fields of activity flourish in periods of change. They attend to understanding, developing and transferring problem-solving abilities to a wide range of shifting circumstances. As they gradually recognize their own unique talents for problem solving they are able to apply these talents to confronting the multitude of questions, puzzlements, frustrations, desires and difficulties intensified in periods of social change.

Uncertainty and risk are inherent to the solving of life's infinite variety of problems. Creative generalists recognize this as a necessary part of the adventure. With the resolution of each problem encountered, they are more and more open to the complexities of a turbulent and changing society, more ready to look a problem straight in the eye with a readiness to convert it into an opportunity.

Through repeatedly confronting problems, a creative generalist learns to recognize, sort out and rearrange the connections between the various parts of a situation. Strengthening some connections and minimizing others is necessary to forming fresh idea patterns (solutions). Creative generalists know that all parts of a situation are interconnected and that changing one connection influences all other parts in varying degrees. They recognize the choices posed by the variety of ways one can work toward overall change in the whole of a situation by *orchestrating* the relationships between the parts. And they recognize that in these choices are opportunities to step toward a preferable future.

The world is full of dreamers, who never quite get around to the doing of their ideas. There are also many doers, who can take someone else's good idea and put it into practice. Creative generalists are different. They have a strong sense of personal mission and are able to *both* visualize and actualize their ideas.

By increasing our capacities to solve problems creatively we will be are more able to *react* to the changing problems we encounter. But we will also be more able to generate the imaginative vision necessary for *proactive* readiness, more able to focus our valuing and use the strength of our persistence to actually make a difference. And with increasing capacity for creative problem solving comes something else…optimism, *informed* optimism.

THE CASE FOR INFORMED OPTIMISM

Optimism is suspect these days. To admit to optimism is to open yourself to accusations of naivety or ignorance. It's true that dealing with persistent social and personal problems is a frustrating job that can easily lead to pessimism. But giving in to pessimism is debilitating. Pessimism leads to impotence through a trail marked by cynicism, burn out, despair and inertia.

In social work we have long relied on compassion and commitment to aid us in the struggle against pessimism. To this struggle the creative generalist brings another essential trait, one Allen calls "informed optimism." He uses this term to emphasize that generalists are optimistic because of what they *know* rather than what they *don't* know.

Creative generalists know that hope is empowering, it's the ally of action. Hope is fed by visions of a better future, and those visions, in turn, are fed by concrete examples of positive changes in the here and now. Though they tend not to capture headlines in the daily newspapers, examples of people working individually and collectively in successful efforts to address such problems as food shortages, health care, neighborhood safety and sexism, exist all around us.[2] These examples do not deny the seriousness or enormity of the problems facing us. Rather, they help point out directions in which we can be moving and unleash the energy we need to get there. They lend substance to hope.

Creative generalists know that each of us have contributions to make and that what we do, matters. As fallible human beings we all, at one time or another, yield to the "yes, but" syndrome. It's a good idea, *but* there isn't enough time, *but* the agency isn't supportive of innovations, *but* we don't have the resources, *but* there is little I can do. With practice, constraints can be treated as elements in the problem rather than stop signs.

Each of us can find our own way, using our special talents, to make a contribution to addressing social problems. Some are inventing alternative energy devices while others are educating the public to the dangers of nuclear power plants. Some are working to restore cuts in the food stamp program while others are organizing community gardens. Some are helping to make medical services more availble to the poor while others are working to reduce the health risks from environmental pollution. There are contributions we make through our informal networks, through our jobs, through the formal organizations and groups we join, through the way we conduct our personal lives. When we see the interconnections between all of these efforts, we begin to appreciate the value of our own contributions. As Ferguson puts it, "Small victories add up to a large cultural awakening."[3]

Finally, creative generalists know that the human mind is our most basic and important resource. And discoveries on brain functioning are enabling us to better utilize the full powers of our minds, helping us to approach problems with better ways of problem solving.

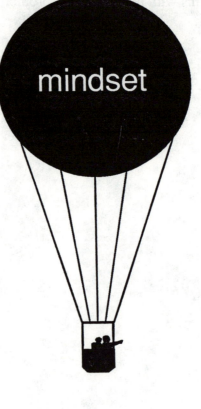

The nature of social work practice

2

Social Worker needed for older adult daycare center. Focus on maintenance of elderly in the community. Responsible for intake, coordination with other services, counseling with individuals and families, and case planning with interdisciplinary staff.

Community organizer. City Department of Human Resources looking for person to provide consultation to neighborhood associations and serve as link between neighborhood groups and city departments. Grant writing experience helpful.

Mental Health Center has opening for an **alcoholism treatment specialist.** Join an interdisciplinary team in providing direct services to alcoholics and their families. Offer community education programs.

Social Worker wanted for foster care unit of County Social Services Department. Duties include recruitment of foster parents, licensing of foster homes, and liaison between agency and foster parents.

Planning consultant. National voluntary health agency seeks person to design and conduct program evaluation studies, identify and interpret trends in health care, and engage in program planning and development.

Social Worker to coordinate Emergency Help Line. Responsible for supervision of a volunteer-based emergency service. Position includes recruitment and training of volunteers, and coordination with police and other health and social service agencies.

In the near future you may well be poring through similar ads in search of a job in social work, the reward for years of diligent study and training in your chosen profession. At least you *hope* it will be a reward. Stories you hear about cynicism, burnout and the "real" education that awaits you may have you a bit concerned. We'll deal with some of those concerns a little later. For the time being, let's see what these ads tell us about the nature of social work practice, about the business that social work is in.

A striking feature of these ads is the great diversity of settings, problems, populations, and activities that social work is involved in. We work in schools, hospitals, public social service agencies, group homes, mental health centers, nursing homes, neighborhood centers, battered women's shelters, adoption agencies, planning departments, and industrial settings to name just a few. Make a list of social problems such as poverty, child abuse, crime, alcoholism, and homelessness—you'll find social workers directly involved in various facets of the problem. Open an office door in a social agency and you'll find a social worker counseling individuals, families or groups. Open another door and you'll find a social worker engaged in the administration of the agency.

This diversity can be traced back to the roots of the profession. We did not start out with a coherent purpose as in law or medicine. In fact, as Carol Meyer points out, social work may be the most complex endeavor to have developed into a profession.[1] You may remember from your history course that one part of social work grew out of voluntarism, philanthropy, agency-based apprenticeship, and a concern with the moral uplift of the poor. Another part grew out of the settlement house movement and was focused on social reform. Each evolved with its separate purposes, responded to different influences, grew in different directions, drew on different knowledge bases, and spawned different methodologies such as group work and family treatment.

Some have suggested that what is unique about social work *is* our diversity, that we are a generalist profession, an almost extemporaneous profession that changes according to societal needs and is willing to be used for a great variety of societal and individual purposes.[2]

Should we regard our diversity as a problem or an opportunity? Should we minimize it or celebrate it?

DIVERSITY AS A PROBLEM

"Diversity" is a positive way to talk about the lack of a clear focus or identity. You have probably already run into this problem. Mention to someone from your home town that you are a teacher, nurse, engineer, dentist or lawyer and they will have a pretty good idea of what you do for a living. Mention that you are a social worker, and there is a good chance they will have a vague image of you as a welfare worker or maybe someone who helps families who are in trouble.

We lack a simple concise jargon-free definition of social work, one that you could pull out and use in conversations with friends and relatives when they ask what you do for a living (or what you are majoring in at school). Some social workers deal with this problem by describing their jobs in terms of settings and tasks. For example, "I'm a medical social worker. I help with the discharge plans of patients in the hospital, arrange for aftercare services, and work with the patients and their families in dealing with the emotional aspects of the illness."

Many social workers believe that the lack of a consensus around a definition of professional purpose will keep social work a fragmented profession and threaten its survival. Several attempts at a definition have been made over the years. Consider the following sampling:

> Social work seeks to enhance the social functioning of individuals, singly and in groups, by activities focused upon their social relationships which constitute interaction between individuals and their environments.[3]

> (Social work is) a helping profession concerned with the relationships between human beings and their interpersonal and organizational environments, with helping to modify or to enhance the quality of transactions between people and their environments,

and with seeking to promote environments that support human well being.[4]

Social work is the professional activity of helping individuals, groups or communities to enhance or restore their capacity for social functioning and create societal conditions favorable to their goals.[5]

(Social work) focuses on the transactions between people and their environments that affect the ability of people to accomplish life tasks, alleviate distress, and realize individual and collective aspirations.[6]

Though they vary in wording, these definitions do reflect a common focus on the interaction of people and their environment. In spite of their vagueness, they do offer direction for clarifying a perspective and sense of common purpose you can share with other practitioners who call themselves social workers.

DIVERSITY AS AN OPPORTUNITY

In selecting a career you may have been concerned that after making a big investment to enter a profession, you might find it didn't hold your interest or it wasn't "right" for you. The diversity that social work offers may have been one of the things that attracted you to the profession in the first place. If you find you don't enjoy working with kids, you can work with elderly people. If you don't like working in a hospital, you could look for a job in a mental health center. If you find out that counseling is not for you, you can explore planning and administration. And in the job you choose, there is often room for shaping it according to your wants and visions. For all of the problems and embarrassment our vague professional identity causes, it does have its compensations.

I mentioned earlier that some people have suggested that diversity *is* our uniqueness, that social work is a generalist profession that is ever-changing and adapting to societal needs. The somewhat vague conception of our professional task (we are concerned with the general welfare of people) allows us to move in many directions and respond to many problems. Along with a commitment to humanitarian values and a pragmatic attitude about getting the job done, this flexibility probably has contributed as much to the survival of social work as efforts to make it a "legitimate" profession.

In Chapter 1 we discussed the fact that our society is in the process of a major transition, a convergence of economic necessity, changing resources and technology, and value shifts. Robert Naisbitt, the author of *Megatrends*, states that in order to grow and thrive, to take advantage of the opportunities present in a transition, businesses must ask themselves what business they are in and what business they want to be in. He cites the decline of the American railroads as an example. Because they steadfastly held on to an outmoded image of what it meant to be in the business of "railroading," they missed the changes taking place about them. If they had redefined themselves as being in the business of "transportation," that image would have enabled them to adapt to and and profit from the very changes that led to their demise.[7]

What does this mean for social work? Much of what Naisbitt says about businesses can be applied to professions as well. The fact that we have not cast in stone a definition of social work, that the nature of the business we are in is the subject of debate and discussion, may turn out to be an advantage rather than a problem. It may place us in a better position to formulate a definition of purpose that makes sense in terms of the transitions that society is going through.

The point I have been leading up to is simply this: We need to approach the task of clarifying the nature of social work in a way that capitalizes on the diversity in the profession, keeps it tuned to societal changes, and draws on the timeless skills, values and wisdom from our past.

CONTRASTING VIEWS OF PRACTICE

The views we hold of the nature of social work influence the way we conduct our practice. Let me illustrate what I mean with two scenarios that contrast different views of social work. These scenarios were developed by Karen Irey.[8]

Scenario One:

A young MSW social worker begins his first job at a small mental health center in Hoovener, Oklahoma. The mental health center is part of a state-wide department that has its central offices in Oklahoma City—150 miles away. At the state office there are many specialists, among whom are social workers, psychologists, psychiatrists, speech therapists, sex therapists, family planners, and alcohol specialists. In Hoovener, however, there is one psychologist, one social worker, and one secretary. The psychologist, an MA who had graduated the previous year from the state university, is the director of the agency. He believes that his job is to see children who are referred from the Hoovener public schools and other schools throughout the county. He usually does a battery of psychological tests for a thorough diagnosis and then observes the children in play therapy.

The secretary answers the phone for both the mental health center and the adjacent family planning and health clinic next door. She sees her job as being a good receptionist and enjoys the time she spends talking with the mothers as they wait for their children in play therapy.

Steve is the new MSW—having just graduated—and is sitting at his desk. He rereads his job description for the fourth time, trying to figure out where to begin—after all, he's always had a supervisor to assign him cases before now. The job description reads: "Provide comprehensive services to low-income families in rural areas, primarily focused on strengthening family ties and roles; do preliminary screening of perspective state hospital patients; provide assistance in identifying and developing necessary community mental health-oriented resources; plan with community agencies on behalf of the released patients, e.g., social and family adjustment, employment, finances; and provide consultation and education for interested groups, citizens, colleges, and community agency staff."

Steve knows how to work with families because of the clinical courses on family therapy that he took at the university. He knows how to arrange the chairs to promote openness and how to use a two-chair role play. Thus he talks to the psychologist about working with the mothers while the children are in play therapy. This is readily accepted by the psychologist and before long Steve has a caseload of mothers, a few fathers, and some children. Steve is very happy; the secretary is upset but no one knows why; and the psychologist really wants to go to graduate school to learn more about diagnosis. Steve is very successful as a family therapist and before long he even has a waiting list.

Scenario Two:

Basically the same scene, but while Steve is reading his job description, his attention goes to the parts on developing needed resources, providing consultation and education, and helping patients reenter their communities after being hospitalized 100 miles away.

He decides that in order to do this he must get to know the community. Thus he sets informal meetings with the town's mayor, the county commissioners, the school principals, and even travels to Oklahoma City to meet with the state senator and legislators from that area. He wants to meet them and let them know that he is living and working in their area, and that he's interested in human needs and problems. He also meets with the psychologist to clarify what his expectations are of a social worker. He tries to plan his coffee breaks at the local drugstore when the town's two policemen, and usually the county highway patrolman, also break for coffee. He drops by the county welfare office, visits the visiting nurses association, shares a game of basketball with the juvenile services workers, and visits the American Indian boarding school at the edge of town. He even discovers two other MSW's in town—one at the boarding school and one at the welfare office.

He soon hears about the local problems with alcoholism, about the teenage group that harasses the boarding school children, and about the drug problem at the boarding school. He is told by several families about the lack of summer employment for teenagers. He is asked by the visiting nurses association to visit some of the homes of their patients to help with understanding what's going on, and several families call on him to get resources for a retarded child or an elderly parent.

Before long Steve finds that he is very busy—he conducts several groups a week on parenting skills; he provides consultation and gets referrals from the visiting nurses association; he is involved with the police, county commissioners, and school officials in organizing a summer recreation and employment program for adolescents; he is called on by almost everyone in town when they want some information on mental health services available in Oklahoma City; he has started a volunteer program to assist patients who are returning from the state hospital; and he has begun a community-wide alcoholism program with the assistance of an alcoholism specialist from the state office.

What leads these two social workers in such different directions? It's their way of thinking about practice. The first social worker holds a view of social work based on a narrowly defined clinical role. The second social worker holds a broader view, a generalist perspective. This view of the nature of social work can be described as a set of ideas for thinking about social problems and the business of social work in dealing with with problems.

WAYS OF THINKING ABOUT PROBLEMS

Creative generalists deliberately view a problem or event in different ways in order to enrich their understanding. Three ways of thinking about problems are particularly useful in explaining a generalist perspective on the nature of social work: pragmatic, holistic, and political. These aspects of a problem were derived from Pincus and Minahan's formulation of a social work frame of reference.[9]

Pragmatic

By "pragmatic" I mean a concern with everyday problems of living and the demands placed on people by various life situations such as divorce, unemployment, and illness.[10] We are pragmatic in the sense that we are concerned with the tasks that confront people in these situations and the resources and conditions that would help in coping with these tasks.

For example, a social worker who is working with an unemployed 30-year-old man who is about to be discharged from an in-patient drug abuse treatment program would focus on such questions as: What plans does he have for housing, work and use of leisure time? What resources exist in the community to help him with these tasks? Will he be likely to encounter any problems in using these resources? What problems will he face in making the transition from the structured environment of the hospital to the community? Does he have a support network of family or friends? Are they able and willing to help? What kind of support do they need?

As another example, consider a school that is trying to integrate a large number of migrant children. Our pragmatic focus would lead us to look at such questions as: What difficulties do these kids face in entering a new school? What problems are created for the teachers in the classroom? How can the situation be turned into an opportunity?

Our pragmatic perspective can be traced back to the roots of social work in the early part of this century. The friendly visitors from the Charity Organization Societies may have been primarily concerned about the "moral health" of the poor, but they did bring food baskets when they came calling. The settlement house workers were concerned with neigborhood conditions and integration of immigrants into the society.

Our willingness to deal with the day-to-day concerns and conditions that face people probably has contributed to the survival of the profession. As we indicated earlier, social work has taken on many tasks assigned by society. In spite of which way the political winds blow, there will be children in need of foster care, families needing assistance with an elderly parent returning from the hospital, and so on. These needs exist in most societies. Even if social work as we know it were to disappear, someone would need to perform these tasks.

Are you comfortable with this pragmatic orientation? Can you take pride in it? Can you see the opportunities for personal and social change that lie in dealing with these problems of daily living?

Holistic

Holistic, interdependence, systems thinking, general systems theory, ecological perspective, eco-systems. Terms like these frequently appear in discussions of the nature of social work practice. Ideas drawn from general systems theory and ecology have proven useful in helping us articulate our focus of concern on dealing with problems.

The definitions of social work cited earlier emphasized that our concern is not just with the person *or* the environment but with the interaction between the two. Viewing people holistically means seeing how all the aspects of their situation fit together, not treating any one aspect in isolation from the others. In working with a pregnant teenager we are not only concerned with her health and medical condition but with legal issues, schooling, her emotional state, family relationships, plans for care of the infant, and so on.

The ecological metaphor and general systems theory call attention to the interdependence of the parts of a system. A change in one part will affect all the other parts. If we were exploring the problem of low reading scores at a school, we would want to consider the school, the teachers, the kids, the classroom, the neighborhood, and the families.

The holistic view also encompasses a shift from linear to multicausality. In assessing problems we do not look for *the* cause. We look for how all the factors in the situation are interacting to maintain the problematic situation. This view opens up multiple possibilities for dealing with a problem.[11]

An important challenge for social work is learning to "see" inter - dependence, to recognize patterns, to become aware of the options that multicausality opens up. A new view of our "outer" reality must be accompanied by new ways of thinking that allow us to see connections, patterns, interrelationships. In a future chapter we will discuss ways to understand and develop these thinking abilities.

Political

I'm referring to the third way of thinking about problems as "political" because it focuses on the relationship between the private troubles of people and the public issues which bear on them. Though this can be considered as an aspect of our holistic perspective, it deserves its own place on our conceptual map.

As Pincus and Minahan point out, an individual or family may be frustrated in dealing with personal troubles when such problems are linked to public issues such as unemployment, racism, or the farm crises.[12] I like William Schwartz's suggestion that social agencies be viewed not just as providers of services but as an arena for assessing the impact of public issues on private troubles.[13]

As an example, consider daycare problems. A single parent who is unable to afford good quality child care has a private trouble. However, the shortage of inexpensive, quality daycare centers or suitable alternatives is a public issue. If you only concentrate on helping a person find a scarce resource, you are only dealing with private troubles. Many private troubles, however, cannot be alleviated without also working on the public issue involved.

This last perspective on problems ties together the historical threads of social work as "cause" (social reform) and social work as "function" (service).

WAYS OF THINKING ABOUT THE BUSINESS OF SOCIAL WORK

Having considered how generalist social workers view problems, the next step is to look at what they do about problems. Pincus and Minahan[14] have suggested several functions of social work that are useful for defining our professional purpose. In this section we have drawn on and modified their conceptualization. Boiled down to its essence, we can say that social work is in the business of:

— Connecting people and resources.

— Creating new resources.

— Making resource systems responsive to people.

— Teaching problem-solving skills to people.

You'll notice some overlap in these categories as we put meat on these barebone definitions. Such are the limitations of conceptual frameworks in tidying up reality.

Connecting People and Resources

— Organizing an outreach effort to identify and provide information to elderly people who may be in need of a nutrition program.

— Working with an agency to simplify application forms, provide child care, and hold evening and weekend office hours.

— Referring a person with landlord problems to a tenants union or a troubled teenager to a drug abuse program.

— Serving as an advocate and helping cut through red tape for a person who is trying to enroll in a vocational training program.

— Assisting a neighborhood association in making application for a grant from the city or obtaining a meeting room in a neighborhood center.

What do the items on this list have in common? They are all examples of activities that involve connecting people with formal resource systems (agencies, organizations, and services).

Many barriers prevent people from connecting with a needed resource. They may not know about the resource system, be aware of its relevance for their needs, or know how to gain access to it. There may be policies and procedures that frustrate people in their attempts to utilize the resource. Practical barriers such as transportation or need for baby sitters may arise. The activities on the list above are all aimed at reducing such barriers and making formal resource systems more accessible.

The connecting that we do with formal systems relies on a knowledge of those systems, an understanding of how they work, an appreciation of the pathways people take to them and the barriers they encounter, an ability to make connections that "stick," and flexibility in serving as a guide, broker, or advocate—whatever the situation calls for.

Much of your knowledge and skill in navigating the world of formal resource systems will be born of your experience with that world. I'm talking here about the informal relationships you develop with people who work in this world, the favors you trade back and forth, the shortcuts and ways of stretching rules you pick up, and the skill you acquire in presenting information or preparing applications in ways that increase your chances of getting what you want.

What does "connecting people and resources" mean in relation to the informal resource system (natural helping systems of family, friends, neighbors and colleagues). It means knowing that Ms. Jones needs help with her yard work and that the Smith boy is looking for a part-time job. It means arranging for a battered woman to stay with a foster mother who needs temporary help around the house. It means carrying a basket of used children's clothing in the trunk of your car which people can take from or contribute to when you make a round of home visits. It means making arrangements for a group of nursing home residents to prepare and teach a history lesson to a fifth-grade class. It means organizing a mutual aid group. In other words, it means linking people who can be resources for one another.

In "service delivery systems" resources are often regarded as "commodities" which are controlled by an organization who "delivers" them to clients in an accountable, effective, efficient and humane way. In "natural helping systems" a resource is more like a "potential" which is released (or energized) though a mutual exchange.

Connecting people and resources in natural helping systems requires an ability to scan the environment, see beyond the usual labels by which we categorize people, and match needs and resources. It requires a "restless curiosity" and a commitment to resource exchange as a basic value by which lives are mutually enhanced.[15] It requires knowing the natural helping systems of the people we work with and the informal systems that exist in the community. ("Community" as used here can be a geographic area or a grouping of people with social, cultural, ethnic or religious ties.)

Connecting people and resources within the informal system can result in a strengthening of the ties in that system as well as dealing with an immediate problem. It presents an opportunity to shift from a remedial to a developmental focus. "I know I should be working toward more developmental long-term goals. But after dealing with matters that need urgent attention there is little time left for anything else." So goes an often-heard complaint. This is why we need to think of alternative choices, where the very same act addresses an immediate need while serving a developmental purpose as well.

I'd like to end this section on connecting people and resources with a brief look to the future. Our society is fast moving into an information age. Computers which can process and generate large quantities of information and link people to all sorts of data banks and electronic bulletin boards are becoming as commonplace in the home as the telephone and TV set. As society becomes more complex, as we are faced with more choices and decisions to make in business and in our personal lives, as we strive to maintain a sense of autonomy and self-reliance, information is a key resource. Linking people and resources can take on new meaning in this context.

Creating New Resources

Our focus on the relationship between private troubles and public issues and our knowledge of the community make us aware of needed resource systems which may not exist. Let's look at a few examples of what social workers do to help create new resource systems.

A YMCA that has served as a shelter for the homeless is closing down. You might get together a group of concerned agencies, churches, and city officials to find a new sponsor for the shelter or help form a new organization for that purpose. Social workers often chair or participate in committees that are initiating new programs or adding and expanding services in existing agencies. They document needs, prepare reports and proposals, and testify at hearings of funding panels and government agencies.

As another example, consider the problem of pregnant teenagers who are reluctant to talk with parents or relatives. You could form a group with these teenagers where they can share mutual concerns, offer each other support, and explore ways of coping with their situation. If such a group met with success, the school system might incorporate it as a regular part of its program. By experimenting with new ways of solving problems and meeting needs within their own work assignments, social workers can create the models on which new programs or services are patterned.

Social workers have been involved in helping form organizations such as neighborhood associations and senior citizen councils where people can work together on common problems and interests. They also serve as consultants to self-help groups that are getting started or changing from a support group to a more service-oriented operation.

The above examples have focused on formal resource systems. Let's turn our attention now to the informal resource system. In some communities natural helping systems may not have developed or may be breaking down. For example, boom-town areas may experience such rapid growth that community traditions have not had a chance to develop. In such an area the social worker at a daycare center might help initiate a baby-sitting coop or a clothing and toy exchange. A social worker at a neighborhood center might work with the police department in establishing a neighborhood watch program.

To give another example, many elderly lose their support system through illnesses and death. Social workers have organized telephone reassurance programs in which isolated elderly people call one another every day to check if everything is all right and to summon help if needed. The worker thus creates a new informal system helping system, linking together those in the community who may have lost such contacts.

Social work, through its community organization branch and settlement house roots, has a strong tradition of creating new resource systems to meet changing needs and organizing people to work together on common problems and interests. Shifts are now taking place in our society from hierarchical to network forms of organization, from centralization to decentralization, along with the development of new communication tools for linking people. These changes open many possibilities for building on our tradition. They challenge us to discover new ways of giving expression to this tradition in the context of our emerging society.

Making Resource Systems Responsive to People

In the course of their work, school social workers relate to mental health centers, courts, child welfare agencies, group homes, neighborhood centers, and medical clinics to name a few. A medical social worker may have contact with nursing homes, homemaker services, visiting nurses, family service agencies, meals-on-wheels, sheltered workshops, vocational rehabilitation agencies and so on. Because we work at the intersection of many formal resource systems we are in a position to see problems in the operation of these systems and in their relationships with each other.

We often see the negative effects of poor communication, coordination and conflicting demands on our clients. Social workers are increasingly taking on the "case manager" role to make the system work better for the client. We also work directly on interorganizational relationships. For example, different application forms and fiscal year dates make life difficult for administrators of agencies that rely on multiple funding sources. A social worker might work with city, county and United Way officials to develop a uniform application and reporting form.

Agency or governmental policies may also have negative effects on the people we work with. Social workers are involved in efforts to modify such policies, humanize the system, and secure client input in the operation of organizations. For example, we have organized residents' councils in nursing homes and worked with parents who are concerned about school closings.

When conflict occurs between or within systems we are often called upon to play a mediating role. It may be a dispute between two factions in a neighborhood association or between the police and a battered women's shelter.

Turning to the informal resource system, we find social workers also engaged in many activities in this arena. We may be serving as an informal consultant to a natural helper in the community, working with a parent and her teenaged daughter to develop a better means of resolving their conflicts, or helping to mobilize neighbors and relatives to provide after-care to an elderly person being released from the hospital. Especially in times of crises, if no central person from an individual's network is available, we may play a very active role in mobilizing family and friends and coordinating their efforts with those of the formal resource system.

By a sensitive blending of the resources of the service delivery system with a person's natural helping network we can augment, support and strengthen that network rather than undermine it.

There is no easy way to summarize all of what might be included in the category of "making systems responsive to people." Social workers take on a variety of system maintenance tasks for society as a whole, and do the same for the institutions and communities in which we work. The school principal is concerned about vandalism in the playground, the hospital administrator is concerned about inappropriate use of emergency room facilities, the neighborhood is concerned about a new group home opening up—such concerns often end up on the desk of the social worker. We are maintenance person, troubleshooter, mediator, and advocate all rolled into one.

Teaching Problem Solving to People

Social workers are problem solvers. Connecting people and resources, creating new resources, and making resourse systems responsive to people can be thought of as professional purposes towards which our problem solving is directed. Yes, social work is in the business of problem solving. More than that, we are in the business of problem solving with people, involving them in the process. This means helping people see their problems from different perspectives, clarifying goals and wants, generating alternative options for dealing with a problem, evaluating the options, developing a plan of action, and monitoring the implementation of the plan.

In the course of problem solving we might be helping people identify their own resources, role playing a job interview to help them practice their interviewing skills, and other such activities. We may be problem solving with a teacher, a pregnant teenager, a committee, an administrator, a family or a self-help group. In each instance we try to be aware of how the characteristics of the person or the dynamics of the system affect the problem-solving process.

Aside from dealing with the specific problem at hand our goal is to help people improve their own problem-solving abilities. Our job, our professional purpose is to promote self-reliance through sharing, teaching, giving away our knowledge and skills around problem solving and methods to involve others in the process.

ENDING COMMENTS

What is social work? We have attempted to answer that question by exploring a generalist perspective on problems (pragmatic, holistic and political) and professional purpose in dealing with problems (connecting people and resources, creating new resources, making resource systems responsive to people, teaching problem solving to people). From observations, experiences and discussions like this one, you will gradually evolve and internalize your own definition of social work.

Becoming aware of and clarifying your personal conceptions is more than an academic exercise. As the two scenarios at the beginning of the chapter illustrated, the ideas about social work you carry in your mind influence your day-to-day practice activities. They are the definitions of social work that your clients, colleagues and others see, experience and react to. They are the definitions that guide the direction of your practice.

There's another reason for clarifying your conception of social work. Steve, from the scenario, was lucky to land a job where his task was to define the nature of his position and determine the kinds of activities he would engage in. Many social workers face a very different task. They work in settings where a lot of their activities are prescribed in thick agency manuals. The prescriptions often have less to do with the nature of social work than with agency policies and procedures, bureaucratic forms of organization, the logistics of providing specific services to a specific client group, complying with local, state and federal policies and mandates, accountability to funding sources, and restrictions imposed by insurance companies. To maintain a sense of autonomy as a social worker in such settings (i.e., to maintain an identity as a social worker as well as an employee of a specific organization), you will need to rely on your internalized definition of social work practice.

Throughout this chapter I have made statements such as, "The business of social work is ..." These statements are more than descriptive. They also reflect what Mike and I believe social work should or could be, what ways of thinking about it we believe lead to good practice. Words like "should," "good," and "believe," imply values. Indeed, any conceptualization of social work is a combination of a framework for relating ideas and a set of values. Any discussion of the nature of social work practice that excludes values is incomplete.

Yes, you've guessed what is coming up. In the next chapter Mike will be dealing with the nature of values, clarifying the values underlying the profession, and proposing a value stance for the creative generalist. The chapter following that will shift from profession to vocation, exploring ways of giving expression to your personal values in this enterprise called social work. You will find help there in framing your personal definition of social work and style of practice.

Social work values

In the last chapter Allen discussed the nature of social work practice and helped us further understand the creative generalist mindset. In this chapter I'll explore social work values with you.

First we'll identify several key concepts. Then we'll use these concepts to better understand social work values. Finally, we'll map out a strategy for responding to an essential challenge social work values pose for creative generalists.

RELATED TERMS AND DEFINITIONS

Let's start by defining three important and related terms, **knowledge, values** and **ethics**. Later we'll add information to refine their meanings, but first let's consider them in the conventional sense. If you looked each term up in a dictionary you'd find some - thing like the following:

Knowledge

We have knowledge about a given subject. It is information we believe to be *true* whether or not we would want it to be that way. It is something observed objectively, something verifiable in our experience and science.

For example if we say, "By the looks of that cloud formation, I believe it's going to rain within the hour," we are believing on the basis of observations about the gathering of clouds before rain that are valid and reliable. We may want it to rain for our thirsty garden or not want the rain to spoil our picnic, but we *believe* it will rain, regardless.

Values

Like knowledge, values are often stated as beliefs. But rather than consider them true in a scientific sense, we use the term value to refer to the way we would prefer, desire or *want* something to be. Values are ideals. They are visionary, something we strive toward. Strongly held values excite our emotions. A fundamental value is an ultimate aim, a state of affairs perceived as highly valuable.

For example, when we say, "I believe in individual freedom," we are stating a value. We are saying individual freedom is important to us, something to strive for, protect and promote, even give our life for.

Ethics

Ethics are *rules of conduct* developed from values. They are principles of action. Our ethics tell us the right and wrong way to go about doing something according to what we value. For example, if we place a high value on individual privacy, we would likely consider it unethical to physically or mentally coerce a client into disclosing personal information.

KNOWLEDGE, VALUES AND ETHICS IN ACTION

Knowledge, values and ethics...like three little kids these terms are easy to tell apart when they're all dressed up in dictionary definitions and quietly sitting next to each other. You know what will happen when we turn them lose in a real-life situation, so we'll have to pay very close attention or we'll never know who's doing what to whom. Imagine we're eavesdropping on the following conversation.

> *"Sure, I know what might happen, but I want him to find out for himself. If he gets into any real trouble, I'll step in. I'm not always going to be there, you know...oh look, here he comes now... and he's got it all over himself...but look at that smile will you...if he throws his chest out any further he'll pop the buttons right off his shirt...I wish I had a camera..."*

Sounds very ordinary doesn't it? A "kitchen conversation," a momentary slice of someone's life. You can picture it being said can't you? It could be a parent or grandparent talking about a five-year-old or adolescent. It could be one seasoned factory worker telling another about breaking-in a new employee. For our purpose let's say it's a mother talking to a friend about her toddler. Now let's take a closer look at what is going on.

We can see that a choice was required that posed a conflict in values. The mother wanted (value) to protect, at the same time knew (knowledge) how learning takes place and also wanted (value) the child to develop autonomy. She knew (knowledge) the survival issue ("I'm not always going to be there...") and used a backup rule to guide her decision (ethics). If trouble *did* develop she would step in to protect her toddler (priority of values).

How could we clarify the mother's values in the situation? We could talk to her about what she believes about being a good parent. We could develop with her a list of what she thinks this involves. For example:

— Parents should protect their children from harm.

— Parents should help their children become independent.

— Parents should not physically or emotionally abuse their children.

In this way we would be clarifying the mother's parenting values and developing a list of ethical guidelines that would be helpful to anyone who shares the mother's basic parenting values.

But I am sure we would also sense something else in the mother…a caring…a deep caring that enabled her to restrain a powerful desire to protect, so that her child might learn and experience independently.

Her actions could be understood as logical applications of parenting principles, but they also reflect a complex integration of commitment, caring, knowing and choosing, a *pattern* of thoughts and emotions. That pattern involved *both* the objective (knowing, choosing, predicting) and the subjective (wanting, fearing, hoping). It was simple and ordinary, yet complex and extraordinary. This mother not only had a practical understanding of how a mother should behave, she relied upon a different kind of value clarity as well. She was able to spontaneously and appropriately respond to a challenge in parenting because she had holistic value awareness, a *readiness* to respond. She had a pattern of values, an overall arrangement of beliefs, a flexible and adaptable image of what a good mother does. She had more than a logical set of ethical guidelines, she had an intuitive *vision*. We would say she did it *on* purpose (logical reason) with a *sense* of purpose (intuitive vision). Her purpose was complete in that it had both logic (as elaborated in ethics) and imagination (an image or vision of how she wanted her child to be in the future).

Have you ever marveled at a certain spontaneous, sensitive and effective action of a mother (or grandmother or teacher or social worker or even yourself) and asked:

> *"How did you come up with that?"…"What made you think of that?"*

> *"I don't know, I guess it just seemed the natural thing to do."…"It just felt right."…"I really didn't think about it in the usual sense of that word…it comes from something I just know."*

What you have witnessed in such an instance is the expression of an intuitive *vision* as contrasted with action based on rationally developed rules of conduct or *ethics*.

In other words there are two directions in which we clarify our values. One is to break them down into specific guidelines. The other is to integrate them into a pattern or direction. Let's nail this point down:

— When we identify a particular value and elaborate rules of conduct that logically flow from that value, we end up with ethical guidelines.

— When we integrate a number of values into an overall pattern we end up with a vision.

— When we integrate our ethics with our vision we get purpose. Purpose should thus include both reason (I did it on purpose) and vision (I am doing this out of a sense of purpose).

— In this complete purpose we find a balanced readiness to respond planfully to anticipated events and spontaneously to unanticipated events.

TWO MODES OF THINKING

Developing ethics involves one kind of thinking (elaborating, detailing, analyzing, categorizing, ordering). Developing vision involves a different kind of thinking (connecting, integrating, interrelating, synthesizing).

These two modes of thinking have undergone considerable scientific scrutiny in the "split-brain" research of the past several decades. I'll discuss them at length in later chapters, but we at least need a brief summary for our work here.

The brain has two complementary yet separate modes of thinking. The left and right hemispheres of the brain have separate functions, and can operate independently as two separate centers of consciousness.[1]

Left-Hemisphere (Rational) Thinking

Left-hemisphere thinking is convergent, analytic, logical, linear, sequential, orderly thinking. Our rational mind controls speech, talks to us, helps us arrange words to make sentences; it is concerned with correctness and error. It classifies the world into identifiable parts; it looks for details; it uses rules, it adds and subtracts, measures, categorizes, evaluates; it deals with the past and evaluates the present from past experience; it is our intellectual, scientific mind, helping us survive with the way things *are*.

Right-Hemisphere (Intuitive) Thinking

Right-hemisphere thinking is divergent, spontaneous, holistic thinking. Our intuitive mind thinks in images, detects patterns. Though not directly involved in speech it gives it emotional inflection. It is more musical and sexual. It makes visual closure, it completes gestalts. It distinguishes shapes in unconnected lines. It is the place referred to when we speak from the heart. It is the "art" in art versus science. It gives depth to our meaning, feeling to our thoughts. It helps form insights, discover relationships. It is analogical and emotional, it is our imaginative, artistic mind. It focuses on possiblity and reaching for what *might be*.

WHOLE-MIND THINKING
AND CLARIFYING VALUES

The relationship of whole-mind thinking to clarifying values is as follows:

— Whole-mind thinking is the balanced use of logical, left-mind thinking and intuitive, right-mind thinking.

— Developing ethics requires an emphasis on left-mind thinking. Developing vision requires an emphasis on right-mind thinking.

— Purpose is a balance of ethics and vision.

— Developing purpose, then, requires whole-mind thinking.

Now, there is an obstacle to using whole-mind thinking that I'll discuss at length in later chapters. Recognize for now that we are a left-mind dominated culture. Our rational mind dominates our awareness. It often takes over functions better performed by our right or intuitive mind. Our imbalanced dependence on rationality results in a compulsion to reduce everything into parts. Our ability to think equally well in terms of patterns, wholes and overall meanings is often severely restricted. Remember then, that developing whole-mind balance requires deliberate, conscious effort to release and encourage the equally active participation of our intuition. But this effort is necessary and important.

Through combining the scientific left mind with the artistic right mind, we maximize our ability to transform the way things are (objective belief) into what they might be (valued belief).

Ethical guidelines and vision should be complementary, interacting extensions of the beliefs we hold as important (values)...but it will take extra effort to fill out that vision end of the business.

SOCIAL WORK VALUES

Now let's turn to the matter of social work values. What are they you ask? This might seem an easy question to answer, but it isn't. Let's take a look at two attempts to answer that question by prominent members of the profession at different points in our history. Both were developed through our National Association of Social Workers.

Values listed in the 1958 *Working Definition of Social Work Practice*:[2]

1. The individual is the primary concern of this society.

2. There is interdependence between individuals in this society.

3. They have social responsibility for one another.

4. There are human needs common to each person, yet each person is essentially unique and different from others.

5. An essential attribute of a democratic society is the realization of the full potential of each individual and the assumption of his social responsibility through active participation in society.

6. Society has a responsibility to provide ways in which obstacles to this self-realization (i.e., disequilibrium between the individual and his environment) can be overcome or prevented.

Values Listed in the 1981 *Working Statement On The Purpose of Social Work*[3]

The purpose of social work is to promote or restore a mutually beneficial interaction between individuals and society in order to improve the quality of life for everyone. Social workers hold the following beliefs:

— The environment (social, physical, organizational) should provide the opportunity and resources for the maximum realization of the potential and aspirations of all individuals, and should provide for their common human needs and for the alleviation of distress and suffering.

— Individuals should contribute as effectively as they can to their own well-being and to the social welfare of others in their immediate environment as well as to the collective society.

— Transactions between individuals and others in their environment should enhance the dignity, individuality, and self-determination of everyone. People should be treated humanely and with justice.

Values versus Ethics Development

The value statements presented above span 21 years of social work practice and are similar to others proposed over the years. No proposed statement of values has evolved into an official value statement for the profession, because we have yet to achieve enough consensus to move from proposal to policy.

On the other hand, we *do* have an official code of ethics. It first achieved official validation in 1960 and has undergone tremendous development over the years. The last revised statement (1979) is detailed beyond our needs here, but I am including a summary of its content.

Code of Ethics: Summary of Major Principles.[4]

I. The social worker's conduct and comportment as a social worker

A. **Propriety.** The social worker should maintain high standards of personal conduct in the capacity or identity as social worker.

B. **Competence and Professional Development.** The social worker should strive to become and remain proficient in professional practice and the performance of professional functions.

C. **Service.** The social worker should regard as primary the service obligation of the social work profession.

D. **Integrity.** The social worker should act in accordance with the highest standards of professional integrity and impartiality.

E. **Scholarship and Research.** The social worker engaged in study and research should be guided by the conventions of scholarly inquiry.

II. The social worker's ethical responsibility to clients

F. **Primacy of Clients' Interests.** The social worker's primary responsibility is to clients.

G. **Rights and Prerogatives of Clients.** The social worker should make every effort to foster maximum self-determination on the part of clients.

H. **Confidentiality and Privacy.** The social worker should respect the privacy of clients and hold in confidence all information obtained in the course of professional service.

I. **Fees.** When setting fees, the social worker should ensure that they are fair, reasonable, considerate, and commensurate with the service performed and with due regard for the clients' ability to pay.

III. The social worker's ethical responsibility to colleagues

J. **Respect, Fairness, and Courtesy.** The social worker should treat colleagues with respect, courtesy, fairness, and good faith.

K. **Dealing with Colleagues' Clients.** The social worker has the responsibility to relate to the clients of colleagues with full professional consideration.

IV. The social worker's ethical responsibility to employers and employing organizations

L. **Commitments to Employing Organizations.** The social worker should adhere to commitments made to the employing organizations.

V. The social worker's ethical responsibility to the social work profession

M. **Maintaining the Integrity of the Profession.** The social worker should uphold and advance the values, ethics, knowledge, and mission of the profession.

N. **Community Service.** The social worker should assist the profession in making social services available to the general public.

O. **Development of Knowledge**. The social worker should take responsibility for identifying, developing, and fully utilizing knowledge for professional practice.

VI. The social worker's ethical responsibility to society

P. **Promoting the General Welfare**. The social worker should promote the general welfare of society.

Why the Difference?

The above listings make it apparent that we have clarified our values into ethics far more extensively than we have clarified them into a vision. Though 21 years separated the two value listings, the second is essentially a restatement of the first. Why haven't we been able to delineate a vision of how we would want the world to be as well as we have identified ethical standards for behavior?

Some believe the source of our difficulty is in our inability to arrive at a consensus on values. Yet, we have been able to derive ethics without this value consensus. In the preamble to our code of ethics we state that we used our fundamental value *(the belief in the dignity, worth and uniqueness of the individual)* to develop ethical guidelines. Why hasn't this same fundamental value served as the basis for establishing an overall vision?

An answer can be found in what we have learned about whole-mind thinking. Earlier I explained that encouraging right-mind participation in thinking takes deliberate effort because we are a left-mind dominated culture. Social work shares this left-mind bias. We, like others in our society, have focused on our science and as Vigilante states, have made a value of science itself.[5] We prefer the language of science and scientific explanations.

In other words, we have extensively developed our ethics because this task is essentially a rational (scientific) clarification of values. We have been unable to clarify our values into a vision because this task requires intuitive (artistic) participation.

Though social work has long stated its inclusion of both science and art in practice, we earnestly developed our science and did little to further our art. We learned to name and label. We worked diligently to define the accountable behaviors of our practitioners. Yet, we have not taken a position on the kind of future we are striving toward.

This state of affairs does not in the least diminish the importance of our effort to develop ethical guidelines for practice. The latest revision (1979) was major, reflecting years of patient work. It has helped us articulate our professional accountability and enhanced our ability to make decisions in practice.

Ethical clarification of social work values *is* necessary, but *incomplete*. Our code of ethics is our *science* of morality. It tells us how we should conduct ourselves. But it will take our *art* to paint a portrait of where we are going. Without one we cannot take the necessary steps. Without the other we wander aimlessly. We need both...in balance.

FINDING THE BALANCE

The social work profession is challenged to balance its ethical clarification of values with development of vision. We need a sense of collective direction to give vitality to our work and to remind us of those seldom acknowledged inner thoughts and feelings that led us to social work in the first place.

We have made efforts to clarify our values by separating and detailing them into ethical guidelines. We now wish to clarify our values toward a vision. Developing vision requires whole-mind thinking with an emphasis on our connecting and pattern-forming intuitive capacities.

Let's therefore begin deliberately thinking about our values in terms of connections. Let's begin exploring our values in ways that tap the special capacities of our right minds. Let's search for patterns, discover relationships, form insights and bring feelings to our thoughts.

We may not have a long list of agreed-upon values to work with, but we did manage to develop ethical guidelines with a generally agreed upon fundamental value and it should serve as a beginning point in this task as well.

MAKING CONNECTIONS WITH OUR FUNDAMENTAL VALUE

The fundamental value of social work is that often stated *belief in the dignity, worth and uniqueness of the individual.* Let's begin exploring it in terms of possible connections, interrelationships and patterns.

Social Work Values Versus Societal Values: Separate or Connected?

Though we call the belief in the dignity, worth and uniqueness of the individual, *our* primary social work value, it is a value central to our society; it is imbedded in our culture. It is our *societal* belief that the individual is more than a resource for the state, more than the carrier of a family name or tradition. It is our *societal* belief that the individual has a right to decide his or her own fate, to have privacy, be protected from harm. The other values we often consider *ours* (self-determination, confidentiality), then, are also values claimed by others in society.

We will not lose our uniqueness as a profession by acknowledging that our fundamental value is same as the one embedded in our society. We *are* unique in our unrelenting efforts to uphold and extend this value in the diverse activity of social work. We *are* unique in our willingness to remind an often forgetful society of its value commitments. We *are* unique in our attempts to actualize this central value in our practice, programs and policies. We need not claim a new value, for we are unique in our attempts to rekindle an existing one, our fanning of already existent embers.

Social Work Professionals vs. Members of Society: Separate or Connected?

Our profession has expended considerable effort in attempting to delineate our unique identity, but understanding our position in the whole of society is also important. We may choose to perceive ourselves as separate from society (self-governing, autonomous, whole, a profession), and acting as an outside force to protect individual rights. But we are also a part of society. In honoring the dignity, worth, and uniqueness of the individual, each practitioner is verifying membership in a profession and a culture.

We will not lose our uniqueness as a profession in recognizing our partness of society. We are both separate and connected. Each of us as individuals is aware of this dynamic polarity. When we look inside we see our separateness, autonomy, wholeness and uniqueness. When we look outside we see that we are connected, a part of family, neighborhood, community and profession. These are simply differing points of view. Both views are necessary.

When we view social work only as separate and unique, we fail to perceive our interrelationships and connections. We begin to approach social work in terms of our job, our career. We concern ourselves with our obligations to do for *others*, to do service for *others*. We concern ourselves with doing a *good* job, an ethical job for *others*...we are paid to be professional altruists, and treat self-interest as a complication. We view the people we work with as recipients of our service and call them clients. We make valiant efforts to behave in a business-like, professional manner...and we achieve technical competence at the cost of meaning and spirit.

When we include social work as a part of society our diverse activity as a profession is directly connected to the world we live in as individuals. In our work we are safeguarding and promoting values of *our* society, the world *we* value as well as the world of the people we identify as clients. What is often posed as professional responsibility can also be viewed as an opportunity to earn a living while problem solving in a world that is ours.

When we recognize our connection to the whole, that we share the same individual rights as others, we might develop insights that better respond to the dilemmas inherent to the words we use to separate (e.g., worker, service, and client). Our rational mind tells us the necessity of such separations and categories. Our intuition helps us soften the boundaries; helps us develop the sensitivity, and wisdom to bridge value conflicts, to fill in the gaps in our logical reasoning.

Separateness and connectedness are paradoxical. When you assume either, it influences your reality. When you assume separateness, you see labels and categories as necessary and right. You see the correct behaviors of a professional as honoring the individuality (separateness) of another. But when you choose to perceive things as connected you also sense rightness. You and the client are in this together. You both have a rightful place in a shared community; the boundaries of your identities (professional and client) temporarily dissolve. It is no longer one motivation of altruism and another of self-interest, but two persons cooperating out of self-interest. When we work to maintain self-determination of the client we are also safeguarding our own individual freedoms. When we work as professionals in the service of clients, we are also working to maintain the category "professional;" the category that feeds us and is *our* chosen route to the good life. Both needs are continually served in our work; our separations are connected.

Separate and connected...we are both. Separateness is the realm of our rational thinking; connectedness is the realm of our intuitive thinking. We are not replacing falsehood (separateness) with truth (connectedness). Rather, we are exercising our ability to see relationships and to search for patterns to counterbalance our sorting for details. In one view we connect for understanding; in the other we separate for understanding. Both views are incomplete in and of themselves, but in balance provide whole-mind resolutions.

Individual vs. Society: Separate or Connected?

We in this society want (value) every individual to be treated as having dignity, worth and uniqueness. We value the diversity of individuals each uniquely achieving their desires, and in turn contributing to the health, strength, and vitality of the whole. We value individual differences; we are a pluralistic society. We want the kind of a world where each individual is fulfilled, happy. Each of us wants the freedom to strive toward that fulfillment, and recognizes the freedom of all individuals must be protected if ours is to be protected. In this sense, we all need the individual to be free and the individual needs a society that values individual freedom (for each of us to have it). Society and the individual are interdependent, necessary to each other...connected.

A person is autonomous and self-governing. Our value of self-determination protects and promotes these attributes of individual freedom. But a person is also a social being. The biology of our growing up includes a long period of dependency, and much of what makes us human (communication, sympathy, self-awareness, conscience) is dependent upon interaction with others. Total individual freedom is an absurd proposition...free from what? From sense of community? What's the difference between autonomy and alienation?

Developments in our society are highly favorable to a detached, fragmented version of autonomy. The traditions that previously connected us to family and community have been traded in on mobility. We are transients seeking individual growth and autonomy. Some of us find it and understand the responsibility that comes with the package. Others get lost in themselves failing to grasp our elemental ties to one another.

Most of us are capable of achieving a balance of autonomy and social responsibility. We recognize the boundary between personal freedom and infringement on the freedom of others. Each of us tries to achieve maximum independence, while acknowledging the commitments beyond ourselves (those circumstances in which you would curb your freedom). At the same time we humans are materialistic, selfish and have established an economic system that promotes these characteristics. We are, indeed, complex and contradictory. We get all tied-up in ourselves, yet remain involved with others. We are preoccupied with our own needs, but find little meaning in life unless we commit to needs beyond ourselves. Tillich considers this paradox a primal law. He believes that every living thing "wants to remain within itself and to protect itself while it moves beyond itself."[6]

Koestler also describes this duality in human nature in his concept of person as "holon," which combines the meanings of whole and part.[7] Each of us views ourself as whole, separate, unique. We have a built-in tendency to preserve and defend our self-identity; to assert "self." Without this our entire social structure would collapse. But we also function as a part connected to a larger system, and have an integrative tendency that keeps our self-assertiveness in check. The favorable condition is of course a balance or dynamic equilibrium of the two. In everyday life both our wholeness and partness are in constant interplay. The holon concept is, then, wholes in a hierarchy in which they are parts...person, family, neighborhood, city, state, nation, world.

In a well-balanced society each individual retains character as a whole, and enjoys autonomy with restraint. Our autonomy is safeguarded, so that society may benefit as we assert our "self" in originality, initiative, and personal responsibility.

The tension between individual and society, (self-assertive versus integrative) has fascinated philosophers throughout history. It is central to the drama of life; it is a creative tension. When we focus on clients and extending service we refer to this natural tension as dilemma. We seek ethics that will resolve such conflict in values so that we may be effective and efficient in our work. Those ethical guidelines offered are then criticized as too abstract...we would like specific instructions. But when we view practice as a creative enterprise in which we help design solution patterns that *transcend* that tension (benefiting both the individual and society), specific rules would constrain our work. In this view the tension between individual and society is our central challenge; it is the arena within which each practitioner tests his or her uniqueness and creativity on a core aspect of life itself.

The literature of social work has ample criticism of our preoccupation with the individual as the primary focus of our effort and typical target of change. This is hardly a secret. Routinely someone takes us to task for this preoccupation and reminds us in no uncertain terms that we have a dual commitment to *both* the individual and society.

Creative generalists shouldn't find it difficult to accept this dual commitment. Indeed, they should be attracted to it as a place to test and develop their creative talents. We know we want a society of individuals who are fully developing their unique potentials. We want creative, healthy, individuals responsible to themselves and others. We are attracted to the words that describe a dynamic, growing person (learning, wondering, sensing, understanding, loving, aspiring).

We also recognize that we must have a society that supports the development of this valued individual, a society that provides freedom with alternatives and choices, a pluralistic society in which there are many decision-making points and a diversity of viewpoints to explore, a society that provides access to information and supports individual expression. And at the same time we know that we want a society with cohesiveness, a sense of direction.

To survive, to renew itself as a living system our society needs the fresh insights of unique individuals...to protect our individual freedoms we need a diverse society. The balance point between the two is, then, an essential place of challenge to creative generalists.

Let me make a practical suggestion in this regard. To keep this challenging and important reciprocal relationship clearly in view I suggest that anytime we see, hear or speak the fundamental value of social work, we mentally add six words that will make it the...

"BELIEF IN THE DIGNITY, WORTH AND UNIQUENESS OF THE INDIVIDUAL *AND A DIVERSE YET COHESIVE SOCIETY.*"

This will keep the central challenge in view so we can begin to clarify our fundamental value into a vision.

CLARIFYING OUR FUNDAMENTAL VALUE INTO VISION

We first need to search for concepts that seem relevant to the central challenge we have identified in our fundamental value. We then need to test in practice their actual fit with that point of tension in our commitment to both the individual and society.

When we do find concepts that help us grapple with that paradox, concepts that suggest practical strategies and excite us to action, we can share them with each other and gradually build our collective sense of vision.

You'll find many potentially useful concepts available. To illustrate my point I have selected one I find especially powerful. It's called "synergy."

Synergy

The process of synergy is recognized by Fuller in natural science, Benedict in social science and Maslow in psychology.[8,9,10] You have undoubtedly heard its meaning explained in the scientific sense. Here synergy refers to the general principle that the whole is more than the sum of its parts. In other words things can be arranged to create wholes that will not behave in the same way as the separate parts did previously. Wholes contain synergistic relationships involving the capacity of persons, forces and ideas to optimize each other, to enhance each other, to attain a state mutually benefiting each other.

Anthropologist Ruth Benedict expanded the meaning of synergy when she introduced it to social science. She used the term to describe a feature she observed in various cultures. She was comparing aggressive (exploitive, uncaring) to non-aggressive (supportive, harmonious) cultures and found the key difference in level of synergy. A low-synergy culture is more aggressive; a high-synergy culture more non-aggressive. High-synergy cultures have more institutions (customs, traditions), that transcend the polarity of individual selfishness and altruism. Synergistic situations are those in which the self-interest of both the individual and the community are served at the same time.[11]

Psychologist Abraham Maslow was studying self-actualizing and highly creative individuals at roughly the same time as Benedict was developing her ideas about synergy in culture. They were friends and at one point Maslow helped test the concept in observing the Blackfoot Indians. In his book, *The Further Reaches of Human Nature*, he describes one of the synergistic traditions he found. He tells of an annual sun dance ceremony and describes a scene like the following.

The wealthy individuals in the village bring their possession to the center of the village. A man with many possessions stands up and boasts of his many accomplishments over the year. He tells how he has done such and such, is good at this and that, is smart, a good hunter and farmer, etc., etc., and how he has accumulated wealth. With great pride (and not to humiliate) he then proceeds to go through all of his possessions, giving them away to widows, orphaned children, the blind, sick, etc. The process is then repeated with other wealthy members of the village.[12]

Consider that person of great wealth who gives it all away every year. He had demonstrated his ability, intelligence, strength and generosity. He kept the benefits of wealth (prestige, power, status, respect), while giving the materials to others. He was wealthy, yet owned nothing. He was loved, respected, admired. Everyone would be happy for his good fortune because of his generosity. What benefitted him would benefit the village as a whole. Compare this to the hoarding of material wealth and the envy and dislike produced in win/lose transactions. High synergy arrangements have this attribute of mutual advantage and cooperation. They are exchanges in which no one is called upon to be unselfish or to put social obligation above personal interest. Low synergy results when one has to lose for the other to gain.

In our culture the competitive nature of industrialization, of education and grading, specialization, and getting-to-the-top, leads to low synergy. But change is in the wind and our renewed interest in barter, skill swaps, partnering, co-ops, and networking are highly synergistic developments.

The synergy concept stimulates our ability to create a vision. The more we use it in daily life, the more we develop our *readiness* to respond to problems with synergistic solutions. Consider just a few of the possibilities.

— Many treat work and play as separate, but a few find ways to turn what they enjoy (play) into their jobs (work). In this way their play *is* their work.

— Synergistic solutions can be found at the program level. For example, in Sweden, many young couples face a housing shortage and many elderly people find themselves with large houses they are unable to maintain. The government now has a program where a large house can be converted into two apartments. The elderly couple live downstairs and rent the upstairs to a young couple. The rent goes to pay off the cost of the conversion so there is no expense incurred by the elderly person(s). This arrangement has the additional advantage helping to create a natural support system for both parties.

— Other opportunities will be found in daily practice. For example, a former student was working in a public social service agency in a small rural community. She had a foster mother on her caseload, who had broken her leg and needed a housekeeper. Another woman on her caseload had been battered by her husband and needed a temporary shelter. There was no money to pay for a housekeeper and no battered women's shelter. The social worker arranged for the battered wife to move in with the foster mother and help out with the housework in exchange for the shelter.

We'll begin to notice many other synergistic possibilities when we look for them and it's important that we also find ways to directly experience mutually beneficial exchanges ourselves. Anyone who barters understands the joy of a trade where both individuals give something they no longer have use for, in exchange for something they strongly desire. Such personal experiences help us gain practical skill in arranging synergistic exchanges and increase our perceptual sensitivity to situations where they might be tried.

SUMMARY AND ENDING COMMENT

If we apply whole-mind thinking to the fundamental value in social work we'll be able to develop a better balance between our ethics and vision for a more complete sense of purpose. In this more complete sense of purpose we'll find an increased readiness to respond to both anticipated and unanticipated events in our future. Concepts such as synergy, self-renewal, health and creativity could be related to our fundamental value to help stimulate the development of a fresh pattern of values for vision. (See Figure 3.1.)

In the next chapter we'll shift our attention from the profession as a whole to you and I as individuals *within* the profession. We'll explore a way to apply whole-mind thinking to a process that aligns our personal values, vision and vocation with trends in our society and profession. In this pattern of alignment we'll find an imaginative and practical guide for our daily problem-solving activity, something I'm calling *vocational style*.

Figure 3.1

Mindset and Values

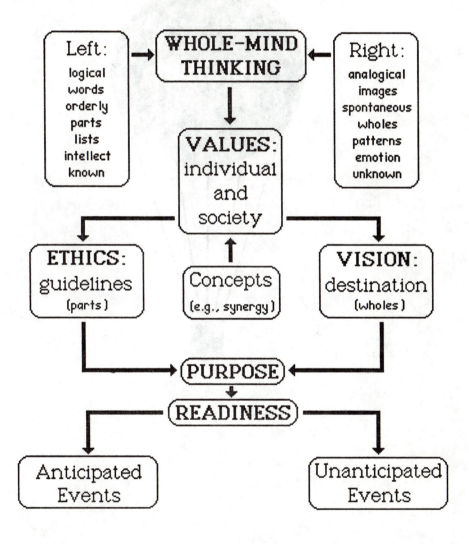

Vocational style 4

In the introduction to Part I of this book (mindset), Allen and I explained that creative generalists are not defined by their activity. Rather, what they have in common is a way of thinking and a predisposition or readiness to act.

In the last chapter (Social work values) I explained this way of thinking is a balance of the left- and right-mind functions referred to as whole-mind thinking. When we apply whole-mind thinking to clarifying social work values we can develop both ethics and vision. Combined ethics and vision give us a more complete sense of purpose. In this more complete purpose we find an increased readiness to respond to both anticipated and unanticipated events.

Throughout discussion balance remained a key concept. Whole-mind thinking is in the balance of left- and right-mind thinking. Our fundamental social work value requires a balanced commitment to both the individual and society. Purpose is a balance of ethics and vision. Readiness is in the balance of our preparedness for both anticipated and unanticipated events.

In this chapter we'll explore another point of balance, one that unifies something we objectively perceive as "out there" with something we subjectively perceive as "in here"...one that integrates our logical choice of a profession "out there" with our intuitive response to a sense of vocation "in here."

VOCATION

We previously established that values are subjective beliefs. They are the way we want, prefer or desire something to be. We feel some - thing about our values, we protect and promote them. When we clarify our values by integrating them into an overall pattern they become visionary, they become elements in our conception of a better world, our *vision* of a preferable future. Our sense of vocation guides us in striving toward that vision.

In thinking about our vocation we begin to connect our personal values with those of our profession and society. Our society's value of individual freedom created a pathway for the development of the social work profession. The profession's valued belief in the dignity, worth and uniqueness of the individual and a diverse yet cohesive society, in turn, can be viewed as a pathway for our personal sense of vocation.

You join a profession. You take courses in it. You get a degree in it and work in it. Profession is outside, vocation is inside. You *have* a vocation. It doesn't require you to become a social worker, or to remain a social worker, but you may find and express it *in* social work.

Vocation is not your job, jobs can be changed. It is not your career, careers can be changed. Vocation is in the meaning of your work. It is in the doing of your beliefs. It is in your approach to job, family, friends and community. It is you, busy being you, and doing what you believe needs doing, which is, in itself, contributing something worthwhile to the rest of us.

You don't *get* a vocation, you don't achieve it like a goal. It's your rational mind that listens to what you want (value) and starts setting up goals. Your intuitive mind, on the other hand, pays attention to the emotional energies of your deepest desires and starts connecting, aligning, unifying, intensifying them into vocation...into something we sense as we work toward a vision. Vocation, then, is like an internal guidance system, a direction finder, our personal homing device.

You become intuitively aware of vocation. You learn to notice cues from your inner self, like the feeling of *rightness* when you are doing something you sincerely consider worth your doing, or the feeling that everything is *coming together, falling into place*. It is in your feeling of *tracking* or *"in-sync-ness"* when with a kindred spirit, someone on a parallel course. It is what you sense when you feel *in tune* with another person. It is *"at-home-ness," connectedness*. It is what is experienced in a synergistic exchange.

Your awareness of vocation is strongest when you are able to align your logic, imagination and emotional energy in doing something you believe in, directing your efforts toward your emerging personal vision of the way things should be. These experiences help you more fully understand what it means to have the *power of intention*, and you learn to recognize it in others as *charisma* or *presence*.

Vocation in work, then, shifts the focus from being a professional to acting upon your beliefs and values. When we have commitment, intensity of desire (value) and visualize the end state of that desire (vision), we activate our internal guidance system (vocation).

FORMING A VOCATIONAL STYLE

There's a way we can turn our *internal* guidance system into an *external* guidance system for the day-to-day practice of social work. I am calling this external form a *vocational style*. Basically, here's how we put one together:

1. We work with, think about, mull over and combine our values, vision and vocation into a *pattern*. Simply put, we have to have a reasonably clear and internally consistent idea of what we want and what it would look like if we got it in order to keep ourselves on the right track. When viewed as a whole this dynamic pattern of value, vision and vocation is our personal *mission*, our commitment to making something happen.

2. Next, we study trends within our society and profession. Every trend poses both problems and opportunities. The vocational style we develop should help us contend with the problems and maximize the opportunities.

3. By aligning our personal mission with trends in our society and profession, we then develop an imaginative and practical vocational style to guide our daily work.

Let's take a closer look at each of these steps.

FIRST STEP TOWARD VOCATIONAL STYLE: COMBINING VALUES, VISION AND VOCATION INTO PERSONAL MISSION

"Combining" is a clue to the kind of thinking needed for developing a personal mission. We are pattern-forming and that requires whole-mind thinking with an emphasis on intuition. Tapping the special functions of our intuition will take deliberate effort on our part because of the overpowering left-mind bias in our culture. Like everyone else, you and I habitually favor the security, exactness and orderliness of our logic. We even seem to trust left-mind words (e.g., goal, objective, profession) more than we trust right-ind words (e.g., vision, values, vocation). Consider the following examples.

Right-Mind Words

Think about how we use the word "vision." On the one hand we know vision is important and necessary (e.g., "He lacks the vision for confronting complex problems."). On the other hand we thwart the efforts of someone trying to develop it (e.g., "...too idealistic, fanciful. My dear you are given to very impractical ideas.").

Everyone hopes someone at the head of the line has a little vision, but typically consider it a rare gift bestowed on the few. With increased understanding of right-mind functions we are finding the contrary is true. Vision can be developed over time like other human abilities. We start by working with our values. We arrange them into mini-visions. We add to these mini-visions over time and integrate them into an overall vision.

Having vision refers to a power to perceive something not present to the eye. ("I had a vision" sounds like a lot of supernatural claptrap to our rationality doesn't it?) Visions often come to us in dreams. (Our left minds really trust dream material don't they?) Considering what you know about intuition, why do you think we often have visions in our dreams? For many, the only time they drop their guard is when asleep. Their left mind is finally quiet and their right mind is freed to paint a few pictures for them. We've kept our intuition fenced off for quite some time now. Maybe if we kicked a few boards out of that fence we could see what our other half is trying to show us without first having to fall asleep.

Even the way we treat our values has a couple of quirks. We are, for example, comfortable in telling each other how we value (subjective belief) personal freedom. But how do we actually react if we happen to experience that value subjectively? If on rare occassion a phrase in a song (e.g., "the land of the free" or "this land is your land") stimulates a feeling response what do we do with it? Do we quickly try to dispell such lapses into emotionalism as unhelpful and unrealistic? Do we dismiss the trigger words as hollow, smaltzy, vague, hypocritical or trite…hardly desirable for the practical and scientific? And it's easy to get things back in control isn't it? All we have to do is recall the many destructive actions taken in the name of individual freedom, the foolish errors and shortsightedness of even those who seem genuine in their efforts to uphold it.

On the other hand we also know that if we wanted to, we could lump our throat and tear our eyes simply by recalling images of individuals we have met, who in times of extreme hardship or physical threat stood firm, ready to make unusual sacrifices (even their lives) for that supposedly vague notion of personal freedom. Consider also your own powerful and sudden feelings of outrage, your teeth-gritting desire for social justice when you hear of a certain abuse, exploitation and disregard of personal freedom.

My point? Each of us is aware that tucked inside our intuitive world of images and emotions is a source of tremendous power. We may at times doubt our ability to control it in rage or passionate desire. Even in milder form, when it unexpectedly bubbles into our awareness we may be embarrassed by it or view it as a weakness to be overcome.

We have learned to restrict that intuitive, subjective world of imagery to a limited and safe range of experience...when to dream, when to laugh, when to be silly, when to love. The rational, civilized and educated adult of the recent past believed for the most part intuition was an unpredictable, overly-emotional, shallow, and sloppy form of thinking. But we are now learning about high quality intuition. We have and are rapidly developing tools for the disciplined use of right-mind thinking. We have ways to better control and channel this source of energy in a balance of whole-mind thinking.

Allen and I will invite you to explore many of these tools in coming chapters. For our work here I suggest only that you anticipate interference from the left ("this is a complete waste of time") and try to keep the channels open to the right. Our left mind talks to us, continually interrupting and criticizing the attempts of our right mind to communicate ideas with images and feelings. To develop a pattern of values, vision and vocation we need balanced thinking, we need to deliberately encourage right-mind participation while holding down some of that left-mind interference.

There's another important ingredient for combining value, vision and vocation into personal mission that I'd like to mention here...*strength of commitment.*

Strength of Commitment

A few months ago I was visiting a friend who was in the final rounds of a struggle with cancer. Above her bed was a picture of three racoons in a tree peering out at you through the leaves. Boldly painted words at the bottom of the picture said:

> "SOME PEOPLE MAKE THINGS HAPPEN;
> OTHERS OBSERVE WHAT'S HAPPENING;
> AND THE REST WONDER WHAT HAPPENED."

Under the circumstances the meaning was especially poignant for me and the phrase "Some people make things happen" stayed glued to the front of my mind.

In large part, social work practice involves *observing what's happening* and then helping those that *wonder what happened.* We watch the world generate problems at a frenzied pace and do our best to lend a hand to those caught in the crossfire. We care about people and recognize that with a sudden shift in circumstances we could also be thrown into the "what happened?" category. We are, in this sense, medics on a battleground. There is no question of the importance of our commitment to this work, but we must commit ourselves as well to *making peace happen.*

A pattern of values, vision and vocation is energized by a *strong* commitment to making it happen. Vivid imagery (vision) comes with passionate, emotionally charged desire (value). (If you want a crystal clear mental image of a plate of home-cooked food, try fasting for a few days.)

How much intensity is required? Say you had invested years of effort and your life savings in a certain project (e.g., growing vegetables in sea water on the shores of a starving country) and were hiring someone to help you complete it. One candidate for the position says, "I believe this is important work and I *really* want it to happen." A second candidate says, "It *will* happen and I want to be there when it does." Everything else being equal, which would you hire?

Highly successful entrepreneurs and business organizations ranging from IBM to Mary Kay Cosmetics recognize the importance of such affirmative commitment...we could do worse than follow their lead. If you're guessing this is just a dose of that old "power of positive thinking"...you're right. In his book *Self-Fulfilling Prophecies*, Russell Jones cites ample evidence in support of this proposition. For example, he reports on the operation of an "anticipation-invigoration mechanism" which excites, alerts and enhances our responsiveness to available stimuli.[1] In short, when you anticipate success you invigorate your power to achieve that success.

A belief that it *will* happen, a strong commitment, fuels our persistence in creating a better world. This is, after all, our world, our time in history. It is a time for envisioning alternatives and making important choices. It is a time for designing solutions that realize our values and a time for making those solutions *happen.*

SECOND STEP TOWARD VOCATIONAL STYLE: STUDYING TRENDS

When developing a vocational style, each of us would, of course, study the problems and opportunities in local and regional trends as well as those of society as a whole. To illustrate the process we'll here limit discussion to several problems and opportunities in a major societal trend, our transition from an *industrial* economy (e.g., steel, automobiles) to an *information* economy (e.g., communications, biotechnology).

Industrial to Information Economy

Our country is midway in a transition from an industrial economy to an information economy. We are struggling to maintain the security of our industrial power, while at the same time carving out a niche in the emerging world of high technology communications.

We are steadily losing ground as an industrial power and are finding it more and more difficult to compete in the world market. The newer equipment and facilities of Japan or West Germany, for example, are more efficient than ours and at the same time costs of upgrading our own industries are prohibitive. The lower labor costs of developing countries give them a competitive edge over us as well.

Robotics, computers and automation are changing the face of our industry with machines taking over assembly functions. Satellite communications, computers and a growing list of electronic innovations are shifting human participation toward generating new ideas, developing technical skills and procedures and "packaging" information to sell to others in the world market.

Problems in trend: access to information

Advances in electronic technologies offer amazing immediacy of information transmission. Though predicted more than twenty years ago, no one really fathomed how quickly we would achieve our current communication systems. Orbiting satellites connect us across the entire planet. New innovations in telephones, printing, TVs, film, computers and a host of other electronic devices tumble into our lives every day.

But we have been skeptical about the many promises of a hi-tech society (e.g., accelerated learning, a bustling economy, and having more control over our own lives). Rightfully so, similar promises were made with the telegraph, telephone and other earlier media advances, but they instead wound up encouraging greater uniformity and centralized control in the hands of the few.

Certainly advances in technology have given anyone with the equipment and technical skill more access to all types of information than ever before. The central question, then, is who will have access to *what* information for what *purposes*? Concerns related to this question differ markedly.

Some view the major concern as increasing governmental surveillance, standardization, regulation and the erosion of individual privacy. In the extreme this is the fear of "big brotherism" or totalitarianism.

Others fear the opposite, that our societal institutions (e.g., national defense, major corporations, banks) have become overly dependent on electronic information systems making them extremely vulnerable to theft and sabotage by criminals, vandals, and terrorists. In the extreme this is the fear of governmental breakdown and anarchy.

A third and again different concern is for those will *not* have equal access to information. For example, will the poor be able to afford the necessary equipment? Will they have the technical ability to use it if made available?

Problems in trend: employment

Though concerns about access to information are often raised, the dominant question regarding the decline of traditional industries in our society and our changeover to an information economy is simply, "What about jobs?"

Even the promise of a bright employment future in the growing communications industry loses its sparkle when we ask how we will retrain everyone for the kinds of jobs predicted? And just how will we cope with supposedly unprecedented layoffs in the near future when our debt-ridden government continues to cut financial support programs beyond bare bones and into the marrow?

Past periods of high unemployment were compounded by sudden inflation and recession cycles. Predictably, our mass anxieties intensi - fied in these periods. Physical and chemical abuse, depression, mental illness and crime increased as well.

If, as some predict, we hit unemployment rates of 50% to 75% in traditional industries within the next five to ten years, social work will surely be challenged with an explosive increase in social problems.

Opportunities in trend: increasing self-reliance

Periods of high unemployment and rapid swings of recession and inflation stimulated awareness as well as anxiety over the last decade. Some began to see the potential disasters in continuing our dependence on a declining industrial economy. Though hardly noticed people were beginning to change.

The inflated costs of building encouraged many to consider the alternative of self-building, and in the process to re-evaluate the meaning of shelter. The inflated costs of new car purchases encouraged many to learn new skills in mechanical repair and to reconsider choices in transportation. High gasoline prices encouraged our acceptance of smaller cars. High food prices encouraged gardening, and with it came a newfound pleasure in growing plants, interest in the nutritional quality of our food. Threats to income encouraged experimentation in barter, and awareness of the benefits of this highly personal form of exchange. Unemployment encouraged a sudden proliferation of budding entrepreneurs and for many a better fit between individual interest and work. Spiraling medical costs stimulated self-care and holistic health alternatives.

In steadily increasing numbers people across the country were responding to economic problems by increasing *self-reliance*.

Opportunities in trend: increasing diversity

Though many have rightfully warned of the potential for increased uniformity and standardization in the computerized future, something very different is happening. There are strong indications that we are moving in an opposite direction...one that leads away from a homogenized, conforming, society and toward a more diverse, open society.

The opportunity is *not* in our advancing technology, but in our changing human consciousness and the way we are *using* that technology. We are thinking, perceiving and valuing differently. Our entry into the age of information and communications is not only worldwide in breadth, it has a new depth and richness. It is not only that we can span great distances in talking to one another, but that we seem to have something worthwhile to say.

A significant number of people are using our new capacities for rapid transmission of information and idea exchange to expand their personal choices, and we are witnessing an amazing diversification of our culture. This diversification is not pointless or haphazard. Rather, individuals are developing their autonomy and making choices that reflect our value of individual freedom.

Opportunities in trend: increased networking

We are responding to the ever present threat of unemployment, inflation, recession and depression with increasing self-reliance. We are responding to the threat of massification in the age of information with increasing diversification.

And in facing our current problems and future threats we have become more and more dissatisfied with the often inflexible, inefficient and unresponsive centralized structures we had created to serve an earlier industrial economy. We searched for and found a new decentralized organizational form, the *network*.

Self-help and mutual aid are proliferating within a new, powerful, flexible, adaptive, interconnected social structure, the network. With it we are spreading out, decentralizing. We are changing from fewer and larger, to multiple and smaller centers of information, power and resources; from federal to state and local, from main office to branch offices.

Self-help groups can be found for nearly any conceivable problem or interest (weight-control, handicaps, retirement, house repair). We are turning away from institutional helping to self-help, and our emerging self-help society not only stimulates diversity, it values it. The "melting pot" helped us build a massive labor force for industrial growth, but we are trading it for the richness of ethnic and cultural difference. We are valuing individuality and choice. It is visible in our art, our foods, our work arrangements, our definition of "family."

Thousands of networks are springing up around issues, politics, hobbies, common problems, common skills, common goals. Look through the lists of any network clearinghouse and you'll find a variety of health networks, educational networks, spiritual and psychological networks, economic and business networks.

Through networks social movements can organize instantly. With rapid communication, news of success travels fast. A creative achievement in any field, anywhere in the world quickly becomes common knowledge.

Satellites immediately report events throughout the world and through the network structure, we can choose to react instantly. Networks are cooperative, self-generating, self-organizing; they connect us directly, horizontally, rather than through vertical hierarchies. Besides offering information and opportunity for collective action, networks are personal. We turn to them for kinship and support. They are *ours*. They are the creative structure that will get us through the rough times of industrial decline. They are a new institution; the most flexible, responsive one we could find to fit our current realities. They cut across constraining bureaucratic and discipline boundaries. They help us sort through information overload to select what we need as quickly as possible.

This new organizational structure, the network, empowers the individual and encourages autonomy. Hierarchies support the values of moving up to get ahead. They produce the competition, stress and tension, we have long heard about. Networking allows for individuals to participate in decisions without the same requirements of delegated authority.[2]

This empowerment of individuals is already having impact on our traditional institutions. Through decentralized networks, home computers, cable TVs, and the vocal consumer, health care, for example, is undergoing a transformation. Holistic health alternatives abound. They are gaining legitimacy in state and federal programs. New entrepreneurs are responding to consumer demand for health concepts that include stress, society, family, diet, seasons, emotions, herbal remedies combined Eastern/Western technologies. More and more people are committing themselves to health-oriented life styles. New tools are available for home diagnosis and treatment. Exercise, diet, visualization, and biofeedback are combined in novel ways as we reach for holistic concepts of wellness.

Private mediation centers have assumed some of the functions of courts. Neighborhood "blockwatch" programs supplement police patrols. Small shifts can be found everywhere. But it isn't the size of any specific shift that's important here. What we are seeing is not the historical "top down" change. Rather, change is coming from the "bottom up." Many people are making small changes. When viewed as a whole, the many small changes cluster and we become aware of patterns, direction, trends.

THIRD STEP TOWARD VOCATIONAL STYLE: ALIGNING PERSONAL MISSION WITH TRENDS IN OUR SOCIETY AND PROFESSION

Self-reliance, cultural diversity and the *cohesiveness of networks*...we are witnessing the revitalization of those values we consider fundamental to our profession...our belief in *the dignity, worth and uniqueness of the individual (self-reliance) and a diverse (cultural diversity) yet cohesive (network) society.*

By supporting these developments in the *what's happening* we are *making things happen.* By participating in the movement of society we can help others respond to problems while at the same time committing our energy toward those developments that reflect our value choices.

This is a "martial arts" strategy. It assumes that you have a lot more power when you aim your energy toward guiding and supporting something already moving in a desired direction, than you do trying to block contrasting trends. It is a "going with the strengths" strategy.

As individual social workers we can make a difference in our day-to-day activities at the local level because that is where a new power for change resides. We are decentralizing and networking, and each of us has the potential for realizing our personal and professional values in the many small changes that are accumulating toward the transformation of our society.

In *"The Nature of Social Work Practice"* Allen talked of viewing the diversity of social work as either a problem or an opportunity. Within the profession you will find trends supporting both perceptions. For some, the professions uncertainties, ambiguities and incompatibilities have been and continue to be a major source of concern.

Creative generalists also recognize some of the difficulties inherent to the diversity of our amorphous profession. But they are also attracted to that diversity, its potentials for adaptive health and the creative expression it stimulates. They require a frame of reference as well, but use a mindset and tools of problem solving that encourage the expression of their own unique views of life, their beliefs about the way things ought to be. Like the proliferating and adaptive entrepreneurs in the business world they are the entrepreneurs of a professional world. They combine values, vision and vocation into a sense of personal mission. They align this personal mission with certain trends in their society and profession and develop *vocational styles*.

VOCATIONAL STYLE

A vocational style is the intuitive counterpart to a rational model for practice. It guides our expression of values, vision and vocation in the everyday world of work and living. It is a flexible, organic form that accommodates our continuing growth. It combines the imaginative with the practical. It combines personal desires with the needs of others. It reflects a *pattern* of alignment, a fit of our individual day-to-day activities with developments we wish to support in our profession and society.

Below I offer three vocational style examples. Each is a beginning sketch, a possibility. Each includes the societal developments we have talked about in its basic pattern. For example, our future may include serious unemployment, financial insecurity and concern about meeting our common human needs. As social workers some of us may work in programs directly related to economic difficulties, but in one way or another all of us will confront the interconnected pattern of stress resulting from a high unemployment situation. Survival is a primary motivating force in human life. In the industrial age survival translates into *having a job* and *earning money*. Employment is the generally perceived means of meeting common human needs for food, clothing and shelter. Most of us assume we will have jobs and earn money to meet those needs. Indeed the "American dream" includes a surplus of money to spend in pursuit of the "good life."

In this "survival plus" formula, earning a living is directly related to individual freedom. Without income how would we acquire the necessities of life, much less be free to reach for its luxuries and pleasures? The dominance of a "having a job and earning a living" headset is, of course, tied to our self-image as a powerful industrial nation, and our continuing failure to regain our past position of power has led to some very gloomy forecasting.

The question of how we could see to it that everyone had adequate money to purchase basic necessities in a depressed economy with the meager resources of a debt-ridden government is difficult to answer. But there *are* answers to the question of how we could help others acquire basic necessities. There are many "small ways" to reduce the tensions that people experience in periods of high unemployment and economic instability. They would be welcomed additions to a growing response already apparent in our society...the desire to increase self-reliance, to diversify and to network.

Of course we would try to help the unemployed find new jobs, but every idea we thought of or came across for insuring food, clothing and shelter could also be made available to everyone (we are after all talking about an age of information and communication). Gardening, food exchanges, neighborhood barter centers...all help restore confidence in our ability to meet our own needs and work together for mutual aid. And we could, of course, find many ways to encourage the networking phenonemon as a flexible and highly responsive way to spread ideas, information and resources throughout our communities.

Now let's take a look at those vocational style examples. In the first I combine the historical idea of converting lead into gold (alchemy) with a more current interest in recycling (trashpicker).

The Alchemist Trashpicker

> *"My son, my son, you could have been a doctor. Instead, you're a social worker. Nothing but a glorified garbage collector. You pick up the refuse, the worn out, the people who no longer work...like broken toys. And, for all of this, you are highly underpaid."*

Perhaps you never heard this from your mother, but if you are in social work you received a similar message from someone; a friend, acquaintance or another social worker. At the point of such an encounter you wish you knew judo or some other martial arts defense so you could deftly side step the accusation, move into your opponent's direction of energy, and with a twist of your wrist leave him or her sitting on his or her posterior with mouth agape and defeat obvious. Instead, you attempt a description of your work and why it is important; or you suggest the other has the value base of a toad; or you shrug your shoulders and wonder how on earth you ever wound up in this unloved profession. Later, you consider with sadness that the trash collector analogy, though crude, does hold up pretty well.

Trash and garbage collectors often prefer to be called sanitation engineers and some social workers prefer alternative labels as well (e.g., mental health worker, psychotherapist, counselor, community organization specialist, probation officer).

Trash collectors pick up our refuse; things we don't want to see anymore; things that look ugly, or smell bad, or might cause disease or remind us of bad times. They haul them to some unseen landfill and cover them up.

People don't like to be reminded of their garbage. They don't want to face the amount of their waste, their errors, the sadness of their broken belongings. They don't like to be reminded that they also will wear down, or someday be seen as less useful, or get replaced by something new or better...and social workers, like trash collectors, remind them.

And just how *did* you end up in this unloved profession? Let me take a few wild guesses.

You pretty much liked people, enjoyed helping someone out when you had the chance and thought you might even get to turn a few social injustices around. You also knew that given the practical realities of a day-to-day job, you preferred talking and problem solving with others to drilling teeth, holding a test tube or labeling rocks.

You knew social workers didn't make piles of money, but they seemed to do all right...and they could live just about anywhere and always manage to find some kind of job.

You heard all the arguments against it...emissaries of the status quo, ineffective bureaucracies, dependency producing programs, but you really didn't have a burning desire to wear a lab jacket or climb any corporate ladders. You never really figured out exactly what you wanted to *be* when you *grew up*. And at least the social work classes talked about *real* things like kids and older people, and mishaps and hopes...and social work seemed like a more open field than the others, less likely to bind you up in a direction or activity you might later regret. You simply weren't ready to get locked into a single course of action. And above all else you wanted the freedom to change and grow, to create your life as you went along. You wanted the security of employment and income, but the promise of megabucks didn't seem as important as a chance to look around some more...try out different kinds of work in different places and hopefully be able to do something decent for other people along the way.

Sure, you met a few jerks in your social work classes, but they seemed a smaller percentage than in your other classes...and you also met people like you, people you enjoyed being with. And if you felt some embarrassment when family or friends back home asked about your major, you also knew that social work with all of its complexity and uncertainty also offered you a reasonable chance for autonomy and creativity in the workplace.

You knew what *others* thought and decided the price wasn't too high. If some social workers were incompetent you could still be competent. If a policy was lousy, you'd find a way to change it or subvert it. If an agency was dehumanizing you'd find ways to make your end of the business more humane. You knew when your *other* friends talked of social work they'd make an exception for you; they believed in you and knew you had something to offer no matter what your career choice.

In short, you trusted yourself, your own inclinations. You looked over the possibilities, had at least a sense of some of the difficulties and bought in. Where others saw only trash, you saw treasure, opportunity, resources.

Welcome my friend, you have high potential to become a full-fledged alchemist trashpicker. Simply in choosing to be a social worker you have demonstrated an ability to disregard what others think when *you* consider something worth your commitment. You may at times be uncomfortable with your image, but essentially you are more internally validating than many others. If you remember this and take pride in it, you will continue to develop your point of personal power, self-reliance and an edge in making life worthwhile. While you relinquish continual need for external approval, recognition and applause, you'll hear more and more from your internal world of curiosity, excitement and optimism.

Other alchemist trashpickers will recognize you. If you were one and standing here right now I'd say, "I'll be damned, another trashpicker," and we'd both know a lot of what's worth knowing about each other without undue explanation or justification. We'd be interested in each other, not in our job titles, money earned or how many times we'd visited Europe, but in how each of us engaged the magical process of alchemy.

Let's take a minute to clarify a more common perception of alchemist trashpickers. Many would think of them as nothing more than junk collectors, people who pile up cast-offs behind the house. To alchemist trashpickers those are not piles of junk, but resources for problem solving. They are "alchemists" in their ability to convert the conventional function of a given trash item into multiple function alternatives. They see alternative uses in everything. Each single trash item has inherent multipurpose when viewed through the eyes of an alchemist trashpicker. Like the alchemists of the past who claimed to turn lead into gold, these modern recyclers turn trash into treasure.

That old door waiting for the trash pickup easily becomes a shed roof, the back of a solar panel, a table top, a mattress support for a homemade bed. It might be dismantled for rare hinges and handles, raw lumber for building and on it goes. The more variety in the alchemist trashpicker's resource pile, the more he or she is able to connect individual items with others to form patterns both functional and aesthetic. Trash pile or resource center…it's all in the eye of the beholder.

Now let's apply this vocational style to social work. Again the "trash" concept is the key. Look for those items others cast off, avoid, don't want any longer.

Consider trash positions. To find and convert them you need to engage the predisposition to trash you exhibited in choosing social work in the first place. You were less concerned with the status others assigned that choice. Apply this ability to disregard the narrow perceptions and status evaluations others use in estimating the worth of various positions and agencies *within* social work as well. Once you break through this barrier, alchemy is at your fingertips.

Imagine a social work employment agency. You already know you'll find a very long line of social workers in front of the counter marked mental health. Same goes for anything else that sounds like heavy-duty counseling. The lines are a lot shorter and less frantic over there on the other end of the room near the sign that says public welfare. Lots of room at other counters as well (e.g., elderly centers, Big Brother/Sister agencies, schools, correctional programs). The point is not that you have to take a lower status position. Rather, you'll find more opportunities for alchemy in positions others consider less valuable.

Primary or secondary setting, big city or small town, slick office or trunk of your car…you'll find many arrows pointing the direction once you decide to look for trash.

One kind of job will have a small description, or state less responsibility, or sound routine, or list *old* sounding words in a goal statement…but the salaries won't vary all that much and you may have stumbled onto a magnificent resource pile.

Let me tell you a few trash and alchemy stories to show you what I mean.

A small town wanted someone to set up a youth center, a place to keep kids off the streets, and so on. Local professionals wouldn't touch it. You know the setup. The first time someone lights up a "joint," the center gets front page coverage and the social worker is a failure.

Well, a couple of students and I took the project on, *after* a little alchemy-thinking. Our argument went something like this: The youth center should not be viewed as a solution (which would be doomed from the start), but a tool for the assessing the extent of the problem. What was the extent of chemical abuse? Who was initiating the current spree of vandalism? Where did kids hang out when truanting?

Framed in this perspective, someone lighting a "joint" in the center would indicate *success* in our getting a chance to find out more about the local chemical abuse scene. The community needed an *ear* held closer to the youth, a finger on the pulse of trouble. The promise wasn't that the center would solve youth problems, but would know more about them. It would help in early detection and development of alternatives *before* everyone got carried away. We would try to *attract* problem awareness in order to defuse critical events. Thus everything we could dream up became a tool for assessment. Saturday dances became a chance to meet, talk, and negotiate with potentially troublesome kids. If trouble did arise, it was our responsibility to know something about it, be close to it, size it up, bring it to the community and *share* in developing solution strategies.

Another bit of alchemy took place in a public school setting. The elementary schools wanted to organize data on "problem" children about to graduate to the junior high level. A profile on each was to be forwarded to the junior high counseling staff, so that they could pick up on special need kids as soon as they got there.

Nobody wanted this one. It would entail the menial work of organizing anecdotal records, teacher reports, psychological reports and social histories on each target kid. A field student agreed to work on this trash project *if* she could report the strengths and assets of the kids, as well as the problems and liabilities. Record review and summaries were still necessary, but she also got to meet with teachers, parents and staff to develop a "strength profile." She asked about capacities, tricks teachers had used along the way to attract the target kids to learning tasks, ways in which teachers and parents found the could develop positive relationships with the kids, etc. She met with teachers individually and then in small groups to develop strategies that would help the kids start off in a favorable light when they moved on to the junior high school. It was both hard work and fun and she had the opportunity to discourage the negative perceptual sets regarding deficiencies while emphasizing strengths and opportunities. Anyone who has read research studies on the impact of perceptual sets in student-teacher relationships can recognize the power in such a simple ploy as presenting the water glass as half-full, rather than half-empty.

One more. Another public school problem. Kids of migrant farm workers posed difficulties for elementary schools along the migrant stream. They had all sorts of achievement problems. They entered each school with low reading and math skills. Records and files were often so late they were of little help to planning. The migrant kids had trouble getting along with peers (low status outsiders). Staff didn't have a sense of the families, history and worklife impacting on the kids and again, nobody wanted this one. Involved (or uninvolved) agencies passed the problem around and previous attempts at coordination and ongoing planning were too time consuming and considered failures. A teacher (alchemists are everywhere when you learn how to recognize one) came up with this little scheme.

The migrant children would be considered "visiting dignitaries." They would carry their own scrapbook of information: typical school information of achievement levels, tests, and also family and pet pictures, stories of "where I've been," etc. When the migrant child entered a new school the teacher would announce his or her arrival and help the child go over the scrapbook information in a class presentation. The child was presented as "traveled," "seasoned," with a "rich learning background." With teacher support, migrant kids became special from a positive perspective. Information moved from school to school in the scrapbook. The kids developed relationships more quickly (pen pals were encouraged). Teachers got to be in a successful, though uncomplicated migrant project, and the kids became more connected to the schools.

My point? Unwanted tasks with histories of failure, boredom or broken promises will often yield extra room to create. They typically will have low success demands, and attaining reasonable goals will seem like major achievements. If you make sure to motivate others and keep your visibility low (the need for recognition and applause), they'll pick up on such projects, freeing you to turn your attention to other trash piles...and they can be found everywhere. The secret shared by alchemist trashpickers is the reward is not in the gold itself. It is in the doing, the toying with possibilites, the magic of a turn-around...the process of alchemy.

The Resource Peddler

Home visiting has been a tradition in social work throughout its history. It was part of an early view of the social worker as a connecting link, a channel of communication between various community services and the clients they served. With a little tinkering and adapting this tradition could become a useful tool for participating in and encouraging networking...so let's do a little tinkering.

First we need to shift from the expert fixer mentality to a networker mentality. The peddler label helps us make this perceptual shift. Like trashpicking, the image of peddling seems a bit humbling until you know its secrets. It strengthens our capacity for internal validation at the cost of a little external validation. You are not going out to *solve* the problems, but to peddle resources through which people will be able to solve their *own* problems (increasing self-reliance). Both have their rewards, but they're different. In one you get a "Hey, you're really good at fixing this." In the other you show how to use a resource and hear people saying, "Hey, we *did* it." Both make us feel good, but the second turns on a different set of lights. You are in these many small ways building the strength of your community. You are valuable to the community for different reasons. You are revitalizing the intuitive meanings in our words "neighborhood," "general store," "town meeting."

And to be honest, I doubt we are really giving up a lot in the way of recognition for expertness. Social workers often find themselves visiting to deliver bad news (your kid is in trouble again) or to ask bad questions (*why* is your kid in trouble again?). Perhaps the peddler image is more a replacement for the meddler image.

So how do you go about becoming a *resource peddler*? Start by establishing a pattern of routine visits. This might easily be adapted to a position where you already are responsible for regular client contact, but could also be developed as a community resource project, research project or an agreed upon way for you to "get to know" the community in a new position. The point is to shift the emphasis from the *assessment* of community problems to the *inventory* of community resources. In your travels you collect, organize and make available information, skills, experiences, where to go, who to see. You encourage barter and swapping. You accumulate, remember, file away. In your mind carry an image of that old time peddler wagon with pots and pans hanging, boxes of hard candies, household tools and supplies. You are becoming a connector, a bridge, a weaver, you are supporting networking.

You'll begin making synergistic connections between people. You'll remember and develop all sorts of talents helpful to this vocational style. An organizer friend of mine used to go into a neighborhood the day before he wanted to meet parents. He'd use the old magic trick of pulling quarters from kids' ears. The next day when he returned to the area the kids would holler, "There he is, that's the man with the magic quarters"…and the parents would talk with him.

You'll learn to pay attention to the many little things (as well as the more important things) people may have or need. Keep track of all formal and informal resources. Pay special attention to helpful and low-cost resources (volunteers, special rates and discounts). Grab coupons whenever you find them. Explore special programs and eligibility requirements. Visit and share ideas with other networks and self-help groups in your region. Talk to the local librarian and carry a list of the "how-to" books available.

And don't forget that once you have a pattern of routine visits established, you also have bargaining power for arranging special deals for your network as a whole.

> *"Say Mr. Theater Owner, I know 100 or more kids that would love to come to a Saturday matinee if a discount were offered."*

> *"Say Ms. Fabric Shop Owner, I know 100 people who'd love to see samples of your material. Any special discounts if they buy as a group?"*

> *"Say Ms. Hardware Store Owner, I know 100 people who are looking for materials to build a neighborhood greenhouse. Sure would be good advertising for someone willing to come up with a special deal."*

How about a few letters? Dear Merchant, I routinely meet with 100 families (of so many men and women, kids, dogs, cars, washing machines). I keep track of "specials" for them. Please send me any pre-release sales flyers, promotions or special discounts you might come up with for this community network.

Want to generate interest and participation in a certain community issue? Here's how a community planning consultant, Steve Webster, suggests using a video camera/recorder in an imaginative way. With each stop you show what previous neighbors had to say about the issue (on camera). If they would like to join the discussion you're ready to get that camera rolling.

How about a library of local "how-to" videocassettes on a variety of skills…go ahead think of all the topics possible.

With practice you'll be like a magnet for possible resources and you'll develop a very important capacity in this resource peddler style. It's something good friends learn to do for each other, but seldom does anyone expand it to a neighborhood or community. It's called "carrying someone in your consciousness." It's what you are saying when you see a card that reminds you of a long-ago and faraway friend. If you send that card, you are telling your friend he or she is in your thoughts. When you take the time to know people (their stories, their worries, what they laugh at, the little things they wish they had to make some special ideas happen), you can make it a point to remember. In each day you'll stumble onto things that recall the people you are "carrying in you mind" and you'll have a resource to suggest next time around.

This is an important capacity in a valued networker. Take the time to listen, to remember, to make connections and when there is trouble, especially *big* trouble, you'll be known and trusted, a welcome participant in the problem-solving effort.

But remember, this vocational style does not require big trouble and big problem solving as a justification. The resource peddler might continue linking, connecting and offering resources for solving everyday problems with major crises few and far between...and like a modern Johnny Appleseed he or she could look back now and then and feel quiet pride for the natural growth encouraged along the trail.

The Community Gardener

Let's pick up on that growing analogy in another vocational style, the *community gardener*. Recognize I am using the term community to refer to any group of people you might think of in that sense (e.g., neighborhood, small town, rural countryside, public housing project, elderly center).

To start I'll clarify two basic approaches to gardening, organic and chemical.

ORGANIC GARDENING
Balance of nature emphasized with gardener *participating* with a natural system of the growth to receive a *share* of the "food" produced.

Complex soil life is a primary concern as the medium through which plant

CHEMICAL GARDENING
Control of nature emphasized with gardener *manipulating* several crucial parts of natural system in order to obtain *all* "food" produced.

The plant and its production are of primary concern. The soil is usually viewed as life develops.

The gardener contributes natural foods (animal manures, vegtable matter, compost, mulch) to soil in a balanced exchange for a share of the harvest.

Bacteria, fungi, insects and weeds are understood as companions in the process of growth; an interdependent self-balancing natural community.

Curious, active, patient gardener, who assumes a "steward" of life role for share of harvest.

Gardener is scientist *and* artist. Observes and records each aspect of garden life (birds, plants, insects, animals, elements) as life-long process of learning to increase ability to maintain balance in garden community. Intuitively "orchestrates" life to increase spiritual as well as physical growth.

Whole-mind thinker, aware of cycles of life, and multi-purpose functions of intricate interconnections of biological community.

Humankind as part of nature. Human activity as collaboration with all other life. Nature as a process in which we will always have a part.

something inert that holds plants upright.

Gardener "feeds" plants artificial petroleum-based fertilizers to speed up plant growth and increase produc-tion of human food, "free" for the taking.

Bacteria, fungi, insects, and weeds. Gardener applies toxic insecticides fungicides, and herbicides to kill such enemies.

"Efficient" gardener who waits for crises and then sprays. Assumes "director" role over food production.

Gardener follows repetitive, cause-effect tasks, ordained by food-production research. Tries to increase labor-saving efficiency and food produced more and more cheaply for human use.

Left-mind thinker, focused only on the steps involved in food production.

Humankind as dominating and triumphing over nature. Nature as a place outside of ourselves, to be exploited as we travel to our rightful place in heaven.

Now...have you noticed some social workers are a lot like those chemical gardeners? You know what I mean. They have this long list of problems or enemies (just like insects in the garden). They have a couple of all-purpose treatments (just like chemical bug sprays), and spend a good share of their lives spraying the hell out of social problems.

Such social workers intend to do good but remember no matter how well-intentioned, the gardener who sprays a poison to kill pests also kills beneficial insects and birds, contaminates the soil and leaves poisonous residues on our food.

How many school social workers consider noise an enemy to learning (like food production) in a classroom, and help the teacher by spraying the enemy with behavior management programs. They feel righteous achievement when they eradicate that noise and increase the efficiency of teaching more "knowledge" into those little plants.

Like soil, a community or family is a balance of living, interconnected parts. Just as spraying to eradicate an insect from a plant produces a dependency in that plant, which in turn attracts more insects, which results in more sprays, and so on, left-mind treatment of people produces dependencies which create more "pests."

The garden has its *own* natural defenses to help each part grow toward its potential; it has its *own* system of checks and balances that we can learn from. We can then learn to build the beneficial aspects; build the strength of the plants so that they become less susceptible to the pests.

Our communities have been weakened by years and years of treating (spraying) for production in a competitive, achievement and profit-oriented industrial world. We have become dependent on centralized synthetic systems (just like the chemical fertilizers, herbicides and insecticides sold in every garden store), and this dependency attracts our pests (inflation, depression, war). Our focus on industrial production like food production has failed to recognize the importance of our interconnections and our communities like chemical gardens are ill, out of balance.

Our media hammers us with crisis words (national debt, illness, crime, abuse) and stirs the kettle of mass anxiety. Chemical social workers with amazing righteousness frantically rush from one crisis to the next, treating symptoms with an armament of all-purpose sprays.

The community gardener, on the other hand, has a different approach. Like the organic gardener he/she is a patient doer who knows how to help a community slowly regain its balance. He/she has an unyielding commitment to the natural growth process, and derives satisfaction from participating in and guiding self-healing mechanisms.

The community gardener:

— doesn't emphasize doing to the deficiency, but encourages the strength.

— doesn't do *to* the community, but with others identifies problems and potentials, and participates in building solution patterns that enable the community to heal itself.

— doesn't spray but connects with others to build a lasting adaptability and responsiveness.

— patiently listens, defines difficulties, refines and redefines them, incubates them, carries them in his/her mind as puzzles, opportunities to create positive and lasting changes.

The problems ahead of us are critical but people are adapting, increasing their self-reliance and building a new sense of community through networks. In such trends the community gardeners see natural self-healing mechanisms. They are drawn to this potential for growth. They know that the art of living is converting problems to opportunities and participate as stewards in a revitalization process.

Schumacher once explained that we already know enough about ecology to keep the earth healthy.[3] We still have enough room and material to see to it that everyone has adequate shelter. We are competent enough to supply everyone's necessities. No one need live in misery...the challenge is clear to community gardeners.

SUMMARY AND ENDING COMMENTS

We've been exploring a way to integrate personal values, vision and vocation with trends in our society and profession to come up with vocational styles for everyday practice.

I sketched three vocational styles to illustrate that the same elements (e.g., self-reliance, diversity, networks) can be arranged to form different patterns reflecting our personal interests and skills as well as job requirements. I also tried to show that a right-mind emphasis in thinking (holistic awareness, imagery, feelings) need not be sloppy and impractical. To the contrary, it can be developed toward very practical, yet imaginative work styles.

There's something else I'd like to add here. In our effort to develop whole-mind thinking we become more open to our intuition. We encourage it to spark ideas that we can rationally work out for practice. The innovations we develop as individuals, in turn, serve as the intuitive spark to the collective awareness of our profession as a whole (or whole-mind if you prefer). Those intuitive sparks might stimulate broad and helpful changes.

Our society is trying to achieve a better balance between its centralized structures and local self-reliance while pushing and pulling its way through a major economic upheaval.

Social work is at the center of this push and pull. We have, for some time, been a vehicle of centralized structures and institutional helping. But we also have roots in self-help. In our early history, for example, we had the settlement house movement. We helped immigrants to this country enter a new society, and emphasized self-help skill, growth of the individual, social participation and the democratic process.

To survive, our institutions will have to adapt and change. Perhaps the spirit and commitment of the settlement house tradition will be renewed in an emerging social work practice. We are all immigrants in a new society. How about a re-settlement house tradition? Maybe we'll even have room for a few alchemists, peddlers, and community gardeners out there...or am I just "imagining things."

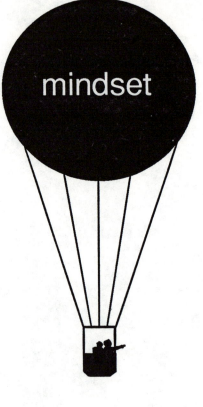

Creativity and the creative generalist

5

The creative *generalist...sounds a bit pretentious doesn't it? But Allen and I aren't suggesting you announce to the world your wish to be referred to as a creative generalist (better keep trashpicker, peddler and gardener to yourself, as well). Rather, we are saying you should think* of yourself as a creative generalist, that creativity is the foundation for what we mean by the *mindset.*

CREATIVITY AND SOCIAL WORK

Social workers are continually pressed to be inventive, resourceful, creative. Too many of the situations they encounter have no ready answers, no quick and easy remedies. Sometimes they draw upon past experience and convert a previous solution to fit a current circumstance. More typically they have to pull together whatever resources they find into a *new pattern, an original form that is responsive to the uniqueness of the situation they are working on.*

Though social workers continually face problems that require whatever creative ability they can muster, the specifics of the phenomenon are seldom mentioned in social work articles or classrooms. Projects, programs and proposals in social work may be described as creative, new, unique, innovative, but do you believe them? Or do you expect the same ideas dressed in new packaging and language?

Obviously, misuse of the word creativity is not a habit peculiar to social work. Look in the Yellow Pages. Almost every item from architectural design to zither repair has someone claiming to do it creatively. The word has been bumper-stickered so often, the promise broken so often, we have come to accept it as suggesting just a little extra flare, flash, pizazz. We live in a world of imitation cheese, reconstituted eggs, and "light" beer...no wonder we accept watered-down creativity.

At the other extreme we find those who talk of creativity as a mysterious power of an intellectual and artistic elite; an elusive and transitory gift for the few. It is something akin to cosmic awareness; doled out by a fickle and stingy universe. Here, the examples of creative individuals all come out sounding like Einstein, or da Vinci, those that breathe rarified air.

The underlying message in this viewpoint? There is little anyone can do about creativity. It comes or it doesn't; some have it, most don't. Marvel at it; appreciate it; look at it; collect, hoard, and sell it; but don't be foolish enough to believe you can *do* anything about what you were born with...or without.

I am, of course, about to tell you something very different. As I explained earlier a left-mind bias and love of science encouraged social work to neglect the intuitive side of practice. Had we looked we would have found an extensive body of knowledge and research on creativity a long time ago. Paradoxically, it is scientific discovery (split-brain research) that has now given creativity legitimacy and challenges our interest.

From our work in earlier chapters you are well aquainted with the creative generalist mindset. You know that it includes *whole-mind thinking* and that this kind of thinking enhances our ability to *form patterns* of imaginative and practical ideas. In the last chapter I suggested using this kind of thinking to develop idea patterns, vocational styles, to help guide our day to day problem-solving activities in social work.

I sketched three vocational style examples for you. Consider how I came up with them. I combined the image of a peddler wagon with the social work tradition of home visiting to come up with a resource peddler that supports our current interest in networking. I used analogy to connect ideas about organic gardening and social work in an idea pattern called the community gardener. The alchemist trashpicker resulted from combining the historical idea of alchemy with recycling. And my ending suggestion that we take our historical settlement house tradition and respond to current needs (we are all immigrants in a new society) with a re-settlement tradition again resulted from a pattern-forming process.

Now pull up your chair and listen close, I'm going to tell you a couple of secrets:

— CREATIVE THINKING IS WHOLE-MIND THINKING.

— CREATIVITY IS "THE PROCESS BY WHICH ORIGINAL PATTERNS ARE FORMED AND EXPRESSED."[1]

That's right, we've been working with creativity concepts throughout the previous chapters. And I'm telling you here, creativity is a lot more than a garnish for serving old ideas, but at the same time it doesn't require mountaintops and cosmic consciousness.

Creativity is a natural ability, a natural human process like physical health. If you want to be healthy what do you do? You work at it. You develop healthy habits. If you want to be creative, you also work at it, you develop creative habits. When you have a habit of thinking creatively you are sharing the mindset of a creative generalist.

Allen and I put the word creative in front of generalist as a reminder of the unique capacities each of us brings to the world of social problems. As we see it creativity is the most important contribution an individual can offer others through the professsion of social work. Consider the words of Gary Davis, a well known author in the field of creativity:

> "Creative thinking is much more than using your imagination to invent lots of new ideas. Creative thinking is a lifestyle, a personality trait, a way of perceiving the world, a way of interacting with other people, and a way of living and growing. Living creatively is developing your talents, tapping your unused potential, and becoming what you are capable of becoming. Being creative is exploring new places and new ideas. Being creative is developing a sensitivity to problems of others and problems of humankind. And being creative is using your imagination to invent lots of new ideas to solve those problems."[2]

So let's do a little exploring and clarifying. I'm not going to tell you everything there is to know about creativity. Instead, I'll tell you a bit about each of the important components of the phenomenon. I'll use terms and concepts familiar to all in the field of creativity, because I am hoping you'll do a lot more reading on your own and this way you'll at least have a general lay of the land.

We'll start with identifying the four key components of creativity. Creativity involves:

— A *creative personality* (creative generalist)

— who uses *creative thinking* (whole-mind thinking)

— in a *creative process* (problem solving)

— to come up with *creative products* (creative solutions).

Now let's take a closer look at each of these components.

CREATIVE PERSONALITY (CREATIVE GENERALIST)

Were you attracted to social work because of its diversity? Would you be interested in a position that has you "wearing many hats," juggling priorities and seldom doing the same activity twice in week? Do you have high levels of energy? Once you chose a course of action do you have the determination and patience to persevere? Do you have a strong desire for independence? When attending school did you try

If you answered yes to many of the above questions you are already well on your way to developing your creative capacities.

Creative individuals are found in all walks of life, but regardless of their chosen activity they share a number of characteristics. Below I'll list several that have an obvious fit with creative generalists in social work.

A Creative Person:

Has an eco-systems viewpoint

While social work was adapting social systems theory to practice, authors in the creativity literature were reporting on the creative individuals ability to employ systems thinking. In 1972, for example, Daniel Noble explained that creative thinking is characterized by thinking in terms of interdependent systems, and suggested (get this) "we need generalist thinkers who understand system interrelationships in our technological culture."[3]

This predisposition to view things holistically is central to the creative individual's ability to link ideas, to combine previously discrete variables into fresh new patterns, to perform alchemy by transforming old ideas (trash) into new ones (treasure).

Is problem-focused

Creative individuals continually search for problem-solving opportunities. They have a heightened sensitivity to problems and life puzzlements. Raudsepp describes this as a "perpetual state of happy dissatisfaction," and Lenowitz reports creative people have a "lower threshold" for problems and see them where others are happy to continue undisturbed.[4,5]

Is persistent

Creative individuals demonstrate a high level of energy, cognitive flexibility and confidence in the face of uncertainty. They will keep coming at a problem with a variety of techniques from different angles; they persevere until they arrive at a creative solution.[6]

Is open to complexity

Creative individuals demonstrate an unusual ability to confront the complexities of life without being overwhelmed.[7] Some consider this a matter of self-confidence. With insecurity the impulse is to take action, to solve a difficulty as quickly as possible. Creative persons are more able to withstand the tension of action impulses, to fend off premature closure in the search for a creative solution.[8]

Of the many descriptions of creative personalities available in the literature, those reported by by Frank Barron and his associates (Institute of Personality Assessment and Research at Berkeley) identify a central attitude difference consistently reported elsewhere.[9] In essence, they found that creative individuals differ from less-creative individuals in the way they choose to perceive the world around them.

> *Open-minded vs. judgmental*: People use their mind to either become aware of something or come to a conclusion about something; and show a definite preference for one or the other. Creative persons have an attitude of open-mindedness where less creative people are more judgmental. The more judgmental you are, the more you desire and search for orderliness; the more open you are, the more flexible, adaptable, and sensitive you are to experience. The more you desire order, the more you are intimidated by change. The more open-minded you are, the more you enjoy the challenge of the unknown.

> *Complexity vs. simplicity*: Creative individuals prefer complexity. They view the chaos of life and its problems as opportunities to create unique solutions. Receptivity to complexity increases the *pattern-forming connections* possible, and thus

increases the likelihood of creative solutions. Those who prefer simplicity seek predictable, clear-cut, conventional solutions. They look for order and planfulness in their life and are often immobilized by anxiety in the face of uncertainty.

Challenge to Creative Generalists

One of the hazards of exploring a phenomenon like creativity involves the use of dichotomies. To clarify we use terms such as creative and non-creative, we describe high-creative ability and low-creative ability. But creativity is a pattern of capacities unique to the individual. Creativity includes an infinite variety of highly personal forms of expression. The *point* of creativity is the expression of individually unique perceptions. Don't get caught up in whether or not you fit some sort of mold developed only to help us understand the phenomenon.

The vocational style examples I sketched for you in the last chapter were creations, not magnificient da Vinci creations but a more *common garden variety* all of us can offer to each other. It's our responsibility as creative generalists to tap our own individually unique talents, to develop and cultivate them in ways useful to ourselves and others. When you are deliberately cultivating your own creative capacities you'll notice a preference for certain forms of expression. These individual preferences will prove a major force in putting together *your* unique vocational style. A number of authors have recognized different patterns of individual creative expression.[10] I'll develop a few of these differences to show you what I mean.

The Improvisor

The emphasis here is not so much on the creative quality of overall solutions as much as spontaneous creativity. This kind of person is a very expressive, vibrant person who stimulates others to create. It is the Jonathan Winters form of humor. If you hand him an umbrella he will quickly recognize many (in this case funny) uses for it. Fluency, adaptability, the ability to spontaneously generate alternative ideas, are the special talents of this creative personality. These talents could easily be adapted into a "Johnny (or Mary) Appleseed" vocational style. Throughout each day this person is planting ideas, uses, unusual perceptions, whether at home, at the agency, with a client. As a jazz musician may quickly improvise, a creative generalist might have similar talent in conversing with others.

The Craftsperson

Here the emphasis is more on the creative product. Satisfaction is in proficiency, technical achievement. This kind of person desires skill and mastery. The vocational style here might be the "Quality Cabinetmaker." It involves a fine-tuned creativity demanding knowledge of tools and patience. Let's say this creative generalist works in a school-age maternity program. Technical creativity would show in the arrangement, timeliness, and unique fit of resources to each individual in the program. It would be reflected in the attention to detail, the sensitivity to changing needs, the skillful organizing and orchestrating of various agencies...the product in this case is is a thoughtful, responsive program for a client with an identified need.

The Inventor

Here the emphasis is on ingenuity with materials; a special talent for making unusual combinatory relationships between things previously separated. The vocational style might be a "Resource-Tinkerer." It involves using old parts in new ways; solving old problems in new ways. This creative generalist would feel right at home in a community resource position. He or she could make excellent use of a special talent for converting traditional resources to meet new needs, and creating resources out of existing but untapped "parts" in the community.

The Innovator

An innovator has a key ability to recognize basic ideas and principles and to elaborate on them; modify and develop them into a variety of alternative approaches. This might be a "Robin Hood" vocational style for the kind of creative generalist who has an eye for quality concepts; "steals" them; and gives them away wherever needed in the community. It involves the ability to quickly adopt and adapt concepts into different solution strategies. For example the fundamental principle of the traditional Big Brothers/Sisters approach could be modified to fit a variety of circumstances that would benefit from an innovative spinoff of this family concept.

The Generator

Some individuals have an ability to form novel ideas at a more abstract and fundamental level. They produce highly stimulating, new principles and assumptions that encourage adoption and innovation by the "Robin Hoods." A sort of "Wise Wizard" vocational style. The originators, stimulators, and skillful alchemists from the world of creative generalists would gravitate to such a vocational style. Wouldn't it be encouraging to find such creative talent in administrative, teaching and staff development positions?

Notice that the above forms of creative expression are not distinctly different, they are differences in emphasis. They certainly do not exhaust the different manifestations of creativity. I pulled them together to encourage your own exploration and experimentation. Watch for your own patterns, preferences, and special talents that may be unified into a coherent, satisfying, powerful and creative vocational style.

The key point here is that creativity involves *choice*, perceptual preference, choosing what to pay attention to. If you chose to see life openly and accept the challenge of its complexity, you will stimulate a kind of thinking, whole-mind or creative thinking.

CREATIVE THINKING (WHOLE-MIND THINKING)

If you asked a roomful of social workers the question, "What is social work?", you'd get answers such as:

> *"Social work is a human service profession mandated by society to remediate social problems, prevent their recurrence, and enhance the quality of life for all of humankind...."*

If we gathered the responses and attempted to select the best answer to the question what would we be looking for? Right, we'd be looking for the most *intelligent* answer. We'd evaluate responses according to correctness, accuracy, thoroughness in terms of the conventional knowledge of social work. The winning respondent would have a *right* answer.

If you asked the group, "How is social work like a lawn sprinkler?", the responses would be different.

> *"Usually at the end of our hose running around in circles."*

> *"Distributes resources so that everybody gets a chance to grow."*

> *"Drowns some and dehydrates others."*

> *"Those standing closest (and hollering the loudest) get the most."*

> *"Not worth a damn if someone shuts the water (resources) off."*

> *"Runs around spraying the hell out of everything, flowers, tomatoes, waterlilies, cacti...the meter spins, the water bill skyrockets, and the owner paves the yard in a program called green asphalt."*

> *"Would like to see the world growing green and flowering, but given four acres of problems, two feet of hose and a quart of water."*

The first question has us *converging* on the right answer. The second question has us *diverging* into different answers. One asks us to think *logically* and the other asks us to think *analogically*.

It is not that one question and answer is better than the other. Rather, the questions and answers are different, and better according to the purpose of the asking.

If the social workers were taking a competitive examination for the one and only social work position in town, you'd likely be better to respond logically with, "Social work is a human service profession...."

If the social workers were attending a conference called "Sort-out or Burn-out," a helpful response to the question, "What is social work?" might be analogical. "Well, social work is sort of like a lawn sprinkler...."

A whole-mind thinker can choose to go with either the logical or analogical direction; that choice is the key ingredient of creative thinking.

Whole-mind thinking is a recent and popular term for what was previously identified as creative thinking. Whole-mind thinking refers to the balanced use of right- and left-mind functions. Though I have identified the basic differences in these functions in previous chapters let's take a more thorough look at them here.

"Split-brain" surgery on epileptic patients in the 1960s and 1970s revealed dramatic differences in the left- and right-brain hemispheres. Each of us has two independently functioning minds. They are complementary, interacting, but different modes of thinking.[11]

> *Left-hemisphere (rational) thinking*...convergent, analytic, logical, linear, sequential, orderly thinking. Our rational mind controls speech, talks to us, helps us arrange words to make sentences; it is concerned with correctness and error. It classifies the world into identifiable parts; it looks for details; it uses rules; it adds, subtracts, measures, categorizes, evaluates; it deals with the past and evaluates the present from past experience; it is our intellectual, scientific mind, helping us survive with the way things are.

> *Right-hemisphere (intuitive) thinking*...divergent, spon - taneous, holistic thinking. Our intuitive mind thinks in images, detects patterns. Though it does not speak, it does give speech

emotional inflection; it is our emotional mind. It is more musical. It makes visual closure; it's the mind that forms images in those gestalt pictures you look at. It forms shapes in those disconnected lines; it "sees" faces in the clouds or the coals of a campfire. It is what you mean when you say you "feel it in your heart." It is our inner artist and poet. It gives depth to our meaning, feeling to our thoughts. It helps form insights, discover relationships; makes connections. It is analogical; it is our imaginative mind. It helps us face the unknown and gives us pictures of what might be.

Though the reality of intuition was validated with the recent finding of its physiological counterpart in the right-brain hemisphere, theorists and researchers in the field of creativity have long known about the two modes of thinking. J.P. Guilford, for example referred to them as "convergent and divergent."[12] The same dichotomy is identified in Weil's "straight and stoned thinking," de Bono's "vertical and lateral thinking" and Koestler's "purposive thinking and thinking aside."[13,14,15]

Whichever term you prefer, whole-mind or creative thinking, remember that creative ideas, solutions, products come from the collaboration of our two modes of consciousness. Our highest creative achievements result from this complementary functioning of rationality and intuition. Creative individuals see more possibilities when solving a problem because they use both rational and intuitive thinking.

You generate with your intuitive mind and evaluate with your rational mind. A sense of the whole (intuition) with defining of the parts (rationality) forms a creative idea.

Our rational mind is our computer. It helps us order reality. It gives us predictability; helps us relate to the knowns of life. Our intuitive mind is our enricher. It forms fresh patterns. It helps us make sense out of the amorphous and paradoxical by establishing workable models. It helps us relate to the unknowns of life.

Our rational mind looks for logical cause and effect. It uses rules, makes distinctions, and evaluates. It is our intellectual mind. Our intuitive mind looks for patterns. It arranges things, puts them together to form images. The intuitive mind holds the key to the "aha!

experience." It makes rapid associations, links ideas in novel ways, transforms past experience and ideas in new ways.

Our intuitive mind presses for new ideas and our rational mind interprets, translates, and verbalizes the results of intuition. It tests the validity of intuitively formed ideas against what we already know of objective reality (knowledge) and incorporates those ideas it finds acceptable.

Emotion and intellect, freedom and discipline, flexibility and preciseness, order and disorder...all can exist in creative harmony in a whole mind. Interplay, harmony, oscillation, our two minds should perform in a natural, healthy rhythm, like breathing in and out. But our society has long suffered an affliction of one-way thinking. Our lopsided preoccupation with rationality has led to fragmented, imbalanced thinking. The effect this has had on individuals varies, but culture is a powerful force on even the most resilient of psyches.

One-Way Thinking

Our rational mind is tuned to biological survival. It relies upon our senses (sight, hearing, smell, taste, touch), to define reality, and perceptually screens out irrelevant information. It focuses on data considered important to survival.

Ornstein offers an interesting example of this sensory screening. The eye of a frog is fully capable of perceiving a wide range of objects. Yet it only transmits four kinds of messages to the frog's brain. No matter how complex the environment the frog eye is wired to transmit only a small number of messages (primarily bug perceptions).[16]

Human senses screen out information as well. Our rational mind relies upon our senses, and is limited to the existing "wiring" for perception. Our intuitive mind is able to imagine and create new realities by "re-wiring" the senses to expand awareness.

When we prevent our two minds from working together this growth in awareness is severely constrained. Without the fantasy and holistic images of our intuitive mind, our rational mind gets rigid, lifeless, mechanical. Without our rational mind to organize and form concrete realities, our intuition gets clogged with unexpended energy and emotions. It waits until our rational waking state consciousness is asleep and pounds at the door of our awareness with nightmare images.

So how do we manage to interfere with this natural, healthy growth process? Culture and socialization are the inadvertent culprits. For example, consider that most cherished of American institutions, public education. In the process of growing up and getting educated most of us have developed a very muscular left hemisphere...to the neglect of the right.

Our exploratory years as preschool children are filled with curiosity, fantasy and openness to experience. Before we acquire language our intuition is fully participating in our growth. But at the same time we want desperately to do good, to be right. We desire the love, recognition and status that comes with doing good and being right. Our parents and teachers offer guidance and we gradually come to learn what is and what isn't. We learn to name, label and define reality; to manipulate it through language. We trade the risk of our earlier perceptual openness for the security of a handle on life. We learn the right thing to do. We learn to see through the puzzlement and inconsistency of life by viewing it through our rational mind.

School strengthens the rational vision bias by rewarding rational vision skills. We are intensively exposed to rule-governed thinking. With increasing vocabulary and command of language we learn the security of unambiguous beliefs...and our intuition is more and more suppressed.

So pervasive is this pattern of rational mind dominance and intuitive mind loss it is referred to as the "4th grade slump" in creativity research. This is the age level at which individuals dramatically start limiting intuitive thinking in their problem solving.[17]

Looking at life through the rational mind helps us keep a grip on reality. It keeps our frog-eye perceptions on track. Outlandish thoughts, irrelevant and irreverant ideas, incorrect perceptions...all are minimized through the power of convention and logic.

Our rational concepts, beliefs and assumptions enable us to pursue happiness, set and achieve goals. They help us to be good scouts and good citizens. They help us keep our noses clean, pay our taxes, be productive, and grow old according to schedule.

Rationality offers order in life. The structure of our beliefs gives us stability. It helps us follow tradition and custom. It helps us avoid the uncertainties of life...but don't forget the cost. With rational mind dominance we also inhibit our expression, lose spontaneity, and mistrust our ability. Our thinking becomes stereotyped and we more and more fear anything that threatens disorder.

Challenge to the Creative Generalist

The challenge to a creative generalist is to maintain the ability to screen reality for order, while at the same time allowing for enrichment of the also present chaos.

A balanced lens of the rational and intuitive becomes an instrument for viewing life, that offers logical structuring with tolerance for unusual ideas and discord. One that allows into our perception the greatest possible richness of experience while moving toward the order promised in a new pattern. With such a lens we are not immobilized by anxiety in the face of uncertainty, but challenged to grow and adapt. We can maintain the openness to experience, the spontaneity, and the wonder of childhood in an overall order of adulthood.

A useful way to develop the balanced lens of rational and intuitive thinking is the deliberate connecting, combining or associating of old ideas to form new ideas. It is the practice of alchemy. Through developing the capacity to link unusual ideas into coherent, useful, new ideas, the individual becomes more open to the uncertainty and chaos of life. With increasing confidence in this pattern-forming ability an individual not only tolerates the unusual, but seeks it to spark the formation of original solutions.

CREATIVE PROCESS (PROBLEM SOLVING)

Problem solving in social work is typically described as a four-stage process: *assessment, planning, implementation* and *evaluation*. This description should incorporate creative process if it is to serve as a guide for the creative generalist. The classic description of creative process also has four stages: *preparation, incubation, illumination* and *verification*. Let's take a look.

Preparation

Creative individuals value creativity, they want to create. They engage problem solving to come up with something unique, novel, original. They begin by gathering whatever relevant and seemingly irrelevant data they can. They perceive the problem in its breadth, importance, level of difficulty, and relationship to other factors. As they formulate the problem they order information and and repeatedly analyze it. They pull new data in to reorganize and restructure the problem so that new possibilities can be generated. They search for patterns. They move the material around, look at it from every conceivable angle, poke at it. They connect, combine and associate ideas hoping to achieve a new synthesis (putting together unrelated concepts). They manipulate information, work it over, push it for that sudden resolution, that creative spark.

Rarely do creative responses come in the earlier rounds of prodding and twisting of ideas. Though the individual is focused intently, continually absorbing new information and reframing old information, frustration mounts. But the tension of struggling with a seemingly impossible problem does not lead to abandonment. Rather it is temporarily tabled, put on *hold*. This precipitates the next stage, incubation.

Incubation

Manipulation of data and ideas has failed to bring about the desired solution. With the frustration of not getting anywhere, the creative individual temporarily drops the problem and turns his or her attention elsewhere. But the intuitive mind continues to wrestle with the problem; searching for additional data, adding associations, juggling variables.

The intensity of commitment to the problem, and the intensity of tension tolerated in the frustrated attempts to solve it, serve as fuel for this intuitive participation. The power of the initial concentrated effort energizes the activity of intuitive process. It determines the extent of uncovering, selecting, reshuffling, combining, and synthesizing of facts, symbols and ideas.

Illumination

Suddenly, in a quiet moment, during an excited conversation, while driving a car or taking a morning shower, a flash appears in the mind of the creative individual. It forms a new pattern of combinations, a new idea, a visualization of a solution.

This is the "aha!" experience. It is central to the creative process. It is the sudden gestalt, the revelation. The tension of earlier frustration is released in the moment of fusion when everything snaps together simultaneously.

Verification

In the final creative process stage the person applies, elaborates and evaluates the insight gained from the illumination stage. The idea is revised and reshaped to meet the changing reality of the problem situation; it is acted upon, tested, evaluated.

Verification is, of course, critical to the specific problem-solving project at hand, but it is also important to the overall development of the creative individual. The resolution of problems, the verification of novel solutions propels the individual into further creative problem-solving efforts. It is a growth process and succeeding attempts are met with greater confidence, commitment, and willingness to tolerate frustration.

Combining Social Work Problem Solving and Creative Process

Now, let's compare the stages of creative process with the stages of problem-solving process in social work.

Social Work		Creativity
Assessment	————	Preparation
Planning	————	Incubation Illumination
Implementation	————	Verification
Evaluation		

From the above listing we can see that in the assessment stage we are also preparing to create a solution. While the word "assessment" emphasizes analytic determination of the nature and extent of the problem at hand, the term "preparation" reminds us to use both rational and intuitive thinking; to hold back our impulses to judge and remain open and sensitive to possibilities. Preparation reminds us to enrich our understanding by exploring the problem from every possible point of view.

Planning is a next logical stage after assessment. In it the solution is developed. Different tasks are organized according to importance and timing. Incorporating the terms "incubation" and "illumination" into the planning stage reminds us to avoid concluding second-rate solutions; to tolerate the uncertainty and ambiguity of complex problem situations; to tolerate the frustration when unable to quickly come up with creative solutions. It reminds us that when we have committed ourselves, the energy of our desire and the frustration we feel mobilizes the pattern-seeking intuitive mind to continue exploration while we shift our rational attention to other matters. It reminds us to hold out as long as possible for the most creative solution we can muster.

Implementation and evaluation, of course, involve trying the planned solution, and determining how well it actually resolved the difficulty. Verification shares this meaning in that the creative idea is tested and verified in action. But it also relates to the growth of the creative individual. Actualizing the creative idea completes the creative cycle. It verifies the creative process to the individual and strengthens the capacity for more complex problem solving.

Challenge to the Creative Generalist

I have several comments to make regarding *labeling* and the steps or stages of a process.

Some try to follow process models as if they are recipes for success. In truth the labels of process stages are only reminders. Regardless of the scheme we use to tell ourselvers of what needs to be done, and when it needs doing, a creative generalist remains flexible. Labels and categories appeal to our rational need for order and predictability. Our intuitive mind knows that nothing in nature is willing to be locked into human categories for very long. We may find moments of comfort in believing we have completed an assessment and are moving ahead into a planning phase, but they quickly evaporate when we remember assessment is required throughout the entire problem-solving process.

We need, then, to consider a stage in a process to be a matter of emphasis in time. Assessment is the *predominant* activity in the assessment stage, and the boundaries between one stage and another are far less than exact.

Yet labels are necessary and important. Look at the words used to describe social work problem solving and the creative process. Without trying to think of correct meanings, what do the words say to you? What does your intuition offer? Any images or feelings? Any humor in those words? Compare "assessment" to "preparation" and "planning" to "incubation," what words hold your interest? Any ideas triggered?

The social work description of process reflects our concern with the scientific method, and is very businesslike indeed. The words are painted in institutional green. The associations are less than exuberant. We "assess" when something is wrong, we get "assessed" and our taxes go up. Assessment is very official sounding.

Preparation suggests action, getting ready to do something, building something. Preparing includes exploring a problem, but intuitively signals that you are already *doing* something about it.

The labels of the creative process actually encourage the kind of thinking necessary to engage the process. For example, play around and associate with the word "incubation." Isn't that what a chicken does to an egg? Isn't illumination something that comes with a lightbulb? Does a chicken seek illumination when setting an egg? Does a chicken get illumination when the egg cracks into a baby chick? Did Edison incubate a lightbulb? Or did he hatch a lightbulb? Or did he seek illumination while incubating an idea? I'll bet when Edison hatched a lightbulb he got ILLUMINATION!

The words we choose to represent what we do, *are* important because they send us all sorts of intuitive messages. If we want to encourage creativity, the language of our process models should reflect this intention. Allen and I recognized this when incorporating the stages of creative process with those of problem solving in social work. We came up with a three-stage process (*preparation, design, verification*) that we'll tell you much more about in later chapters.

I have one more point to make about process labels before moving on. It has to do with the incubation and illumination stages identified in the classic description of creative process.

When reading different books and articles on creativity you'll notice many of the examples given are of *technical* problem solving. Now, if you commit all of your creative energy to solving a technical problem, if you box yourself off from much of the world of daily confusion, if you grind away long enough, you will, sooner or later, get one of those lightning bolt illuminations. Many of the examples of creative scientists and inventors are like this. Such individuals often worked for many years on one or several related problems. This focus of interest was then reflected in their description of a tremendous dam up of tension later released in an explosive revelation.

The nature of the creative experience in social work is usually quite different than that of the scientist or inventor. A creative generalist who comes to a field like social work is drawn to problems that are seldom technical. Rather, they are social problems and pose a special creative challenge.

In social work we square off with complicated human conditions, multiple problems hidden in understated "situations of concern." Such situations are loaded with diverging values and emotions and the different interconnected problems within them continue to develop and change whether or not we are present to notice.

Social situations come with clusters of related problems, problems of all shapes and sizes. Typically you're preparing, incubating, illuminating and verifying in different pieces of the overall puzzle at the same time. And the illuminations are often of the "why didn't I think of that before" level of intensity. Now and then you will get one that will roll your socks up and down and you'll certainly remember the experience...but don't underrate the continual, day-to-day accumulation of "got its."

To commit, to focus energy, to tolerate complexities and frustrations are very much a part of the creative experience in social work, but take pride in the special emphasis you have chosen. It's as if at birth each of us are given a 100 amp battery of creative energy. We are free to use it (or not) in any fashion we desire. The battery is self-replenishing with use and has a lifetime warranty.

One individual chooses to illuminate like a lighthouse beacon. The sparks fly when hooking up to the battery and when the light flashes it is seen for miles. Another decides to illuminate differently, choosing tiny lights like those you've seen on Christmas trees. This creative generalist patiently begins stringing these tiny lights in every nook and cranny of human experience, in back alleys, backwoods and remote farmlands…and leaves a trail of flickering illumination. Neither choice of illumination diminishes the other.

A creative generalist in social work is challenged to develop a *common garden variety* of creativity. A kind of creativity that is effective and resilient in the world of people and daily life problems. When vocation leads a creative generalist to social work, the problems encountered will be complex social problems. Collaborating with others, engaging them in problem solving, forming agreements, and transferring skills are only part of an overall challenge to our creative capacities.

CREATIVE PRODUCT (CREATIVE SOLUTION)

What do we mean when we call something creative? If you were holding an object in your hand, what would lead you to consider it the result of someone's creativity? If you hear someone answering a question, what makes you think, "Well, that's an intelligent response."? How would the answer be different if you had thought, "Now, that's a creative response."?

The question would, of course, have to have some difficulty before you'd conclude intelligence *or* creativity. But you'd be referring to the correctness, accuracy, thoroughness, of the answer if you considered it intelligent. The respondent knows a lot (of what is known) about the topic at hand. Intelligent answers are thus right answers.

For you to consider the response creative, it would also have to be appropriate to the question, but you would see it as something good rather than correct. Intelligence refers to rational thinking. It is a label we use within a system of logic and the external reality, the world of right and wrong, true and false. Creative responses include participa - tion of the intuitive mind. They are felt as good or bad. The demand for correctness is not as tight in estimating creativity, but certain criteria do have to be present.

It doesn't matter if it's an answer to a question, an omelet, a house design, a dance, a kitchen utensil, a painting, a woodworking tool, or a social work project proposal, a product (solution) must have certain attributes before the creativity bell rings. It must have *fit, novelty, alchemy and elegance.*

Fit

A creative product is not correct in the usual sense of the word, but it must be appropriate to the question or problem; it must be pertinent, relevant; it must *fit*. The question is not does the solution fit or doesn't it. Rather we are considering the *extent* of its fitness as we would in the case of physical fitness. The extent of problem resolution found in a product to be its level of creative fitness. Fit, then, reflects the individual's sensitivity. A solution without fit would be irrelevant, bizzare, unhelpful.

Novelty

Nearly everyone would guess that a creative product must also be somehow different, unusual, new, original; it must be *novel*. The novelty of a product indicates the individual's ability to form new and yet relevant patterns.

Alchemy

Remembering the alchemist trashpicker should help with this one. A creative product should show that ideas were changed, converted or *transformed* from one direction to another; recycled into a new form. Something was associated, combined, connected with something else resulting in a novel idea that fits the problem. A new synthesis was formed, and it reflects the abilities of an alchemist.

Elegance

William Gordon tells us that an *elegant solution* "to a given problem is one where the solution is the simplest in proportion to the complexity of the variables involved."[18]

Elegant solutions have simplicity, poise, grace. They offer the most impact for the least expenditure of energy. In a multiproblem situation an elegant solution solves not only the immediate crisis, but connects and has positive effects on all sorts of related problems; it has a lot of *serendipity* value. What catches our attention is how complexity is condensed into simplicity. The elegance can be found in this economy of motion and powerful resolution, like poetry.

Examples

Now that you have the basic idea behind the standards for a creative solution let's test them out with several examples.

> Japan was suffering devastating floods. Swollen rivers wreaked havoc and destruction to communities as they tore a path to the sea. Rising water levels promised even more serious calamity. Community volunteers attempted sandbagging to dam against the flood waters. Continual rain, muck and inaccessible dam sites made trucking of sand and bagging a futile solution. One creative problem solver came up with a unique alternative. Using pillow-shaped plastic bags the volunteers scooped up flood water, sealed the bags, and created dams. The communities were protected by damming the water with water.

Apply the creativity "indicators." Did the solution *fit*? Yes, it responded directly to the obvious problem. What if someone would have said, "With all this roaring water, why don't we advertise whitewater rafting as a tourist attraction?" In other circumstances, this might have been a creative idea. (If someone did suggest it to the Japanese villagers I hope they knew how to swim). The plastic pillow dams had a powerful connection to the problem at hand.

Was the solution *novel*, original, unusual? Were you surprised when you read it?

Did you sense *alchemy*? Somehow the ideas of "zip-lock" freezer bags, or plastic bread bags or plastic bottles were combined with burlap sandbags; and were then converted into a wall of plastic and water that dammed the floodwater.

Did the solution have *elegance*? I'll say. Consider the complexity involved with conventional sandbagging. People sloshing back and forth dragging heavy bags of wet sand against a forceful current...stumbling, falling, tiring quickly. Now visualize them pass - ing empty plastic bags; opening them; letting the raging water fill them; and settling them down to build the dam. Complexity to simplicity...how poetic...to stop the water with water.

Here's another one.

> Duke Ellington and his orchestra were performing in a large outdoor
> arena. The place was packed with people. Ellington was
> conducting about midway through one of his arrangements. A few
> sensitive ears in the audience noticed the distant rumble of an
> arriving jet transport. Gradually the sound increased until everyone
> was aware of this outside threat to the musical performance.
> Ellington shifted the tempo of the music, adjusting it to the coming
> thunder. The music prepared for it and at the point where the jet
> was directly overhead the music embraced it; included it in a grand
> pattern of musical harmony. As the jet continued its course beyond
> the hall the music gradually released it... and the shock wave of this
> spontaneous event; this transformation of dissonance to harmony,
> hit the audience as they erupted into applause.

Fit? You bet. *Novelty*? To be sure. *Alchemy*? Absolutely. *Elegance*? Enough to bring an elated audience to its feet.

I enjoy hearing and telling stories about clearly elegant solutions such as these, but creativity does not require catastrophy or crowded music halls. Creative solutions of the common garden variety develop in the context of your work, without anyone else really noticing. They sometimes spring up spontaneously as intuitive hunches; *seeds* for elegant solutions.

Let's try another example. This one won't send the creativity indicators into orbit quite like the previous ones. (We can all aspire to one of Ellington's crescendos, but why not practice whistling every chance we get?)

> It's your first child welfare case as a social work student. It's one of those multiproblem family cases with many agencies involved. The father is depicted as tough, aggressive, hostile. He has (very) physically thrown several past social workers out the door. You're supposed to get the parents to work with a coordinated agency effort, but nobody has any suggestions on how to relate to the father. You have several contacts with the mother...she is interested and willing to cooperate, but doubts her husband ever will.
>
> On the next visit the door opens to show mother and FATHER sitting at the kitchen table playing cribbage (cards). You find yourself wanting to switch goals from "developing a strategy with mother on how to get father to cooperate" to "exiting from the home with your skin, teeth and facial characteristics intact." But in the moment you are standing there facing the couple at the table your intuition presents an image to your mind. You grew up with card-playing relatives and imagined the same kind of easy, card-playing talk with these two at the table. You quickly decide to try something. You take your coat off and ask if you could play a few hands with them. The mother nods nervously; the father grunts without looking up from his card hand. You play for about an hour, only talking card-talk. When leaving you ask when you could come to see the mother in the next week, and make your arrangements.
>
> On the next visit, the father again happens to be there...with the cards and cribbage board. To make it short, that card game becomes your ritual opening, your *connection*; that kitchen table becomes your discussion, planning and bargaining table. The kids like to hang around to watch, so you are able to observe the relationships within the family and know better what would work in what situations. The agencies get their cooperation, and you learn to trust your intuition.

Did the solution have *fit*? Yes, you found a place of equity with a person who had previously been defensive with those in authority, and developed a simple game of cards into an instrument of communication and decision-making.

Was it *novel*? The idea of playing cards is conventional, but the product (working through a problem and eliciting cooperation for participating agencies) of the card-playing was novel in this circumstance.

Was *alchemy* apparent? Again, I say yes. It may be tempting to view the card-playing as a technique of relationship building. But it is important to recognize the card-playing was converted into a beginning ritual for discussion at the table. It is not the card-playing itself that has special meaning. Rather your readiness, your scanning the environment for an opening, your willingness to seize the opportunity to make it happen, are what makes a rather ordinary event creative.

The solution was also elegant, simple yet complex. It not only solved the difficulty of eliciting the father's cooperation, it opened opportunities for relating with the kids, observing family interaction and offered a gathering point, a context for future problem solving.

Challenge to the Creative Generalist

The attributes we have been exploring are not standards for strict evaluation of someone's creative effort. Fit, novelty, alchemy and elegance are rule-of-thumb indicators. They are subjective and will be present or absent in varying degrees in a variety of creations. They are meant to be tools of *discovery*, rather than *judgment*. The more you are able to recognize creativity in the accomplishments of others, the more you'll be able to support and strengthen a phenomenon that we need desperately, and yet remains in short supply.

Discovering the creative abilities of others increases sensitivity to the many opportunities to be creative in our own lives. The many small creative solutions help us develop an edge on living so that we have less time for depression, or burnout, or the fear that we might lose our job. Through them we can begin to convert life's routine problems into challenges for creative thinking. Each of the multitude of difficulties we face every day can be viewed as opportunities for exercise and practice.

SUMMARY STATEMENT

We began this chapter with creativity defined as "the process by which original patterns are formed and expressed."[19] We found this process involves:

— A person who is open to experience rather than judgmental; and willing to face the complexities and ambiguities of life.

— A person whose attitudes encourage creative thinking; the balanced use of rational and intuitive thinking.

— A person who applies creative thinking to problem solving through preparation, incubation, illumination, and verification.

— A person who consistently comes up with solutions characterized by fit, novelty, alchemy, and elegance.

This person is to our way of thinking a *creative generalist*.

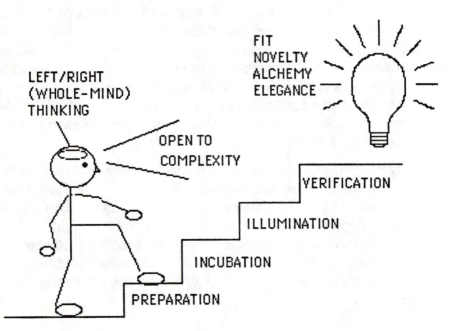

Part
Two

TOOLS

Part II
tools

In Part I, Allen and I explored the *mindset* of a creative generalist with you. Now we'll take a look at some of the *tools* of a creative generalist..

CHAPTER 6: TOOLS FOR CULTIVATING CREATIVITY

In this chapter I show you a number of ways to increase creative thinking in problem solving. We have learned to shut the door on our intuition, and we can learn to open it again. It's all back there waiting. We don't have to construct some elaborate machinery to get in. All we need to do is squirt a little oil on our rusty hinges…and *push*.

You don't even need any special shoes or clothing or diet supplements. We've got all the necessary equipment built in, free for the using. All it takes is a little determination. After all, that orderly little judge of ours (rational mind) has enjoyed our attention for quite some time now…banging the gavel on relevant and irrelevant ideas, day in and day out. In moments of daydreaming (intuitive thinking) we may hear beckoning music from the other side of that door. We may glimpse flashing images of possibility when it is slightly ajar. But with a loud rap of the gavel court is quickly back in session.

When we deliberately open that door to welcome our free-spirited artist (intuitive mind), we can expect some very noisy admonishments. That little judge of ours is articulate and commanding.

"This is a courtroom for the serious business of life. Get that sloppy, distraction out of here and SHUT THAT DOOR."

Life can be more than a courtroom for survival where we judge the present from the perspective of the past. It can also be a theater in which we orchestrate sounds and images toward a possible future...we need only request (firmly) a court recess (defer judgment) to change the setting at will.

CHAPTER 7: THE CIRCLES MAP

Here, I tell you about a very special tool for whole-mind thinking. It is useful for logically organizing complex information and at the same time stimulates our intuitive pattern-forming abilities. It is a multipurpose tool. It helps us increase our perceptual openness, flexible persistence and ability to associate and visualize. It is also a practical tool for working with other individuals, small and large groups.

The circles map is *both* practical and imaginative, it facilitates *both* rational and intuitive thinking. Take a look to find out why the shortest distance between where you are and where you want to be is *not* a straight line when you're following a circles map.

CHAPTER 8: THE PROBLEM-SOLVING RELATIONSHIP

In this chapter Allen invites us to explore an often misunderstood tool of social work, the relationship.

One of the most popular ideas Allen and our colleague, Anne Minahan, presented in their book, *Social Work Practice: Model and Method,* is what they called the "four-systems model." It was a major step in bringing the generalist perspective to our understanding of the relationship in practice.

Allen reviews the development of the four-systems model and guides us through the perceptual shift necessary for converting the *helping* relationship to the *problem-solving* relationship.

We find an important element of uniqueness for social work in Allen's clarification of the problem-solving relationship, and learn that an emphasis on empowerment instead of nuturance does not lead to insensitivity. Rather, it stimulates a new sensitivity, one markedly different than that prescribed in the many other helping professions.

With this perspective on the social work relationship we are encouraged to utilize the tools of creativity and circles mapping in ways responsive to our personal desires for self-expression, while at the same time transferring our skills to those with whom we collaborate in problem-solving activity.

Join Allen to find how the problem-solving relationship enhances our capacity for synergistic exchange.

tools

Tools for cultivating creativity

6

In this chapter we will work on integrating the creativity concepts of the last chapter to clarify ways in which each of us can develop our unique creative capacities.

HOT AND COLD THINKING

We know that creative thinking is whole-mind thinking, a balance of rational and intuitive thinking. In cultivating creativity these left- and right-mind modes of thinking are not approached as discrete categories. Rather, they are treated as ends on a *continuum* of thinking. Creative solutions are found by individuals who are able to move freely on this continuum of thinking, who are able to adjust the flow of their thoughts toward the left or right according to what's needed at a given point in a problem-solving process.

A useful analogy here would be a hot and cold water faucet. We vary the *blend* of hot and cold water for different uses. When we want to *increase* the temperature of the water blend, we *turn down* the cold water and *turn up* the hot. When we want to *decrease* the temperature of the blend, we *turn up* the cold water and and *turn down* the hot.

In whole-mind thinking, then, our intuition is a hot flow of thinking and our rationality is a cold flow of thinking. We *turn down* the cold and *turn up* the hot when we want to increase pliable, flexible ideas (e.g., a "hot"idea, in the "heat of the night," a "hot" flash). We reverse this procedure when we want to firm up or solidify our ideas (e.g., "cool" logic, a "cool" headed decision, in the "cold light of dawn," "cold and calculating").

Notice how developing the analogy this way gives you a qualitatively different understanding of the whole-mind concept. For example, in the "heat of the night" may not at first seem logically connected to right-mind thinking. But reflect on this a minute. Heat refers to passion and emotion is the domain of our right mind. Night is darkness and darkness is the unknown. Our intuition forms recognizable patterns of the unknown.

Consider "cold and calculating" is the same way. Cold is intuitively understood as the absence of emotion (rationality) and calculating is a capacity of our left mind.

Using analogies to think through ideas like this, beckons the participation of our intuition. It turns up that hot water faucet, changing the blend of thinking for a different kind of understanding.

Now, the handles on those water faucets could be thought of as *tools* for increasing and decreasing the water temperature. In the same way, there are tools that help us increase and decrease our rational and intuitive flow of ideas for blending or balancing in whole-mind thinking

Indeed, to explain the use of tools in cultivating creativity I just *used* an important tool known as the *analogy*. I asked myself, "How rational and intuitive thinking like a water faucet?" to help explain the use of tools for blending our flow of ideas appropriate to our needs at a given point in the problem-solving process.

Most of the tools for cultivating creativity emphasize *turning down our rational mind* and *turning up tour intuitive mind* . In other words, most tools for creative thinking help us *increase* the heat of our ideas. Why? You already know why don't you? The tools are helping us counterbalance that old left-mind bias in our thinking.

In our culture, rationality is well developed and intuition is underutilized. In problem solving, our dominant, rational mind pressures us to hurry up and make that judgment. It dislikes the disorder of problem situations and compels us to pick a solution, clean up the mess and get things back in order again. We need to *increase* the participation of our intuitive mind to see more possibilities in ambiguous information. We need its special capacity for combining, recombining and synthesizing information into fresh patterns, for making knowns out of the unknown.

Tools for *turning down* our rational mind help us hold back our compulsion to make premature judgments. They help us to keep our *perceptions open* and increase our ability to *tolerate complexity*.

Tools for *turning up* our intuitive mind help us increase our powers of *association* (combining, connecting ideas) and *visualization* (imagery, imagination). They help us cultivate our capacity to *form and see patterns*.

A BASIC TOOL FOR TURNING DOWN THE LEFT MIND

Earlier, I gave you an example of analogy. It is the most essential and powerful tool for turning up intuitive thinking. Let me now show you a corresponding tool for turning down rational thinking. This one was first introduced by Alex Osborn in the 1950s. He called it the "deferred judgment technique" and used it to minimize criticism and evaluation in his popular "group brainstorming" sessions. Since that time the importance of deferring judgment has been well-documented in research and training programs.[1]

Deferring judgment takes a little discipline. We have learned to be severe critics of impractical or unrealistic ideas. We often hate to admit even to ourselves, that we have such ideas...such wild, unrelated, unacceptable notions. Judging is a supported and very popular pastime. (Think of all the critics and analysts in the newspapers or on TV.)

In reading the following, you'll likely hear some griping from your left mind ("What's he driving at?" "Am I missing something?" "This isn't making any sense."). Just turn down the volume a bit. Avoid unnecessary conclusions. Tell that little judge of yours to wait a minute, keep your perceptions open and try to look for different patterns of meaning without immediately deciding whether or not they're relevant.

Deferring Judgment Example

"To Bee or Not To Bee..."

"What do you want to BEE when you grow up?" "What are you gonna BEE when you graduate?" I've always had a lot of trouble with BEE questions. When I finished high school I thought I had three choices: go to the factree, go to the armee, or go to collitch. I didn't want to BEE a factree worker; I didn't want to BEE an armee worker; so I got to BEE a collitch stewdent.

It was enough for me to BEE a collitch stewdent without worrying about what I would BEE after I was a collitch stewdent, so choosing a collitch was easy...I just went to one.

I went to Oshkosh where they make collitch graduates, beer and overhalls...they really make good overhalls.

In the registration line they gave me a big packet of materials on PLANS and you were supposed to choose one according to what you wanted to BEE when you graduated. You can guess I was having a lot of trouble with those PLANS...but I stayed in line anyhow.

It was a long line leading to a counselor sitting at a table. You were supposed to announce to the counselor your chosen PLAN, major, and minor. The counselor would then let you register. It all seemed a very serious business and the other people in line must have known what they wanted to BEE. They just walked right up, told the counselor and got to register.

Now, the lines were arranged alphabetically, and I remember the person ahead of me was named Harper. We talked a little, and it was obvious Harper knew a lot about the PLANS, majors, and minors. When he got to the front table he looked that counselor right in the eye and said, "PLAN 4, major-psychology and minor-sociology."

The counselor let Harper register and I found myself standing at the table...and she said, "WELL?"...and I said, "Boy, what a coincidence. I'm doing PLAN 4, major-psychology and minor-sociology." I didn't know what sociology was, but figured if it was important they wouldn't call it a minor....

Discussion of Beeing Example

Well, how did you do? How many times were you aware of evaluating? How many times did you say to yourself that it was irrelevant or that it was difficult to find the point? Did my CAPS and mispellings irritate you? Was it all a little too cutesy; too down-home? Too forced? Too fake-comfortable? Too many periods...?

Or did you defer judgment? Did you trust that sooner or later I would get around to making a point? Did you patiently wait for ideas? Maybe you even got a kick out of my directly, honestly, openly *wasting your time* with a lot of mumbo jumbo about BEEing...in this case you'd have to admit I got away with fooling around right in the middle of a textbook.

But I wasn't simply fooling around. The story does have a message of sorts. It approaches the topic of deferring judgment in an indirect, roundabout way. It reflects different perspectives on deferring judgment and invites your emotions and imagination with a story rather than making a clear, direct, logical point.

When you were a child did you ever do a "hidden pictures" puzzle? You'd find an assortment of hidden animals, boats or people drawn into a scene. The Bee story was like that.

The mispellings were pretty easy to contend with. They formed a simple pattern and didn't deviate far from convention. But did you sense any intuitive connections within the mispellings? They were formed with sound (e.g., stew-w-w-dents) and they also suggest intuitive images. Registration is like a giant stew, with participants bumping into each other (e.g., like vegetables denting each other in a boiling stew). A classroom of people who would really rather be doing most anything else have a collective itch...or collitch. Registration situations are treated with such seriousness. Everyone is so busy, busy, busy (like bees); long moving lines like bees swarming to get into the hive.

You've experienced similar situations...the lines, the counselor, the serious-sounding PLANS. Did you feel any connection to the confused person repeating the plan of the person ahead of him in the line?

Maybe you picked up a few messages at other levels of awareness. The counselors in our lives often present decisions as serious and binding. The main character of the story resisted that decision and treated the plan as less than critically serious. He trusted he would get other opportunities to form a meaningful plan in the years ahead. We are often asked to order ourselves, to help somebody process us through a program (e.g., education). There are elements of craziness in such order (e.g., students asked to know what they want before experiencing and understanding the choices). In this view the central character may have demonstrated a strength. He wasn't just an uninformed blockhead, he was holding out, deferring a choice (judgment). He did manage to get through the process without yielding to the pressure for closure...and somehow remained optimistic and largely unaffected in the face of ambiguity.

USING TOOLS IN THE DIFFERENT STAGES OF PROCESS

Now that you have the basic idea of how the tools for turning down the left mind (e.g., deferred judgment) and tools for turning up the right mind (e.g., analogy) work, let's briefly tie them into the different stages of process. You'll find many tools are useful throughout problem solving, but some of them are especially helpful at various points *in* the process.

In the last chapter I mentioned that Allen and I had developed a three-stage description of the problem-solving process (preparation, design, verification) to integrate the stages in creative process (preparation, incubation, illumination and verification) with the stages of social work problem solving (assessment, planning, implementation and evaluation). Part Three (Process) of the book is a chapter-by-chapter discussion of this process. It includes detailed descriptions of each stage and many suggestions for incorporating both left- and right-mind thinking into social work problem solving.

Here I'll just highlight the process stages to show you how certain tools can be especially helpful in each of the stages.

Preparation

In this stage we are identifying a problem. We are trying to keep our *perceptions open* to increase the number of elements available for later *association* into creative solution patterns. By increasing the amount of data and information available for pattern forming, we are also increasing complexity and ambiguity. This in turn increases our experience of tension, frustration and the desire to get on with it, to take action on a solution idea even if we know it is second rate. To avoid premature closure we try to maintain our *flexible persistence*.

Tools especially helpful in this stage, then, are those that increase our *perceptual openness* and *flexible persistence*.

Design

In this stage we are searching for and attempting to generate *idea patterns* that will form creative solutions. This is the period of incubation and illumination in creative process.

Tools that increase our powers of *association* (combining ideas) are, of course, helpful here.

Verification

In this stage we are *doing* the creative idea pattern in the concrete reality of the problem situation, we are testing out the solution pattern developed in the design stage. The analytic and assembly powers of our left mind are, of course, emphasized in verifying the worth of our solution. But our powers of *visualization* also serve as a rudder through the trials of implementation. A vision of the solution helps us keep our commitment and energy focused as we modify and adapt to fit the practical world.

Tools that enhance our ability to visualize are especially relevant here.

AN OUTLINE OF THE TOOLS

Now, let's take that closer look at the turning down the left-mind and turning up the right-mind tools for *perceptual openness, flexible persistence, association* and *visualization*. Below is a brief outline of what we'll be covering.

I. TOOLS FOR TURNING DOWN THE LEFT MIND

A. Tools that encourage *perceptual openness*.

1. Deferring judgment.

2. Breaking initial idea patterns.

3. Shifting perspectives.

4. Challenging assumptions.

B. Tools that encourage *flexible persistence*.

1. Taking charge.

2. Writing ideas down.

3. Setting ideas aside.

II. TOOLS FOR TURNING UP THE RIGHT MIND

    A. Tools that encourage *association.*

        1. Using analogies.

        2. Forming connections.

    B. Tools that encourage *visualization.*

        1. Forming clear mental images.

        2. Developing imagination skill.

        3. Image talking.

        4. Recalling dreams.

TOOLS FOR TURNING DOWN THE LEFT MIND

Perceptual Openness

It's important that we develop our perceptual openness to enhance our creative problem-solving abilities. We want to notice more, be more open to multiple meanings, see beyond conventional meanings, see with both our rational and intuitive minds.

When someone is trying to be more aware, to "see" more, they often understandably look "harder." Rational thinking in this sense magnifies like a microscope. You look more closely at the parts, the detail.

Turning down left-mind thinking to increase perceptual openness involves changing the original image, shuffling the parts in an effort to reconnect them into new wholes. Instead of a microscope we are here using a kaleidoscope. You turn the kaleidoscope to cause shifts in the colored fragments (bits of information). New patterns are formed (intuitive mind), which can then be analyzed (rational mind).

You increase perceptual openness by asking yourself to turn, shift, and switch information. When you ask yourself, "How can I see this differently?," you *will* begin to see it differently. All the circuitry is there, built-in, ready to go…you only have to push the right buttons. You increase perceptual openness by reminding yourself, cueing your consciousness.

Four tools (cues) are quite helpful:

1. Defer judgment.

2. Break your initial idea patterns.

3. Shift your perspective.

4. Challenge your assumptions.

Let's explore their use. Look at the following gestalt picture. Do you see an old or young woman?

Figure 6.1

Whichever you see first, look for the other. When you have perceived both the old and young woman, switch back and forth several times (if you are stuck for hours, you can use the aid I have included at the end of this chapter).

Notice how you must *break* the first image (idea pattern) to see the second. The difficulty is not so much seeing the second image as letting go of the first one (initial patterns are tough little devils aren't they?). It helps to deliberately *shift your perspective*, change the way you are looking at it. Do you sense the tension, the frustration when you are letting go of one gestalt (destructure), and the relief when you see the second gestalt (restructure)? Letting go of the connections in the first image produces disconnectedness which is felt as tension. This tension is then released into a "Got it!" or "Aha!" when a new pattern is connected.

Let's try another exercise.

Situation: Three men dressed in tuxedos are standing in front of a large vault room. The gold-colored door is open and the three men are looking inside. In the center of the room is a four-foot marble pedestal. Sitting on top of the pedestal is a black velvet cushion. On the cushion is a peanut.

Instructions: Take the next 5 minutes and tell what might be happening in the peanut situation. There is no right answer. Be as creative and whimsical as you want. Develop alternative stories if you have time.

Okay, do you have a few? Now let's talk about the exercise in terms of breaking patterns, shifting perspectives, and challenging assumptions.

I've used the peanut exercise with various groups of people over the years. Most responses conclude the peanut's importance (some sort of mystical or magical peanut, the last real food in the universe, the peanut is really a UFO, etc.).

Why is that? Why do so many responses signify the peanut as central to an important event?

Key words lock-in assumptions of importance with the peanut as central character. Words such as tuxedos, gold, vault, pedestal, suggest importance, wealth. The peanut sits an a *velvet* cushion, which is *on top* of a pedestal. The idea of being "on top" of a cushion, sitting "on top" of a pedestal casts the spotlight on that single peanut. The assumption is formed without really thinking about it.

The situation, then, is presented in such a way that it triggers a quickly formed assumption. We can increase alternative possibilities rapidly by *challenging that assumption*, looking at the scene differently, and breaking those initial patterns.

For example, the marble pedestal might be a piece of antigravity equipment used in a magic act. It was left in the theater after the show and the custodian put it in the vault room storage with other props and equipment. It kept floating around, banging into other very expensive materials, so the custodian grabbed a velvet cushion from another piece and tied it to the pedestal. The cushion not only softened any bumps into other equipment it actually settled that floating pedestal right down to a standstill. The custodian was going out the door, noticed a slight pedestal movement, reached into his pocket and found one peanut. He tossed that peanut and it landed squarely in the middle of the cushion...and the pedestal stayed at rest.

The next morning three men rehearsing for a musical were looking into the room for their instruments. One of them said to look at the peanut sitting there. They were about to pick it up to see why it was so important...

Notice in this version the assumptions of importance have been challenged. The pedestal is the item of importance. The men just happened to see the peanut. The vault is a storage room.

I'm not saying this is a *better* story than one with the peanut as central character, rather that many possible stories can be generated once initial assumptions are challenged.

In the old/young woman gestalt you had to let one image go to perceive the other. Here you also must shift your perspective to get unusual combinations. The kaleidoscope forms new patterns as you turn it...but you *do* have to turn it.

Each time you exercise your ability to defer judgment while looking at something from a different perspective, you are developing perceptual openness. Each time you consciously decide to look at something differently you'll notice attributes previously unavailable or hidden.

In the creativity literature you'll find many exercises that, like the peanut story, are helpful to developing your ability to see things differently

Flexible Persistence

I've worked with a lot of people in creativity workshops and seminars. Many quickly respond to suggestions to become more aware, sensitive. To toy with ideas. To work exercises, puzzles. But they start resisting and backpedaling when the going gets a little rough.

> *"I don't get it...I'm getting bored...can't we try a different one?"*

Yet those who stick it out, those who *persist*, gain the awareness and ability to work through those feelings of boredom, to repeatedly engage the necessary frustrations of creativity.

There's a well-known phase in group brainstorming referred to as the "plateau phase." At first a group is actively participating in generating ideas. Lots of conventional ideas come to mind and everyone is eager to get theirs into the pot. Then responses dwindle. After a short period of sporadic ideas...deadly silence. They have scraped off the obvious, the conventional. *If* they now stay with it they'll begin to find novel, unusual responses.

I believe more people turn away from creative enterprise at the plateau phase than at any other point in the creative process. It is then that we feel frustrated, when we believe the well has run dry.

Creative individuals accept frustration as necessary to the problem-solving process. They deliberately hold out for an elegant solution. Others yield prematurely to the pressure for closure. They fail to stir the caldron of possibility enough to come up with the internal rewards, the "aha's," which would, in turn, wet their appetites for more creative activity...which leads to greater toleration of frustration...and longer "holding out"...for even more elegant solutions....

Some like to believe creativity just flows from the soul. But when you think about it, a period of stress in the process makes more sense.

Consider the recent upsurge in physical exercise in this country. Physical exercise is certainly stressful. If you are a jogger, you have come to accept heavy breathing, leg cramps and sweat as part of the growth process. You recognize that jogging stresses the muscles and organs and "tells" them to grow and accommodate your desire for increased physical strength. Stress for the sake of creative growth makes the same kind of sense.

Indeed, our current TV commercials would suggest we have moved from merely tolerating physical stress to welcoming it. We no longer struggle with weightlifting, we invigorate ourselves by "pumping iron." Handsome athletes grin at us while announcing they "like to sweat," it gives them an "edge." A health studio full of people doing aerobics with weight belts is pictured and we hear the sound of rhythmic, labored breathing in the background. In the next scene three attractive, bouncing, enthusiastic, smiling, and very trim women pass by in slow motion...Sure we know it's a commercial hype for the studios, but our attitudes *are* changing.

Just wait, when the need for *creative* frustration becomes common (and profitable) knowledge, we'll likely see grinning TV personalities telling us how terrific it feels to "pump your brain" at the local creative thinking studio.

Look how lucky you are...you have the chance to be ahead of the pack...maybe you'll own that studio.

Now that you're properly motivated let's talk about increasing flexible persistence with three tools:

1. Take charge (resist closure and commit energy).

2. Write down ideas (capture them, "hold" them on paper).

3. Set ideas aside (incubate them).

Taking charge

It is important that you consciously acknowledge your participation in the creative process. *You* are allowing mental elements (singly or in small clumps) to remain disconnected in your mind long enough to bring about new, harmonious, integrated patterns (elegant solutions).

You already know what this will feel like. The disconnectedness will produce tension and a part of you will start griping. In the introduction to Part II (Tools), I said we have learned to *shut the door* on our intuition, and we can learn to *open* it again. We oil the hinges with breaking patterns, shifting perspectives, and challenging assumptions. Our perceptual openness opens the door; it takes flexible persistence to hold that door open.

Your rational mind in this sense is like a very orderly, tidy business office. You're working away on some problem in there and you notice it's getting a bit stuffy (your initial solution patterns). You defer judgment and open (perceptual openness) the door for fresh ideas. You feel a cool breeze as a few idea fragments float gently into the room. Papers flutter on your desk, and you hear the voice of your rational mind say,

> *"Shut the door will you?…the papers are going to get messed up…come over here and sit down so we can get on with the solution I gave you."*

You stay at the door, holding it open. The breeze grows into a wind. Ideas of all shapes and sizes are tumbling in the door. The curtains are flapping…papers lift from the desk and shelves in a great swirl of white…it feels like the beginning of a storm…book pages turn with a snapping sound…the desk lamp rattles in place…you stand with your hand on the doorknob, tense but excited...your hair is blowing...it is difficult to see clearly, but you know your office has gone from tidy to mess; order to chaos...and now that other part of you is hollering.

> "HEY, DUMMY, SHUT THE DOOR...LOOK AT THE MESS YOU MADE...ARE YOU CRAZY?...WHAT'S THE MATTER WITH YOU?...WE'LL NEVER GET THIS STRAIGHT AGAIN...THIS IS SERIOUS...LOOK AT ALL THE TIME YOU'RE WASTING...IT WAS JUST FINE IN HERE, SAFE AND SECURE...MY SOLUTION WAS GOOD ENOUGH...THIS ISN'T GOING TO GET US ANYTHING BUT TROUBLE...NOW WILL YOU SHUT THE DAMN DOOR?!!!

If you're not prepared to respond, you'll find yourself on the floor picking up those papers, trying to find the initial solution...and the door behind you will be *shut*.

My point? consciously *take charge*. This is, after all, *your* mind we are talking about.

> *"Sorry, that solution of yours just wasn't good enough. I deserve more and I'm holding this door open until something better comes up. We'll get things straightened up again later. I know I can rely on you to help. And while I'm at it, I may as well tell you things are going to be a little different in here. You can grump around all you want. I'm going to have a lot more creativity in my life from here on...and if that means having to put up with some of your yammering and racket...well so be it."*

That part of you (sitting there in your rational mind) will quiet down, when it knows the strength of your intentions and will comply much more easily after you come up with a few elegant solutions. Remember, developing creative ability is a lot like building muscle, it's a growth process. You won't get any major cramps if you don't start right off with a marathon run. Pick a number of smaller problems to work on, just like daily workouts.

Maybe your bedroom or office isn't arranged just as you'd like it...start there. Look around for a few "good" problems to work on. "Good" problems are those like a sudden windfall of money and you now have a problem of how to spend it; or a sudden chunk of free time and you wonder how to use it. These will have plenty of stress for muscle-building, but are less intimidating and therefore easier to hold from premature closure.

For example, say you have a good problem of where to go for a two-week winter vacation. You have saved a sum of money and are all set to head out of the cold snow country into a warm, tropical climate. Where should you go?

You look at a few travel brochures and find you have saved just enough to cover a trip to Jamaica. On first appraisal it seems a good solution, but you have time and decide to generate a few alternatives before buying the tickets. You start to "reframe" the problem. It isn't simply how to spend your vacation time. Sure, you saved just enough to cover the Jamaica trip, but do you really want to blow the whole wad on that one trip? You ask yourself what you would most enjoy on such a trip and conjure images of a beach and warm water, seeing new sights, meeting people, reading and relaxing in that tropical environment...but couldn't you do these things in California, Florida, Arizona, at lower cost? Should you hurry somewhere to "start" your vacation (plane)? Could you "start" the vacation before traveling and consider the travel to a destination (car, bus, train) an opportunity to see new sights, meet people, read and relax? Maybe you might travel for only one week and do the second week at home (reading and relaxing...and saving some of your hard-earned money)?

The more you explore and question, the more possibilities emerge. No single pattern is quite elegant enough and you feel the frustration of not deciding. Your left mind starts griping about how this is an unecessary hassle...and how you better go get those Jamaica tickets and be done with it. "Wait a minute," you think, "I'm going to hold out a bit longer...something's bound to turn up."

You continue to explore alternatives related to the key elements of money, time, warm climate, meeting people, reading and relaxing.

You want the most your money can buy, the best possible use of your two-week vacation period. You want to select a place that will contrast with the January chill, warm your spirit, get you through a case of midwinter doldrums. You hold out some more. You search, get confused, incubate, search some more...and then one morning whie you're eating breakfast and reading the paper you hear an idea quietly step right in the middle of your paper-reading thoughts...

> *"Instead of going to get what you want, why not stay where you are and ask it to come to you."*

> *"What? What's that you say? What's that supposed to mean...'ask it to come to you'...(no answer offered)...does this mean I shouldn't go anywhere???"*

> *"See?," says that neat and orderly part of you. "That's what you get when you hold out...ludicrous ideas...you better get those tickets or they'll be sold out and you'll be miserable...that's what you deserve for all this waffling around."*

> *"Now just hold on I want to explore this a little," you respond.*

It's still unclear to you, but you sense possibility in that idea, "...ask it to come to you." Other things you have wanted pop into your mind. You had wanted to redecorate or add something to this little house of yours, but had never connected this desire to your winter vacation. You really like the house, but had simply assumed you had to *go* somewhere during your vacation to get a real picker-upper.

Suddenly you imagine bringing the tropics right into your house. It quickly shifts into a little sauna, window greenhouse, work-out-and-relax addition just off your bathroom. A nice little wood-heated sauna... You would get to see new sights, right in your home...you could have a warm climate, right in your home. You could read and relax, spend your money and yet keep it (investment in property). You could meet people by having a January tropics party. Maybe even a small hot-tub could be worked into the deal...

In the above example of solving a good problem I tried to show the importance of taking charge. When you hold off that part of you that wants the security of an immediate decision other possibilities are automatically set in motion. When the possibilities are charged with energy (desire, frustration, will), they often form solution patterns responsive to needs and desires beyond the range of the immediate concern. It is as if their vigorous movement magnetically attracts a number of nearby unfulfilled needs, unresolved problems.

When you see that the solution coming is also responsive to some of your other concerns, wants, questions, you feel exhileration, you sense the poetry of your own summary power. Each time you practice solving smaller, good or less loaded problems, the experienced "aha" of a multifunction solution stimulates further creative problem solving. You develop habits of seeing things differently and resisting closure, because you want more of those elegant solutions.

Writing ideas down

How many times have you written a "to do" list of chores for the day, only to find later that you accomplished everything on the list without ever looking at it...but you didn't stop making out lists did you? The list was there if you did need it, it was your security. The process of writing it was also helpful to you, since each item was a summary of other thoughts. The words and short phrases you listed captured some of your thinking and held it on the paper.

When problem solving, your intuitive mind transmits all sorts of ideas, fragments, possibilities...collect them, round them up, be a packrat...let your analytic mind begin tentative ordering by writing things down. The process of writing and ordering will drain off the tension of incomplete ideas, it will relieve some of that pressure for premature closure. You are also conserving the energy it takes for unecessary memory and recall...you are *making room* for more ideas.

When you resist closure you are telling your analytic mind to hold off, to wait. Writing idea notes to yourself is asking your rational mind to work *with* your intuitive mind in a new kind of collaboration.

Your intuitive mind is seeking patterns. Many fragments will bubble up into your conscious awareness. Let your rational mind assign them tentative words. Acknowledge the words as important by *writing them down*...give them a concrete reality.

Remember, your intuitive mind doesn't sequence ideas for you. It doesn't evaluate them and send timely instructions. It's busy seeking patterns, forming images while you are consciously attending to something else. You'll get the spark of an idea...capture it, hold on to it, jot it down on something.

Get a stack of notepads and make sure they are handy (e.g., put one next to your bed, in the bathroom, in your car). Think of your intuitive mind as a cosmic antenna. Write down whatever you get so that your rational mind can ask better questions...which will lead to more creative answers.

Build idea banks, get some shoe boxes and label them with project categories. Collect your notes, and idea messages as they come in and deposit them in your boxes. Dump them out on the floor routinely and see if any patterns are emerging.

Pick a few broad, open categories for practice. How about your "someday" house? Look for all the ideas you'd like to incorporate into its design. How could your dream house reflect all of your unique needs and desires? What would it look like? How would things be arranged? Get a big box for this one. Sketch out everything you think up. Be your own architect. Visualize living in your sketches.

Pick a time and place to be alone each day. A special time set aside each day...just for you. How about an extra hour each morning? Set that alarm one hour earlier for meeting with your best friend, your creative self. Think things over, jot down notes, muse on ideas, create lists. The more you "get" the more you'll persist in the search. The more you practice, the more flexibly you'll approach initial ambiguities.

Set ideas aside

To understand this suggestion it is helpful to view the creative process in terms of what we know about *energy fields*.[2]

Our scientific understanding of energy fields underlies our electronic technology, the electrical stimulation of a heart to start it beating again and our extensive brain wave research.

Consider a simple demonstration of the effects of an energy field. If you sprinkle sand on the sounding box of a violin and draw the bow over the strings, the energy field produced by the sound vibrations will arrange the sand into geometric patterns. The patterns vary according to pitch, intensity, etc. A similar thing happens when you pass a magnet under a surface covered with iron filings. The magnet acts on these particles, they begin to move and suddenly they spring into geometric patterns around the magnet's force field.

Now let's slow down the process and try to picture what's happening. As we move the magnet closer and closer to the metal particles, they become charged with energy. Each particle becomes a magnet in miniature and begins to attract and repel other particles just like the poles of the magnet. As the magnet comes closer we see the particles begin to move. They are in a state of accelerating tension, acting on each other as the magnetic energy increases. At a certain point a chain reaction occurs and the metal particles form harmonious patterns.

In the creative process whole-mind thinking is like that magnet. The preparation stage is like drawing the magnet of whole-mind thinking closer to the problem, question or circumstance. We begin to manipulate the mental particles. With increasing attention the energy field builds intensity. Energy flows from the creative field to the idea material. We experience tension in the bumping, chaotic action of the mental particles. Our analytic mind works feverishly to form those geometric patterns, but it is like moving those metal particles with a tweezers. We feel tired and confused. It is time to *set the idea fragments aside* (incubate them) for a while.

We turn our conscious attention elsewhere, but at another level of awareness the pattern-forming process continues. When we later return to the problem we find fresh new ideas to work with. Or, sometimes without warning, we instead sense a creative possibility coming just before it bursts into our thoughts. The earlier tension is spontaneously released into that pattern of resolution and we experience relief, AHA!

With practice, creative tension can be accepted calmly with alert, sustained attention. There is a balance point between the *taking charge* (to persist) and deliberately *setting ideas aside* (to incubate). It becomes easier to recognize that balance point as we come to understand and accept the creative tension experienced when we focus our energies to destructure problem patterns and restructure them into solution patterns.

TURNING UP THE RIGHT MIND

Tools for cultivating creativity both *turn down* rational thinking and *turn up* intuitive thinking. We select and apply them in the process of creative problem solving according to requirements at the time. In the preparation stage we are attempting to maintain our perceptual openness and flexible persistence in the face of mounting frustration and ambiguity. The tools we use at this time are helpful in turning down our rationality, in fending off the tension and pressure to close on a solution or plan. Challenging assumptions, shifting perspectives, breaking idea patterns and taking charge are ways to deliberately subdue our dominating rational minds.

When we capture initial ideas by writing them down, we are relieving some of the left-mind pressures for closure by tentatively ordering and naming ideas as they emerge. This reduces some of the confusion and allows room for more of the complexity of right-mind possibility-thinking.

Association

Tools for *association* turn up the pattern-forming process of intuitive thinking. In the design stage of problem solving they help us move the bottled-up energies of frustration through incubation toward release in the "aha" of illumination.

Of course, we are speaking of a matter of emphasis here. We may use tools of association to stimulate our intuition, but they also help us contend with our rationality both in terms of a specific problem-solving activity and our long-term creative development. With the tools that turn up intuition we are also inviting our rational mind to use a mode of thinking approximating the integrative process of our intuition. By deliberately thinking in terms of similarities, connections and patterns we are welcoming our intuition, but at the same time are tempering our predilection for ordering and analyzing.

Our rational mind already utilizes *logical* associations in processing information (knife-bread-peanut butter-jelly). It makes conventional connections. By drawing upon your intuitive mind you'll make more *unusual* connections. Rational associations combine ideas within a single context (shoe: shoe-lace, shoe-sock, shoe-horn, shoe-foot). Creative associations jump around from one context to another (shoe: horse-shoe, shoe-fly-don't-bother-me, a-h-h-h SHOE! ("god bless you"), shoe-bee-do-bee-do.

Arthur Koestler believes all creative activity has this special associative pattern.[3] He coined the word "bisociation" referring to the connection of one plane of thinking to another.

Koestler explains that humor is a form of creativity. A joke compels us to perceive a situation in two self-consistent but incompatible frames of reference at the same time. The comic "bisociates" the two and we perceive the punch line as a delightful mental jolt...the leap from one plane to another. Our response to this collision is a reflex "ha-ha."

In invention the bisociation of previously separate areas of knowledge and experience is a form of synthesis rather than collision, and leads to an "aha" rather than "ha-ha" response.

In an artist's painting, bisociation is reflected in the juxtaposition of the familiar and the eternal which results in an "ah-h-h" response.

Creative achievements in humor, science, and art are different, but the same special pattern of association is fundamental to each.

You may be shaving, or driving your car, or talking to a friend when suddenly an insight pops into your mind and forms a pattern of associations, a new idea, a picture or vision. Whether a nifty solution to one of your smaller puzzlements or a thunderclap of intuition that will transform your lifestyle, you experience joyfulness over this flash of insight, this "aha" event.

The term "aha experience" was coined by Gestalt psychologists to indicate the euphoria which follows the flash of illumination when bits of the puzzle click into place. It is a signal that you have *combined* previously *unrelated* mental structures in such a way that you will get more out of the new whole than you put into it. The whole is not merely the sum of its parts, but an expression of the relations between its parts and each new synthesis leads to the emergence of new patterns of relations.

How many existing (and accepted) patterns of information could be rearranged into new ideas? The number of basic elements in music or a story plot are limited, but the *arrangements* of the elements, the new combinations, continue to entertain us with songs and stories year after year.

Increasing our ability to associate ideas is a matter of attitude. Choosing to think in terms of associations is a habit of mind.

Look at the following figure.

Figure 6.2:

Use your fingers or scraps of paper to block out the A and C. Next block out the 12 and 14.

The ability to associate is built-in. Your mind *wants* to form a pattern. It will accept imperfect parts and see them as if they were perfect in order to form the pattern, and name the parts. Is the center of the above figure more a 13 or B? It really doesn't matter, does it? You will see it according to its context; its relation to other parts of the arrangement.

Whatever you decide to combine will be the challenge to your built-in associative ability. To develop this ability you can practice making combinations that stretch your associative muscles. You can train your mind to accept more and more complex combinations, through successful exercises.

Using analogies

In the beginning of the chapter I explained that *analogy* is the basic tool for turning up our intuition. Let's try thinking about tools for cultivating creativity with analogy and see if we can make some different associations.

To form an analogy you associate seemingly unrelated things by asking how one is like the other. Here I am asking, "How is cultivating creativity like cultivating a garden?"

In gardening you cultivate after your recently planted seeds sprout up through the soil. Using a *tool* (e.g., hoe) you disturb the soil around the young plants in an effort to rid it of weeds. The weeds compete with your young plants for available nutrients and energy. Cultivation *turns down* competitive weeds and releases the nutrients to the plants you want to grow. You cultivate as part of an attempt to establish the best possible environment for the growth of your seed sprouts. You know you can't *force* the seeds to grow; you can only set the conditions which favor their growth.

Weeds are vigorous growers. Year in and year out they adapt to the special climate of your garden. When you turn them down (hold back or defer their growth) by cultivating, you are throwing the competitive balance in favor of your seed sprouts. You also *stimulate* (turn up) the growth process of your plants; you fertilize, mulch and water them. You know certain plants enjoy growing in proximity to certain other plants, and use your knowledge of "companion planting" to give them the benefit of such *associations*. For similar reasons you plant according to the cycles of the moon. You patiently observe the unique growth patterns of each of your plants and tie some to stakes, supporting the forms they have chosen. Once the sprouts gain size and strength, they will be better able to cope with those tough kids down the block, the weeds.

Deferring judgment is like cultivating those weeds. When unusual ideas sprout up through your intuition, you want to give them a chance by deferring quick judgments. You turn down intruding weed thoughts such as, "This will never work...that's irrelevant...what a foolish thought...stop the fantasy and get back to reality."

You know you cannot *force* creative ideas to grow; you can only set the conditions which favor their growth. You combine or *associate* your emerging idea with other ideas to stimulate its growth. You *visualize* where it might be heading and draw upon other known or "solid" concepts for support (like staking your plants).

Just as you allow seeds a chance to grow before thinning to the best seedlings, in creativity you allow intuitive ideas a chance to build strength before thinning them with the judgmental eye of your rational mind.

Of course, any good gardener will tell you there's more to gardening than holding the weeds down. Throughout the process from seed to plump, ripe tomatoes you watch closely. You keep your perceptions *open* for the constantly changing conditions in the garden. Sunshine, rain, heat, cold, insects, wind...new conditions, new patterns...all are beneficial when in balance. The gardener attempts to maintain this balance of environmental conditions.

At times, the garden environment seems an overwhelming system of complex interrelationships. Long chains of interdependence from the microbes and bacteria in the soil to the nitrogen released in a lightning storm seem almost beyond understanding. The frustrations of too much or too little moisture or sunlight, a sudden onslaught of devouring insects or plant disease...and the gardener is momentarilly tempted to give it all up and head for a supermarket. But he or she doesn't and learns to accept the complexity, to adapt to critical events, to develop the *flexible persistence* of a seasoned gardener.

Each season the gardener *prepares* and *designs*. Each season the garden keeps its promise. Lush foliage, vibrant colors, heavy fruits, different varieties, different patterns form a new garden reality. Each season is both new and a reaffirmation of the eternal miracle of growth. It is a *verification* of the process...and for the gardener who participates, an opportunity to express "self" in a celebration of life.

Differing uses of analogy

It's easier to intuitively grasp the many interconnected aspects of creative problem solving when capturing them in images of gardening than when reading them in a list. There's a qualitative difference between the direct (logical) and indirect (analogical) descriptions. Most of us enjoy the images of growing plants and it's also helpful to perceive the "growing" of creative ideas with the same positive attitude.

Let's work a bit more with analogy and consider some of its different uses. In the last chapter when I asked, "How is social work like a lawn sprinkler?" I was selecting a lawn sprinkler as a random object to trigger associations that would open up different viewpoints about the profession.

In other words, I made the initial arrangement by posing a random object (lawn sprinkler) next to something we all have many thoughts about (social work). Then by searching for similarities we associated all sorts of ideas about social work. If we wanted to explore further, it would be easy to pick up a few other words or objects that one sees when imagining a lawn sprinkler (hose, faucet, grass, rose bush, rainbow). Or someone might have said, "I see social work more like a paper crinkler than a lawn sprinkler." Or "Lawn made me think of fawn, and I see social work like a fawn because...." We could have selected any other random words to move our associations and discussion in other directions. (How is social work like a letter opener, a hard-boiled egg, a derby hat, a broadway show, a rainy afternoon, a record player?)

The analogy is, then, an extremely versatile tool for encouraging associations, and it serves as the basis for many of the popular creative-thinking techniques.

For example, William Gordon devised a method of group problem solving he calls "synectics." The (Greek) word synectics itself means the joining together of different and apparently unrelated elements, and analogy is used as an underlying operational mechanism. Three forms of analogy Gordon uses as tools for group discussion are personal analogy, direct analogy, and fantasy analogy.[4]

In personal analogy the individual "becomes" a part of the problem. Say you kept loosing your car keys. Personal analogy would have you asking yourself, "If I were the keys how would I keep from getting lost?" Personal analogy helps you know the problem differently by empathic identification with it. Einstein tells of using this form of analogy to "become" part of his mathematical formulations.

Direct analogy is the actual comparison of parallel facts or knowledge. Nature is often suggested as a source of useful parallels regardless of the problem at hand...animals, birds, flowers, insects, etc. Davis offers an example with obvious social work connections. He tells about a creativity workshop for retired people where many expressed concern for their personal safety. The direct analogy, then, becomes how do animals, plants, birds, etc., protect themselves, and how can these ideas help the elderly? All sorts of camouflages, electric shockers, sprays, tape recorded screams and alarms, were generated.[5]

Fantasy analogy has us ask the question, "How in my wildest fantasy would we desire this problem to be solved?" For example, Gordon describes the invention of a vapor-proof closure for space suits through someone's fantasy analogy of having trained insects do the work of closing and covering.[6]

Forming connections

Over the years a variety of other tools for *forming connections* have been derived from the analogy. For example, "Forced Relationship Techniques" described by Charles Whiting, and "Random Juxtaposition" described by Edward de Bono show that relationships and possibilities emerge when a common element (known problem) is juxtapositioned (arranged) with a random element.[7,8] "How is poverty like an old shoe?"..."How is Reagan like an artichoke?"..."How is social work like the Goodyear blimp?"..."How is reading this paragraph like a bar of soap?"

When using analogies with random words it is especially helpful to first use another well-known device, the *attribute list*.[9] Before associating the random word you first generate its attributes. For example, in the social work and lawn sprinkler association, you would make note that a lawn sprinkler spreads water over a certain area according to the amount and pressure of water transmitted by the faucet and hose. Typically a lawn sprinkler spins in a circular motion. It is often constructed of metal and plastic parts; is typically colored green. It must be monitored to prevent overwatering. It must be moved around to adequately cover entire area.

Our intuitive mind communicates through pictures and images. It is therefore helpful to add whatever support you can think of when arranging analogies. For example, page through a magazine when selecting random objects for an analogy. The visual aid of the magazine pictures will invigorate your associative power and quickly help you remember attributes.

The Yellow Pages are also helpful. Say the question or problem at hand is, "How do you think we should relate to her?" You randomly point at plumber, window glass installer, dog groomer, to develop alternative approaches.

Myron Allen offers another connecting tool that incorporates attribute listing. He calls it "Morphological Synthesis" and it involves creating lists of attributes and arranging them so that each attribute is posed next to all others.[10] For example, let's say we are designing the waiting room in a new social service agency. We want the design to reflect consideration of the clientele who will use it and the overall purposes of the agency. We develop lists of possible colors, textures, room shapes, sounds, views, furniture, etc. When we pose each proposed item for the room against each color, texture, shape, and so on, we'll generate an amazing list of alternatives.

Often waiting rooms reflect the business furniture suppliers' concept of durable comfort. (Because of this it's difficult to tell if you are waiting to see your dentist or waiting to talk to a loan counselor at the bank.) Waiting rooms in social work could encourage feelings, initiate relationships, reflect agency sensitivities and priorities, suggest thought patterns (a picture on the wall can suggest a perception to consider). We *do* have a choice between music and Musak. We don't use the business furniture suppliers' concept of durable comfort in furnishing our homes. If we want clients to feel "at home" in agency waiting rooms, why not use a tool such as "Morphological Synthesis" to move beyond the six plastic chairs, a bowl of goldfish and three copies of Family Circle magazine?

Remember, when using tools such as in the various "forced relationships," the random objects or words you arrange are simply *devices* to initiate possibilities. You don't owe that lawn sprinkler anything. It serves only as a starting point for chains of associations. When ideas peter out, go back and pick another random word. Actually, when solving a particular problem a series of forced relationships with a variety of random objects is often more productive than devoting the same amount of effort to just one forced relationship.

Creative thinking tools can be quite effective when used individually or in small groups...and if your social work group participants think such methods are a silly waste of time, you might suggest that the Kleenex pop-up tissue was invented in a Synectics training session, and literally thousands of consumer products result from deliberate use of analogical techniques. When you begin exploring the literature on creativity, you'll find many tools, techniques and exercises that have obvious relevance for social work practice. I strongly encourage you to use them routinely. Just as daily physical exercise helps train your body, daily workouts with creativity exercises help train your mind.

Hundreds of exercises are available that would help you sharpen your creativity tools. Through them you will become aware of the many subtle differnces in thinking stimulated by tools broadly defined as turning down rational thinking or turning up intuitive thinking. For example, Eugene Raudsepp has written several books that offer a variety of helpful and fun paper-and-pencil exercises.[11] Let's sample two of his exercises that help train our ability to *form connections*.

Instructions:

Fill in the blank with a word that relates to each of the other words.

Examples:

Sleeping   contest   spot   shop   _____

Answer: Beauty (sleeping beauty, beauty contest, beauty spot, beauty shop).

Style   love   jacket   span   _____

Answer: Life (lifestyle, love life, life jacket, life span).

Now try the following:

bug	rest	fellow	cover	_____
cross	baby	blood	ribbon	_____
tooth	talk	potato	bitter	_____
alley	date	snow	spot	_____
studies	work	science	welfare	_____

A	B	C	D	
belt	magic	market	head	_____
hunter	light	wind	stand	_____
beater	head	roll	rotten	_____
shave	quarters	call	down	_____

Answers can be found at the end of the chapter.

If you had trouble with the fifth set of words, you are in desperate need of practice (excuse me). This is a sample of the first of seventy-five exercises Raudsepp offers in *Creative Growth Games*. With succeeding exercises of this type he gradually increases the level of difficulty.

Consider for a moment how the kind of thinking you use in working through this simple exercise trains your mind for social work practice (e.g., when trying to find common denominators for cohesion in working with a small group of adolescents).

Another of Raudsepp's exercises has us making connections in a slightly different manner.

Instructions:

> Fill in each of the three spaces between the two "key words" with words which have a meaningful relation with the word preceding and following it.

Examples:

> Dark _____ _____ _____ shovel
>
> *Possible answers* Dark color white snow shovel
>
> School _____ _____ _____ run
>
> *Possible answers* School guard house dog run

Now, try the following:

Star	_____	_____	_____	before
Lemon	_____	_____	_____	dog
Fire	_____	_____	_____	scared
Dog	_____	_____	_____	white
postage	_____	_____	_____	knee
White	_____	_____	_____	about
Short	_____	_____	_____	out
Blood	_____	_____	_____	color
Light	_____	_____	_____	test
Blue	_____	_____	_____	ball

Example answers can be found at the end of the chapter.

Although this is another combinatory thinking exercise, it taps a different thought process than the first. Again, consider the kind of thinking represented and the fit with practice (e.g., linking needs to resources, making a relevant referral, trying to find the best route for getting from here to there).

When you work through the wide array of exercises offered by authors such as Raudsepp, Adams and de Bono, you not only train your thinking, but also discover and strengthen some of your own unique thinking talents.[12,13]

Visualization

Our rational mind is the locus of our logic, reason, analysis, reading, writing, and language. Our intuitive mind is the locus of our symbols, emotions, rhythm, pattern-seeking, and visual imagery.

Our rational mind speaks to us in words, our intuitive mind shows us pictures. When we deliberately exercise visual thinking we again invite our rational mind to participate in a process that is predominant in our intuitive minds.

All of us are used to visualizing in some contexts, such as dreaming, selecting paint for redecorating a room, solving a problem where shapes and spatial arrangements are important, or when we are describing the appearance of a person or place. But in terms of utilizing mental images in the process of creating many of us are practically visual illiterates.

If I would ask you to put the coffee on would you image the coffee pot or simply respond to the word in your mind? If I said, "How are your folks doing?" would you first visualize them or would you automatically respond with words formed in your mind? Who of us do you guess are the best visualizers? Who would you guess are the most imaginative? Artists, poets, actors, writers, and kids, right? Why are they that way? You already know the answers, but I'll plod along anyhow.

The schooling process and our culture stresses rational, objective thinking. Visualization, imagery, fantasy, imagination, dreams, daydreams...all are subjective, intuitive experiences. Like the rest of the functions of our intuitive mind our ability to visualize suffers from disuse, we have *learned* to keep it to a minimum.

"Stop daydreaming and pay attention. This is important."

"Don't worry honey, it's not real...it's just make believe...it's only your imagination."

"Are you off on one of your pipedreams again?...you'll never amount to anything if you spend so much time in fantasy"

Well we learned how not to use it and we can learn to use it again. It's built-in, remember? We all can visualize just as we all can speak. Some people are better speakers than others. Why? Because they develop the skill...they practice.

Visualization is critical to the formation and capturing of creative ideas (A picture is worth...) and also plays a central role in the expression of those ideas in objective reality (verification). Mental images guide us in following through on the "aha!" idea, they help us *make it happen*.

It doesn't matter if an image is real or imaginary. If it has strength (strong commitment), if we hold it in our mind's eye (vision), if we believe in it, our body, mind and actions will be affected toward making that image happen. What we lack through disuse is the ability to form and hold strong images. To increase our ability to visualize, then, we need to practice.

Form clear mental images

Mental images are recorded from sensory information. Visualization thus involves not only seeing, but also hearing, touching, tasting, and smelling. Sensory combinations enrich visual imprints. For example, if I ask you to shut your eyes and think of the smell of an orange as if you were peeling one, you would likely visualize peeling an orange first to identify the citrus fragrance.

To practice forming clear mental images you first need to develop a list. Then you go down each item on the list, closing your eyes and visualizing each item. Be sure to include a few simple shapes (to build clarity), sounds, tastes, etc. Let me list a few as examples.

— a bright red circle

— your name written on a blackboard

— someone calling your name

— children at a playground (see and hear)

— a green square

— holding hands with someone

— biting into an apple (see, hear, taste, touch, smell)

— the sound of a jet plane

— a bowl of ice cream (dress it up and taste it)

— a loaf of hot bread

— a mooing cow

— doing dishes (sight, sound, touch)

— petting a dog

— pine scent

— a cup of hot chocolate (with marshmallows)

— a blue triangle

— the face of a friend

— thunder

— the smell of gasoline

— a group of friends laughing at a joke

It would also help build clarity if you would select a few simple shapes (fruit or square, circle, etc.). and draw them on a large sheet of white paper. Look at them a while and then close your eyes and visualize. Stick with it; practice a little each day.

Develop imagination skills

Developing your imagination is like putting individual images into scenes; pictures into a motion picture. For example, in your mind's eye you are walking down a street in your home town. It's a sunny spring day. Feel your movement, add a variety of sights, sounds, smells, tastes (children running past, laughter, fresh-cut lawns and flowers, a car going past and someone waving).

After you have achieved clarity (you are *in* the scene, you *hear* words spoken to you), begin changing roles. Role-play different personalities (select some of your favorites). Add drama and adventure. Sound childish?...it should. Remember, you are trying to regain abilities lost through disuse.

Image talking

Your rational mind is your verbal mind. It uses words and talks to you constantly. You speak, read and write words. You build verbal power. Here we are trying to beef-up our intuitive abilities. Our intuitive mind visualizes and shows us pictures. Talking to ourselves with images, drawing pictures, builds visual power, just like writing notes to ourselves in words builds verbal power.

When problem solving try sketching pictures, doodles, designs, rather than just words. Don't get caught up in whether or not your drawings are "good." Remember, you are simply "talking" with your intuitive mind through images.

Use sketches to represent ideas. Try drawing rather than writing your shopping list. Carry a notebook around with you and sketch ideas whenever you get a chance. Have some butcher paper at home so you can really get expansive now and then. The point is you are not simply drawing. You are developing a way of thinking and communicating with your intuitive mind.

Instead of listing goals as words, sketch a picture of yourself having achieved that goal. Design your dream home, sketch the kind of furniture you'd like to see in it. Draw a map of where you are and where you might be going.

If you enjoy cooking, design some sort of utensil that would make a certain job easier. No one will see or evaluate what you draw, so *free up*.

Try carrying on a conversation with your intuition through pictures. On a vacation day sit down and decide what you (and your intuitive friend) might like to do. Sketch possibilities and pick one (be sure to take your friend along).

Recall dreams

Dream recall, like drawing, is a tool for increasing visualization power. It is also a tool for getting to know your intuitive self and regaining balance in thinking and perceiving.

In dreaming you are communicating directly with your intuitive mind. You are asleep. Your rational mind with its unrelenting focus on the external world; with its incessant yammering, pushing, shoving...is asleep. Your body is quietly being replenished. Here you stand face to face with your creative inner world; a landscape of tremendous potential for learning and growth.

I don't have to prod you to exercise dreaming, to make it a daily habit. You'll dream whether or not anyone tells you to. You'll dream whether or not *you* want to. You'll dream whether or not you remember your dreams, or attempt to learn from them. Like I've often said, your intuitive powers are right there, built-in. Dreams are a proof of that.

We have always known intuitively, that something important happens in that world of dreaming. Dream research over the past decade has confirmed this. We know that dreams connect us somehow. They are a frontier of learning. My treatment of them here will be brief, but I encourage you to explore further on your own.

Dreams shows us firsthand how our intuitive mind processes information when freed from the logical reasoning process of the conscious rational mind. Dreams show us that pictures are very important in conveying information. If you increase your use of drawing and sketching as a tool for developing visual power, and at the same time practice remembering and recording your dreams, you'll find they quickly work together. In other words, the images you draw, and consider important representations of things you want and "believe" will happen, will be picked up in the dream world communication system, to be enriched, and interelated with other wants and possibilities.

You will find much more elaborate and helpful information elsewhere, but let me offer a brief list of points for practicing dream recall.

1. Be sure to have a notebook, or tape recorder available at bedside.

2. Tell yourself (auto-suggestion) just before going to sleep each night, "I will remember my dreams."

3. If you wake during the night, write down the main points and the entire dream will usually come back to you in the morning.

4. Practice observation in your dreams to increase clarity in both your visualizations and recall. Look for the setting, the people, the action, the color, the feeling, and the words.

5. Think over your dreams each morning, (read notes, read over past dreams).

6. Be practical about it. Skip the heavy diagnostics. Look simply for the basic lesson of the dream. When you get unusual symbols reduce them to your common terms.

7. Need I remind you? Persistence will pay off.

If you practice forming clear mental images, imagination skills, image talking and dream recall you'll rapidly reclaim the powers of visualization helpful to doing the creative idea, verifying it in concrete reality.

ENDING COMMENT

Well, that's about it on the tools for turning down the left mind and turning up the right mind. I do have another tool for you. It's a tool that works well for encouraging both left- and right-mind functions.. It's called the *circles map* and you'll find it in the next chapter.

EXERCISE ANSWERS

Answers to Connections Exercise 1

Bed, blue, sweet, blind, social, vitamin, black, head, egg, close.

Example Answers to Connections Exercise 2

Star light day long before

Lemon yellow paint house dog

Fire escape fast run scared

Dog tag laundry wash white

Postage stamp foot sore knee

White wash clean face about

Short fall down cast out

Blood test paper white color

Light cigarette smoke screen test

Blue sky high jump ball

Young Woman/Old Woman Gestalt Picture

The Young Woman   The Old Woman

The circles map 7

In the last chapter we looked at a variety of tools for developing creativity. In this one we'll explore the use of another tool, a tool useful to both left- and right-mind thinking tasks that I call the circles map *or sometimes "doing circles."*

The circles map is helpful for logically organizing and analyzing data. It can be used to describe, order, outline and prioritize information. At the same time it stimulates our intuition. It encourages "possibility thinking" and a more balanced awareness of part-whole relationships.

In the discussion of this chapter I'll illustrate different ways to use the circles map. Because of page dimensions, I have to limit the number of circles I use in any one map. Such constraints are unnecessary when you are practicing on your own. So, be sure to have large sheets of paper (e.g., flip chart, newsprint, butcher paper) or a blackboard available.

A VISUAL AID

I first started doing circles in the "pre-generalist" days. Like others at the time, I was diligently trying to incorporate systems theory into my teaching of social work methods. Drawing circles on the blackboard to illustrate concepts seemed the obvious thing to do. It took time and continued practice before I began to recognize the multipurpose power of this simple tool.

Circles and systems are easily connected. If I asked you to visualize a system and draw it on the blackboard, what would you come up with? Chances are you'd imagine a solar system—spherically-shaped objects, invisibly interconnected, moving around a center or nucleus like a sun.

If you hold that solar system image in your mind for a minute its pattern will serve as a beginning "template" for drawing a circles map. You name the system with a key word or phrase in the center circle (like the sun). You label other circles around the center circle to represent subsystems (like planets orbiting the sun). Additional points of information specific to the various interrelated subsystems understandably orbit them (like the moon orbits earth).

In other words a circles map is, in essence, a way to visually represent an infinite variety of part-whole configurations. For example, you could use it to describe a theory or idea, design a 30-day diet menu, organize a "to do" list, or sort out a problem situation.

Let's try out a simple example. Say you were making plans for how to best use your coming Saturday. You write "Saturday" in the middle of a sheet of paper and while gazing at it begin to think of things you'd like to accomplish in that time period. You randomly jot down and circle key words and phrases as they pop into your mind. You're not trying to organize at this point. It's more like pouring the big and small desires and possibilities tucked away in your mind onto the the Saturday circle. Let's say Figure 7.1 represents some of your thoughts.

Figure 7.1

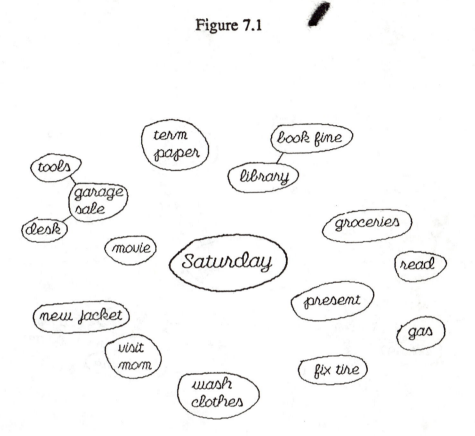

After looking at this random arrangement of possibilities around the Saturday circle for a while, your mind automatically begins to order and cluster idea fragments. Some needs are high priority and deserve a prominent place in your Saturday plans. Others vary according to such factors as time required versus importance, location and distance to travel, fun potential, "killing two or more birds with one stone," and so on. Whatever your process of elimination and prioritizing, let's say you now sketch a second circles map (see Figure 7.2).

Figure 7.2

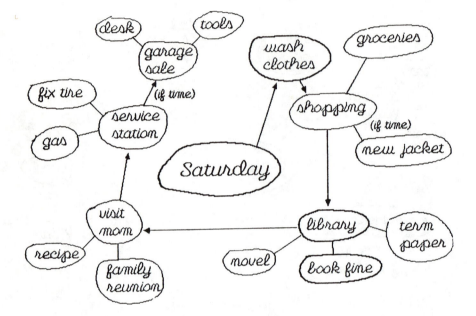

Notice how you indicate high priority by size and outline of circle, relationships by location of circles, direction or sequence of activity by arrow connectors and options with words on the connecting lines. In this case you have a circles map that is similar to a flow chart. In other uses it will look quite different.

Notice also that in this example you used the circles in two stages: first to stimulate, associate, and generate possibilities and then to organize, design and visually represent your plan. Emphasis on stimulation or organization will also vary according to circumstances and your reason for doing circles at the time.

Let's try a different kind of example. This time let's focus more on the organizing function of the circles map.

Say you are responsible for a three-hour in-service or staff development seminar at your agency. You have agreed to discuss creativity. Using some of what we talked about in Chapter 5 let's first sketch a simple overview circles map. You'd probably do this on a flip chart before the session (see Figure 7.3).

Figure 7.3

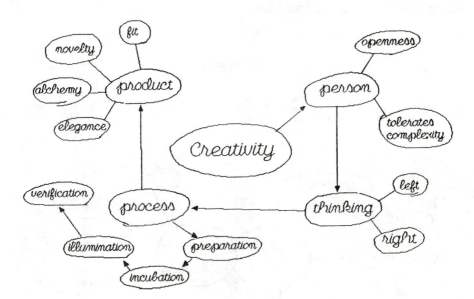

Notice again the use of circle size and position to indicate part-whole relationships and arrow connections to show direction or sequence. I'll introduce other symbols for visual communication as we continue.

Let's say you use this circles map on a poster to guide your presentation in the three-hour session. You would use it to highlight the overall topic and could refer to it throughout discussion. It would help you organize your discussion periods and keep on task. You would "pull out" circles that you wanted to talk more about and sketch more detailed maps of them on a blackboard or flip chart. At the same time participants would have a visual aid to refer to, something to help keep them aware of the whole of the topic during digressions, specific exercises and breaks.

For example you'd likely want to "pull out" the creative-thinking circle for elaboration on the blackboard. You'd here sketch out something like that in Figure 7.4:

Figure 7.4

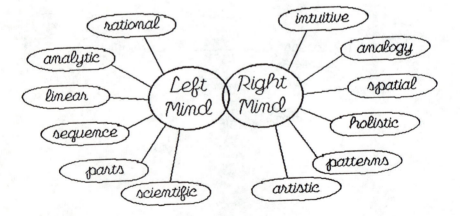

Notice that this time overlapping circles were used to indicate the strength of a relationship. Let's say it's time to involve participants in a few exercises. You might draw (or have drawn in advance) a circles map of the tools we discussed in Chapter 6 (see Figure 7.5).

Figure 7.5

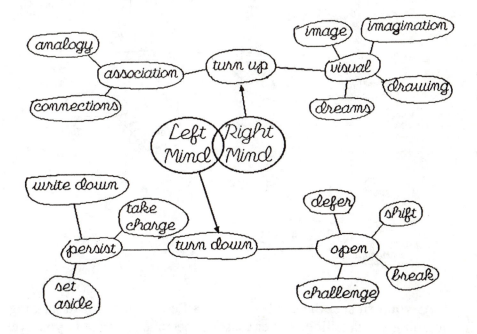

If you wanted to instead emphasize the use of creative thinking tools in a problem-solving process you might consider a circles map more like that in Figure 7.6.

Figure 7.6

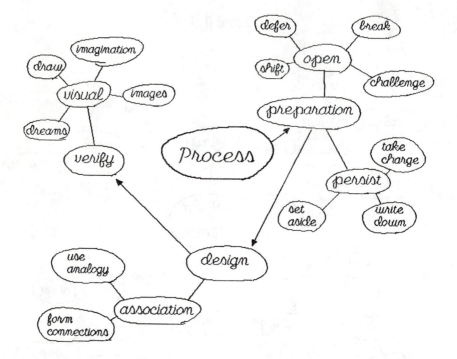

As you can see, the circles map is a flexible tool for describing, outlining and detailing. Other uses will become apparent to you over time. In a learning setting it consistently encourages participants to see interrelationships, connections and patterns in whatever the topic at hand. It offers a quick sense of the whole in complex topics and a grasp of key relationships within that whole. It also increases participant interaction, questioning and idea generating. It's much more adaptable for rearranging ideas than a conventional outline and encourages moving ideas around to search for different relationship patterns. It facilitates "zooming in" and "scanning across" information for different perspectives and understandings.

COMMUNICATIONS

If you imagined yourself leading that creativity session in the above example (pointing at a circles map while talking, sketching maps on the board to respond to questions or process exercises and rearranging circles to elaborate interests emerging in the group) you probably have a sense of how the circles map is a tool for communicating as well as understanding. I'll tell you a bit more about this.

In the early 1970s I assumed responsibility for developing a *field unit* that would demonstrate a generalist approach to social work in the public school setting. This experimental project was called a field "unit" rather than field "placement," because students were not placed with professionals in agencies. Instead a faculty member (in this case, me) worked directly with students in the field. Concepts and methods emphasized in this field unit were, of course, a generalist perspective, problem solving, creativity and doing circles.

In field meetings we sorted problem-solving activities with the circles process. We assessed and strategized with circles. Students did circles to organize classroom papers. They learned to collaborate with clients in doing circles. We established a consulting team that traveled around the state offering problem consultation to other school social workers through doing circles. We presented staff development seminars and a variety of workshops that utilized the circles map. Several school social workers got release time to join us in our problem-solving activities, and we carried rolls of butcher paper and portable blackboards to and from various meetings to insure resources for doing circles.

In short, the circles map underwent extensive experimentation and development during the six years of this field project (plus six additional years in other classes and field projects). It was a primary tool for communications and management in assessing, planning and generating ideas and collaborating with clients.

The experiences and understanding gained through this broad range of involvements serves as the foundation for what I'll now explain about doing circles in problem solving.

PROBLEM SOLVING

Why did doing circles become so important? Why did mapping out ideas, questions, problem information and resources with circled summary words and phrases become an integral part of an experimental field unit? Why did it catch on so quickly and become a trademark of participating students and professionals? Because it *works*.

It's not just a new technique for specific professional tasks. It has a broad range of usefulness including personal problem solving. Field unit participants often requested consultation time with the group to do circles on an idea, question or problem. Let's take a look at an example.

The Apartment Problem

One of the students was having a problem in living arrangements. She lived in an older building (one she could afford). In her spare time over the course of a year she had completely redecorated her apartment. She was very handy and had made many small repairs (electrical outlets, cracks in walls, etc.) She stripped the paint from the woodwork, wallpapered the bathroom and repainted each room. She put up new curtains and steam-cleaned the carpeting. Because she enjoyed this kind of work and made it a hobby, she also knew how to find bargains on paint, wallpaper, yardgoods and other decorating materials.

It was the end of her first year lease agreement. Though she had anticipated a small increase in rent, she was caught off guard by the amount the landlord was now asking. Considering her tight budget she simply could not see how she could afford to stay.

She complained to the landlord that it was unfair to be penalized with an outrageous rent increase after she had worked so hard to redecorate the apartment. He apologized and explained that another tenant in the building had agreed to pay the new rent for the chance to move into her apartment if she decided not to sign a new lease agreement.

The student had one year left until she finished her degree and then would be leaving the community. She enjoyed the location of the apartment (accessibility to campus, shopping, lake). She liked the older neighborhood because of its quietness and stability. She couldn't afford to stay and was worried about finding another rental within her budget. The time and expense of hunting for one, plus the cost and hassle of a move also bothered her. She was concerned about how much this development would interfere with her summer job. She considered another loan to cover the increased rent, but already felt over her head in debts and wasn't even sure she could arrange one.

While the student explained her situation to the group another student was at the board drawing circles. The beginning map looked something like Figure 7.7.

Figure 7.7

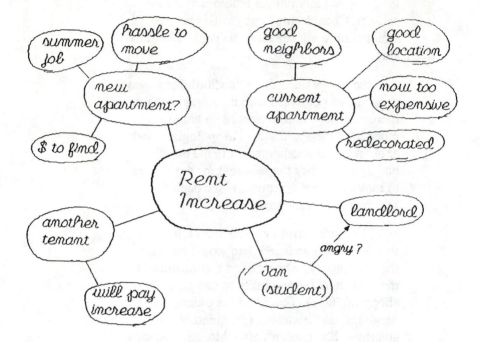

Questions were asked to clarify information and fill out the circles map. For example, someone asked why she had put so much effort into redecorating an apartment when she would only get to enjoy it for a couple of years. She explained it was her self-help therapy for handling the pressures of going to school. She had a flare for such work, and would probably have a number of redecorating projects going wherever she lived.

Someone else asked about the landlord. The student said she was first angry with him, but later understood his position. He had bought the apartment building on a shoestring, was holding down two jobs to cover repairs and loan costs, and really needed the extra rental income.

The questioning continued for a time, but the pauses and silences became more frequent as participants began searching for possibilities.

Someone rolled her eyes and suggested the student get therapized for her "fixer-upper compulsions" before she gets addicted to another apartment (laughter). Someone else said if she really needed a quick fix he'd be glad to let her redecorate his apartment when he was gone on weekends (more laughter). Another quipped she should probably quit social work and open a redecorating business (more laughter). Then someone suggested if she had been a little faster she could have managed to redecorate all the apartments in the building and hers wouldn't have been such a great deal (more laughter). These comments were circled on the board, and things quieted down again.

Then someone said that the student really was very talented, and if she would advertise her skills some landlord would surely give her a break on the rent. Someone else interrupted this comment (excited) and suggested she should make that kind of proposal to her current landlord. Others caught the direction of this suggestion and pitched supportive ideas.

In essence, they believed the student should propose to her landlord that over the next year she live in and redecorate the apartment vacated by the tenants who planned to move into her apartment.

Well, she made her proposal and it worked. The tenant in question was an elderly couple on the second floor, who wanted a first floor apartment. The landlord would pay for all supplies to redecorate the vacant apartment (if she agreed to use her skill in finding bargains). He would help her move into it and he would cut her original rent payment in half for the labor she contributed. He considered it a great deal. He had seen a sample of her ability, and wasn't looking forward to the probable loss of a month's rent to clean up and rent the vacated apartment.

The Apartment Problem: A Synergistic Solution

Remember those indicators of creative solutions (fit, novelty, alchemy, elegance)? This solution was creative and synergistic. The student, landlord and tenants in the situation all benefited.

Creative solutions are often synergistic, because synergy is elegant. A synergistic solution has a lot of impact on a situation with minimum practitioner involvement (energy expenditure). When a solution strategy is recognized as beneficial by the different people in a situation, they commit energy to the changes necessary without the continual effort of the practitioner.

Obviously, synergistic solutions won't be found in every social work situation, but you'll never find them if you aren't looking. With whole-mind thinking, a radar antenna for mutually benefitting arrangements and a tool such as the circles map you'll find more synergistic solutions than you thought possible.

In the student apartment situation, it was initially tempting to view the landlord as an adversary. He raised the rent and thus *caused* the student's problem. Yet her problem (higher rent) helped solve his financial difficulties. The tenants might have been adversaries for offering to pay higher rent for the redecorated apartment, but the student's problem helped solve the elderly couple's difficulty in getting to and from their second floor apartment.

Assuming adversaries in this situation might have led to suggesting win-lose strategies, e.g., trying to get landlord to hold off higher rent for one year through argument or, if possible, legal pressure; appealing to the elderly couple to withdraw their offer.

The field unit participants valued synergy, and therefore did not immediately identify adversaries. They instead used the circles map to first consider the motivations of others in the situation as *attributes* of the problem. Attributes of a problem *may* turn out to be either assets or liabilities to problem solving. They may include adversarial relationships, but they may *also* be potential resources for synergistic change.

From past experience unit members had learned the benefits of *challenging assumptions* in problem solving. They knew that making the concerns of others a center circle gave them a better chance at finding mutually beneficial solutions. In this case, putting either the landlord's financial problem or the tenant's physical problem in the center circle *shifted the pattern* from "problem" to "solution."

The Apartment Problem and Relationships

Words such as warmth, empathy, sensitivity and caring are very much a part of the language of social work. Practitioners often focus on positive relationships as a key to success in problem solving. The creative generalist, on the other hand, concentrates on the problem to be solved and views the relationship more an *outgrowth* of successful problem solving than a *prerequisite* to it.

For example, in doing circles on the apartment problem, one of the participants commented on the student's compulsion to redecorate and another suggested that she quit social work for a decorating business. When focusing on the etiquette of sensitive relating, such comments might be considered sarcastic or unfeeling. But in this situation it reflected "ground rules" pertinent to problem solving and using the circles map.

After the group used the circles map to organize and detail the presenting problem situation, they shifted gears and began generating unusual connections. They were deliberately toying with the problem, saying whatever ideas popped into their thoughts. This playfulness about a serious problem is not an insensitivity to the presenter's feelings, but a deliberate and agreed upon attempt to open things up, to increase flexibility.

Everyone (including the presenter) was searching for intuitive associations and knew they would likely stumble on a few ideas that would stimulate laughter. The joking comments that an outsider might consider in bad taste were actually sought by the group.

Koestler says humorous "ha-ha's" sit right alongside creative "aha's".[1] The field members knew very well that laughter is often an indicator that someone may have found the thread of a connection for the group to weave into a creative solution pattern.

AN ORGANIZATION AND STIMULATION TOOL

In the apartment example the participants shifted gears from organizing to generating connections in using the circles map process. They were demonstrating an important aspect of this multipurpose tool. As I mentioned earlier, it can be adapted for a variety of uses on a continuum from organization (left-mind emphasis) to stimulation (right-mind emphasis), depending on the requirements of the selected problem and stage in the problem-solving process.

Organizational Uses

There are many ways to use the circles map for organizing (describing, presenting, sorting out, analyzing) information. Complex interrelationships can be summarized in a visual pattern. In previous illustrations you saw how size of circles, and arrow connecting lines can show relative importance, relationship and order. The distance between circles is also varied to indicate differences and similarities. Relationships of critical importance can be expressed with varying amounts of overlap.

In an article titled, *"Diagrammatic Assessment of Family Relationships,"* Ann Hartman identifies a tool for family assessment similar to the circles map. She calls it an "eco-map" and suggests using solid connecting lines for important relationships, dotted connecting lines for tenuous relationships and jagged connecting lines for conflictual or stressful relationships.[2]

In a similar way we have experimented with a variety of connecting lines (thick, thin, dotted, +'s, -'s). Sometimes we write key words on the connecting lines and we found that using different colors for both connecting lines and circles is especially powerful visually.

Depending upon your purpose for doing circles, such variations can be used to represent whatever range of relationships you consider important. For example, arrow connectors can indicate necessary order or steps in an activity, changes over time, direction of preferred development and level of reciprocity in relationships.

Stimulation Uses

The circles map can also be used to stimulate the unusual associations necessary for building creative solutions. It will help you generate a multitude of choices through the language of your intuitive mind (images, spatial arrangements).

Here you are seeking a toehold on the unknown, you move across the circled words using them as stepping stones to a new idea pattern. The circled words attract related ideas like a magnet. You gaze at them. You wonder, you muse. You are collecting insights, waiting for inspiration.

Your pattern-seeking right mind isn't logical, it may transmit seemingly irrelevant images and feelings. Remember that anything may become useful. If you find yourself thinking of lines in a song or if you suddenly imagine a shape or picture, get it written down on that circles map. Remember, you are trying to attract, excite and tease out possibilities. Your left mind may start doubting the process.

"Nothing is happening...this isn't getting me anywhere."

But persist, be playful and patient. Doodle with your pencil or go back and clean up a few previous circles and lines, look at them in a relaxed, yet attentive fashion. There is no right or wrong here. When you associate seemingly random thoughts words and phrases around the circles you'll soon sense coherent patterns forming.

Gabriele Lusser Rico recommends a "clustering" process for creative writing that is essentially the same as using a circles map and random juxtaposition for stimulating new ideas.[3] Working with circles and creativity tools on such tasks would, of course, be a good way to develop your skill.

Say, for example, you have a paper assigned in one of your classes. You pick a topic that you want to present in a strong proactive statement, but you can't seem to find the right words to convey this meaning. Combine the circles tool with analogy. Ask yourself a question like, "What color is proactive?" Without judging, put a color down next to the word in a center circle. Let's try the color red (see Figure 7.8).

Figure 7.8

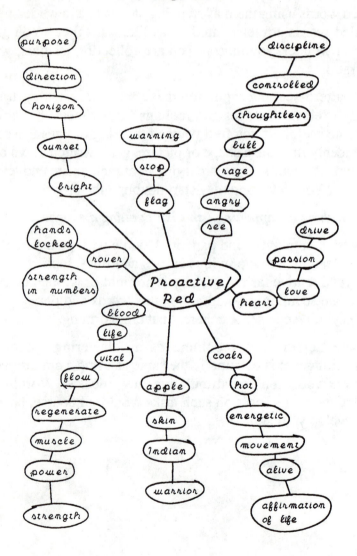

Notice how patterns form in those associated words. Move them around and try different combinations. I'll give an outrageous example of sentences drawn from those associations.

> *"This is not an issue for the cautious. It will demand our concerted effort, our strength and power. Have we lost our ability to care passionately? Can we not accept this challenge as warriors? We will learn to discipline our rage, to focus it. And with its heat we will forge a steel hard conviction to bridge the chasm between the way it is and the way it damned well better be."*

At times you'll sketch a circles map primarily to organize your thinking or activity. At other times you'll engage the process because you want to stimulate ideas. When doing circles throughout a problem-solving process, you'll find you continually move back and forth from organization to stimulation according to the need for convergent or divergent thinking.

RELATIONSHIP TO CREATIVITY

On the surface the circles map is a simple and obvious device. It doesn't intimidate. You can use it, for example, as a shorthand device for gathering and recording information in an interview. In this application it is an easy skill to acquire and transfer to others. But with continued practice you will also think of different applications.

On first appraisal the circles map is like a screwdriver. It helps "fasten" bits of information together in building replicas of the external, objective reality. But it is also the artist's paintbrush; a tool for capturing, drawing out and expressing the internal, subjective reality.

The circles map is a tool both simple and complex, orderly and flexible, rational and intuitive. It has practical elegance. It helps us in those aspects of problem-solving requiring a practical task orientation, those daily chores, those "to do" lists. At the same time it is elegant.

It triggers our imagination, energizes our collaborative work with others and encourages the transfer of creative problem-solving skills.

It also encourages use of creativity tools. Let's take a closer look at the relationship of the circles map to perceptual openness, flexible persistence, association and visualization.

Perceptual Openness

When we increase our perceptual openness we are able to see more in assessing problems. We become more sensitive to the interwoven complexities of problem situations. We increase the quantity and quality of what we know about a given problem, so that we have a rich supply of elements to later combine and associate in our search for a unique pattern, a creative solution.

Techniques for developing perceptual openness are typically reminders to defer judgment, to hold back our quick-to-judge, rational mind long enough to allow for increased intuitive awareness. We remind ourselves to break those first judgments, those initial idea patterns, to look at things differently by shifting our perspective and to challenge our original assumptions about what we believe is happening.

In the apartment example I mentioned a way to challenge assumptions by temporarily considering one of the related outer circles to be the center circle (e.g., seeing the components of the student's problem through the problem of the landlord or tenant). Because the circles are connected with lines, yet spatially separated, they also encourage such shifting of perspective.

In an outline your eyes follow the structured order (*A* then *B* then *C*, and so on). This leads us to assume importance and the proper sequence of activity. The circles map offers order as well, but the connecting lines, size of circles and spatial arrangements can be varied to remind us of the tentativeness of our early conclusions. It is easier to break initial idea patterns.

Doing circles offers a framework that enhances perceptual openness. It helps the creative generalist maintain a balance in openness and closure according to the requirements of a given task.

Through spatial arrangements, circled pieces of information can be grouped to form weak gestalts of similarity. Proximity suggests relationship. At the same time, spatial distance can be used to separate pieces of information suggesting differences and distinctions.

When you step back and view the whole constellation of circled ideas orbiting the central question, different patterns of relationship emerge, different clusters of information can be recognized and noted through variations in connecting lines and colors.

Any combination of elements can be viewed as separate, grouped or integrated into wholes. The process of doing circles is more open than outlines, lists and narratives. It encourages looking things over before selecting a route. It helps hold the door open to choices.

Flexible Persistence

With flexible persistence we are able to handle the increased complexity and ambiguity that results from deferring judgment. We are able to tolerate the natural tension and feelings that we may never get the mess put together again. We learn to take charge of our energies and write things down in an effort to hold back our rational desire for premature closure.

When doing circles you are capturing intuitive ideas and writing them down. The circles are like the shoeboxes for collecting ideas I suggested in the last chapter. They hold the ideas for you and free your attention to search for other possible ideas and resources.

In doing circles you use key words and short phrases rather than the longer more detailed language of outlines and narratives. Our left mind speaks to us. It likes to take command whenever a language task comes up. Through the circles process, the left-mind need for order is partially met, but held in check by the language of the right mind (images, spatial arrangements, patterns).

The creative tension of part versus whole, separate yet connected, remains, but much of the left-mind censorship is relieved. When viewing the circles map you perceive both wholes and parts. You can focus on detail for left-mind analysis and separate spatially for the purpose of distinction. You can then shift your viewpoint to scan across the whole to let your right mind process ambiguities and unknowns into beginning patterns of possibility. The circles map thus encourages dynamic viewing; moving in to detail a component circle with smaller descriptive circles, backing out to scan the whole and pick up any subtle changes that may have resulted. This movement from part to whole and back to part again, builds the sense of taking charge, making it easier to tolerate the creative tension in part-whole relationships.

Unnecessary tension is also relieved because in forming circles of information you are *doing* something. You are tentatively arranging random thoughts. You feel a sense of direction because you trust your ability to create a form and build upon it. Ideas first trickle in, then flow. Writing a name in a circle creates an image for the right mind to connect. At the same time writing and naming is a left-mind function. Doing circles is encouraging balance and cooperation between your left and right minds with a mix of language, associations, openness and tentative ordering, focusing and scanning. Doing circles...left and right...like breathing in and out.

Association

Associative or combinatory thinking helps us restructure the mess into new, more coherent patterns. When we increase our powers of association we are able to discover alternative solutions more quickly. We learn to use analogy and a variety of techniques such as, random juxtaposition or morphological synthesis to stimulate and strengthen our combinatory thinking, our ability to associate ideas.

The circles map enhances the techniques of association. To use random juxtaposition, for example, select distant circles for association. Filling the space between one circled word and another is similar to the linking exercises you practiced in Chapter 6. You can create analogies by adding circles of random words such as in the proactive/red example.

In minimizing language detail and using circle images to capture ideas, you are already encouraging right-mind participation, you are simulating its pattern-forming process. When you scan an arrangement of circles your right mind will be seeking connections, perceiving parts that will attract and group other circled ideas. It is your right mind that bridges the spaces between circles and ideas. It will make associations that are initially out of the range of awareness of your left mind. Doing circles is a self-organizing process. When you recognize a pattern (aha!), it will be charged with feelings of "fit" (the same as when you recognize the second image in a gestalt picture).

Visualization

Visualization is an important ability for the creative generalist. When we increase our powers of visualization we are better able to receive the messages of our intuitive mind. Our intuition communicates through images, it searches the unknown to discover and form patterns and transmits these as images.

Tools for increasing visual power help train our rational mind to be more receptive to intuitive images. They help "tune our receivers." The more we practice forming clear mental images, imagination, drawing and dream recall, the more able we will be to utilize our intuition. Visualization helps us hold onto a creative idea while our rational mind works out the details. It serves as a focal point for the tension energy released in resolution (aha!), which in turn serves as fuel for the expression of that idea.

Visualization and imagery are powerful tools for shaping reality. Consider the way you accept visual cues in movies (e.g., passage of time, a dream sequence). In comic strips universal symbols are used to express ideas, emotions, movement.

Doing circles helps us develop our ability to visualize. The circles map is after all a visual representation in itself. Each circle represents what Koestler calls a "holon" (whole and yet part).

The circle is also a symbolic visualization. It is recognized across cultures. It is an archetypal symbol that many believe taps the deep recesses of intuitive awareness. Jung was convinced that archetypal symbols lie deep in our collective unconscious and stir our feelings because they touch the core of our concerns (e.g., life, death, sexuality).[4] The image of a circle is in that sense an energizer.

The circle is an also an organic shape. It is one of the first figures drawn by a child...what better symbol for "toying" with ideas. It is the shape of an egg...what better symbol for incubating and hatching ideas?

A TOOL FOR DIFFERENT SYSTEM SIZES

The creative generalist focuses on problem solving and works with differing sized systems (individual, small group, organization and community) according to the requirements of the problem at hand.

Earlier, I discussed the development of the circles map in the field unit. Over the years we found it a valuable tool in working with different system sizes. Let's take a look.

Worker and Individual

When working with an individual the circles map is an important tool for collaboration. Picture yourself doing circles with an individual. You are both working from the same side of a table. You are looking down at the map you are developing. What does a map do? It shows alternative routes. It's something you like to have along when traveling from a situation over here to a different one over there. It's something you pull out and look at when you lose your direction. Remember the student and her apartment problem? She asked the field unit to do circles with her, because she was searching for alternatives. She wanted to get her "bearings," a sense of direction.

The circles map emphasizes the problem circumstance, rather than personal inadequacy. The two of you are "getting the problem out on the table," you are figuring out the puzzle in front of you. You are not doing something *to* the other person. You are both doing something *to* that problem on the table.

In the beginning activity of problem solving the circles map encourages optimism. Something is already being done, something concrete is happening, the problem is being understood. The circles map communicates the message that "you and I can put this together." It emphasizes design. When design is emphasized the client is no longer the "poor soul with the problem." He or she is active as the "problem expert," making sure the circles are accurately labeled and determining the relevancy of proposed solutions.

In successive contacts the circles map serves as a summary of development, a record of tasks accomplished. It offers the security of ritual. It can be used to "open the meeting" to "get down to business." It conveys the message that problems can be converted into solutions, that they can be broken down into manageable pieces without losing sense of the whole.

Worker and the Small Group

Staff, task, team and other group meetings are often win-lose affairs. You know what I mean…one person makes a suggestion, the next tells why it won't work and offers an alternative. The next tells why that one won't work and so on. It's as if the unstated assumption of such gatherings is that one idea must lose for another to win. Incomplete ideas wither from lack of group support. Half the people present don't participate and continual fault-finding constrains those that do. Individuals search suggestions of others for deficiencies so they can argue for *their* idea.

This is the "survival of the fittest" approach to communications and decision making. The idea that survives a barrage of criticism is the strongest and deserves to win. Ideas presented early in a meeting typically get lost in the shuffle and late ideas have a better chance of convincing a bored group. Recording devices such as "minutes" more reflect outcomes than alternative ideas and process. ("After much stimulating discussion the committee decided to have a subcommittee further assess the extent of the problem.")

The circles map, on the other hand, encourages open communication, individual participation and idea building. Various patterns of ideas are recorded and can be referred to throughout a meeting. The attention of the group is on the circles map in front of them, and quiet group members often find it easier to speak toward that visual display of ideas (rather than having all eyes of the group directed at them).

The circles map shows ground already covered and individuals used to winning through repeating the same basic idea throughout the meeting are kept in check. Gaps in information and ideas are also in view and individuals are typically supported in their efforts to help fill these out. It seems as if group members perceive a completed circles map as an achievement in itself, and they thus encourage each other in developing a good one. Digressions are more tolerated, since everyone knows the circles map will "remember" the key points they are working on. Circling everyone's ideas gives each individual a sense of acceptance and participation in the idea-building process.

The circles map facilitates the use of open communication techniques. For example, a technique for encouraging speculation and building idea patterns involves shifting the usual emphasis from finding deficiencies to searching for strengths.

Group members are asked to scan each idea presented for points they find attractive. They then attempt to "hitchhike" or "piggyback" those ideas with their own connecting ideas.

The circles map encourages this structure for idea building. Members may continually scan the visual summary of ideas. They may return again and again to build upon and fill out different possibilities.

Through valuing and building on each others ideas, each individual is acknowledged as a contributor. Each becomes more willing to communicate raw data and incomplete notions that then serve as springboards to the associative thinking of the total group.

A useful technique for generating alternatives is putting ideas *on hold*. In win-lose communications a reasonable idea is often aggressively protected from any further generation of possibilities. The circles map puts each idea on hold, allowing continued exploration without fear of losing the "only thing we have come up with." If indeed, no better ideas are found, the original suggestion is verified. If, on the other hand, a new idea seems promising it can be combined with the original suggestion, adding to its power.

Worker and Large Group

When working with an organization or community group having a hundred or more members, a social worker often considers the size of membership a liability in terms of problem solving. Picture yourself in a room exploring problems with that many people and what do you see? Looks more like a political convention than a problem-solving session, doesn't it? But that liability could also be viewed as an asset.

When searching for creative solutions the complex and variable perceptions of a large group can be viewed as a rich diversity of pieces to combine into unique patterns. In this view the concern is not with the actual complexity of perceptual variation, but how to best orchestrate it toward those creative solutions. The circles map is a valuable tool for this orchestration. When combined with several other techniques it encourages us to accept the challenges of working directly with large groups. Let me explain.

I have often used a large group problem-solving format similar to the one I will briefly describe for you (please check sources cited for detailed instructions). We have tested it with groups ranging from 50 to 150 participants. With increasing size you must, of course, pay more attention to structure, timing, organization and details (e.g., room accommodations, handouts, learning resources).

Let's say we (five or six field students and myself) have agreed to act as "process consultants" for an organization desiring a day of problem solving. Everyone within the organization (e.g., administrators, staff, cooks, bus drivers) will attend. We have arranged to use an elementary school building for the day-long session. We plan to meet with the total group (say 100) in the school gymnasium, and will use classrooms for small group activities. The day of the session would run something like this:

8:30 AM:

> Large group meets in the gymnasium. We introduce ourselves and explain our role is to organize and facillitate their problem-solving activities for the day. We are not experts on their organizational difficulties, but will help them guide the process of problem solving. We give a brief overview of the day (the mechanics of the different activities, the morning emphasis on problem finding and afternoon emphasis on solution finding).

9:00 AM:

> We ask the large group to join small task groups in designated classrooms. There they will identify priority problems with a "Nominal Group Procedure" developed by André Delbecq.[5] With a series of round-robin discussions, voting and recording results on large sheets of butcher paper, this procedure insures individual participation in identifying and prioritizing problems. It also emphasizes acceptance and understanding of individual contributions, rather than evaluation and criticism.

10:30 AM:

The small groups return to the main meeting room. Each group reports their final three priority problems. We draw circles charts on the priorities while the groups are reporting. Problems are clarified, restated and clustered. The intention is to use the circles map process to develop a final list of four priority problems reflecting the interests of the total group. If this cannot be achieved through discussion, voting can be requested. The final four problems are converted into questions. For example, difficulties with a food service program might be changed to, "What can be done to upgrade the food service program?" Each question is then written at the top of a large sheet of butcher paper.

1:00 PM:

After lunch the total group assembles in the main meeting room. We have placed the four priority questions (written on butcher paper) at different locations in the meeting room. Using a "Cybernetic Sessions" procedure developed by John Hall and Roger Dixon, each location is designated a "station."[6] Participants are each given an itinerary card that shows where they should be (station) and when they should be there (time period). A process consultant is assigned to each station to record ideas (circles map) and to review what has been said previously as new participants come to the station. By following the itinerary card, each participant works at each of the stations and always with a different grouping of participants.

Each period lasts approximately ten to fifteen minutes. With four priority questions we would schedule eight periods (roughly two hours). At the end of a period, half of the group at a station is asked to move to the next station. The remaining half maintains continuity

of discussion with incoming members in the next
period. The new members bring fresh ideas and the
departing members are dispersed into new groups.
With this procedure many diverse viewpoints can be
gathered in a short period of time. It also helps
participants gain a broad perspective on the identified
problems from working with so many different people
at the various stations.

We ask the participants to observe the rules of "brainstorming" in
generating possible answers (solutions) to the question at each station.
Brainstorming, originated by Alex Osborne, has four requirements:[7]

1. **Defer judgment**

2. **"Free-wheel" ideas**

3. **Hitchike each others ideas**

4. **Push for quantity**

The last two periods are devoted to selection of the best three
solutions listed. If not apparent on the circles maps, voting is used to
accomplish this selection.

3:00 PM:

Large group is reassembled. Circles maps are
posted in front of the group.
Consultant/recorders (with help of participants)
summarize the ideas considered best from each
station. Ideas are clarified through discussion.
If each station produced three solutions, a
dozen circles maps would be discussed. Some
of the solutions may have obvious overlap and
are integrated into a new circles map. Usually
solution patterns are complete enough by the
end of this round of discussion to be taken

home by the organization and detailed there for
implementation. Sometimes the energy level is
especially high and we may suggest
participants return to their original small groups
for a final planning and elaborating session.

For many of the reasons stated throughout this chapter, the circles
map is a helpful tool for participants in a large group problem-solving
process. It helps them sort out and organize the priorities and
stimulates ideas for solutions. But the circles map is also important to
the "process consultants" in such an event. For example, I do not
particularly enjoy speaking in front of a 100 or more people. Keynote
speaking engagements give me sweaty palms and nightmares.
Working with the circles map is quite different. Here attention is on
the board. I am serving as a recorder, a funnel for ideas from the
group. The participants have committed time and effort to the process.
The ideas represented in the circles are theirs. In other words they are
interested, motivated. You are not pressured to be entertaining, you
do not feel as much "on stage."

When you are drawing circles and participants are making comments
from behind you, the intimidating size of the group fades from your
awareness. You find yourself hollering back over your shoulder as if
there were only a handful of people involved.

*"I must be getting dense, could someone tell me what
that word means again? Is that idea close enough to
this one over here, so we can put them into the same
cluster? We have a mighty lonely looking circle over
here...will someone help fill it out a little?"*

ENDNOTE

In this chapter I've explained the circles map, a useful tool for
organizing and stimulating ideas. It works well with different system

sizes, encourages whole-mind thinking and the expression of creativity.

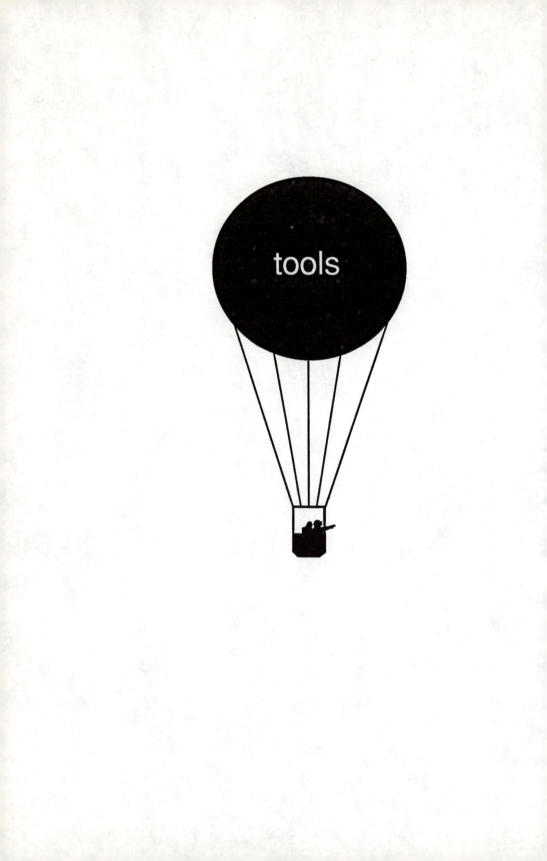

tools

The problem-solving relationship

8

In any problem-solving effort you are likely to be relating to many different people. For example, in a foster home case you might be dealing with foster parents, natural parents, school teachers and psychologists, court workers, physicians, other social workers, a speech therapist and a lawyer. Your work with all these people, not just the "client," is crutial to accomplishing your goals.

In 1973, my colleague Anne Minahan and I developed the four-systems model to account for the social worker's connections with the various people in a given situation.[1] Looking back, the development of this model was a first step in bringing a generalist perspective to bear on the issue of relationships.

I will begin this chapter by discussing the four-systems model. Viewing relationships with the creative generalist mindset, I will then propose a further step in our thinking—a shift in focus from the "helping" relationship to the "problem-solving" relationship.

THE FOUR-SYSTEMS MODEL

The four-systems model gained widespread acceptance because it helped social work shift its attention from an almost exclusive concern with the worker-client relationship to a more encompassing view that better fit with generalist practice. The model also helped clarify some important practice issues. Let me explain.

Separating Client System and Target System

In Chapter 1 we noted that the late Sixties was a time of unrest and social action. Social workers were admonished to not "blame the victims" but to serve as their advocate. Welfare rights groups, tenant unions and other such groups were being organized everywhere. In this environment the message was clear: in order to help a client, the "target" might be someone other than the client. The person or system we needed to influence or change might be a landlord, an administrator, a city council member, or a social worker at another agency. Anne and I saw the need to conceptually separate the client system from the target system.

We defined the "client system" as the person or persons who voluntarily seek our help, are the expected beneficiaries of our work, and have developed a working agreement or contract with us. The "target system" was defined as the people who need to be influenced to achieve the goals of the client system. The two systems may overlap (as when a couple wants our help in dealing with their marital relationship) or they may be different (as when you are trying to convince an employer to hire a client).

Though referring to people as "client systems" and "target systems" may seem a little awkward, the language did serve a purpose. The term "system" emphasized that the client could be an individual, family, group, community or organization. The term "target" was a reminder to make a conscious decision about whom you need to influence.

Aside from breaking the assumption that the client is necessarily the target, our model brought into question the use of the term "involuntary client." That term is often used when referring to people who are unwilling participants (e.g., people on probation or parole, or a parent accused of child abuse). Uncomfortable as it may feel, it is more honest to acknowledge that they are actual target systems (and only potential client systems). If you are able to carve out some areas where the person does request and sanction your help, then he or she can be considered a client.

At times you may find yourself in a situation where it's not clear who your client is. Suppose you were hired by a nursing home administrator to organize a residents' council at the home. And suppose the residents push for changes that the administrator opposes. Are the residents or the administrator your client? When facing conflicting expectations you will need to clarify your agreements with the people involved.

The four-systems model also helped put in perspective some differing stances around relationships. While caseworkers had been emphasizing the value of collaboration, many community organizers were stressing the need to understand and work with adversarial and bargaining relationships. The fact is, in any one situation you can be involved in all types of relationships. While collaboration and mutuality are desirable in relating to the client, your relationship with the target system may take on an adversarial or bargaining stance.

The Action System

The third system in our model is the "action system." This system refers to the people the social worker works with and through to accomplish the goals of the client. Through the action system you mobilize and coordinate a wide array of resources and bring them to bear on the problem. One-to-one relationships, mutual aid groups, committees, family units, case conferences, and neighborhood organizations are all examples of possible action systems. As you can see, the action system may be limited to worker and client but more often includes other people as well. It may meet face to face or have its work coordinated by the worker. It may or may not include the client and/or target system.

Thus the action system concept helped broaden our approach to relationships. It emphasized the need for flexibility in deciding on the appropriate size and type of system to work with. It called our attention to the dynamics of action systems such as case conferences and committees as well as one-to-one relationships. It suggested that the social worker must often go beyond the personal resources he or she brings to the situation.

The Change Agent System

The fourth system we defined is the "change agent" or agency system. "Change agent" was a popular generic term in the Sixties for referring to anybody involved in bringing about change. (I stopped using the term after somebody at a workshop I was conducting pointed out that change agents were also employees of the New York City subway system who sold turnstile tokens.)

Defining this system called attention to the influence of the employing agency on the worker's activities and the fact that the agency may itself at times be the appropriate target system. Practice models often ignored the agency context.

Summary

The four-systems model has served two main functions. As a sorting tool it was responsive to professional concerns. When Anne and I wrote our book, we were looking for ways of bringing social work together. Caseworkers, group workers and community workers all had their own jargon. The four-systems model provided a common language for talking about the people with whom we worked. It was flexible enough to be applied across many different situations, problems and fields of practice. Sorting people according to the four systems helped clarify the situations we were dealing with and tasks we needed to attend.

The model also provided an impetus to generalist practice. It helped break assumptions that were constricting our thinking (e.g., the client is the target, the one-to-one therapeutic relationship is the primary tool for helping), opened up options and choices in dealing with problems, and shifted the focus from person to problem. For many social workers it served to validate the way they were already approaching practice. Creating choice and opening the field of action made social work more attractive to creative generalists.

FROM "HELPING" TO "PROBLEM SOLVING"

Social workers who are engaged in administration, planning, organization, and social policy carry a client relationship with the system in which they are involved. So do social workers who are engaged in counseling. However, a common assumption is that the relationship established with the client in these two contexts is (and should be) fundamentally different.[2] In other words, the assumption is that working with a school principal on a problem of vandalism or a hospital administrator on referral mechanisms is fundamentally different from working with a mother who is troubled over her son's poor grades in school or her husband's alcoholism.

I want to invite you to temporarily let go of the apparent logic of this assumption and explore an alternative point of view with me—a point of view that builds on the assertion that social work practice is a problem-solving process.

Consider what Compton and Galaway say about relationships:[3]

> Relationship...develops out of purposive interaction, out of
> the business with which the worker and the client (or other
> system) concern themselves. It cannot be presumed that the
> client is looking "for a helping relationship" when entering
> the social work situation but rather that the client comes out
> of concern about a problem in which the professional
> relationship is instrumental in working toward a solution.
> This means that we do not speak of the worker's
> "establishing a relationship" or "offering a relationship;"
> neither do we speak of needing a good relationship before
> difficulties can be discussed. The relationship comes out of
> the communication about difficulties. It grows and
> develops out of purposive work. The professional
> relationship as an affective, experimental interaction should
> develop as necessary to the task. It is not necessarily

friendly; sometimes the problem is worked out in reaction and
anger, in conflict as well as in collaboration or bargaining.

Since the business or task of social work is problem solving, the
relationship that develops should grow out of the requirements of good
problem solving. If you recall from previous chapters, problem
solving requires withholding judgment, shifting perspectives on
problems, and tolerating competing points of view. These same
requirements are there if we are problem solving with the school
principle over the vandalism problem or the parent over her troubles
with her teenage son. A shift in focus from "helping" relationship to
"problem-solving" relationship reminds us to bring these essential
qualities to all our working relationships.

GUIDELINES FOR
PROBLEM-SOLVING RELATIONSHIPS

How do you foster a problem-solving relationship? The guidelines I
present here come from applying the mindset of the creative generalist
to the issue of building productive working relationships.

Pay Attention to Problem Solving

Social workers deal a lot with feelings, their own and those of
others. In fact, the phrase, "How do you feel about that?" has almost
become a symbol of being "social worked."

And many social workers agonize over the appropriate balance
between detachment and involvement in their relationships. It's like
walking a narrow ledge separating two abysses. One is being overly
emotionally involved, over-identifying with the client, feeling
sympathy and pity rather than empathy, being so caught up in the
situation so as to be unable to help. The other abyss is being overly
objective, to the point of being distant, cold, unfeeling, uncaring,
relating to the client as just another "case." In fact, the literature on
burnout portrays such behavior as a coping mechanism for dealing
with the emotional strain of the job.

When we rivet our attention to the problem-solving process itself (rather than the relationship) and immerse ourselves in the problem, we automatically develop a kind of objectivity appropriate to productive relationships. This type of objectivity does not result from the use of any techniques. Nor is it a sign of being disinterested in or insensitive to feelings. Rather, when you direct your energies toward a problem, you don't generate the same *kind* of feelings as when you aim your energies at the person or the relationship itself. Let me give an example of what I mean.

Once I taught a class which was the second semester of a required two-course sequence. Due to a variety of mishaps, the group had three different instructors the first semester and were very upset by their experience. So the first day of class I was confronted by a group of students who for the most part did not want to be there, who were still harboring bad feelings from the previous semester, and who were very vocal about their feelings. Many of them were about to graduate and would have preferred to take an elective course rather than another required course. It became apparent that almost anything I proposed as a class activity would be met with the kind of opposition and skepticism that makes failure a self-fulfilling prophesy.

I quickly dropped my prepared plans for the first session and began to do some problem solving with the class. We worked out alternative ways for students to complete the course requirements. This resulted in an entirely new format. The next day a student from the class stopped by my office. She said she hoped that I wasn't upset or offended by the anger of the students. She thought it wasn't fair that it was directed at me.

Her remarks made me realize that I actually did not feel bad or feel personally attacked. It wasn't because I was being professional and rising above those feelings. The fact is, I had gotten wrapped up in seeing the situation as a challenge. Could I take some basic principles I had been teaching the first semester (e.g., you can't make anybody do anything they don't want to do; the element of choice promotes acknowledgment of personal responsibility; utilize, rather than fight, the force of resistance) and use them with the class to guide the problem-solving process? Could I use the class as a live case example? Could I use this as an opportunity to establish my credibility and the validity of my beliefs?

Yes, when I'm personally attacked, I get defensive. On one level of reality, that is what might have been taking place. But the reality of the situation as a challenging problem was also there and that is the reality I chose to relate to. Therefore, I experienced the feelings appropriate to confronting a challenging problem rather than feelings appropriate to being attacked. The situation turned out to be a good learning experience, led to some good relationships with the class, and resulted in my experimenting with some course options I would not normally have considered.

Invest Yourself in the Problem

Most of us can share frustrating experiences we have had dealing with service people such as auto mechanics, plumbers, carpenters, and doctors. Our complaints would probably include not enough exploration of the nature of our problem, selling a particular solution rather than exploring the pros and cons of different alternatives, sloppy work, putting efficiency and the "fast-fix" ahead of quality and care, and not being responsible or reliable. The rise in the do-it-yourself movement in repairs is only partially a response to rising costs. It also comes from the realization that it is difficult to find a service person who will put the same quality of thought and workmanship into your project or problem as you will yourself. And you have to live on a daily basis with their solutions.

Fortunately many of us have also had occasional positive experiences. The man who serviced my oil furnace is a good example. He was an old timer who had worked in the business for years. He took pride in tracking down problems and working out inexpensive, sound solutions. If a part wasn't functioning right, he would take it as a challenge to find a way to repair it, even improvising a component before resorting to replacing it with a new part. Using a new part was like a sign of defeat. He would cuss when hitting an intractable problem but stay with it until a solution was found. Then, with pride in his voice, he would show me the clean-burning flame and explain how the repair was made. My questions were not received as a challenge to his authority but as an invitation to display his knowledge and ingenuity. I'm sure he attended his customers' furnaces no differently from the way he attended to his own furnace.

So what does this have to do with social work relationships? Well, I liked the old timer, trusted him, had confidence in him, felt he was concerned about my problem. Isn't this how we hope our clients feel about us when we have a good relationship with them? The furnace man never took a course in interpersonal skills nor spent any time working on our relationship. My feelings toward him were a result of his approach to and concern with my problem.

Invest yourself in the client's problem, approach it with the care, conscientiousness and responsibility with which you would approach your own problem or that of a good friend. These are the "techniques" of relationship building.

Engage Your Curiosity

Though you cope with relationships throughout your life, when you enter social work training they become a subject of scrutiny. You often start by examining differences between personal and professional relationships, and are taught to disentangle one from the other. Interpersonal skills labs teach you to identify the behavioral components of good relationships (e.g., paraphrasing what the client says and maintaining eye contact) and have you practice them. Armed with these newly acquired techniques you're ready to go out and form good relationships.

Now picture yourself in a situation where you *are* interested in what somebody is explaining to you. For example, a good friend might be telling you about a problem she is having. If you looked at yourself, you would probably notice that you were maintaining eye contact (because you were really tracking with the person) and that you were asking for clarification (because you really wanted to understand what she was saying). In other words, you already possess many of these interpersonal skills. They are brought out when your curiosity and interest are engaged. You can therefore approach the issue of building good relationships by asking, "How can I look at the situation so it actually does hold interest for me? How can I engage my curiosity?"

One way of engaging your curiosity is to assume that you already have some kind of connection with the other person, even if you never met before. You then look for what that connection might be. Another assumption that can arouse your curiosity is that there is something we can learn (or some way we can benefit) from all relationships. Let me give an example.

Think of the kind of person you hate working with, whose behavior drives you up the wall. You know that this person has a right to your help, but it's so hard to be tolerant. "Anyone able to have patience with such a client must be a saint," you think to yourself.

The two assumptions might lead us to raise some questions: Why did I bring this person into my life at this time? Why did I activate my connection with him or her? What am I supposed to learn from this encounter? What message is this person bringing me? What links can I discover between this person and situation and other people and situations in my personal or professional life?

From the other side, you might ask why *you* are being brought into that person's life at this point. What unique things do you have to offer that person?

When you are able to get your head into this frame of mind, a tolerance for the person develops. This doesn't result from a belief that you *should* be tolerant. Rather, it occurs because of your assumption that the person has something to offer you (or you have something to offer her or him) and you're curious to find out what that is. There is a puzzle here which you want to figure out. Or, like a round-robin story, you are interested in where it is going next. Your curiosity and interest evoke the tolerance which lets you stick with the situation.

Acknowledge Your Self-Interest

Closely related to the issue of making the situation interesting to you is the issue of your self-interest. We are taught that being professional means you are there to meet the client's needs, not your own. Of course you should not be meeting your needs at the expense of the client (e.g., getting satisfaction from making decisions for other people). Nor should you be putting your problems and needs ahead of theirs (e.g., you are obliged to attend a case conference regardless of whether you are in the mood to do so). But being professional does not mean you have to *deny* your self-interest, only that you not act selfishly. In a working relationship self-interest and collective interest (be the "collective" a relationship with another person or a whole community) need not be in conflict. Barter relationships where each person gets a good deal are an example. The questions to ask ourselves are: How do I create a context where mutual needs are met? How do I view the person as a resource to me? What can I learn from him or her? How does the situation provide an opportunity to express my vocational style? Acknowledging your self-interest is necessary to creating synergistic arrangements.

Good working relationships grow out of recognition that the people you work with are resources to you as well as the other way around. If complementary self-interests and needs are met, such a relationship will develop a mutual and collaborative nature. Relating to people around their strengths rather than deficiencies, facilitating solution-finding rather than providing solutions, identifying similarities with rather than differences from the people we work with, building linkages rather than maintaining boundaries, sharing responsibility for outcomes—these are the elements which build productive relationships.

The fact that you get paid for "helping" sometimes obscures the reciprocal component of working relationships. It is helpful to remember that you are not getting paid to feel or act caring and understanding. You are paid to engage people in a problem-solving process and discipline yourself to serve their best interest. That is what you are obligated to do and are accountable for. Facing lonely, unhappy people who are in need of love, caring and intimacy makes us face the limitations of what we can offer another person in a social work relationship. We may feel bad about this, but it shouldn't negate the value of what we do have to offer. (I sometimes have a picture in my mind of the social worker as a battery which people hook up to for an emotional charge. It doesn't take long to get drained when you are jump-starting people all day. The "battery model" is not an appropriate one for social work.)

Discover Satisfaction in Problem Solving

In earlier chapters we stated that the creative generalist gets satisfaction from the problem-solving process itself, from the process of exploring problems, generating solutions, overcoming obstacles, recognizing potentials, engaging people in the process, opening up new perspectives, locating the right resource. I'll illustrate my point with an analogy.

> Sam's car breaks down on the road and John pulls over to see what's wrong and lend a hand. After locating the trouble, John improvises a needed part out of some wire and tape that should last until a permanent repair can be made. Sam is, of course, very appreciative. If John were a social worker, he might derive satisfaction from the fact that Sam changed from being frustrated and depressed about the car to feeling good that it was working again. As a generalist, John also derives his satisfaction from meeting the challenge of the problem and getting the car going again. He takes pride in his craft.

I'm not saying that creative generalists don't enjoy gratitude. It's nice when it comes, but it is not the end they are working toward. If Sam was a nasty cuss and drove away without even a "thank you," John would probably still find satisfaction in his work. And he may even have learned something about cars that will be useful to him in the future.

The issue of where your satisfaction comes from is related to "burn out." We may find ourselves dealing with people who want no part of our services. We are continually proving ourselves and establishing our credibility to taxpayers and other professionals. In this type of climate, if we are dependent on making people feel good to feed our satisfaction, then we are likely to burn out quickly. Can you find satisfaction in the challenge of dealing with problems others have not been able to or don't want to deal with?

Be Yourself

Think of a professional you had a good experience with, someone you admired and respected, someone who was helpful and made you feel good about yourself. Chances are that one of the things you noticed is that such a person didn't seem to be playing a role. The person inside that professional was acknowledging and talking directly to the person in whatever role you occupied (student, client, patient). If this person was your next-door neighbor, she or he would probably act the same way.

In discussing vocational style, Mike emphasized the need to integrate your personal and professional self. Remember to bring your interests, talents and unique personality to your relationships. Don't forget to be who you are in the professional world of clients, agencies and service delivery systems. In fact, work at creating opportunities to express your unique self.

Mike is fond of telling a story about a group of delinquent teenagers he worked with. As a school social worker, Mike was supposed to "do therapy" with those kids. So he formed a group and took them to the mountains for some "Huckleberry Finn" exploring. In order to participate in these trips the kids had to agree to work on changing behaviors that were getting them into trouble at the school (e.g., skipping school and disrupting classes). The outings were attractive enough to them that they were willing to honor the agreement. In the course of the outings they could talk in an informal way (like they might do on a fishing trip with a favorite uncle) about anything that concerned them.

This synergistic arrangement managed to satisfy the needs of the school and the kids, while at the same time allowing Mike to work in a manner he finds comfortable and enjoyable. It's an example of how to create *contexts* where you can put to use who you are (strengths, interests, attributes) in working with people.

COLLABORATION AND CONFLICT

In a problem-solving relationship you and the other person are collaborators in a problem-solving process. However, collaboration does not preclude confrontation or conflict. Indeed, as Bennis, Benne and Chin point out, conflict and confrontation can often lead to collaboration.[4] They view collaboration as an achievement, not a gift. They say it is often achieved through open confrontation of differences, through conflicts faced and resolved, through limited areas of collaboration growing into larger areas of collaboration as fuller trust develops.

Likewise, collaboration does not preclude unilaterally taking charge now and then. "Just tell me what to do!" Being overly tired and in the midst of moving, I began bickering with my wife. Every decision about where to put things became a monumental discussion and waste of time. The only way out at that moment was for one of us, the one with the most energy, to take charge. There are moments like that in all relationships. Often in an emergency or crises the person involved may not be in a position to participate in joint decision making. Being told what to do may be the most helpful thing. In mediating a dispute we often have to take charge in setting up the ground rules.

Relationships sometimes start out from a bargaining stance. Earlier in this chapter I mentioned that when you are working with another person who doesn't want to be there, as in probation and parole, you may have to enter into a bargaining framework to achieve a working agreement. In serving as a broker or advocate for a client we are often bargaining with the target system. The creative generalist will look for opportunities for synergistic exchanges in such relationships.

Finally, you may encounter situations where the goals of both parties are in complete opposition. When the target system is outside the client system, you may be collaborating with the client in developing a strategy to deal with the target system. In such cases your only recourse may be to power tactics such as boycotts, protest demonstrations, open confrontation, threats, and court orders. Such tactics are aimed at equalizing the power of both parties, and increasing the costs to the target system of maintaining its position. Even if these tactics don't result in an outright win, they may induce the adversary to bargain with you.[5]

RELATIONSHIP BARRIERS

Differences in race, sex, ethnicity, social class, and sexual orientation between worker and client can act as a barrier in developing a good problem-solving relationship. Fortunately, steps can be taken to reduce such barriers. Trust is an important ingredient in effective counseling. Research indicates that in spite of racial, sex and class differences, trust can be developed when a worker is perceived as competent, possessing expert knowledge, reliable, and having good intentions. Further, workers can establish trust when they acknowledge the differences in race and sex, avoid racial and sexual stereotyping, display awareness of racial, sexual and class experiences and oppressions, and at the same time focus on the personal experiences, life situation and aspirations of an individual client.[6]

Many of these suggestions fit well with the guidelines for fostering a problem-solving relationship. Adding a sensitivity to and understanding of racial, social class and other differences to these guidelines will help you to work effectively with different client groups. In addition, the tools for cultivating creativity discussed in Chapter 6, particularly those for deferring judgment and maintaining perceptual openness (challenging assumptions, breaking patterns and shifting perspectives), are relevant here.

Stereotypes are dependent on closed perceptions. The creative generalist is able to challenge assumptions and break thought patterns that perpetuate stereotypes. The ability to shift perspectives, see situations from different points of view, can be used to increase your sensitivity to cultural differences and the plight of minority groups. The requirements of effective problem solving reinforce the requirements for bridging racial, sexual, class and other differences between worker and client.

Social work's fundamental value, respect for the dignity, worth and uniqueness of the *individual*, ties our concern with minority groups to the very mission of the profession. But don't forget the other side of that value, the importance of a diverse yet cohesive *society*. The two are linked together—to promote one we have to promote the other. The issue then goes beyond bridging or tolerating racial, sexual and cultural differences. As social workers our commitment must extend to protecting and fostering the diversity necessary for the health of the society *and* the individual.

SUMMARY AND ENDING NOTE

I began this chapter with a discussion of the four-systems model. It was a beginning step in bringing a generalist perspective to bear on the issue of relationships in social work. The model contributed to broadening social work's focus from an almost exclusive concern with the one-to-one client relationship to the full complement of relationships with all people connected to the problem situation. By distinguishing between client and target system and introducing the notion of action system, the model helped open our options in dealing with problems. It helped shift our attention from person to problem.

The "problem-solving relationship" represents a further step in developing an approach to relationships which is congruent with a generalist perspective on practice. In contrast to the "helping relationship" with its therapeutic roots, the problem-solving relationship grows out of the demands of the problem-solving process and the value stance of the creative generalist. It utilizes the problem-solving skills of the generalist in connecting with people and building productive relationships.

Problem-solving relationships are fostered by paying our attention to the problem-solving process rather than the relationship, investing yourself in the problem, engaging your curiosity, acknowledging your self-interest, discovering satisfaction in problem solving, and being yourself. To these guidelines it is important to add an understanding of racial, sexual, class and other differences between worker and client.

In a problem-solving relationship the client becomes a partner in the problem-solving process instead of an object of help or recipient of service. An emphasis on empowerment instead of nuturance does not lead to insensitivity. It stimulates a new sensitivity appropriate to the mission of social work.

Part III
process

Parts I and II introduced you to the mindset and tools of the creative generalist. Part III will explore how these are applied to the problem-solving process in social work.

PROCESS PHASES

In an earlier chapter, Mike mentioned that we developed a three-phase description of the problem-solving process: preparation, design and verification. We did this to integrate the stages in creative process (preparation, incubation, illumination and verification) with the stages of social work problem solving (assessment, planning, implementation, and evaluation). The labels we chose for the phases serve as reminders to engage whole-mind thinking throughout the process.

Preparation

The focus of the preparation phase is on gaining an understanding of the problem situation and assembling the data and information you'll need in the design phase. The aim is to frame the problem in the way that best prepares you to design an effective and efficient (creative) solution.

We chose the label "preparation" for the first phase because "assessment" implies a predominately analytical look at the nature and extent of a problem. Our rational mind does, of course, play an important role in this phase. It concerns itself with the orderly collection and categorization of data and the systematic weighing of factors that help us decide on priorities. But we rely on our intuitive mind as well. Perceptual openness increases our sensitivity to data about the problem and enables us to view a situation from many different perspectives. Flexible persistence helps us tolerate the resulting complexity and avoid premature closure. The more inclusive term, "preparation," suggests *getting ready* for a journey through the problem-solving process, preparing to *do* something.

Design

The next phase, "design," focuses on generating ideas for solutions and shaping those ideas into a workable plan of action. One aspect of design uses our intuitive power of association to generate ideas and combine them into idea patterns which serve as the basis for creative solutions. Another aspect emphasizes rational thinking in evaluating the feasibility of ideas and detailing and sorting them into goals, objectives and tasks. Our rational mind transforms idea patterns into blueprints, and sequences the tasks that need to be performed.

The term "design" helps us maintain an ecosystems perspective by reminding us that solutions, like problems, are patterns of variables. In designing a solution we are rearranging an existing pattern (the "problem") into a new pattern (the "solution"). The use of the term "design" also reinforces a philosophical stance of the creative generalist. Many social problems are framed as resource problems (e.g., shrinking oil reserves, budget deficits). Often such problems can be more effectively dealt with if conceptualized as design problems (i.e., designing solutions that reduce the need for scarce resources, that use existing resources in the most efficient and ecologically sound ways, and that help us recognize the potential of new resources).

Verification

In the verification phase, our understanding of the problem and proposed solution are put to the test. We verify our ideas by implementing them. Combining implementation and evaluation in a single phase emphasizes the need to continually monitor our interventions and make necessary readjustments as we go along. In addition, verification calls for confronting the unexpected, evaluating outcomes, and concluding the problem-solving process.

The evaluative component of verification has both a quantitative side (concerned with measuring the amount of something) and a qualitative side (concerned with the essential character or meaning of something). Just as creative problem solving requires whole-mind thinking, an holistic approach to evaluation requires an integration of qualitative and quantitative research strategies. The term "verification" reminds us of the need for both kinds of evaluation.

FLEXIBILITY IN USING PROCESS MODELS

There's much to be said for process models. They are a useful device for organizing and presenting a mass of information on how you get from point A to point B. They help keep us on track and remind us of tasks we need to accomplish along the way. And process models appease our rational need for order, predictability and control.

On the other hand, process models have their limitations in representing reality. With a mechanical process like an assembly line, we can determine the precise moment that a certain task must be performed, how long it will take, and when the final step will be finished. Or, if we are dealing with a technical problem (such as designing a brochure), the stages in the process may be clearcut.

In social work, the situation is quite different. We interact with people in our problem solving. The problems we deal with are embedded in ecological systems; as one part changes it affects the other parts. Unanticipated events occur. Aspects of the problem get better or worse on their own. No matter how thorough our preparation and how well designed our plan, we are always working with limited data and understanding. We have limited control over what happens once a plan is set into motion. The responses evoked by our actions alter our understanding of the problem. In turn, we use this new understanding to modify the solutions we designed.

As much as we might like to treat process models as step-by-step recipes for success, they simply don't work that way when problem solving with people. It is necessary to remain flexible and regard a stage in a process as a matter of relative emphasis over time.

Problem solving with people is more an organic than mechanical process. Unlike machines, people adapt to their environment. When we think in terms of organic process we are recognizing timing, natural cycles, evolving patterns, elements combining at higher levels of complexity, and maturation. We guide organic process rather than control it; we cooperate with events rather than dominate them.

LEARNING PROCESS MODELS

While engaged in any process—walking, eating a sandwich, writing a book, or doing social work—you are consciously aware of only a small part of everything going on. In fact, total awareness of everything occurring could easily immobilize you. Do you remember learning to drive a shift car or skiing for the first time? There seemed to be so many things to keep track of all at once. After a bit of practice, however, it all came together more naturally or automatically.

The only times you are aware of everything in a process are when you first learn it or when you try capturing it in written form. (Did you ever read a description of the physiological process involved in walking or reaching for an apple?) In this part of the book you will be both reading about and trying to learn a new process. Though it may initially appear a bit overwhelming, with practice you'll gain mastery of the tasks and lose the self-consciousness that slows you down. Further, of the many techniques and procedures to be discussed here, in any particular situation, you'll only be using those appropriate to the problem. Consider too that the problems you deal with will vary in complexity. In some instances the preparation phase may only last 15 minutes, while in other cases it will take weeks.

Remember these points if you get bogged down in the details of the chapters that follow.

CHAPTER HIGHLIGHTS

Chapter 9: Setting the stage

The problem-solving process gets underway when you become aware of a problem and decide to do something about it. In this chapter I explore the well-travelled pathways that link social workers with clients, as well as the trails that creative generalists carve out themselves. I detail the tasks involved in setting the stage for problem solving in social work.

Chapter 10: Preparation (data)

The success of the problem-solving process depends a great deal on the adequacy of your preparation. In this chapter I present an overview of the preparation phase and discuss methods of gathering data.

Chapter 11: Preparation (problems)

The work of preparation is continued in this chapter. I discuss ways of organizing data that help us understand problems and determine problem priorities. I also demonstrate how to generate different perspectives on a problem.

Chapter 12: Design (ideas)

The first step in the design process is generating ideas for dealing with the problem. Once ideas are generated, they need to be combined into a rough pattern, detailed in the context of practical realities and organized into a plan for implementing the solution. I cover these aspects of design in this chapter.

Chapter 13: Design (solutions)

This chapter reviews the remainder of the design phase. I discuss how you orchestrate the various people and systems that need to work in concert to carry out the solution. The topics I cover include action systems, working agreements, and target systems.

Chapter 14: Verification

Transforming a solution from idea to reality requires more than carrying out the tasks specified in a plan. In this chapter I discuss confronting the unexpected, monitoring the process, evaluating outcomes, and concluding the problem-solving process.

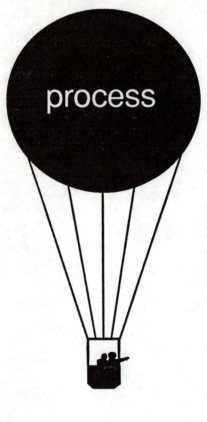

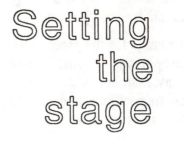

Setting the stage 9

In setting the stage for the problem-solving process in social work you'll be called upon to play three different parts. I will refer to them as your three "selves:" your employee (of organization) self, your social work self, and your vocational self.

The concern of the organization (as bureaucracy) in the initial phase of practice is with intake and the tasks related to processing people into the system. Your "employee self" carries the responsibility to address the organization's goals. Your "social work self" is concerned with engaging people in the problem-solving process and fulfilling such professional purposes as connecting people with resources and sharing problem-solving skills. Fighting for air time with your other two parts is your "vocational self." It has its own agenda, wanting to get involved in situations that offer opportunities to express its values and employ its style. You'll be challenged to keep these three selves in balance, finding synergistic solutions that at the same time meet the needs of the agency, the client and yourself.

OVERVIEW

The problems we engage in social work most often come to our attention through the different pathways that connect organizations and potential clients. We are positioned to react to what comes our way. The creative generalist is challenged to find ways of balancing a proactive and reactive stance. In this chapter I will explore both the usual ways the social work process gets started and the strategies that creative generalists employ in taking the initiative to engage problems.

Setting the stage for the problem-solving process involves a number of tasks: preparing for initial contacts with people, making a preliminary assessment of the situation, balancing a readiness to act with an avoidance of premature closure, and deciding on next steps in the process. These tasks will be discussed in the second half of the chapter.

The agency or organization in which you work greatly influences how the stage gets set. Therefore, I will start the chapter with a discussion of the organizational context and the issues it poses to the social worker.

ORGANIZATIONAL CONTEXT

Social work is by and large practiced in institutions and organizations. While you may view your initial contact with a potential client as a preliminary step to the the problem-solving process, from the organizational perspective it marks the start of the *people-processing* process. What does that mean to you as social worker? What problems and challenges does the organizational context pose?

Professional vs. Organizational Task

The term "intake" is commonly associated with the initial phase of practice. However, intake is a bureaucratic *people-processing* task of service delivery systems rather than a part of the problem-solving process in practice. Organizations develop intake policies to screen applicants, determine if they meet eligibility requirements, and gather data needed for agency records. The decision to serve an applicant may depend as much on the needs of the agency as on the needs of the person.

Kirk and Greenley have pointed out that to survive, organizations need clients.[1] Beyond any fees they may bring, clients are indirectly a resource because they justify organization claims to funding. However, clients may be a liability as well as an asset. Clients with difficult problems may require special attention and strain scarce resources such as staff time. If they fail to show improvement, it could affect the organization's reputation, jeopardizing future funding. The multi-faceted and ambiguous nature of many social and personal problems allows the organization to exercise discretion in how a problem is defined (categorized). By this mechanism the organization can adjust "eligibility requirements" to their needs.

As an employee of an organization, your job may involve the "taking in" of people into the system, helping turn people into applicants, and applicants into clients. This may include such activities as filling out forms with the person, checking eligibility requirements, classifying problems, explaining agency policies and procedures, and determining fees. In the social work literature you can find discussions on how to help people assume the role of "client." However, the bureaucratic task of intake should not be confused with the professional task of connecting people with resources or the goals of social work at the initial phase of practice.

Connecting People and Resources

In Chapter 2, I talked about connecting people and resources as one aspect of the business of social work in dealing with problems. Operating out of regard for this professional task (in contrast to serving as the organization's gatekeeper) has consequences for how you view the initial contact and your responsibilities to the potential client.

It's important not to let the initial point of entry or your organization affiliation overly constrict your view of a person's situation. The agency where a person winds up may be purely accidental. Many problems are multi-faceted and could fit within the domain of several different organizations. Also, the functions of an organization may not be clear to a potential client or a referral source. In a family with multiple problems, happenstance may determine through which point the family enters the service delivery system. If the teenage son is picked up by the police for stealing a car, the probation and parole social worker may be the family's first contact. If the father lost his job and got depressed, a mental health center might be the point of entry. If the mother took ill and was hospitalized, they might first be involved with a medical social worker.

While at the first contact your "employee self" is occupied with intake, your "social work self" says, "Here's a person with a problem. Regardless of my particular job at my particular organization, what can I do to be helpful, to see the person gets connected with the appropriate resources?"

Most of us have experienced incidents such as the following:

> You've been anxiously waiting in line for the past hour. If you don't get your registration materials in the next ten minutes, you are going to miss an important job interview. Finally, it's your turn. But with disbelief you hear the person behind the table telling you that you are in the wrong line. You should be in the line to the right. No matter how much you plead or protest, she won't get your materials. And the person at the table to the right makes you go to the back of her line to "wait your turn just like everybody else."

I hope I didn't upset you by reviving bad memories. If I did, calm yourself down by recalling a more positive incident. One happened to me last week. In the midst of a busy day, I had to take a long bus ride across town to pick up a tax form I urgently needed. When I arrived, the clerk told me that he was sorry but they didn't stock those forms at this office. Somebody had given me the wrong information over the phone! Just as my blood pressure was about to rise, he quickly added, "Let's see what I can do about it." He took my name and address, made a few phone calls, and arranged for the form to be mailed to me that afternoon. I was still annoyed at the waste of time, but this small act of unexpected kindness dissipated my intense angry feelings.

How would you deal with a potential client who was "waiting in the wrong line," or showed up at the wrong office? What responsibilities do you feel once you are aware of a person's problem? Beyond organization requirements and professional duty is the value issue that Mike brought up in Chapter 4. What kind of community would you like to live in? How are your acts contributing to building that type of community? In effect, what the clerk at the tax office was communicating to me was, "I acknowledge our connectedness as fellow human beings. I am responding to you out of that connection rather than from our separate roles as clerk and taxpayer."

Spend a few moments problem solving with the person. Acknowledge his or her frustration. Make a phone call to set up an appointment at another agency. Write down travel directions. Small gestures can make a big difference.

Bureaucratic Organization and Providing Services

Agencies are not evil entities which delight in making life difficult for workers and clients (though sometimes it appears that way to us). Many characteristics we complain about are actually byproducts of what we demand of agencies and organizations.

It's instructive to look at the evolution of alternative agencies and organizations. Many start out as an informal group of people who are concerned (perhaps "upset" or "outraged" are more accurate) over some problem or social condition that society is neglecting (e.g., missing children, abused women, AIDS victims). Some are formed by people who share a problem or an ideological interest in a problem. Initially the focus in such groups is on mutual support, self-help, information sharing, consciousness raising and advocacy. They might meet in an old storefront with scavenged furnishings and posters covering the walls—a ragged, yet comfortable, "lived in" feel. The drab environment gets transformed by people's energy, commitment and feelings of solidarity. Everyone works hard, nobody gets paid. It's an all volunteer effort aided by a few donations of needed supplies.

As the group meets with success and gets its message across it attracts more people and uncovers more needs in the community. A small demonstration grant is secured to provide some minimal services. Soon there are increasing comments such as: "We need to get more organized," "Our communications seem to be breaking down," "The person who's supposed to answer the phones never showed up today," "I'd like to keep helping, but I've got to feed my family," "What we really need is a couple of full-time paid positions," "We'll never get any United Way funding until we have an accounting system that shows our costs per unit of service."

Many organizations, such as battered women's shelters and drug abuse programs, started with a small group of concerned volunteers and evolved into organizations administering large annual budgets. A network form of organization is appropriate when mutual support and information sharing are the goals. When a group is trying to perform some task (e.g., lobby for a bill in the legislature) or provide a service to people (e.g., counseling, temporary housing), then some form of bureaucratic organization is necessary. It's part of the cost of doing business. There are ways that bureaucratic structures can be modified to reduce the conflicts that arise between the goals of efficiency (productivity), worker satisfaction, and client satisfaction. But the bureaucratic form of organization is tied to service delivery, to arranging for the right services to get to the right people at the right time.

We shop the large supermarket because we want the convenient hours, the variety of items, the cost savings, the parking—in short, because we want better service. At the same time we miss the personal touch we got at the Mom and Pop grocery stores we abandoned. What does "better service" mean in our social agencies, and what are the costs we pay for it? Are some of the services we provide ones that people could be providing for each other via informal networks? We need to raise such questions in our search for ways to humanize the bureaucracy.

Organization Environments and Practice Models

I've mentioned that intake requirements of organizations can influence social work goals in the initial phase of practice. Funding sources also influence practice activities. For example, most insurance companies only pay for mental health counseling with the client, not for the time a worker spends with collaterals such as teachers, neighbors, and relatives. You can bet that in agencies where insurance company payments are an important source of revenue, practice models that heavily rely on the worker-client relationship will be encouraged.

But professional and practice models in turn do influence organizational structures. Chris Argyris and Donald Schön point out that professions create controlled or "artificial" environments that are designed to permit standardized application of the techniques of the professional, enable the professional to realize objectives as he/she sees them, control the task, and render the behavior of others predictable.[2] The hospital, physician's office, and medical laboratory constitute the artificial environment for the physician. The lawyer's courtroom, the teacher's classroom, and the social worker's agency represent similar structured environments.

These environments include formal, structured interactions among professionals and among professionals and clients, and sharp role differentiation. Terms such as "plaintiff," "defendant," "patient," and "client" describe people in terms of the artificial environments created by the respective professions. Much of the authority of professionals comes from their knowledge of these settings, their certification to practice in them, their understanding of the language spoken in them, and their ability to negotiate them.[3]

We have become more aware of how institutions such as schools, hospitals and courts can work in opposition to their stated purposes—discouraging learning, breeding illness and interfering with justice. Exploring ways to make the system work better for the potential client may take you beyond bureaucratic structures and processes—you may find yourself confronting aspects of the artificial environment that exist to support professional activities and claims.

For example, radical (in the sense of "root") reforms, such as schools without walls (using the community as classroom) and home birthing, challenge basic assumptions of artificial environments such as who is qualified to practice in them and what kind of physical structure is necessary.

In the same vein, Froland and his colleagues, writing on prospects for partnership between human service agencies and informal helping networks, has suggested several changes that such agencies must make in their approaches to service provision if a partnership is to be successful.[4] Summing up these changes, the authors state that a partnership will be best accomplished by emphasizing policies of gradual decentralization, destandardization, and deprofessionalization. True, these strategies make accountability and coordination more difficult as well as raising other problems. But every arrangement has its own costs.

DIFFERENT BEGINNINGS AND SOCIAL WORK TASKS

We have taken a look at how the organizational context helps set the stage for the problem-solving process in social work. We are now ready to explore ways the process gets initiated and identify the social work tasks associated with these different beginnings. Consider the following scene:

> 8:30 AM — Arriving at the office you glance at your calendar and notice two new cases scheduled for this morning. Your 9:00 appointment is a 53-year-old widow, who called the mental health center "to talk with someone about my depression." That's all the information you have about her. At 10:30 you will be seeing a couple with their 9-year-old son. He has been in and out of foster homes for the past three years. The school counselor, concerned about the child's "lack of motivation" and failing grades, referred the family to the mental health center. The parents signed an information release form with the agency application. You have reports on your desk from the school and the child welfare worker that you want to review before you meet with the family. At 3:30

is the second meeting of the agency taskforce on teenage suicide. The group is looking into what the agency can do to get its services to these troubled youths.

Depicted in this scene are some of the different pathways that connect social workers with people and problems. Let's take a closer look at each of these pathways.

The Potential Client Comes to You

A common beginning occurs when a person(s) you don't know voluntarily initiates contact with you (shows up at your office or agency, or calls for an appointment for help with a problem). In such instances you are starting from scratch. Your task is to:

— Clarify the problem that the potential client is requesting help with.

— Determine what the person's goals are and what you are being asked to do about the problem.

— Identify the options for dealing with the person's request and clarify what can be expected of you and the agency.

— Depending on which option you and the person select, end the process, refer the person to another source of help, or come to an agreement on the next steps in the process.

Notice my use of the term "potential client." In discussing the four-systems model, I cautioned against assuming the person who initiates contact is the client or target system. Any designation of "client" at this stage should be considered tentative. It depends on what you and the people involved determine the problem to be.

The Potential Client Is Referred

Sometimes "referred" just means that a person who is voluntarily seeking help got in touch with you through a third party (e.g., a doctor, a friend, or a social worker at another agency). Often, however, when people are referred it means that someone else thinks it's a good idea for them to see you. The "someone else" may have the power to require the person to see you, as when a judge orders a delinquent teenager to attend a drug abuse program. Other times the third party may be acting out of concern about the potential client as when the teacher notifies the school social worker that Helen has been coming to school ill for the past few days. Or the potential client may be coerced into coming, as when a woman threatens to leave her husband unless he seeks help for his alcoholism.

When a third party is involved, you will need to determine how the potential client regards the referral and views his or her own situation or problem compared to the person making the referral. When you initiate contact with the person who has been referred, you will have to clearly explain why you are there and share what information you have from the referral source.

The initial exploration of the problem usually involves both the referral source and the person who has been referred. As a result of your exploration you might determine that the referral source is the appropriate client or target system. For example, the adult children of an elderly widow contact a family service agency. They are concerned that it is not safe for their mother to be living alone. Not being able to convince her to give up her apartment they would like the worker to talk to her. After looking into the matter the social worker may conclude the children need help in accepting the mother's position rather than the other way around.

In certain settings such as hospitals or schools, the referral path may be the main one used to connect you with potential clients. Those who control the referral process such as doctors or principals can determine which people and problems will reach you. Therefore, it is important that you have some input into the referral policies and procedures.

A Situation is Referred

At times there may be situations or problems that are referred to you, rather than a specific person. For example, a principal might ask your help in dealing with high truancy rates in the school; a nursing home administrator might be concerned with low staff moral; the merchants in a neighborhood may ask you to do something about increasing incidents of vandalism.

In these cases your initial clarification of the problem occurs with the person making the referral. You will then initiate contact with the various people related to the situation. You will have to decide at what stage to involve which people in the problem-solving process. The earlier people are involved in the exploration of a problem and the development of a solution, the more committed they become to the effort. Some people or groups might feel offended if not contacted at the beginning and may cause trouble down the road. From the start it is helpful to be thinking in terms of potential client, action and target system members.

Initially those making the referral (the principal, the administrator, the merchants) are the client system. They requested your help in dealing with a problem. When possible you'll also establish an agreement with the target system (truant school children, nursing home staff, neighborhood kids) on the nature of the problem and secure their sanction to work on it with them. In other words, you'll aim to make them your client or include them in the client system. Your original client may be incorporated into the action system or drop out of the picture.

Recruiting Clients

Sometimes agencies engage in "outreach," taking the initiative in making the initial contact. Your agency or organization may actively seek out potential clients who don't know about the programs or services you are offering or who may encounter some barrier in using them. These outreach efforts include screening programs, door-to-door canvassing of a neighborhood, booths or information tables at shopping centers and community events, talks to clubs and organizations, public service announcements in the media, hot-lines, feature stories in the newspapers, and building links with other organizations like police and detox centers. Such activities may be aimed at increasing the number of referrals or the number of people who voluntarily initiate contact with the organization.

In outreach efforts it is possible for the goal of problem identification to be subverted into the goal of "selling solutions." Whether we recruit potential clients for an assertiveness training group or a baby-sitting exchange, there is always the danger that our enthusiasm for our "product" will lead us to make the problem fit the solution rather than the other way around. In raising public awareness about a problem there is often a thin line between consciousness raising and creating a market for our services.

TAKING THE INITIATIVE: PROACTIVE STRATEGIES FOR THE CREATIVE GENERALIST

The various pathways that connect social workers with problems and potential clients serve organizational and professional purposes. But for the creative generalist, something is missing.

Creative generalists are proactive, sensitive to problems, aware of opportunities. You might read an article about barter and see the potential for a clothing and toy exchange at a daycare center you work with. Or, in the course of getting resources for clients, you may become aware of the need for coordination among several food pantries in town. Or, a fire at a rundown hotel used as a shelter for welfare clients may evoke enough community concern for you to get the city to look at the need for temporary housing. The initiatives you take give expression to your values, visions, priorities, interests—your sense of social work as vocation.

In the world of social agencies and "service delivery systems," acting on your own initiative poses some challenges. Organizations are usually structured to be reactive, to respond to situations presented to them (e.g., self-initiated contacts by potential clients or referrals). As we have noted, policies and procedures are established to screen and process potential clients through the organizational system, and the organization sanctions the worker's activities in this regard. Organizations are less likely to be structured to initiate activity, to be proactive. There is less expectation and sanction for workers to respond to their own awareness of a problem (especially if the organization itself is contributing to the maintenance of the problem). You will have to rely on your personal vision of the mission of the profession for the initial sanction to deal with such situations. There are several strategies creative generalists employ in setting the stage for the problem-solving process.

Using Alchemy

Do you remember the "alchemist-trashpicker" Mike described in his discussion of vocational styles in Chapter 4? He or she deliberately took on problems others didn't want to deal with, such as the youth center in the small town and the school kids of migrant farm workers. The "alchemist-trashpicker" saw opportunities in those problems where others just saw headaches.

Using your perceptual openness and power of association you can discover many ways to convert the problems you are *required* to work on into the problems you *want* to work on (or at least reduce the gap between the two). Let's look at another example. Suppose you were working for an agency that served elderly people. At the agency, recruitment and retention of volunteers to visit nursing home residents has been a continuing problem. Though you don't have much interest in the problem you have been assigned to work on it. What you would rather be doing is setting up an educational/support group for adult children of elderly parents. You believe that this is a very much needed resource but the agency won't free up enough of your time to set it up.

What to do? You start thinking like a creative generalist. How can I link the support group project with the volunteer problem? Not being able to come up with any clever solution, you decide to let the whole thing "incubate" for a few days. Then suddenly at a staff meeting, during a discussion about field work students, the "light bulb" clicks on. Why not organize the educational/ support group in a way where each of the participants has a "field experience." The field experience could consist of a six-month stint as a volunteer visitor to elderly nursing home residents. Discussions of their volunteer experiences would not only be a way to supervise the volunteers but a great way to bring out concerns they have about dealing with their elderly parents. They could also learn a lot from the residents about relating to elderly people. They would become knowledgeable about services to the elderly and in turn be a resource to people outside the group.

The more you operate out of your sense of vocation the more you will notice opportunities to give expression to you own values. Suppose you are a school social worker. While eating lunch with a group of teachers in the school cafeteria the conversation turns to the difficulties they are having in getting records of students who have been transferred from other schools. You have heard this mentioned before as a problem. So you make a mental note to talk with the school principal about it. You have been looking for a way of getting involved with the problems stemming from the transient student population at the school. Judging from the referrals they send you, the teachers seem to view you mainly as a resource who will design treatment programs for kids who are disruptive in the class. This situation might provide a chance to broaden their view of your role in the school.

Practice using alchemy. It can get to be a habit you'll enjoy.

Building Your Own Pathways

Earlier in the chapter I described some typical pathways through which potential clients find their way to social workers. The creative generalist does not simply sit at the end of the path waiting for potential clients to show up. To exercise some control over their situation, generalists also establish their own informal network of pathways.

Consider the people at work you get to know, the relationships you tend to cultivate. Who do you stop to chat with, whose problems do you take an interest in, who do you feel some connection with, who do you have a beer or coffee with after work? These informal relationships, which are not confined to other professional staff, reflect who you are as a person. They reveal more of your "vocational self" than your "professional self." As a result, the information you obtain and the problems you are exposed to through this informal network are more likely to relate to your vocational interests.

For a number of years I served on the board of a Jewish Social Service agency. One of the programs it sponsored was a weekly hot lunch social-recreational program for elderly people. Some of the board members could not understand why the agency social worker, who had an MSW degree, spent so much time with that program. "Couldn't it be handled by a volunteer or someone with less training?" they asked. A visit by some board members to the program proved instructive. They observed the social worker continually circulating among the participants, greeting them, inquiring how they were doing, asking why Sara hadn't come last week, finding out about a problem Ida was having with her landlord, listening to a story about Ruth's visit with her children, arranging for Harry to take a few people along the next time he went to visit his wife at the nursing home, and so on. The social worker had, in effect, developed her own intake system that reflected her personal style. This system, which supplemented the more formal intake system of the agency, reached people who would not otherwise have contacted the agency or considered becoming a "client." The board was satisfied that the worker was making good use of her time.

When you can't be "where the action is," you can build pathways via those in the community who do have linkages to the people and situations with which you are concerned. For example, in poor rural areas families may have more regular contact with a veterinarian than a physician. Some vets have participated in a program educating farm families on diseases transmitted from animals to humans and making referrals to physicians when necessary. When you take the time to get to know a community, you will become more aware of such potential pathways.

Planting Seeds

Once again nature provides a helpful analogy. The seeds I am referring to are, of course, ideas for activities or programs you wish to develop. There are two styles of planting seeds. The "organic generalist" will thoughtfully select a fertile spot for planting. He or she will then nurture the seed, seeing that it is exposed to the best conditions for facilitating growth. A carefully placed comment at a meeting, a gentle reminder during a coffee break, and your idea may be on its way to germination.

The other style is more like a wildflower which casts hundreds of seeds to the wind with the expectation of one or two of them finding an hospitable environment. If you are the "Johnny Appleseed" type of generalist, you'll be mentioning your idea for a barter center (or whatever) to anyone you come into contact with who might have the slightest interest. Sooner or later, in one form or another, the idea may take root.

TASKS IN SETTING THE STAGE

Regardless of how the problem-solving process gets initiated there are a number common tasks in setting the stage:

— Preparing for initial contacts with people.

— Making a preliminary assessment of the situation.

— Balancing a readiness to act with an avoidance of premature closure.

— Deciding on next steps in the process.

Preparing for Initial Contacts

When a potential client initiates a contact you may not have any lead time to prepare for the interview. Your only preparation may consist of your past experiences with similar situations and the checklist of goals to be accomplished at initial meetings that you keep in mind. In many instances, however, you will have some preparation time. The preliminary assessment of the situation may require more than one interview with the potential client and additional contacts with other people associated with the problem. When a referral source makes the initial contact or when you take the initiative to address an issue, you will have some time to think things through. In a setting such as a school or neighborhood center you will already know people in a variety of ways.

As you gather experience in this process you will develop your own list of useful tips that make your initial contacts easier to deal with and more productive. What follows is a list that grows out of our experience.

Visualize the worst and best case scenarios

If you are nervous about an upcoming meeting, have to present someone with bad news, or have to raise a sensitive issue, you may find yourself procrastinating in making that phone call to set up the initial meeting. You may worry how this or that will turn out. To get over this hump it is useful to think about the "worst case scenario," i.e., what is the worst thing that could happen. (This should be a simple task. For some reason people usually find it easier to imagine and generate pictures of what could go wrong than what could go right.) You then say to yourself, "O.K., how would I deal with it? Suppose I make a fool of myself, or the person gets angry at me, or… Will I survive? What are ways I could respond?" By facing up to the worst case, and psyching yourself for it, the rest goes easier. This technique can also be used in helping clients prepare for encounters they are reluctant to face.

A word of caution here. Visualization is a powerful tool for shaping ideas into reality. If you dwell too much on what can go wrong, you may be helping to bring about the very situation you are trying to avoid. So, also picture the contact in your mind as you would like it to go. This will actually help you visualize in a most graphic way what needs to be done in the interview.

Positive visualization taps into the energy of the "self-fulfilling prophesy."[5] Street-wise community organizers know that when they are advocating for their client or cause, they need to make it easy for the "target system" to say yes. This includes coming in with positive expectations as well as supplying the target system with reasons for supporting the request and ways to save face.

Develop a game plan

A plan is the analytical counterpart to your visualization. Having a game plan means knowing what your goals are, what you hope to accomplish, being prepared for possible problems you might encounter, knowing how you intend to reach your goals. In the course of carrying out the plan you will alter it in response to unanticipated circumstances that arise. However, having a game plan will give you a sense of security and help you come across as a thoughtful and competent person.

When your initial contact is with a group, you may need to find a way for each person to have a chance to state their perceptions of the issue or problem. In a family experiencing conflict you may have to establish some ground rules so each person can tell their story without being cut off by other family members. At the first meeting of a new task force you might go round robin, getting each member's perception of the task facing the group.

Be yourself AND be aware of others' values

A student of mine was concerned about an upcoming interview. Would the potential client view her as young and naive? How could she overcome this perception? Rather than looking at her inexperience as a problem we decided to look at it as an attribute. We then reframed the issue as how to make use of this attribute in the interview. One suggestion that came out of the class discussion was for the student to explain to the potential client that she was a student in training and that she would appreciate his help. Would he mind giving her some feedback after the interview? Did she get at his concerns? Were the next steps made clear?

For some potential clients this approach might be a good means of involving them as an active partner in the problem-solving process. The feedback session might produce valuable information about the problem or situation that was missed in the interview itself. In addition, you might actually inspire the person's respect by showing you have enough self-confidence to acknowledge your limitations.

Commenting on what makes a good community organizer, Nicholas Von Hoffman once stated in an unpublished speech that nothing is so reassuring as a person who acts like himself or herself. When you are willing to accept yourself as yourself, other people will be too. Von Hoffman warns that if you were raised in a small Midwestern community and are now working in a ghetto area, using the slang terms of an urban slum will make you sound either idiotic or patronizing.

It is important to sort priorities when the goal of expressing your personal freedom seems to conflict with respecting the values of the community or people with whom you are working. If a friend invites you to a church service and you know that the people there would be offended by jeans, you would wear a regular pair of slacks even though you are more comfortable wearing jeans. If you are advocating for a group before a zoning board, and you know your testimony would be more credible if you wore a tie, then wear the tie (or find a job that doesn't require you to testify at hearings). Your goal is to help the client's cause, not to express your personal freedom of dress. Respecting the values of others need not conflict with being yourself. There is a difference between pretending to be someone you are not and dressing in a certain way in order to avoid unnecessary problems that get in the way of your goals.

Understand the ways
people experience the initial contact

The act of seeking or being offered help with a problem holds different meanings to different people. The meaning will vary depending on the circumstances leading up to the initial contact, personality characteristics, and cultural norms. The variety of reactions you may encounter (hostility, relief, embarassment, anxiety, enthusiasm, hopefulness, etc.) reflect the different meanings associated with the initial contact.

In discussing the problem-solving relationship in the last chapter I stressed the value of shifting attention from person to situation. Focusing on the situation and the positive resources in the situation (avoiding deficiency-oriented thinking) is a way to deal with reactions to the initial contact that get in the way of problem solving.

In my class I use an article, "Another Sleepless Night," written by a mother of a developmentally disabled child.[6] It describes her odyssey in searching for help and her frustrations at finding professionals who kept diagnosing and measuring her child's deficiencies but not his potentials. A student in my class who was working at an adult congregate living facility for developmentally disabled persons read this article and was very moved by it. The following week she had an occasion to interview the sister of one of the residents. One of the first questions she asked the sister was what accomplishments of her brother she was most proud of. The sister was visibly surprised by the question. She stated that in all the years she had been dealing with social workers nobody had ever asked her that question. It lead to some new insights about the brother and helped establish a good working relationship.

Some people fear that asking for help will be viewed as a sign of weakness or incompetence. (Did you ever notice how some people will travel for miles in the wrong direction rather than stop and ask for directions?) Focusing on a person's deficiencies feeds into such fears and increases resistance.

We often encounter people who don't exactly welcome us with open arms. It is useful to regard resistance as motivation in a direction different from where whe are headed. Acknowledging the resistance is a good first step in dealing with it. We should view the resistance from the point of view of the information it contains, and look for ways to hook into the other person's motivation. A woman accused of child neglect may resist talking about her parenting skills, but be motivated to discuss ways of getting a better paying job. Discussion of her financial situation may lead to its impact on her ability to provide for her child.

Making an Initial Assessment

In the next chapter I will describe in detail how to gather data and explore problems. Our concern here is with getting just enough of a picture of the situation to know what our next steps should be. Making an initial assessment of a situation involves a lot of sorting of information. Pulling out your note pad and "doing circles" will help in the sorting process.

Description vs. evaluation

Pincus and Minahan point out that description and evaluation are often intertwined.[7] As an example, suppose a teacher said that John has a disrupting effect on the class. What does this statement tell you? What specifically does John do in the classroom? Under what circumstances? How often? What is the response of the other children? How does the teacher deal with the situation? If you view a problem as a condition or situation that someone is evaluating as undesirable, it will help you sort out the facts of the situation from how it is being evaluated by those involved.

Prioritizing problems

Potential clients may come with a host of intertwined problems. They may feel overwhelmed and not know where to begin. You can't attack a whole range of problems at once. It's important to partialize, to pick out with the potential client a specifically defined problem (the problem-to-be-worked) as a starting point.[8] Sorting out the problems in the situation and prioritizing them may itself constitute the initial problem-to-be-worked. "Doing circles" with the potential client can prove very helpful, giving them a perspective on the situation and a handle on how to begin coping with it. Problems can be prioritized on the basis of what's causing the most immediate pain, what the potential client sees as most urgent, what part of the problem the potential client and others can immediately start working on, and what needs to be done before other steps can be taken.

Different views

I mentioned earlier that, when the potential client is a family or other group, you should be prepared to give each member a chance to give their view of the problem. Even when the potential client is an individual, others connected to the situation may have very different views of it. Sorting out these different views and getting some consensus on the matter may be the initial problem-to-be-worked.

In identifying the problem-to-be-worked you will also be clarifying goals of potential clients, what they hope will happen, what they expect of you or your organization. When the potential client system is a group such as a family or neighborhood association, conflicting definitions of the problem will result in conflicting goals and expectations.

Clarifying wants

The initial contact may concern something you want of others, e.g., participation on a committee or help with a problem you have encountered. When students in my field unit bring in problems for consultation, they are asked to think through in advance what they want out of the session, what kind of help they need. Suppose the issue was poor attendance at a group the student is leading. What is the student looking for from the consulation? Ventilating feelings of frustration? Program ideas for the group? Help in deciding whether to discontinue the group? Support for a decision already made? How to deal with a feeling of failure? It may not be clear at the beginning what you are looking for. But starting with a focus on what you *want*, you can generate a list of alternatives like the ones above. Reviewing the list can help clarify the nature of the problem you are seeking help with.

Going through this kind of "I want" clarification will help sensitize you to difficulties others may have in expressing their wants. You can use the same process in helping others clarify their wants. Put each item in a circle and look for the connections. When you are dealing with a group, such as a family, you can often get at the heart of a problem or conflict by asking each person such questions as, "What would you like to see happen? What would make you feel better about the situation? What do you consider a fair compromise?"

Problems vs. solutions

Sometimes you may be initially presented with a solution rather than a problem. A woman asks your help in finding a nursing home for her mother. A principal wants you to start an assertiveness training group. These are solutions. What problem is the nursing home placement or the training group a solution to? It may well be that the solution you are asked to implement is an appropriate one. Having said that, let me now add that often the solution is not appropriate. In getting an initial picture of the situation you need to distinguish between problem and solution, what the difficulty is and what the person wants you to do about it. You need to explore what alternative solutions were tried or considered.

Your perceptions vs. others

You'll be developing your own view of the situation as you gather information about it. You have to be careful that your perception of a problem does not blind you to what the potential client sees as the difficulty. Suppose a mother that you started working with last week calls for your assistance. She just found out that her teenage son has been arrested by the police for selling drugs. If you get too caught up in all the contributing problems in the family (e.g., alcholism, unemployment) you might miss the point that to the mother and the kid, the central problem at the moment is how to deal with the consequences of the arrest.

Balancing a "Readiness to Act" with an "Avoidance of Premature Closure"

In an earlier chapter Mike described a natural tension that occurs in problem solving. When you increase your perceptual openness through right-mind thinking, your left mind fights to "shut the door" and tidy things up. If you yield prematurely to pressures for closure, you lessen your chances of finding a good solution.

While making your preliminary assessment of the situation you may often find yourself facing internal and external pressures for closure. You will be pressed to DO SOMETHING! about the problem. These pressures may of course be quite legitimate. Common sense dictates the necessity for quick action in a crisis situation. And intervention cannot always wait upon a complete understanding of the situation. Our knowledge base is never complete. Sometimes you need to intervene in order to produce data for further analysis. Finally, people often use the excuse of needing more time to study the problem as a tactic to delay or to avoid dealing with a problem.

But sometimes you may be pushed prematurely into pursuing solutions by your own low tolerance of ambiguity or a desire to get people off your back. You'll need to evaluate the pressures you face and balance a readiness to act with an avoidance of premature closure.

You can help avoid premature closure by responding to situations in ways that keep your options open. Initially we don't know who our client or target system will be. When you get a note from the teacher that John is fighting with other kids in class, there are many ways to respond, e.g., call him to your office, observe him in the class, talk more with the teacher, contact the parents, read prior school records. Even though you may be keeping an open mind on the situation, others may read your behavior differently. Simply calling John to your office may signal to him and his peers that you have labeled him as "the problem." Holding an initial meeting with one member of a feuding family or community group may result in other members believing that you have "taken sides." Such perceptions would rule out your being able to assume a mediator role.

Treating data as tentative also helps you keep open. Your initial point of entry into a problem represents only one perspective on the situation. Further, the information you gather arrives in a certain sequence. This sequence greatly influences how later information is interpreted and formed into patterns. The circles map is a useful tool for holding information in tentative patterns, rearranging the pieces, and overcoming the effects of the sequence of arrival of the information.

Deciding on Next Steps in the Process

The initial contact can end on a number of different notes:

— The difficulty may be resolved in the first session with no need for any further contact.

— You may refer the potential client to another resource.

— An additional meeting might be arranged to further explore the situation.

Whenever there is to be continuing contact, it is useful to develop a preliminary agreement with the person that identifies the problem-to-be-worked, the initial goals, what each person has agreed to do at or before the next meeting. This need not be more than a simple explicit verbal agreement or understanding, but it is a useful way to clarify things at the end of the meeting.

Setting a specific time limit on the initial exploration and a time to reconsider the agreement is important. For example, my field unit negotiated a preliminary agreement with a local Head Start organization over a problem stemming from forced staffing cuts. The agreement specified what the field unit would be doing over the next three weeks to gather information about the problem and the kind of cooperation we needed from the organization. At the end of the three-week period we would meet with representatives from the organization, share our findings, and generate some options for dealing with the problem. If at that point they felt they wanted to pursue one of the options we would negotiate a new agreement on how to proceed. The same process can be used when dealing with an individual or family around a personal problem. The built-in time limit for reconsidering the preliminary agreement removes some of the worry about "what I'm getting myself into." It provides a face-saving way to part if things don't work out.

SUMMARY

Problem solving begins with an awareness of a problem and a commitment to deal with it. This chapter has discussed how the stage gets set for the problem-solving process in social work. We explored the impact of the agency context, typical pathways that connect potential clients and agencies, strategies creative generalists employ to maintain a proactive stance, and tasks involved in starting the process. The stage has now also been set for the remaining chapters which will focus on the preparation, design and verification phases of problem solving.

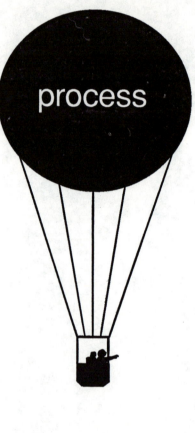

Preparation
(data)

10

Once you have become aware of a problem, made a preliminary assessment, and decided to commit yourself to it, the stage has been set for the problem-solving process. You are now ready to begin the preparation phase.

This chapter will focus on data gathering. The next chapter will explore ways we process data to understand a problem. I'll begin this chapter with an overview of the preparation phase.

OVERVIEW

In the preparation phase you'll gather data about the problem situation. You'll discover key components and dimensions of the problem, systems in which the problem is embedded, resources in the situation, and potential client, action, and target systems. You'll explore various hypotheses and assumptions about the problem. You'll sort and organize information, generate different perspectives on the situation, and frame the problem in different ways. Your understanding of the problem prepares you for the design phase where you will be generating ideas for dealing with the problem and shaping those ideas into workable solutions.

In Chapter 6, *Tools for cultivating creativity,* Mike used the problem of where to go for a winter vacation to illustrate some points about perceptual openness and flexible persistence. Let's use that example again, this time as an analogy for the preparation phase. The decision to take a vacation sets the stage for the problem-solving process. Once the decision is made, you start gathering data about alternative destinations and modes of travel. You check how they fit with what you want from a vacation and consider the relative costs. You immerse yourself in the problem, sorting the information in different ways, exploring different options. Like the person in Mike's example, all this activity may result in seeing the problem in a very new light, e.g., "How can I get a warm climate to come to me?" This way of looking at your problem leads you to consider staying at home and spending your vacation money on a sauna or small greenhouse.

I stated earlier that problem definition is the bridge to solution. As the vacation example illustrates, the way you define (frame) a problem determines the kinds of solutions you consider. Problem framing is therefore an important element of preparation. When you were setting the stage for the social work process, you also asked, "What is the problem?" Then, however, you were interested in identifying the problem in order to determine if it was appropriate for you to deal with it. Now you are interested in understanding the problem in order to frame it in a way that will lead to an effective and appropriate solution.

The key to creative preparation is maintaining perceptual openness. In the preparation phase you will be called upon to maintain openness in how you gather data about the problem, what you regard as data, meanings (information) you extract from or attribute to data, how you organize and sort data, and how you shift perspectives and frame the problem.

Diagnosis and Labeling

At one time the terms "study," "diagnosis" and "treatment" were used to describe the stages in social work problem solving. There is an important difference between the aims of diagnosis and the aims of the preparation phase.

Diagnosis is still closely associated with the medical field where it means identifying a disease by its signs or symptoms. The aim in diagnosis is to label a person or problem according to characteristics associated with a specific diagnostic category. The label serves as the link between problem and solution. This way of problem solving can be very efficient as long as clear-cut diagnostic categories have been established and specific effective treatments are associated with specific diagnoses.

For the kinds of problems social workers deal with however, there are few clear-cut categories and very tenuous connections between label and treatment. The label may in fact serve to hide our ignorance or create the illusion of understanding.

In the preparation phase our aim is to individualize the situation, gain an appreciation of its unique aspects (rather than place it in a category), and arrive at a *mutual* understanding of the problem with the potential client. We familiarize ourselves with the specific context (e.g., people, resources, contraints) in which we are problem solving. Our social work eco-systems perspective steers us away from attempts to pinpoint *the* cause of a problem. We direct our attention to the interplay of the various factors in the situation in order to discover different options and approaches for dealing with the problem. The way we define or frame the problem forms the link between problem and eventual solution.

An organization or program may require that a formal diagnosis be made. For example, many insurance companies will not pay for mental health counseling unless an official diagnosis is made by a psychiatrist. Or a student may have to be labeled "slow learner" in order to participate in a certain program. In the last chapter I discussed how agencies can use the process of classifying a person's problem to gain control over intake. Such labeling can be detrimental if it creates perceptual biases that emphasize deficiencies over capabilities. However, the need for a diagnosis can be dealt with as a problem to be shared by you and the potential client.

Suppose you are a social worker in a school which has received funding for a special class for "slow learners" from low-income families. A screening process was set up and a number of eligible students were identified. It is your job to contact the parents and get permission to enroll their children in the program.

There are several ways to approach the labeling issue with the parents. You can help them consider the trade-offs of access to special resources in exchange for putting up with having their child labeled a slow learner. Or perhaps the referral can be written up in a way that raises questions about the validity of the label and poses participation in the program as further assessment, an opportunity to identify and label *potentials*, not just deficiencies. There may be some positive sides to the label. A student in the special class might get reinforced for making a certain amount of progress and get to experience success and feelings of competence. The same amount of progress by a student without the label might be considered inadequate. Further, if the child makes enough progress to have the label removed (or simply outgrows it), it would be viewed by the school as a real accomplishment. You could work with the parents on ways they can obtain more information about the program and how the labeling is treated by the staff. Perhaps they could talk about the situation with other parents who have had experience with such programs in the past or who also have questions about giving permission for their child to participate in the program.

The point is, you don't have to sell the program to the parents or smooth over any angry feelings about the labeling issue. If the situation is viewed as a problem by the parents, you can engage them in problem solving around it. See them as a client rather than as a target system. Put the problem rather than the parents or child in the center circle and do a circles map with them.

Dealing with Open Problems

One reason it's difficult to employ clear-cut diagnostic categories in social work is that we are usually dealing with open problems. Let's take a few minutes to review the distinction between open and closed problems.[1]

Closed problems are ones where the boundaries are well known and fixed, the variables comprising the problem are finite and identifiable. There is often one right (i.e., logically correct) answer or solution to a closed problem. The solution is usually predictable and arrived at through a conscious, controllable and logically reconstructable process, utilizing some set procedure. Remember those algebra problems ("A man is rowing upstream at 5 miles per hour. If the stream is moving at 3 miles per hour, at what time will he arrive at his dinner party in Toledo?") you spent endless time with in high school? Those are examples of closed problems.

With an open problem many of the variables comprising the problem are not known and/or not capable of being measured. The boundaries (contraints) may change during the problem-solving process. There are many possible solutions to an open problem. The process of solving an open problem often involves the production of novel or unexpected ideas. No preset formula of detailed sequential steps can be followed. "What should I do when I grow up?" "How can we lower the dropout rate in the schools?" "What should be the priorities of this agency?" are examples of open problems.

Cartwright points out the paradox in the field of planning (equally true in other fields) that the most sophisticated analysis tools are those which are appropriate for closed problems, while the majority of problems increasingly tends toward complicated open problems.[2] When planning a road meant basically finding the shortest distance between two points (allowing for the terrain) and "costs" meant how much money it would take to build the road, sophisticated planning tools could deal with these closed problems. Today, planners must take into consideration the environmental impact of the road, social costs, and effects on development in the immediate area as well as in other parts of town. Will the road relieve traffic congestion or will the new development it encourages attract so much traffic that congestion will again be a problem in a few years? How should the road be viewed in relation to policies promoting public mass transportation and renewal of downtown neighborhoods? In other words, the planning of a new road is becoming recognized as more of an open problem than a closed one.

Some problems, like the rowboat one, are closed problems by nature and best solved by treating them as such. For most of the problems you encounter in practice, whether you treat them as open or closed is a matter of perceptual choice.

It is tempting to define problems as closed so that we can employ our sophisticated methodologies. Defining problems to suit the methodologies of the practitioner is something that has occurred throughout the history of social work (as well as most professions). Boundaries are built into the methodology or theory which seek to reduce ambiguities from the start. A behavioral therapist might view the acting out behavior of a child through a predetermined set of variables such as frequency of types of behaviors and kinds of reinforcements. The variables studied derive from the nature of the theory being used rather than the nature of the problem. (The problem is closed by predetermined parameters.) We are not saying to avoid such theories, just to avoid their premature use. They should be called upon *after* the problem is understood, when possible solutions are being discussed.

In preparing to deal with an open problem you may find yourself raising such questions as: "If everything is connected to everything else, how do I put any boundaries around a problem or my activities in understanding a problem?" "Where do I draw the line?" "How do I know when I have enough information, when I understand the problem well enough to proceed?"

Earlier in the book Mike discussed tolerance of ambiguity and a preference for complexity as important traits of the creative generalist. We often erect boundaries (constraints) and/or fail to challenge them because we don't like to live with ambiguity and complexity. But effective problem solving requires that we do so. As we will see, appropriate boundaries are determined in the process of exploring the problem and clarifying your objectives and goals with the potential client system and others. You'll have to draw on your flexible persistence and take charge to prevent you rational mind from closing the problem too soon.

WHOLE-MIND THINKING IN DATA GATHERING

To understand a problem you need to look at it with both your rational and intuitive minds (whole-mind thinking). Your rational mind identifies the parts, examines the details, assesses the impact, analyzes the dimensions. Your intuitive mind develops a feel for how the parts relate to the whole, grasps at the meaning of pieces of data, immerses itself in the problem, turns the problem inside out.

Data gathering likewise employs whole-mind thinking. As a kid I remember being impressed that my parents, by just looking into my eyes, could usually tell when I was sick. A parent's intimate knowledge of his or her child results in a perceptual sensitivity to small changes in behavior or demeanor that signal ill health. Such changes might well go unnoticed by others. If the child is taken to a clinic, the doctor will want to know the child's temperature and perhaps order some additional tests.

What we have here is an example of the two sides of data gathering. In the one case, data is gathered by a device (e.g., a thermometer) especially designed to elicit certain kinds of data. The data has meaning for the doctor independent of his or her relationship to the child. In social work the devices used to collect data include structured interviews and observations, questionnaires, evaluation forms, and content analysis of existing material such as agency records or minutes of committee meetings. When we speak of skill in relation to this kind of data gathering we are referring to skill in the design of the device (e.g., the way you sequence questions in an interview or the catagories you create to record your observations) and skill in the use of the instruments. This side of data gathering relies heavily on our rational left-brain thinking.

On the other side of data gathering, rather than using some device to collect data, you allow the data to *find you* by becoming a more sensitive instrument *yourself*. The skill we are talking about here involves training your powers of perception and association and exploiting the potential of chance happenings. Your closeness and connections to the data, your intuition, your right-brain thinking all play a big part.

The challenge to you as a creative generalist in applying whole-mind thinking to the task of collecting data is to blend together both modes—using devices to find data and being aware of the data finding you.

Pincus and Minahan describe a scene where a social worker, armed with agency forms, sets out on a home visit to gather data on a problem a mother is having with her children.[3] The worker also needs to determine if the family is eligible for the agency's program. During the course of the interview the children come home from school. Shortly afterwards there is another disruption—a glass of milk comes crashing to the kitchen floor and a fight between the kids breaks out over who is to blame. Before the interview ends, a neighbor stops by to borrow some eggs.

One social worker might use these interruptions to gather his or her thoughts and fill out the forms. If the worker has had a busy day and is late in returning to the office, he or she may become irritated by the interruptions. Another social worker, who regarded these events not as interruptions but as opportunities, might come away with much more data about the family. How did the mother greet the children when they came home from school? How did she handle the fight? How did the kids respond to her? Does the neighbor seem like a good friend?

Becoming more aware of the data that is "finding you" will enrich your understanding of a situation. Regard everything as potential data. Pay attention to what isn't as well as to what is. What is not said in an interview should be treated as data as well as what is said. What you are not shown on the tour you are given of a nursing home may may be as revealing as what you are shown. A casual conversation may yield more data than a formal interview.

AWARENESS OF RESOURCES

Gathering data on the resources in a situation is an important aspect of the preparation phase. Unfortunately, we are usually more aware of deficiencies than resources. Therefore, in discussing ways of letting data find you, I will be emphasizing awareness of resources.

A resource is anything which can be put to use to help solve a problem, meet a need or achieve a goal. Resources can take the form of information and other intangibles as well as material things. For something to become a resource, we have to *perceive* its utility for the task at hand. Sometimes this is easy, as when we are dealing with resources that are "labeled" for specific uses (e.g., visiting nurse service, homemaker to assist elderly persons, Alcoholics Anonymous). At other times a needed resource may not exist (there is always a shortage of formal resources) or we may not be sure of the most appropriate resource for the problem at hand. We may have to use whatever we've got and improvise. We may be looking for something with a goal in mind, but not know exactly what it is that we are looking for until we find it.

What makes something a resource is not its innate characteristics but our ability to view those characteristics *in relation to* our needs or goals. This involves learning to open our perceptions so we can see something as a potential resource, use association to envision the connection of the resource to our problem or goal, and engage our flexible persistence to stick with our search.

Let's look at some principles and techniques that help maintain your perceptual openness to resources.

Use your Biases

Much has been written in the literature on biases that enter into the process of collecting data. Data are the raw material that we convert into understanding. Pincus and Minahan state that, since there is no way to collect *all* the possible data about a problem, there is no way to avoid the selectivity which goes into data gathering.[4] It is possible to intentionally or unintentionally gather only data that supports your initial assumptions and biases. Much of the literature stresses ways of minimizing the effects of your biases.

Let's consider the issue from another point of view and regard a bias as a preferred way of loking at something. You have probably heard of the phenomenon of the "self-fulfilling prophesy" and the "placebo effect" (what you look for or what you expect is what you get). These are well documented and very powerful forces.[5] Why not use their power to our advantage? If we believe that the people we work with possess untapped resources, and the strength of our belief makes it more likely that we will find what we are looking for, so much the better. These are the kinds of biases we want to bring to our data gathering.

View People (Including Yourself) in Terms of Attributes

The biggest block to seeing the resources around us is our tendency to engage in deficiency-based thinking. I'd like to illustrate this point with an exercise. It goes like this:

> Put this picture in your head: *Homebound Elderly Person.* Now, thinking like a social worker, write down anything that comes to mind, anything you associate with *Homebound Elderly Person.*

You might want to take a moment right now to try this.

The list you generated may include:

— Lonely

— Meals on Wheels

— Need for transportation

— Health problems

— Visiting Nurse

— Help with housework

— Financial aid

What social workers tend to see when they look at a homebound elderly person is a bunch of deficiencies on the one hand, and formal services and programs for meeting those deficiencies on the other.

When I use this exercise in class, I assign some readings the week before which discuss how professionals often turn needs into deficiencies, relate to people around their deficiencies, and try to "fix" what is wrong with them. This approach is not only strongly rooted in the "medical model" but in our sincere desire to help people and alleviate suffering as well.

So strong is deficiency-based thinking that even after reading and discussing those articles, students still generate a list of deficiencies and formal services. To break the pattern of this type of thinking you have to break the kind of valuing you attach to people's attributes.

The next part of the exercise goes like this:

> Instead of thinking of *Homebound Elderly* as a pathological condition to be remedied, DEFER JUDGEMENT and picture it in your mind in purely neutral descriptive terms. Now write down as many ATTRIBUTES of *Homebound Elderly* that you can think of.

Again, you may want to take a few moments to try this yourself.

The list you now generated might look like this:

— Always at home

— Wants to meet people

— Talents not being used

— Able to answer the telephone

— Lots of idle time

— Have disabilities which curtail mobility

— Reads a lot

The next step in this exercise is to take these attributes and generate ways they can be turned into resources. This is helped along by thinking of what needs other people or groups may have for those attributes, and how they can be a resource (remember the concept of synergy). For example, take the attribute of always being at home and able to answer the telephone. Many organizations can't afford a telephone answering service but have a need for someone who is home a lot and can take messages. So do Neighborhood Watch programs, which are dependent on a good telephone network to alert the neighborhood in case of trouble. So do Helping Hand programs, where houses along a school route are designated as places where kids can stop in case of trouble. Elderly people who enjoy reading might provide a newspaper article clipping service for some community organization.

When visiting a homebound elderly person, whether you see with your bias of deficiencies or your bias of resources will influence what you find.

Look for Multifunction Resources

In the example above, listing the person's attributes helped us discover new resources by breaking the pattern of turning needs into deficiencies. Attribute listing is also a helpful tool for breaking the pattern of associating a given resource with its usual function. It can also help us look beyond the usual functions associated with a person's formal role or status.

There is an exercise in the creativity literature which asks you to think of as many uses as you can for a pile of bricks. Since we usually associate bricks with building, the most common ideas generated are things like building a fireplace or outdoor grill. Or its most familiar characteristic, its weight, often suggests uses such as a doorstop or paperweight. In other words, its usual or obvious function or characteristic tends to blind us to other possibilities.

If we make a list of the attributes of a brick such as volume, color, shape, porosity, ability to absorb heat, and hardness, each attribute or combination of attributes opens up possibilities for additional uses.

They say that "necessity is the mother of invention." You've all had some kind of experience such as using a table knife when you coulnd't find a screwdriver or otherwise improvising a resource or tool when the one you needed wasn't available. A good mechanic or plumber is one who can improvise a needed tool or part. He or she "sees" what needs to be accomplished and views the attributes of the resources around them in terms of those characteristics that might serve that function.

For example, a social worker sees an ad for a foreign language movie with English subtitles. He thinks of this as a resource for a children's group he is leading which has a deaf child in it. A probation officer is helping a teenaged kid explore job possibilities. The teenager has a good relationship with an English teacher at an evening school he is attending. The teacher agrees to use the manual for the nurse's license exam to help the boy with his reading skills. At the same time, discussion of the content of the manual with the teacher will help the boy explore his interests. An English teacher, a foreign language movie, *anything* can be a resource. The more you expand your perceptions to look at things in terms of attributes, the more you engage your associative powers to form new patterns, the more you will begin to see the relevance of the data finding you to the problem or goal you are working on.

Commit Yourself to Your Goals and Keep Them in Your Consciousness

I'd like to explain this principle through an analogy. Did you ever have a headlight on your car burn out? You drive around with one headlight for some time, knowing you have to get it fixed soon before you get ticketed by the police or cause an accident. Suddenly you begin to notice many cars on the road with only one headlight. You've never noticed so many before. Is there suddenly an epidemic of blown headlights? No, there have always been that many. It's just that you are now taking notice of them because you are carrying your headlight problem around with you in your consciousness.

Or maybe you've had the experience of learning a new fancy word and all of a sudden you run into it all over the place. What about making a decision you have procrastinated on or making a commitment to some goal and suddenly you start running into people who are helpful to you, or run across a useful article in the current issue of some journal you are reading.

These are not simply examples of coincidence. Our minds take in only a small fraction of everything happening around us. This selectivity is necessary for survival. Without it we'd soon go insane from overload. Though we are often unaware of the selectivity taking place, we can learn to direct it.

Did you ever hear the expression "commitment enlists providence?" Tice explains this phenomenon by postulating that when we establish and affirm an intention and create a vision of an end state, we "program" our subconscious minds to selectively perceive anything that could help us achieve our purposes.[6] He observes that even when we begin with no idea of how to achieve our goal, we will gradually see the means we need through the filter we set up which will selectively bring to our attention events, people, and other resources which could be useful to us.

So keep your data collection needs and goals in your consciousness. At the most unexpected time or place you may run into what you are looking for.

DATA COLLECTION DEVICES

Social workers use a variety of data collection devices including interviews, observation, and analyses of existing written materials. In this section I'll introduce you to these devices and suggest ways they can be used or adapted to fit your particular circumstances.

Interviews

The individual interview or group meeting is probably the most widely used data collection tool. Information obtained by interview is often more complete than written forms of questioning since the interviewer is there to clarify questions, probe ambiguous answers, and tailor the style and pace of the interview to fit the person. The biggest limitation of interviewing is probably its reliance on the verbal ability of the person or group members.[7]

Directive vs. nondirective

It is usually helpful to let clients tell their story in their own way and in their own pace. Broad questions such as, "What can I do for you?" or, "Can you describe to me what happened?" can be used to get things started. Follow-up questions get at the details. Though there may be certain information you need to obtain, the order in which you cover it is kept flexible and responsive to how the interview is developing.

At the opposite extreme is the directive interview where the worker sticks to a scheduled set of questions. This way of structuring the interview is often necessary when collecting data for research or administrative (record-keeping) purposes. It is easier to analyze and summarize the data from a community survey if all respondents are asked the same questions in the same way.

Setting ground rules

Interviews or group meetings can be structured by establishing ground rules for content and participation. For example, suppose you were conducting a meeting of an agency task force. By making explicit the issues that were (or were not) appropriate for the group to consider, you could either prevent the discussion from wandering all over the place or help open up an overly constrictive view of the group's task.

When interviewing a family you might ask each person to take a turn explaining how they see the family's problems. To prevent interruption and argument, family members are requested to wait their turn and state their point of view without passing judgment on what other family members have said.[8] How well the family is able to handle such rules provides further information for the worker.

Physical setting

Some people view a home visit as an intrusion while others welcome the convenience of not having to make arrangements for transportation and child care. Some people feel intimidated by the formal official setting of the worker's office while others are motivated to talk there. By negotiating the location of the meeting you communicate your sensitivity and ensure that the interview is conducted in a setting comfortable to the other person. Also, people show different sides of themselves in different settings. A conversation held in a neutral location or on the respondent's turf (such as a coffee shop) may reveal a more natural side of the person.[9] This is especially true when working with teenagers.

The physical layout of your office is another factor to consider. For example, a desk becomes less of a barrier when the client is sitting in full view of the worker rather than in front of the desk.[10]

Pictures

It is said that a picture is worth a thousand words. It can also stimulate a thousand words. A resourceful student I knew was assigned to work with a depressed, reticent, elderly hospital patient. He took a Polaroid picture of her and asked her to tell him about the person in the picture—what she was thinking about, how she was feeling. This technique got the patient talking.

Putting together a collage that represents a person's current life situation or aspirations is another good use of pictures. In a similar vein, I once asked a class to draw a picture of their ideal social agency. People took turns explaining their pictures. A lot more information was obtained than would be from a regular discussion of their experiences of working in agencies. Use of devices such as these should be preceded with some comments about overreliance on verbal communications and the value of expressing thoughts in pictures. People are often self-conscious about their drawing skills and may not have drawn a picture since grade school. However, with a little encouragement and humor most people are willing to give it a try.

Programming the interview with activities like the ones described above adds a rich dimension to the information you are able to obtain.

Questionnaires

Questionnaires and other forms of written data gathering can be used in a variety of ways. One main advantage of the questionnaire is that it saves time and effort compared to other data collection methods. With a minimum of personal contact you can gather information from a large number of people. Questionnaires can also preserve the anonymity of the respondent. When people must openly share their views, the data obtained may be colored by the presence of the worker or others.

Against these advantages you need to weigh the disadavantages of questionnaires. This method of data collection is dependent on people's ability to read and write, and their motivations. People are often reluctant to fill out questionnaires and may provide only terse answers to questions. The questions themselves may be misunderstood or interpreted differently by different respondents. These factors have to be accounted for in your data gathering plan.

As with interviewing, questions vary on where they fall on the directive to non-directive continuum. Questions can be highly structured and sequenced with predetermined response choices, or very open-ended.

Group administered questionnaire

Questionnaires are often useful when you need to determine the knowledge or attitudes of a group. Suppose you are starting a support group for relatives of cancer patients. A quiz covering basic facts about the nature of the disease and its treatment could be given out at one of the meetings. Instead of collecting and grading the quiz you could review the answers, allowing people to assess their own understanding, clarify their misconceptions, and request further information as needed.

I mentioned earlier that the use of questionnaires helps avoid group members biasing or influencing each other's answers. For example, in a budget committee you might ask each person to write down the criteria she or he believes are important for allocating scarce funds. By collecting the answers, you can get an idea of the degree of consensus in the committee without certain prominent members being able to influence the results. Similarly, when interviewing a family, each member can be asked to write down three things he or she likes about each family member and three things he or she dislikes. Reading the responses anonymously and asking the family to guess who wrote it is sometimes used as a way of opening up discussion in the family.[11]

When conducting an evaluation of a program or service, respondent anonymity is often necessary to get honest replies. Self-administered questionnaires may be the only route to go in such situations.

Diaries and logs

Some people like to express themselves in writing and find it a more comfortable way of communicating than verbalizing their thoughts in an interview. People can keep diaries which describe their reactions to important events or the results of things they have tried. Behaviorists often ask clients to record in a daily log the frequency and circumstances surrounding specific behaviors. This not only produces baseline data for planning and evaluation, but also increases the person's self-awareness.

Projective techniques

Instead of posing direct questions, projective techniques elicit a person's thoughts by asking for a response to a purposefully ambiguous stimulus. The sentence completion test is one such device. Unfinished sentences related to some topic are constructed and the person is instructed to complete the sentences. Some examples: "When I get angry I _____." "The trouble with this agency is _____." "My life would be better if_____."

Another example of a projective technique is the Twenty Statements Test. Used primarily to explore self-image, this device asks people to describe themselves in 20 brief statements. Responses can be grouped into such categories as physical traits (e.g., short, fat), affect (e.g., depressed, happy), roles or reference groups (e.g., student, Christian, middle class), and behavioral characteristics (e.g., nervous, shy).

These tests, along with other forms and questionnaires, can be administered during your meeting with the person or assigned as a task to be completed prior to your next session.

Observation

Almost all your activities provide opportunities for gathering data through informal observation. As Simons and Aigner point out, this does not involve being clandestine so much as it involves being astutely aware of what is taking place in your surroundings.[12] However, observation is usually considered a method of data collection when used in a planned way. Like other data gathering devices, there are options in how it is structured. The situation being observed can be a real-life situation or one contrived by the worker. Observations may be systematically recorded on a detailed form or written up in impressionistic notes. The worker can decide to be a participant or non-participant observer.

As a data collection technique, observation has its own strengths and weaknesses. Pincus and Minahan point out a number of advantages and disadvantages.[13] Observation provides data that is relatively independent of people's verbal ability, insightfulness or biases. Data can be collected without placing any demands on the system under study. In fact, observation can often be used regardless of the system's motivation or willingness to cooperate. On the other hand, some events may simply be inaccessible to the worker. Certain kinds of data, such as attitudes and motivations underlying behavior, are not subject to observation. And the worker's presence, as a participant or non-participant observer, may influence the behavior of the system being studied.

Recording observations

When working with a family or other group, your knowledge of group dynamics and your past experiences help you formulate questions which guide your observations. For example, if you are trying to understand the power structure of a committee, you might pay attention to which members support one another on which issues, who contributes what kind of information, whose ideas and comments are sought on which topics, and how disagreements are resolved. Developing a list of questions prior to your observation will sensitize you to pertinent data.

There are also a number of devices for recording data on social interaction that have been developed for research studies.[14] These devices can be adapted to practice.[15] Structured observations recording the frequency and duration of types of selected behaviors are regularly used to evaluate behavior modification interventions. Use of such recording devices usually confine you to the role of non-participant observer.

Structuring the situation being observed

Most of the time you will be observing a natural situation such as a committee meeting or a classroom in a school. Occasionally you can increase the likelihood of obtaining needed data by structuring the situation you are observing.

In the structured family interview the family is given a task contrived by the worker, such as planning a family vacation. The task is designed to elicit certain kinds of interaction, or interaction around certain issues. The family may be divided into various subgroupings (such as parents alone, children alone, or only male members) for purposes of observation.[16]

Minuchin and Montalvo report on a family where the parents related derogatorily toward their children—five boys ranging from 7 to 14 years of age.[17] The boys were asked to try to find something positive to say about each other while the worker and the parents went behind a one-way mirror to watch carefully for relationships and labels used toward the child most consistently portrayed by the parents only as an "idiot, a dull kid." It turned out that the siblings warmly and respectfully related to this child, and were providing buffers to the parents' labels.

Role playing

In an interview or group meeting, role playing can often be used to provide data for observation. For example, in a training school for delinquent teenage girls, I once set up a role play of a court hearing at which a girl is sentenced to the institution. The teenagers played the roles of the judge, the girl, the parents, and the probation officer. The role play not only produced useful information on how the girls viewed their situation, but was an activity in which the girls enjoyed participating. Role playing often stimulates discussion.

As another example, suppose you're working with someone who has experienced difficulties in job interviews. In addition to just asking what kind of problems she or he experienced, you could break into a role play taking the part of the employer. A five-minute role play can sometimes produce as much information as a half-hour interview.

Observing the physical environment

While most of your observations will be directed at people and social interaction, they can also be turned to the physical environment. Pincus and Minahan offer several suggestions of what to look for in studying organizations and communities.[18]

A simple walk through a neighborhood may reveal many things about it. The kinds of food stores, pictures showing in the movie theatre, and newspapers sold at the newsstands tell you much about the ethnic composition. The history of the community is revealed in such symbols as a synagogue which has been converted into a church, and multiple mailboxes on single family homes (indicating conversion to rooming houses).

In studying organizations, status symbols such as size of the office and desk, carpeting, and nearness of reserved parking spaces to the entrance can tell you about the place of an individual in the organization's heirarchy. The furnishings and decor of public institutions often reflect the value the community places on them.

Look around when you visit an institution such as a home for the aged. Do all the rooms look exactly the same, or do they reflect the individuality of the person living in them (through pictures, bedspreads, a chair brought from home)? How up to date are the newspapers and magazines in the dayroom? Are easy to read clocks and calendars in view? Are the dayroom chairs lined up in a row against the walls or arranged in conversational groupings? Such observations give clues to the institution's philosophy.[19]

Existing Written Materials

Sometimes you will be able to find useful data in existing written materials such as case records, newspaper articles, police reports, minutes of committee meetings, surveys and census data. Because these documents were usually written for a purpose unrelated to the problem you are exploring, the data they contain may be incomplete or in a form that is difficult to use. Further, documents can paint a distorted picture, reflecting the selective perception of the author. In spite of such limitations, existing written materials can offer easy access to potentially useful information with little or no involvement required of the system under study.[20]

Individuals and families

Case records are usually available on people who have had previous contact with your agency. School and medical records, as well as records from other agencies, can be obtained with the permission of the client.

Many social workers have mixed feelings about the use of such material prior to the first contact with potential clients. On the positive side, it can acquaint you with their situation and avoid the necessity for requesting information that is already available and annoying for the person to have to repeat. On the negative side, the material may so color your view, that you lose the ability to form your own fresh first impressions of the person and his or her situation. In fact, a case record often reveals as much about the person who wrote it as it does about the person who is the subject of the record. Therefore, these records should be used with caution.

Some information on individuals may be a matter of public record. For example, suppose you were working with a neighborhood association on the problem of poor housing conditions. You could obtain the name of the owner and the value of an apartment building from mortgage and tax records kept by the city. Data on previous citations for building code violations might also be available. The voting record of the city council person representing the area could be examined to determine his or her stand on issues of concern to the neighborhood.

Organizations

There are many written sources of information on agencies and organizations. Suppose you have an interview for a job in a social service agency where you would really like to work. Reading the annual reports of the agency and applications to funding sources can give you a picture of the agency's philosophy, goals, problems and priorities. Such information can help you present yourself in a way that would make you a more desirable candidate for the position. Suppose further that you got the job, only to discover a lot of conflict between subgroups of the staff. You might gain some insight into the problem by reading the minutes of previous staff meetings and directives and memos issued by the administrator.

As another example, a social worker was serving as a consultant to a community group which needed the support of the city's Human Services Resource Board for a project they were developing. She did a systematic review of the minutes of past board meetings noting such data as who attended, items discussed, what subcommittee recommendations were made, who supported what issues, who voted with whom on what issues, what kinds of objections or questions were raised about proposals, and under what circumstances issues were put up for vote, tabled, or sent back to subcommittee. The review uncovered useful information on key board members who needed to be influenced and ways of approaching them.[21] Just as systematic recording can reveal information not detected by more casual observation, a planned method of analyzing written materials may yield more information than a casual reading.

The usefulness of existing written materials depends a great deal on the connections you make between them and the problem you are exploring. A number of years ago I worked on a project that explored the potential impact of converting the numerous county mental hospitals in the state into local treatment centers. Up to that point active treatment cases were sent to the two state hospitals while the county facilities were operated as custodial institutions. Data on the county hospitals were sparse, but we did have statistical records on all patients treated at the two state hospitals. These records included information such as county of residence, diagnosis, severity of illness, type of treatment, and length of hospitalization. Looking at this data we realized that the state hospitals in effect served as *local* treatment facilities for those patients living in the surrounding communities. Different patterns of hospital usage were found for them compared to patients living further away. The comparison provided information that was useful for planning purposes and making projections on the utilization of the proposed decentralized treatment centers.

PLANNING A DATA GATHERING STRATEGY

I've discussed a variety of data collection devices available to you as a social worker. In planning for your data gathering Pincus and Minahan suggest that you combine data gathering with other goals, examine the demands placed on the system under study, use more than one means of data collection, evaluate your sources and check your sample.[22]

Combine Data Gathering with Other Goals

You will often have (or be able to create) choices in ways to collect data. The methods you select can be designed with a dual purpose in mind—to have a beneficial effect on the situation as well as to elicit needed information. For example, part of the business of social work in dealing with problems is sharing our problem-solving skills with people. When gathering data in an interview, let the person know the reasoning behind the questions you are asking (e.g., "I'm asking about Mr. Baum's stake in the situation since we'll need his support at some point."). The explanation for your questions helps the person understand how you are approaching the problem and the hypotheses you are exploring. You are sharing knowledge and information with the people as well as gathering data from them.

Pincus and Minahan point out that a neighborhood survey might be a means to stimulate an awareness of existing problems, provide a new neighborhood group with a task which can give it a feeling of accomplishment, help the group members learn some organizational skills, and provide an opportunity to develop broader contacts in the community.[23]

To cite some other examples, visiting some older adult daycare centers with an elderly client is not only a way to collect information about the different centers but also a way to explore the person's concerns about participating in such a program. Having a teenager make phone calls from your office to find out about job training programs also provides an opportunity to teach him or her to overcome fears about talking to people on the phone. A structured family interview, where each person gets a chance to tell their side of the story while other family members must listen, can serve as a problem-solving model for the family.

Examine the Demands Placed on the Systems Under Study

Filling out a lengthy questionnaire is not only time consuming but often regarded as a burdensome task. Gathering information on a committee by observing meetings and reading minutes of past meetings places no demands on the system under study. Data gathering techniques vary in the nature and extent of the participation required by others. The feasibility of using a particular technique will depend on the participants' perception of the legitimacy and reasonableness of the demands, how motivated they are, and the kind of relationship you have established with them (collaborative vs. adversarial).

Use More Than One Mode When Possible

Every method of data gathering has its own advantages and disadvantages. By using a combination of methods the disadvantages of any single technique can be minimized. This very obvious point is often forgotten in practice. Our reliance on the direct interview can obscure other modes of data collection which can replace or supplement an interview

Evaluate Your Sources

Consider some of the reasons you might be interviewing a school teacher. If you were looking for potential members for a task force, you might be gathering data about the teacher herself. Or you might be after the teacher's view of some problem at the school. Or you might be interested in the progress of a particular student you are working with.

The validity of the same source of information may vary depending on the system your are interested in. If the teacher felt she was being blamed for a student's behavior she might downplay the problem in an interview with the social worker. On the other hand, you might get some accurate information from the same teacher if you were gathering data on the problem of obtaining records of students transferred from other schools.

It is sometimes helpful to distinguish between the person (or system) you are studying and the person (or system) from which you are collecting data. In reading over a client's case record you might learn as much about the person who wrote the record as you do about the client.[24]

Check Your Sample

How adequate is your sample? Practitioners as well as researchers need to be able to answer this question when analyzing their data collection procedures. Suppose a client complains about a job training program. What would you conclude about the program? Is this person's experience typical? Do the majority of participants in the program feel that way? You'd want more than one opinion before drawing any conclusions about the program.

When conducting an interview or observing someone, you are likewise exposed to only a *sample* of the person's behavior. Did you catch the person in a bad mood? Is the setting of the interview making the person nervous? Is the person trying to make a certain impression on you? Keeping such questions in mind will help you avoid jumping to premature conclusions.

ENDING NOTE

In this chapter I have provided an overview of the preparation phase and discussed ways of gathering data. Sometimes data collection gets dominated by the need to fill out forms.

"Forms, forms, forms. Help! I'm drowning in paperwork!" Perhaps you've heard that desperate cry emanating from the hallways of a social agency. In the course of exploring a problem you will be collecting much data about the situation. Some of it will be data you need for problem solving. Some will be data the agency needs for its own purposes. Bureaucracies have ferocious appetites for data. The data they need may have more to do with legal or statutory reporting requirements, insurance companies, agency accountability, administrative planning and so on than with the specific problem or situation of concern to you.

The creative generalist is challenged to prevent bureaucratic data needs from overshadowing his or her own data gathering needs related to the problem at hand. It will take more than a little alchemy to meet this challenge, but you can begin in small ways. You can attempt to convert agency requirements for filling out forms into more productive data gathering sessions with people. Though they may become a routine and boring part of your work, you must avoid becoming humdrum in asking the questions and recording the answers. Filling out forms is a problem shared by both you and the potential client. The forms should be worked on from the same side of the table, filled out in full view of both, questioned and wondered about by both.

Join me next in Chapter 11 where we will continue our exploration of the preparation phase.

Preparation (problems) 11

The last chapter provided an overview of the preparation phase and explored methods of data gathering. As we move on to consider what we do with that data in understanding a problem, I want to make a distinction between "data" and "information." Data becomes information when you attribute some meaning to it. Information doesn't reside in the data but in the questions you ask of the data, the perspectives from which you view it, the ways you arrange it. Understanding a problem involves converting data into information.[1]

ORGANIZING DATA ON PROBLEMS

One way of extracting meaning from data is by arranging it into configurations that create order. We do this with the aid of techniques that help us sort the data according to the parts of the problem, arrange the data in ways that make it easier to explore relationships within and between the parts, and visualize and construct different representations of the problem.

The mind is like an automatic pattern-making machine, creating order and meaning out of arriving data.[2] Once a pattern gets established it is difficult to break, even when new data doesn't fit the pattern. In exploring a problem we want to shift from automatic pilot to manual controls and take charge of the patterns being formed. There are several techniques that help us take charge. They utilize different combinations of rational and intuitive thinking.

Problem Outlines

An outline is a way of sorting data according to the different dimensions or parts of a problem. The categories of the outline reflect the social work perspective on problems we discussed in Chapter 2 (pragmatic, holistic, and political). An outline can be used as a checklist, reminding us of aspects of a problem we may have overlooked.

Don't expect the outline I present to fit every problem you encounter. You'll need to use it flexibly and adapt it to your own situation. It is merely suggestive of what to include. As you gain experience with certain types of problems such as domestic violence or developmental disabilities, you will learn what important elements of these problems need to be considered in your outline.

Key people or systems: A good starting place is a listing of the key people or systems involved in the situation. Eventually you will sort these people into client system (who has engaged your services), action system (whose aid you are enlisting in the problem-solving effort) and target system (at whom your strategies are directed). Legal, medical, financial and other aspects of a problem will suggest particular systems to include in your outline.

The situation of concern: As I discussed before, it is often difficult to obtain a clear statement of the problem. You are more likely to get evaluations of a situation rather than a description. What you want to include here are data that reflect how the situation might be described in non-evaluative terms by someone who doesn't have a stake in it.

The situation perceived as a problem: Problems reside in people's perceptions of a situation. How do each of the people involved see the events taking place? How do each define the situation as a problem? What life tasks confront the people involved? What concerns do they have about the situation? What would they like to see done about it? You will have gathered some of this data during your initial contacts.

Parts people are playing in the problem: What are each of the key people or systems doing that seems to be contributing to the problem or preventing it from being resolved? What are people doing that seems to be helpful in dealing with the problem? What characteristics (sex, ethnicity, social status, occupation) affect the way people view and interact with the problem?

Dynamics of the problem: What are the sub-parts of the problem? How do the sub-parts feed into each other? How are outside systems and conditions affecting the problems? What is the relationship of the "public issue" to the "private trouble?" Are there particular times, places or events associated with the occurrence of the problem?

History of the problem: How long has the problem been going on? Is it cyclical in nature? What has been tried in the past to deal with the problem, under what conditions, and with what results?

Extent of the problem: How extensive, serious or pervasive is the problem? What aspects need immediate attention?

Obstacles: What seem to be the major roadblocks to solving the problem? Who benefits from maintaining the problem? What resources or conditions would facilitate dealing with the problem? What constraints are there in dealing with the problem?

Resources: What resources are available to deal with the problem? Who is motivated to work on it? How can those motivations be harnessed?

Matrices

While outlines help us identify the parts of a problem, we also need ways to relate the parts to each other. A matrix is a simple tool for this purpose. In a matrix, two or more dimensions of a problem are laid out in relation to each other. For example, suppose you are dealing with the problem faced by a young mother who is recuperating after a serious operation. One dimension is the sub-problems in the situation—how to arrange for childcare, housekeeping, transportation to the clinic, possible loss of a job due to long absence from work, insufficient funds to cover medical costs. Another dimension is the key people and systems who are or could potentially be resources in the situation. A matrix composed of these two dimensions is shown in Figure 11.1.

Figure 11.1: PROBLEM-RESOURCE MATRIX

PROBLEM

PERSON OR SYSTEM	Childcare	Housekeeping	Job	Money
Mother				
Sister				
Neighbor				
School				
County Social Service Dept.				

Filling in the boxes of the matrix helps us see more readily how key people might be used as resources, for which problems adequate resources exist, and where the "holes" are. Also, by forcing us to look at every possible connection the matrix may stimulate new ideas. For example, we may have thought of the neighbor as a resource for child care. But putting "neighbor" and "job" together might lead to the discovery that the neighbor works part time at a place that currently has some job openings.

Circles map

In Part II we devoted an entire chapter to the circles map and discussed why it is a major tool of the creative generalist. As you might have anticipated, it is an indispensable tool in the preparation phase.

Let's review some of the features of the circles map that make it such a powerful tool for organizing data. By constructing a visual representation of a problem or situation (using such cues as size of circles, placement of circles relative to each other, and types of connecting lines) the circles map has great summary power. It can hold large amounts of data and capture complexity, while giving a feel for the whole of a problem. The circles map also allows you to focus on one aspect of a problem without losing the sense of the whole. You can zoom in and scan across data, making it easier to discover relationships of the parts of a problem to each other and to the whole.

Working with people individually or in groups, the circles map is a tool for simultaneously collecting, recording and ordering data. Inviting participation in constructing the maps also increases the likelihood of arriving at a mutual understanding of the problem.

In Chapter 6 we offered some examples of the use of the circles map and referred you to an article by Ann Hartman which explains their use in assessing family relationships.[3] Social workers who use the circles map to lay out a client's personal network (family, friends, neighbors) find they are able to gather a lot of information about the person in a very short period of time. Making note of the nature of the relationships within the network, types of resources and directions in which those resources flow is a good way of getting an overview of the client's situation. It is also helpful to clients in taking stock of their situation and developing new insights. Understanding a person's natural helping network is important for the planning process.

The personal network map can be elaborated to include major systems the person is connected to (e.g., school, work, legal system, church) and additional notations such as stake in the problem and motivation to work on it. The circles map sharpens social work's focus on the interaction of people and their environment.

While mapping personal networks is a helpful tool for understanding a person, I want to emphasize that there is a difference between assessing a person and assessing a problem or situation. In social work the "center circle" is the problem or situation rather than the person. For example, consider the circles map Mike did on the student apartment problem in Chapter 7. While knowledge of the student's skills and attributes was important to understanding the problem, the assessment focused on her situation rather than on her as a person.

PRIORITIZING PROBLEMS

In exploring a situation you may identify a number of interrelated problems. For example, a family situation may involve trouble with the kids at school, alcoholism, and financial difficulties. A neighborhood association may be concerned about traffic safety, public transportation and vandalism. Since you can't do everything at once, you and the client need to determine which problem to start with. Two factors go into this decision: the desires of the client and strategic considerations.

Client Preference

At times what the client wants is very clear. For example, in a crisis or emergency, immediate needs for food, shelter, safety or medical care will likely demand your attention. Or some aspect of a situation such as resolving a child custody dispute or dealing with creditors may be most pressing and the client will readily let you know his or her concern. In some instances, however, the client may have difficulty stating what is most important. You may have to engage in "active listening." What emphasis do you pick up in the way the client describes the situation? What seems to arouse the most emotion? What issues does the client keep returning to? You don't want to draw conclusions from such observations, but use them to reflect on priorities with the client. "You've mentioned conflicts with your brother-in-law several times. How much of a problem is it for you?"

When working with a group, it's often useful to use a structured method of helping the client system identify priorities. For example, with families you could use the method where each person takes turns saying what he or she would like to change in the family, or writes down a list of the three most important family problems. Such methods ensure that each person has input into setting priorities.

With large groups or organizations, the nominal group technique mentioned by Mike in Chapter 6 works very well.[4] Suppose a newly formed neighborhood association asks for your help in setting priorities for the coming year. Being aware that in open meetings a few vocal people can dominate the discussion, you suggest the following procedure:

Step 1 Each person at the meeting is asked to write down a list of at least three neighborhood problems he or she is most concerned with. Specifying a minimum number helps prod people's thinking.

Step 2 Go round robin in the group, each person offering one item from his or her list. The items are recorded verbatim on a blackboard with no discussion permitted. Continue round the group until there are no new items offered.

Step 3 The listing is reviewed to clarify the items and make sure everyone understands what they mean. Items covering more than one problem can be separated and similar items can be combined. Some people may be tempted at this step to criticize the choices of others or defend their own items. Be a strict monitor and don't allow any evaluative comments. Remind the group that they will each have a chance later in the process to present their point of view.

Step 4 Each person picks the three most important problems from the list and rank orders them, giving three points to the most important item, two to the second most and one to the third most. You then tally up the points. Other variations include rank ordering all the items, rating each item on a scale from one to five (from *not important* to *very important*), or simply selecting a given number of items from the list.

Use of this type of procedure will help broaden the participation in a group where a few members dominate discussion. After the problems are prioritized, small groups can be formed to discuss the top items.

Strategic Considerations

I've discussed various methods of identifying what problem in the situation the client regards as most pressing or important. In deciding on priorities we also need to take into account which problem, if resolved first, would have the greatest overall positive effect on the situation. For example, suppose you are working with a woman who is concerned about her boyfriend's alcoholism, getting a better paying job, and meeting new people. She is most troubled about the alcoholism, but the boyfriend's refusal to acknowledge the problem and the woman's fear of confronting him may not make it feasible to tackle that problem head on at the moment. An alternative might be to first focus on taking some nightschool classes in order to improve her job skills. The classes might be a way to make new friends, and being gone a couple of nights a week may take some of the pressure off of dealing with her boyfriend. A better paying job might also improve her self-esteem, perhaps opening her up to alternatives in her relationship with her boyfriend that she is now hesitant to consider. When it's not feasible to work on the most pressing problem, you can pick one that has the strongest linkages to it.

Let's look at another example. Suppose you are working with a neighborhood association. Because of the apathy of neighborhood residents, and previous setbacks, the morale of the group is very low.

This must be taken into consideration in deciding which neighborhood problem the group should take on. Since a success would bolster the group and give it confidence in tackling other issues, a problem with high success probability might be considered a priority. If attracting new members is important for the organization, then it might be best to go with a problem that touches the greatest number of neighborhood residents or is likely to produce the most publicity.

One final example. Suppose a fire at a downtown YMCA has destroyed half the available temporary housing for the city's homeless. Though adequate housing for this group of people may have been a long standing problem, the fire suddenly raises community concern over the issue. The timing may be ripe to pull out those proposals for dealing with the problem that have been sitting on the shelf for lack of support.

Timing, feasibility and the *linkages* among the problems in the situation—these are what I call strategic considerations in determining priorities. Combined with client preference, they help you and the client decide which problem to focus your energies on. Drawing a circles map of the problems in the situation will help reveal their interconnections. This tool is especially useful when the client experiences the problems in the situation as "one big muddle." Not knowing how to disentangle them from one another or where to begin in dealing with the situation may be the main difficulty facing the client. In such instances, reviewing and sorting out the various problems in the situation becomes a necessary first task.

FRAMING PROBLEMS

We have discussed ways of ordering and organizing data to understand the problem or situation you are working on. Sometimes the very way that the data has been organized (how the problem has been defined or framed) hampers our understanding and prevents us from finding a solution. The problem may need to be redefined and seen from a fresh perspective to get a handle on it. Your data may need to be *disorganized*. You may need to identify and challenge assumptions that lock certain patterns into place and overcome blocks that constrict your view of the problem. In the course of the preparation phase you will go back and forth between organizing data and redefining the problem.

A problem can be considered a gap between where you are and where you want to be. Problem definition is the bridge to solutions. We usually have or can create choices in how we are defining or framing a problem. Different definitions lead to consideration of different solutions. In this sense, problem definition and solution finding can be considered a simultaneous process. You can develop an ingenious solution, but if it solves the wrong problem, it won't do any good.

A flexible attitude toward defining problems and a willingness to shift perceptions, challenge assumptions and break patterns are essential for effective problem solving. Problem redefinition is hampered by overcommitment to a particular approach, excessive logic, unwillingness to speculate, excessive deference to experts, and other perceptual, emotional and cultural blocks.[5] The techniques discussed below can be considered as ways to overcome such blocks.

The "How To" Technique

This is one of the simplest, yet most effective, techniques I have run across. What you do is state the situation or problem in as many different ways as possible, all starting with the words, "How to..." These words tend to keep the definitions action focused and specific.

Suppose that you are working with a committee dealing with housing conditions in a central city slum. A concern of the committee is that children are getting lead poisoning from eating paint chips peeling from the wall. If you asked the committee to think of as many ways as possible to frame the situation as a problem, starting with the words "How to...," you might generate a list that looked like this:

— How to prevent lead poisoning in children which is caused by the ingestion of paint chips.

— How to get kids to stop eating paint chips.

— How to educate parents to the danger of eating paint chips.

— How to get companies to stop manufacturing paint that contains lead.

— How to enforce building codes that prohibit the use of lead paint.

— How to get quicker medical care for children who get lead poisoning.

— How to immunize kids against lead poisoning.

— How to prevent kids from being hungry.

— How to make paint chips nutritious.

— How to make paint chips taste so bad that kids won't want to eat them.

— How to keep paint from peeling.

— How to keep kids busy enough so they won't eat paint chips.

— How to get influential people in the community concerned about the problem of kids eating paint chips.

I stated earlier that problem definition is the bridge to solution. The different definitions on the above list imply different strategies and different "target" systems (e.g., kids, parents, landlords, housing inspectors). We often define problems in terms of how to prevent people from doing something (e.g., kids from eating paint chips or skipping school) rather than how to help them do something they are motivated to do (e.g., make paint chips nutritious or turn the community into a classroom). It's much more difficult to deal with problems that are framed the former way. Sometimes there may be little choice but to constrain someone's behavior, but other definitions of the problem should be exhausted first.

Another thing we can observe from the list is that some "how to's" represent broad statements of the problem (e.g., how to prevent lead poisoning which is caused by ingestion of paint chips) while others represent more specific definitions (e.g., how to make the paint chips taste bad). Problem solving involves a successive movement from global to more specific definitions.

Even if you don't deliberately generate a "how to" list, you can still be *listening* for different definitions of the problem in your discussions with people. The more you practice generating such lists, the better you'll get at identifing alternative definitions.

You can generate "how to's" by yourself, with another person, or in a group setting. When in a group, make sure people don't start evaluating each other's definitions. And encourage "outrageous" items such as "How to make paint chips nutritious." Suggestions met with laughter usually indicate a novel perspective on the problem (like the punch line of a joke). The item may not be practical, but the perspective it opens may prove useful to explore.

What is the Problem a Solution to?

Problems and solutions are often different perspectives on the same situation. To a group of teenagers, hanging out on the street corner is a solution (where can we go to meet friends and get away from the house?). To local merchants, who are concerned about attracting customers to a downtown location, the teenagers behavior may be viewed as a problem.

Posing the simple question, "What is the problem a solution to?" can open new perspectives and help generate alternative definitions of the problem. If eating paint chips is a problem, we can ask, "What is eating paint chips a solution to?" Hunger? Boredom? The possible alternatives suggest hypotheses to be checked out with further data gathering. The problem of eating paint chips might get converted to the problem of how to prevent hunger or boredom.

In a similar vein it is often useful to view a problem as an opportunity. The lead poisoning may provide an opportunity to mobilize community support for stricter enforcement of housing codes in general. Sometimes you link your wants or objectives to the problem at hand. Suppose you have to do a research project for your social work degree and don't want to do it, can't get enthused or just plain don't have a topic you want to study. You have a problem. Start with what you are currently interested in doing, e.g., exploring job possibilities after graduation. Use your associative thinking to link the two. How can a research project be an opportunity to explore the job market for yourself. A study of how recently employed social workers found their jobs might fit the bill. Asking what the problem could be a solution to, will help reveal the opportunities hiding in the problem.

Problem-Purpose Expansion

This next technique is a form of means-ends analysis based on the work of Gerald Nadler.[6] It helps you clarify your objectives and make sure you are solving the right problem. To illustrate the technique, consider the following problem:[7]

> You are traveling north for an important meeting. Your employer is sending you to learn about a new product he would like to buy and market. On one of the lonelier stretches of road about twenty miles from your destination, your car blows a tire. You pull over to the side of the road and go to the trunk to get out the jack. After assembling the jack under your bumper you discover that the latch which holds and releases the main support is broken. You want to fix the latch on the jack.

The initial problem formulation is "to fix the latch on the jack." This formulation leads to such solutions as finding a new latch and improvising a latch from another tool. With the problem-purpose expansion technique you restate the problem in the following form:

I WANT _____,

IN ORDER _____.

Thus the car-jack problem could be restated as:

I WANT to fix the latch on the jack,

IN ORDER to raise the car.

This reformulation leads you to search for ways of raising the car, e.g., borrowing a jack or looking for two small ramps. The reformulation process can continue as follows:

I WANT to raise the car,

IN ORDER to fix the tire.

Solutions: Patch the tire; dig a hole in the ground beneath the tire.

I WANT to fix the tire,

IN ORDER to get to the meeting on time.

Solutions: Call to say you will be late; call to ask someone at the meeting to pick you up.

I WANT to get to the meeting on time,

IN ORDER to get information on the new product.

Solutions: Reschedule the meeting; send a different representative.

Each reformulation further clarifies the main objective and suggests new approaches to the problem. As this example illustrates, the less constrictive you are in the way you formulate your problem, the greater the range of possible solutions you open up.

As a further example, let's look at the following situation involving a student who was conducting an investigation of a child neglect complaint. She found that the mother, a single parent, was taking adequate care of her four-year-old daughter. However, the child was isolated from other children and the student thought it would be beneficial for the child to participate in a daycare center. The mother was hesitant about the suggestion. The problem the student brought to class for consultation was: How to get the mother to enroll her child in day care. Viewing the problem from the mother's perspective, her resistance was understandable. She saw the daycare center suggestion as leading to involvement with the "welfare department" and as an affront to her abilities as a mother. Recognizing that the original framing of the problem was in a negative form (how to get someone to do something they didn't want to do), we did a reformulation:

I WANT to get the child enrolled in a daycare center,

IN ORDER for her to be able to socialize with other children.

We then generated ideas on ways for the child to have a socialization experience. One solution called for getting the mother connected with a babysitting pool. This idea would not only solve the problem of exposure to other children but provide some respite for the mother and expand her circle of resources. It was a suggestion that the mother did like and adopt. The reformulation led away from solutions that would have exacerbated the problem to one that had positive spinoffs.

Sometimes you can clarify your objectives by simply engaging in some wishful thinking. Ask yourself (or the client) to complete such sentences as: "What I really want is…," "What I would really like to do (or see happen) is…," "If I could remove all the constraints in the situation, I would…," "If I had the power to change things, I would…."

Substituting the words "I want" for "you should" in discussing a problem can be helpful in shifting perspectives (e.g., "You should pay attention to what I say," vs., "I want you to pay attention to what I say"). It changes the focus from a tone of moral imperative to a straightforward statement of need. It opens up exploration of getting your wants met, as opposed to the more constrictive formulation of getting someone else to comply with your demands.

Challenging Assumptions

The nine-dot problem offers a good illustration of the effects of unchallenged assumptions on problem solving. The problem is presented in Figure 11.2. Give it a try before looking up the answer at the end of the chapter.

Figure 11.2: THE NINE DOT PROBLEM

Connect the nine dots with no more than four straight
lines without lifting your pencil from the paper

Looking at the answer, you'll notice that the solution requires challenging an assumption that people almost inevitably make in approaching this problem, namely that you have to work within the boundaries defined by the nine dots. This is not a restriction imposed in the statement of the problem but one that people tend to impose with their perception of the problem. And it is this unnecessary assumption that prevents the problem from being solved. The alternative solutions to the problem each suggest other assumptions that could be challenged.

Challenging assumptions is a way to generate alternative perspectives on a problem. But to challenge an assumption you have to be aware that you are making one. How do you do that? The techniques for reframing problems discussed earlier are also ways of identifying assumptions. (Challenging assumptions, breaking patterns and shifting perspectives are, of course, all interrelated. One leads to the other.) The "How to..." list you generate or list of ways that the problem is a solution can be scanned for assumptions. You can also write down a brief statement of the problem and review it, raising questions about each word or phrase in the statement as you go along. Staring at the word or phrase is actually a good stimulus for generating questions.

"What information do I have that supports or refutes this assumption or hypothesis?" "What kind of data would help me place confidence in the way I'm looking at the problem?" The assumptions you identify and hypotheses you generate determine what further data you need to collect.

Combining the Circles Map with Other Techniques

I already reviewed the power of the circles map as a tool in organizing data. It can also serve as a stimulation tool in shifting perspectives. By changing your center circle or otherwise rearranging the circles you can often develop a new perspective or generate a new way to frame the problem. Circles maps are often used in combination with the other techniques described in this chapter. To illustrate how the various problem-framing techniques work together, I'll take you through an exploration of a problem.

> In a geriatric ward of a mental hospital, housing about 20 patients, the staff is concerned about patients who wander into the rooms of other patients by mistake and cause a disturbance. At any one time there seem to be 3-4 patients who have difficulty finding their own rooms. Sara, the ward social worker, is asked by the administrator to come

up with a plan to help these patients find their own rooms and present the plan at next Friday's staff meeting.

A week has almost past. It is late Thursday afternoon. Sara still hasn't come up with anything to present at tomorrow's staff meeting. In hopes of stimulating some ideas she walks through the ward and occupational therapy room and jots down a list of items which catch her eye. The list turns out like this:

> 1 public address system
> 1 small tape recorder
> a variety of old magazines
> a head nurse with a good singing voice
> 1 box of Christmas tree lights
> 12 plants
> 1 student psychologist who likes elderly people
> 5 10x12-inch mirrors
> 600 feet of string
> 4 boxes of crayons
> a large pad of drawing paper
> 3 overworked nurses aides
> 2 boxes of assorted candy
> 1 bowl of assorted fruits
> 17 safety pins

Back in her office Sara ponders the list and tries to think of a plan for dealing with the problem.

Suppose you were Sara. How would you solve this problem? Take a few moments to generate some ideas. Practice deferring judgment. Don't censure your ideas or worry at this point about how practical they are. When you finish your list, I'll share with you the solutions typically generated when I present this problem to classes and workshop groups.

Here is a typical listing which comes from brainstorming groups:

1. Put a colored patch on the patient and the same color patch on his/her door.

2. Put a different plant in each room to make the room easier to identify.

3. Tie one end of a string to the patient and the other end to his/her door.

4. Have the student psychologist set up a behavior modification program which uses the candy and fruit to reward patients when they find their own rooms.

5. Lock the doors of the patients who are being disturbed.

6. Use Christmas tree lights to point out paths to different rooms.

7. Put a mirror on the door and a picture of the patient next to the mirror. If the faces match when they look in the mirror, then they will know it's their room.

8. Have the head nurse sing into the PA system a song to the patients which gives them directions to their own room.

9. Make a party for the staff so they can relax.

The first point this example illustrates is that pressures of the job can lead us into jumping directly from an initial problem statement into developing solutions. The whole idea of the preparation phase is that we need to explore and understand a problem before looking for solutions. Otherwise we may end up solving the wrong problem, acting on unverified assumptions, or developing ineffective solutions.

Did you raise questions in your mind about the nature of the problem when you generated your solutions? Did you spot any assumptions about the problem or appropriate target systems in the list of solutions? Let's go through the process of exploring the problem and then we'll return and reexamine these solutions. In exploring the problem we'll move back and forth between organizing data, reframing the problem, and identifying further data needed to clarify the problem.

I'll be illustrating the use of the various techniques presented in this chapter. In practice, you are not likely to use all of them on the same problem—one or two will usually be sufficient. My purpose here, however, is to give you a better feel for the use of these techniques by showing the similarities and differences in the information they produce. Let's start with a circles map (see Figure 11.3):

Figure 11.3

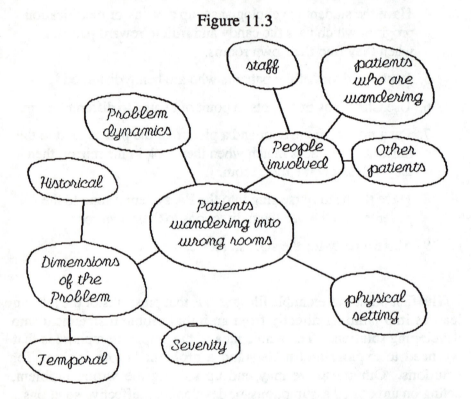

The situation occupies the center circle. The labels for the other circles come from adapting the general problem outline to this specific problem. At the same time we record the information we have, we also begin to generate questions about each circle and identify further data needed to gain an understanding of the problem. For example, how do the people involved view the situation? Could the physical setting be affecting the patients' behavior? Are there certain times of the day or week when the problem is worse? Out of this first round of questions the data-gathering plan begins to evolve. As we reframe the problem we uncover assumptions and formulate hypotheses that need to be checked out. This further shapes our data gathering plans. In gathering data we would of course rely on several modes, including interviewing, observation, and use of existing records.

Another way to begin exploring the problem is to review the initial statement of the problem, underlining the words and phrases that need clarification or contain assumptions that need to be check out. Let's try it.

> In a geriatric ward of a mental hospital, housing about 20 patients, the staff are concerned about patients who wander into the rooms of other patients by mistake and cause a disturbance. At any one time there seems to be 3-4 patients who have difficulty finding their own rooms. Sara, the ward social worker, is asked by the administrator to come up with a plan to help these patients find their own rooms and present the plan at next Friday's meeting.

"the staff are concerned" - Who on the staff are concerned? All of them? How much of a problem is it? Who has actually complained about it? What specifically concerns them about the situation?

"by mistake" - How do we know it is by mistake? What are some competing explanations? What evidence supports the different explanations?

"cause a disturbance" - Who is disturbed by their behavior? The staff, other patients, the patients who are wandering? What kind of disturbance is caused?

"3-4 patients" - Is it the same patients each time or do all of them exhibit this behavior at one time or another?

"social worker is asked to come up with a plan" - Is it the social worker's responsibility? Should she be working alone or involve others in developing a plan? Is there a common solution to this problem or does a separate plan have to be developed for each patient?

"to help the patients find their rooms" - Is this the most appropriate way to frame the problem? What are some alternatives?

"next Friday's staff meeting" - Why this time limit? Is the staff meeting the best place to present the plan?

The circles map and problem statement analysis helps us raise questions about how the situation is being viewed. To generate alternative views we can pose the question, "What is the problem a solution to?"

Viewed as a solution, wandering into the wrong room may be a way to deal with boredom, wanting more social contact with other patients, wanting attention from the staff or help in finding their rooms. These explanations could be added to the more obvious ones involving lack of motivation or cognitive abilities.

At this point we might make use of a matrix to help organize our thoughts on ways of viewing the patients' behavior. Down the rows of the matrix we could list the competing explanations or assumptions. The columns of the matrix could be used for categories such as data supporting the assumption, data refuting the assumption, additional data we need to collect, and ways of collecting the data. The matrix would be one way of assuring that we systematically explored each of the assumptions.

Another perspective shifting question we discussed earlier is, "What is the problem an opportunity for?" The ideas this question stimulates will depend a great deal on your ongoing "agendas." For example, one of your concerns as a social worker in this setting might be that the staff is not involved enough in joint problem solving with the patients. Such a concern might lead you to frame the problem as, "How can I use the situation to set an example of ways that staff and patients can work together on ward problems." Or you might be concerned that the physical environment of the ward is drab and dehumanizing. If you can show that the physical environment contributes to the problem (e.g., the doors to the rooms all look the same and the corridors are not easily distinguished from one another), you might be able to support a request for painting on the basis of the patients' health and safety. Such agenda items come from your internalized definitions of social work, your values and your sense of vocation.

Reviewing the circles map may suggest additional opportunities the problem presents. For example, let's deliberately shift our focus from the patients who are wandering into the wrong rooms to the other patients on the ward. Put these patients in the center circle for the moment and consider how the problematic situation might be a resource in helping them. When these patients return to a community setting, they will need to deal with people they don't want to see who knock on their doors. In teaching them strategies for dealing with the wandering patients they can learn some valuable social skills at the same time the ward problem is being dealt with. You might also set up some kind of buddy system where the patients who are closer to discharge can be in a helper role for the more confused patients.

A circles map of the different opportunities presented by the situation is a good way to organize this information. It will help you notice connections between circles (new patterns) that will be useful in designing solutions.

Another reframing technique we've discussed is the Problem-Purpose Expansion. With this technique you start with the original statement of purpose and reframe as follows:

I WANT to help the patients find their rooms,

IN ORDER to eliminate the disturbances on the ward.

I WANT to eliminate the disturbances on the ward,

IN ORDER for the ward to run more smoothly
and ease the pressures on the staff.

The Problem-Purpose Expansion reframing could take a different direction:

I WANT to help the patients find their rooms,

IN ORDER for them to learn socially appropriate behavior.

I WANT them to learn socially appropriate behavior,

IN ORDER to speed their release from the hospital.

The first direction leads toward solutions that involve staffing patterns and ward procedures. The other direction focuses on treatment goals of patients. The fact that the same problem can lead you in both directions suggests that the solution might need to address both aspects.

Last, but not least, let me reintroduce that trusty workhorse, the "How to..." technique. If you recall, this technique simply asks us to restate the problem in as many different ways as possible, starting with the words "How to".

1. How to help the patients find their rooms.

2. How to prevent the patients from leaving their rooms.

3. How to prevent them from wandering into other rooms.

4. How to increase the tolerance of others on the ward for their behavior.

5. How to get staff more time to deal with the wandering patients.

6. How to make the wandering serve a purpose.

7. How to make the patients' rooms attractive enough that they will want to find their own rooms.

8. How to help the patients identify their own rooms.

9. How to arrange the ward so rooms are easier to find.

10. How to help the staff keep track of the patients.

Arranging the "How to" list into a circles map will help you identify the different perspectives on the problem and different assumptions about it represented in the list of items. To construct the map, you pick out items that seem to be related and jot down each related group of items around a blank circle. For example, items 5 and 10 both mention staff. Items 4 and 6 are similar in that they *don't* focus on eliminating the wandering behavior. A partial circles map of the "How to" list is shown in Figure 11.4. Rather than arranging items according to predetermined circles (organizing function), the purpose here is *to discover* the designation (category) for a circle by looking for the commonality in related items. Once we discover a category, we can generate other items that would fit that category.

Figure 11.4

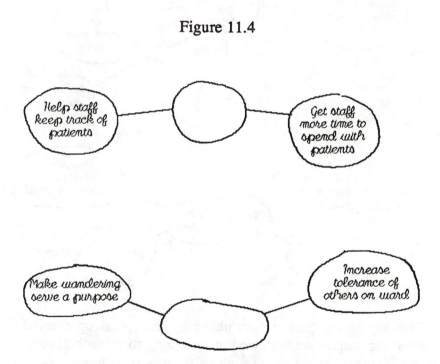

The staff circle could be labeled "staff as target system" or "making it easier for the staff to deal with the problem." Our attention is shifted from the patients to the staff. We would now generate some additional items that would fit the category such as, "How to get more staff," or, "How to prevent the staff from getting upset over the problem." The other circle could be designated "making the problem not a problem." Here our attention is shifted from eliminating the offensive behavior to eliminating the perceptions or context in which it gets so labeled. Additional items from this category might include, "How to insure that patients only have access to their own rooms, How to eliminate private rooms, and How to set up a buddy system among the patients." Our circles map would now appear as in Figure 11.5.

Figure 11.5

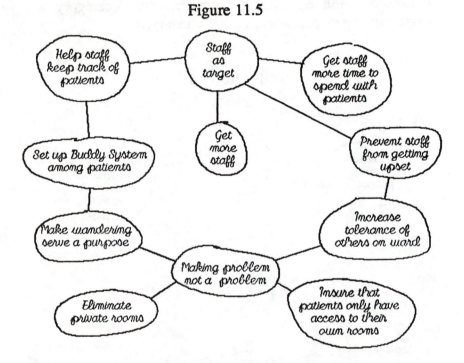

The key to the preparation phase is perceptual openness. The various techniques we reviewed in the wrong room problem are ways of maintaining openness through shifting perspectives, challenging assumptions and breaking patterns (or reminders to do so). Having explored the problem, go back now to the original list of solutions we generated at the beginning of the example. You should more easily spot the assumptions and perspectives on the problem that the various solutions contain. You'll note a bias toward attributing the problem to the inability of the patients to recognize their rooms and viewing the patients as the target system. Though our exploration of the problem might lead us to such a conclusion, we need to consider other alternatives to make sure we are on the right track. A solution might be quite novel or original (e.g., the one about use of a mirror on the door) but if it solves the wrong problem it's not worth much.

I mentioned earlier that you won't need to employ every technique on a given problem. You'll use them selectively, especially when you get stuck. The more you practice perceptual openness the more it will become a natural way of thinking for you. Together with the circles map as an organizing and stimulating tool, you'll be prepared for the preparation phase.

KNOWING WHEN YOU ARE FINISHED PREPARING

After you've collected data, organized and reorganized it, developed an understanding of the situation, established priorities and framed the problem, you may still find yourself bothered by a few nagging questions, "Did I draw the 'right' boundaries around the probem? Did I collect enough data? Did I frame the problem appropriately?"

We are always operating with a less than complete understanding of the problem. In the design phase we will continue adding to our knowledge of the problem and revising our understanding. In the preparation phase we want enough of an understanding to set some direction for the design phase. The problem outline can be used as a checklist to see if you have covered the various aspects of the problem. In the last chapter, I suggested you could analyze your data collection methods by examining the demands placed on the system under study, looking at the advantages and disadvantages of each method used, evaluating your data sources, and checking your sample. Such an analysis will help you place confidence in your data.

The most important outcome of your preparation is the way you frame the problem. Ultimately, the test of your problem formulation is its utility in the design phase—does it provide a basis for developing a plan that can resolve the problem. There are, however, some questions you can ask at the end of the preparation phase to review your problem formulation. I'll conclude this chapter with a brief discussion of these questions.

Does It Agree with the Client's Way of Thinking?

The way the problem is framed should make sense to the person, should be congenial to the person's way of thinking and categorizing reality.[8] We want to arrive, with the potential client, at a mutual understanding of the problem. In this chapter I've given examples of ways to collaborate with potential clients in activities such as drawing a circles map. By actively involving the person in gathering data and exploring the problem you will be continually checking out your perceptions with him or her.

If you negotiated a tentative working agreement with the potential client to explore the problem and examine options, then you should specifically set aside time to review what you've both done, take stock, and decide on the next steps.

Does It Feel Right?

Sometimes when you hit upon a way of framing a problem, something "clicks." You intuitively sense it's a useful definition. Allow your intuitive side to participate along with your analytical side in evaluating your formulation of the problem.

Does It Avoid Unnecessary Assumptions?

There are few problems that don't have some built in constraints. However, problem solving is often hampered by *unnecessary* assumptions which we build into the definition of a problem. A good redefinition eliminates needless constraints and opens up many avenues to possible solutions.

Does It Go with the Grain?

A good problem formulation "goes with the grain." It frames a problem in a way that utilizes motivation and other resources in building a bridge to a solution. What we label "resistance" is often motivation toward a goal which is in opposition to our goal. Thinking in terms of resistance leads to strategies of applying an opposing force that is stronger than the resistance. Thinking in terms of motivation leads to strategies which build on or utilize the force of the motivation.

The principle here is similar to the martial arts strategy of using the resistance to your advantage rather than fighting it. Reframing is a way we do that in problem solving. I've mentioned before that many problems in social work get formulated as how to prevent someone from doing something they want to do, or how to get someone to do something they don't want to do. Problems framed this way are the most difficult to solve.

Focusing on assets rather than liabilities helps in developing a positive framing of a problem. For example, student social workers who regard their status only as a liability might define their problem as, "How to overcome or minimize the effect of my low student status?" This definition points to solutions which involve concealing the fact of being a student. If the problem is redefined as, "How can I use my student status as an asset?" other possibilities open up. Some clients find it easy to work with student social workers because of their age or because they aren't seen as entrenched in the agency. Other people like working with students because of the access they have to the resources of the university. Field assignments can be developed which build on these assets.

ENDING NOTE

In the past two chapters we have journeyed through the preparation phase of the social work process. Collecting data, organizing it in different ways to uncover the information in it, prioritizing the problems in the situation and reframing them prepares you to start the work of designing a solution. We are now ready to consider the design phase.

Figure 11.6: STANDARD ANSWER AND ALTERNATIVE SOLUTIONS TO THE NINE DOT PROBLEM[9]

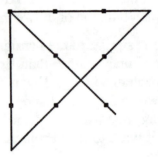

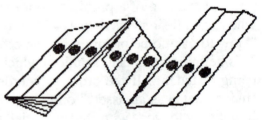

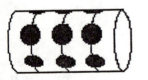

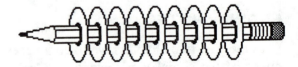

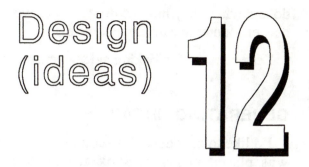

Design
(ideas)
12

In the preparation phase, your task was to understand the pattern of people, systems, events and contexts we call a problem. In the design phase your task is to form a new arrangement of these variables into what we call a solution.

The priority problems identified in the preparation phase and the way we framed those problems provides the starting point for design. The first step in the design process is generating ideas for dealing with the problem. Once ideas are generated they need to be combined and connected into a rough approximation of a new pattern. Then they are detailed in the context of practical realities and organized into a blueprint (plan) for implementing the solution. These parts of the design phase will be covered in this chapter. The design phase continues with the orchestrating of the various people and systems that need to work in concert to carry out the solution. This aspect of design will be the topic of the next chapter.

WHOLE-MIND THINKING AND DESIGN

As in the other phases of the social work process the creative generalist is called upon to employ whole-mind thinking. Flexible persistence, associative power and visualization are especially important in generating ideas and connecting them into patterns. Our critical, judgmental, rational mind also plays an important role. While deferring judgment is necessary for generating ideas, the scrutiny of our rational mind is welcomed in evaluating our ideas and detailing them into a plan for action. Is the plan feasible? Are the goals and objectives clearly spelled out? Does everybody know what they have do and when they have to do it? Have we anticipated difficulties we may encounter in carrying out the plan?

Let's start out by looking at idea generation.

GENERATING IDEAS

I'd like to introduce this section with one of my favorite stories. It was placed in my mailbox at work one day by an anonymous contributor without any indication of its source.

> Some time ago, I received a call from a colleague who asked if I would be the referee on the grading of an examination question. He was about to give a student a zero for his answer to a physics question while the student claimed he should receive a perfect score and would if the system were not set up against the student. The instructor and the student agreed to submit this to an impartial arbiter, and I was asked.
>
> I went to my colleague's office and read the examination question, "Show how it is possible to determine the height of a tall building with the aid of a barometer."
>
> The student had answered, "Take the barometer to the top of the building, attach a long rope to it, lower the barometer to the street and then bring it up, measuring the length of the rope. The length of the rope is the height of the building."
>
> I pointed out that the student really had a strong case for full credit, since he had answered the question completely and correctly. On the other hand, if full credit were given, it could well contribute to a high grade for the student in his physics course. A high grade is supposed to certify competence in physics, but the answer did not confirm this. I suggested that the student have another try at answering the question. I was not surprised that my colleague agreed, but I was surprised that the student did.
>
> I gave the student six minutes to answer the question, with the warning that his answer should show some knowledge of physics. At the end of five minutes, he had not written anything. I asked if he wished to give up, but he said no. He had many answers to this

problem; he was just thinking of the best one. I excused myself for interrupting him, and asked him to please go on. In the next minutes, he dashed off his answer which read:

"Take the barometer to the top of the building and lean over the edge of the roof. Drop the barometer, timing its fall with a stopwatch. Then, using the formula $s = \frac{1}{2}at^2$, calculate the height of the building."

At this point, I asked my colleague if he would give up. He conceded, and gave the student almost full credit.

In leaving my colleague's office, I recalled that the student had said he had other answers to the problem, so I asked him what they were.

"Oh, yes," said the student. "There are many ways of getting the height of a tall building with the aid of a barometer. For example, you could take the barometer out on a sunny day and measure the height of the barometer, the length of its shadow, and the length of the shadow of the building, and by the use of a simple proportion determine the height of the building."

"Fine," I said. "And the others?"

"Yes," said the student. "There is a very basic measurement method that you will like. In this method, you take the barometer and begin to walk up the stairs. As you climb the stairs, you mark off the length of the barometer along the wall. You then count the number of marks, and this will give you the height of the building in barometer units. A very direct method.

"Of course, if you want a more sophisticated method, you can tie the barometer to the end of a string, swing it as a pendulum, and determine the value of g (gravity) at the street level and at the top of the building. From the difference between the two values of g the height of the building can, in principle, be calculated."

Finally, he concluded, that although there are many other solutions, "the best," he said, "is to take the barometer to the basement and knock on the superintendent's door. When the superintendent answers, you speak to him as follows, "Mr. Superintendent, here I have a fine barometer. If you will tell me the height of this building, I will give you the barometer."

At this point, I asked the student if he really did not know the conventional answer to this question. He admitted that he did, but said that he was fed up with high school and college instructors trying to teach him how to think, to use the "scientific method," and to explore the deep inner logic of the subject in a pedantic way, rather than teaching him the structure of the subject.

What does this story about physics have to do with social work? While the solution to the problem required a knowledge of physics, it also required creative problem solving. The resourcefulness shown by the physics student is the same quality we hope to develop in ourselves as problem solvers in social work. The knowledge base we need as social workers of course differs from other professions and differs from setting to setting within the profession. It's the problem-solving process that forms the common thread.

Given what you now know about creativity, can you imagine the thought processes in the physics student's mind? He displayed a lot of perceptual openness in framing the problem and viewing his resources. The stated problem was, "Show how it is possible to determine the height of a tall building with the aid of a barometer." The student challenged a number of assumptions in the problem, namely:

"... with the aid of a barometer" meant that the barometer had to be used for its customary purpose of measuring air pressure.

"... with the aid of a barometer" meant nothing could be used in addition to the barometer.

The only association between the height of a building and barometers is the fact that air pressure decreases with height (and therefore that the only way to demonstrate a knowledge of physics was to make use of this association in the answer).

Perhaps he used attribute listing to see the barometer in a multifaceted light. Barometers have weight, a fixed length, and monetary value, among other attributes. He then might have looked for connections between these attributes and the objective of determining the height of a building. Note that framing the problem with the phrase "*determining* the height" rather than "*measuring* the height" opens up a wider range of possible solutions.

New ideas are the products of new connections. How did our clever physics student make such connections? He could have first brainstormed ways of determining the the height of a building (e.g., by using a ruler, marking off units as you climb the stairs)and then could have looked for ways of substituting the barometer (e.g., it has a fixed length, measure in "barometer units"). New uses for the barometer could have been suggested by linking a random object like a piece of string with the attributes of a barometer (e.g., string + small heavy object = pendulum). He could have thought about people who would already know the height of the building (or have access to the information) and how to "pay" for the information with a barometer (an object with monetary value). He could have used a direct analogy such as, "How are ways of determining the distance between two cities like determining the height of a building?" (Ask someone who knows the distance or look it up on a map. Who could I ask about the height of the building or where might this information be recorded?)   The student could have used a personal analogy ("If I were a barometer, how would I go about determining the height of a building?"). He could have visualized himself walking around the building, barometer in hand, to see if the scenes suggested any ideas.

In truth, I doubt that he used any of these tools in a conscious way, given the short time he had to work on the problem. Earlier in the book we mentioned that such tools are, in effect, cues to use the full power of our intuitive mind. The more practice you have with them the more you will begin to employ intuitive thinking as a matter of course.

Let's return to social work now. Designing a solution usually begins with a search for ideas on ways of approaching the problem. Of course, you will consider existing empirically tested procedures or interventions in the solution you design and adapt them to fit your unique set of circumstances. But their availability should not overly constrict your initial search for solution ideas.

Of the many tools for generating ideas discussed by Mike in Chapters 6 and 7, brainstorming is probably the most widely used. It has great versatility, is well suited for working with individuals or groups and embodies many principles of intuitive thinking. Therefore, I will elaborate here on its use.

Brainstorming

While you can brainstorm on your own, it's usually more effective (and much more fun) to brainstorm with other people. All you have to do is follow four simple rules designed to create a climate conducive to intuitive thinking in problem solving:

1. Defer judgement.

2. Free your imagination.

3. Go for quantity.

4. Build on ideas of others.

While the rules themselves are simple, getting people to follow them is another matter. It is helpful to introduce brainstorming by explaining the rationale for each of the rules.

Defer judgment

As Mike emphasized in previous discussions, deferring judgment is essential to turning down our rational mind. I usually explain the first rule with the help of a brief exercise devised by Edward de Bono:[1]

Look at this picture of a wheelbarrow and give me your comments about it (See Figure 12.1).

Figure 12.1

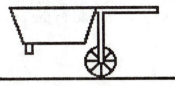

I record the responses on the blackboard. They are usually of the sort:

> The placement of the wheel makes it difficult to balance.
>
> It is hard to steer.
>
> Would tip over if left alone.

Though you only ask for comments, what you get is a list of what is *wrong* about the design. I point this out to the group and tell them that when the same picture with the same instructions are presented to a group of children, the responses tend to be very different:

> Since the wheel is near your foot, you could easily kick off any mud.
>
> Much easier than the usual wheelbarrow for going around corners.
>
> Pushing down is less likely to strain your back than lifting.
>
> Easier to tip over a low wall or into the middle of a hole.
>
> You could have a spring on the wheel strut which automatically weighs every load.

The children don't view the design as simply good or bad. While the design as a whole may not be feasible, the children identify interesting aspects of it which suggest ways to improve the design of a wheelbarrow. For example, a second wheel could be added to the conventional design which would make it easier to turn a tight corner or follow a narrow path such as a plank on scaffolding. The suggestion about tipping could lead to the use of a hinged wheel (see Figure 12.2).

Figure 12.2

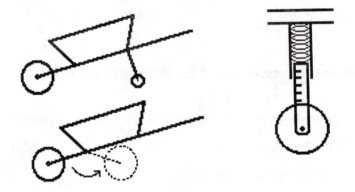

The wheelbarrow exercise sensitizes people to the first rule of brainstorming, *defer judgment..* When someone in the group involuntarily blurts out "Hey, that's a good idea!" or "We don't have the resources for that," he or she will often be chided in a joking way by other group members. Remind the group that they will have ample time afterwards to critique the ideas. When criticisms comes up, ask people to put their thoughts "on hold" until later.

Free your Imagination

The second rule, *free your imagination,* is meant to encourage people to think of offbeat or even outrageous ideas that they would ordinarily never bring up in a serious discussion. Such ideas often evoke laughter. Usually such laughter is a way to dismiss an idea as ridiculous. In a brainstorming session, laughter should be taken as an indication that a different perspective on the problem is being offered. While the idea itself may not be feasible or have merit, it may open up a way of approaching the problem that hasn't been considered. For example, while generating ideas for a workshop, someone suggested that participants crawl on the floor. While this had nothing to do with the content of the workshop, it did call attention to the need to plan for physical movement and lead to ideas on ways to build movement into the workshop format.

Go for quantity

The more ideas you come up with, the more likely you are to hit upon a useful one. This is the rational behind the third rule, *go for quantity*. When generating ideas, you'll often hit a plateau and run out of steam. This is a natural phenomenon, and you should warn the group that it might happen. You can help people break beyond that point by encouraging some deliberately wild or outrageous ideas, anything right off the top of their heads. This often loosens up the group and stimulates another round of ideas. Suggesting some kind of quota ("Let's get three more ideas to fill the blackboard") will often suffice to shake loose a few additional items.

Build on the ideas of others

You've probably observed that in productive problem-solving sessions people build on each other's ideas rather than merely offering competing suggestions. The fourth brainstorming rule, *build on the ideas of others*, encourages people to relate their own ideas to ones previously generated and to think of ways of modifying, adapting or combining ideas on the list. Such combinations or modifications often lead to new ideas which are superior to the ones that sparked them.

Be sure to appoint a recorder who lists the ideas on a blackboard or poster paper. It is very important that people be able to see the list. It is easier to play with the ideas when they are in front of you, and by keeping them constantly visible none of the ideas get lost. When you are done generating ideas you review the list with the group to clarify the items. For each item the group can indicate what similar ideas come to mind, what are some useful aspects of the idea (just like the wheelbarrow example). The review phase itself may produce some new ideas.

The next step in the design process, after generating ideas, is forming them into a rough pattern that will serve as the basis for a blueprint of the solution. Let's now look at how ideas are combined into patterns.

CONNECTING IDEAS

We have said that the circles map is a useful tool for associating ideas and combining them into new patterns. It can be used to record ideas as they are generated (looking for possible connections as we go along) or to review and organize the ideas from a brainstorming session. The circles map helps you see connections between various ideas, helps reveal strategies to the problem that underlie the ideas, and suggests ways of combining ideas into an overall strategy. I'll use an example to illustrate the process of generating and combining ideas.

> The manager of a large office building has been receiving an increasing number of complaints about the building's elevator service, particularly during rush hours. Several of the larger tenants in the building have threatened to move out unless the service is improved. In response, the manager recently inquired into the possibility of adding one or two elevators to the building. Although it would be feasible, the only elevator company in the area has a six-month backlog of orders. As an assistant to the manager, you were asked to come up with a plan *to get two new elevators installed within three months.* You must present the plan at the next staff meeting.

A typical brainstorm session I conducted on this problem resulted in the following sequence of ideas:

— Locate an out-of-town company to do the job.

— Form your own elevator company.

— Bribe the elevator company to install the elevators on time.

— Burn down the buildings which are ahead of you on the schedule.

— Negotiate a swap with a company that has less than a three-month wait, perhaps compensating them with money.

Notice that the bribe suggestion led to another illicit suggestion, burning down other buildings. This suggestion, as you might expect, was met with laughter—an indication that a different approach to the problem was being offered. While burning down other buildings is not a serious solution, it did suggest looking at ways of getting ahead of others on the waiting list (e.g., negotiating a swap). Often in brainstorming groups you'll be able to trace this kind of idea development.

To open up our "solution space" we could reformulate the problem using the problem-purpose expansion technique:

I WANT to get two new elevators installed within three months,

IN ORDER TO keep the tenants satisfied.

"Keeping the tenants satisfied" is now the new objective and brainstorming is again employed to generate ideas.

— Encourage flexible work hours to stagger the demand for the elevator.

— Encourage use of the stairs.

— Put trampolines on the street and have people jump out the window.

— Give people parachutes.

— Attract companies that use computers and have few employees so there won't be as big a demand for the elevators.

— Educate people to the health benefits of exercise, especially walking up steps.

— Start a health club in the building.

— Put a restaurant in the building so people won't have to leave at lunchtime or dinnertime.

— Build a parking ramp that circles the building.

— Build bridge to the building next door and use their elevators.

— Charge a fee for riding elevator to discourage use.

— Reduce the rent of tenants who use stairs.

— Give people something to do while waiting for the elevator.

The items on this list are specific examples of different general approaches to the problem. If we used a circles map to group the items according to their underlying strategy, the main circles on that map might look like the ones in Figure 12.3. Items from the "How to" list would then be attached to their appropriate circle, and additional items related to the circle could be generated.

Figure 12.3

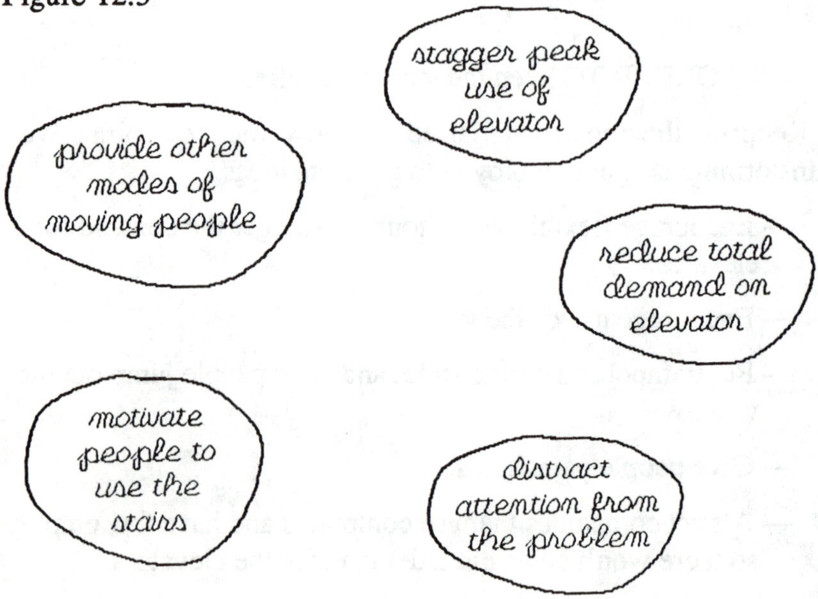

When all the possibilities are laid out in the circles map, we can begin to see *connections* between the ideas. For example, the health club idea can be linked to several of the strategies. For the price of installing an elevator, you might be able to build a fitness center. Climbing stairs can be part of the fitness program. If people came in early to use the facility or stayed after work, it would have the effect of staggering work hours. The tenants might not only see it as a desirable tradeoff for an additional elevator, but it might help attract new tenants if some of the old ones left. With consciousness about the importance of exercise and fitness, and evidence linking it to productivity, companies might encourage employees to use the facility. Posters and displays about various health issues, located near the elevators, might distract people from thinking about how long they are waiting for the elevator.

As the example illustrates, exploring the connections between ideas with tools like the circles map increases our chances of designing a solution that reflects the standards for a creative product (fit, elegance, alchemy and novelty).

SHAPING IDEAS INTO PLANS

In moving from ideas to concrete plans we have to detail them, and evaluate their feasibility. Here is where we especially appreciate our left-mind ability to break things down into component parts, focus on details, order and sequence things, and critically evaluate ideas "in the cold light of day." The vision generated by our right mind gets transformed into a blueprint for action.

Goals, Objectives and Tasks

The concepts, "goals," "objectives" and "tasks," are useful analytical tools for detailing ideas. They form a hierarchy in moving from abstractions to greater levels of specificity.

Definitions

A goal statement is a declaration of intent. Your goal might be to find a more satisfying job, get to know your neighbors, obtain an MSW degree, buy a new bicycle, or start a health club. Such goals get formulated in the process of generating and connecting ideas. Notice that goal statements tell you where you want to end up tomorrow, next week, next month, next year, or five years from now (short-term vs.long-term goals) but not how to get there.[2]

Goals are reached in stages, piece by piece, step by step. Each step can be thought of as an objective.[3] Thus objectives are more specific and immediate than goals. If your goal is to improve your school grades, an objective might be to raise your math grade to a "B" by the middle of the semester. If your goal is to get an MSW degree, an objective might be to find out the requirements and costs of different programs. When you formulate objectives you are determining the steps necessary to reach your goal.

Tasks are the specific actions you take to accomplish an objective. If the objective is to raise a math grade to a "B" by the middle of the semester, the tasks associated with this objective might be to spend one hour a day studying math and to locate a tutor for help with difficult material. If the objective is to find out the requirements of various MSW programs, the task might be to phone or write the schools for information. When you specify a task, you are determining the actions involved in taking the next step.

Clarity and specificity

Clarity is important, whether you are formulating goals, objectives or tasks. When intents are not clear, it leads to vague goal statements such as "revitalizing the neighborhood." If you are not sure where you want to go, it's hard to plan your journey. Even a small clarification such as "making the neighborhood attractive to young families," or "creating a more viable business climate for local merchants" is a big improvement. You can see how much easier it is to formulate objectives from such statements. If your goals are too vague, you probably need to do some further work in generating and connecting ideas.

What I said about clarifying goals applies equally to objectives. When your objective is "to see that all building code violations in the neighborhood are taken care of by the end of the year," it is easier to identify the actions you need to take (tasks) than when your objective is "to improve housing conditions." A good test for how clear and specific your objectives are is to ask, "Can I easily determine when or if the objective is accomplished?" If the answer is no, you should go back to the drawing board. You may have a goal masquerading as an objective.

Clarifying tasks involves similar considerations. Compare the following tasks: (1) Inform the neighborhood about the proposal. (2) Ask to speak about the proposal at the next meeting of the neighborhood association and get volunteers to distribute flyers door to door. If the task is specific enough, someone not familiar with the problem should have a clear idea of what needs to be done to perform the task. If the actions called for are not clear, you may have an objective disguised as a task.

Means-ends chain

Goals, objectives and tasks. Sounds like a neat, tidy and logical scheme, doesn't it? (Did you expect less from the rational mind?) Of course, when you're dealing with a relatively simple situation, you may wonder what all the fuss and bother is about. But the first time you're caught in the mire of a complicated problem you'll begin to appreciate the power of these concepts to give you a handle on the situation and sort things out.

Like most such schemes, they work best with a little flexibility, if you follow the spirit rather than the letter of the law. Let's look at some problems you may run into when applying these concepts in practice. Consider the following statements:

1. I want to improve my life.

2. I want to do better at school.

3. I want to get higher grades.

4. I want to raise my grade in math.

5. I want to raise may math grade from a "C" to a "B."

6. I want to raise my math grade from a "C" to a "B" by the end of the semester.

We would all agree that number 1 is a very vague goal while number 6 is a very specific objective. But how far can you clarify a goal before it actually turns into an objective? How far can you clarify an objective before it turns into a task? Further, if you started with number 2 as a goal, then number 3 can be considered an objective. But in relation to number 4, number 3 might be considered a goal.

Sometimes you may get the feeling that this conceptual scheme is adding to your confusion rather than abating it. Distinguishing between goals and objectives, and objectives and tasks, may seem like an exercise in splitting hairs. When this happens, the following should help you put things back in perspective.

In moving from goals to objectives to tasks you are forming a means-ends chain. At any point in the chain, if you ask the question *why* am I doing this, it points you upward in the chain toward your goals. If you ask *how* am I doing this, it points downward toward your tasks. Think of goals, objectives, and tasks as three levels in the means-ends chain with somewhat overlapping boundaries. The important point is to be able to connect a specific activity you are undertaking to an eventual goal you wish to reach, and vice versa, rather than making sure every link in the chain is precisely categorized.

Representing the means-ends chain in a flow chart is often very helpful in thinking through goals, objectives and tasks. I'll give an example after we discuss one final point, feasibility.

Feasibility

So we have made our ideas clear and specific and ordered them into a means-ends chain. Is our rational mind satisfied? Not yet. Now that we are clear on what we propose to do, it wants to know if it is feasible to do it.

Feasibility refers to the likelihood of being able to achieve your goal. In simplest terms a goal is feasible if the resources for change are greater than the barriers. Resources can include such things as time, energy, motivation, knowledge, money and sanction. Simons and Aigner distinguish between two types of barriers, constraints and obstacles.[4] Constraints are barriers not very susceptible to modification (e.g., a law that prohibits picketing in a certain area or a husband who absolutely refuses to participate in marriage counseling). Obstacles are barriers that are subject to alteration (e.g., a client's lack of knowledge of legal procedures or lack of transportation). Constructing a simple "balance sheet" listing the supports and resources on one side and the barriers on the other may help you weigh the factors.

There is a continual assessment of feasibility as you move down the means-ends chain. A goal might seem feasible at first, but as you begin to identify objectives and specify tasks, you might discover that you don't have adequate resources, or that there are certain barriers you didn't think of before.

Garvin and Seabury suggest playing the devil's advocate when helping people consider how realistic their goals are.[5] "It's an attractive job, but how are you going to get around the college degree requirement?" While such comments are inappropriate when generating ideas, they are useful when discussing feasibility. You are not trying to talk the person out of the goal. Rather, you are helping him or her to consider all aspects of it, and test commitment to it. By specifying what goes into accomplishing a goal, the person is encouraged to honestly express how far she or he expects to be by a given deadline.

VISUAL REPRESENTATIONS OF SOLUTIONS

In Chapter 11, I discussed the use of matrices and circles maps to construct visual representations of a problem or situation. Such representations enable us to maintain an overall view of a problem or situation in spite of the complexity or amount information involved. A visual representation (blueprint) of a solution or plan can likewise be very helpful.

There are often several different objectives related to a particular goal, and several different tasks associated with each objective. For example, suppose you are working with the family of an elderly person being released from the hospital. The goal is to enable her to recuperate at home. A chart of the various tasks and objectives might look like Figure 12.4.

Figure 12.4

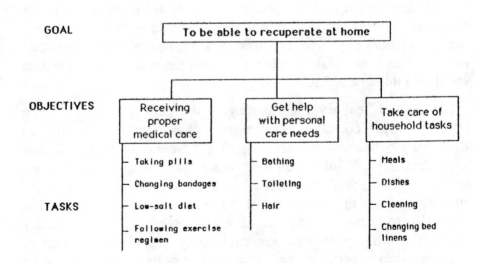

This kind of blueprint helps insure that we won't overlook any important tasks. It is also very useful in the next part of the design phase where the focus is on putting together an action system (who will do which tasks to make sure the objectives are accomplished).

As another example, consider the elevator problem I discussed earlier in the chapter. Suppose the idea of establishing a fitness center in the building seems to hold a lot of potential. The building manager likes the idea and so do the tenants you've talked with. So now you have a goal—to get a fitness center established in the building. A partial list of the objectives associated with this goal include determining the specific features the tenants want in the center, figuring out the best location for it, determining the relative costs and benefits of owning and running the facility vs. renting space to an existing fitness center enterprise, and negotiating rental or construction contracts.

The actual list of objectives involved in establishing the fitness center would of course be considerably longer. When you add the tasks associated with each objective, the list would become unwieldy, making it difficult to organize and keep track of the work that needs to be done.

In the earlier example, where the goal was to enable the woman to recuperate at home, there were relatively few objectives and they needed to be worked on simultaneously over a relatively short time span. In the current example, some objective need to be accomplished before others. A flow chart can be contructed where objectives that need to be accomplished during the same time period are grouped on the same level. Another device to portray the sequencing of objectives is a time-line matrix. The objectives (and associated tasks) are listed down the rows and the time span the project covers is listed across the top. This way of blueprinting a plan helps you keep track of progress and see that tasks are accomplished in proper sequence. If you were organizing an outreach project, you'd want to know that the literature for distribution would be ready by the time the volunteers were trained.

Some objectives call for making decisions which will affect the shape of the plan. Flow charts can be constructed which highlight the decision points and diagram alternative paths to a final destination. In such flow charts the convention is to use boxes to designate objectives or tasks, and diamonds to designate decisions. Continuing with the fitness center example, one objective was to determine the best location in the building for the center. The tasks involved might be finding out the size and type of space requirements for a center, surveying space in the building currently available and reviewing tenant rental contracts to identify space that might be available in the near future. Based on this information you would decide if an appropriate space in the building was available for the fitness center. If it were, you could go on to the next objective. If not, you would have to look into alternatives for remodeling or adding on to the existing building. A small segment of the flow chart for the entire project is shown in Figure 12.5.

Figure 12.5

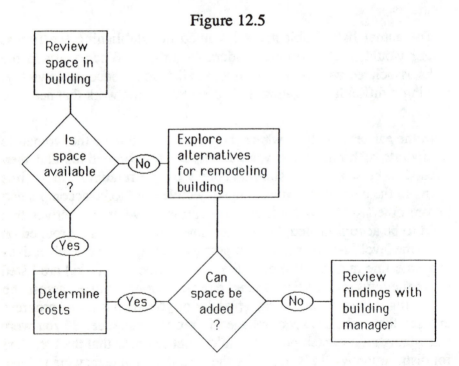

The kind of flow charts and diagrams I've been discussing are most often used as tools in project and program planning where a large number of interrelated objectives and tasks need to be coordinated. While most of the solutions you design will not be as elaborate, these tools can be adapted and scaled down to fit your needs. And there is another important reason to understand and practice using these tools. The disciplined use of rational thinking harnesses the power of our left mind, just as the the disciplined use of intuitive thinking harnesses the power of our right mind. Sloppy thinking in either realm leads to ineffective problem solving.

ENDING NOTE: ON TECHNIQUES

I'd like to conclude this chapter with a few observations on the role of techniques in social work practice. Earlier in the chapter I mentioned that after generating ideas on ways of approaching a problem, you may want to incorporate various empirically tested procedures or techniques in your design. A technique is a specific standardized method to accomplish an objective (e.g., placing chairs in a circle to promote interaction in a group). In effect, a technique is a solution that has general applicability (a circular arrangement of chairs will promote interaction in a wide variety of groups across a wide variety of settings).

The field of social work has experienced a great deal of pressure to specify exactly what it is that practitioners do when they *do* social work. Researchers want to know so they can operationalize our interventions ("inputs," "independent variables") when evaluating practice models. Administrators want to specify what social workers do so they can determine the amount of training a person needs for a given position and be able to justify funding requests. Professional organizations and licensing boards want the information so they can administer competency tests and certify advanced and specialized levels of practice. Educators want to offer curriculums that prepare students to be competent practitioners.

This pressure has understandably resulted in a tendency to clarify the practice of social work in the direction of a body of techniques (parallel to the tendency to clarify values in the direction of ethical guidelines). But there is a lot more to "doing" social work than applying techniques. Our actions encompass two other forms of "doing" which I call "devising" and "acknowledging."

When we *devise* an action in response to a situation we are applying a principle or concept to it rather than a technique. Do you recall the example of a social worker who had on her caseload a battered woman in need of temporary shelter and a foster mother in need assistance because of a broken leg? The worker arranged for the battered woman to stay with the foster parent in exchange for help with the household chores. We wouldn't call such an arrangement a technique. Rather, the worker took the concept of synergy and the principle of resource exchange and applied it in the specific context of this problem. She devised a response which gave expression to her philosophy of practice.

Things are continually happening in a practice situation, regardless of what you do. *Acknowledging* involves seeing and using the opportunities that arise in all situations. Suppose you are driving a client to a clinic appointment when suddenly your car stalls. The client gets out to look under the hood and in a few minutes has the car going again. This incident prompts a conversation about cars and you learn a lot about the client's interests and talents that you didn't know before. You also sense a more relaxed atmosphere as the client feels good about being the one in the "helper" role for a change. Again, we wouldn't call stalling your car a technique for exploring job interests or improving relationships. Rather, you acknowledged the opportunity for exploring job interests and improving your relationship that the situation presented.

Creative generalists know that the techniques they incorporate in their solutions will need to be supplemented by the actions they devise and acknowledge. In this chapter I have explored the first part of the design process: generating ideas, combining ideas into patterns, and shaping ideas into a blueprint for a solution. Join me in the next chapter where I discuss the remaining tasks of the design phase.

Design (solutions) 13

We have said that both problems and solutions are perceptual patterns. When a pattern is not working well, we call it a problem. When we rearrange the parts into a new preferable pattern, we call it a solution. In the last chapter I talked about generating ideas and forming them into a kind of blueprint (goals, objectives, tasks) for the newly developed pattern. Once such a blueprint is developed, the emphasis in design shifts to getting the blueprint ready for implementation.

> Who do you want to participate in solving the problem? How will you bring them together? (*Action systems*)

> Does everyone know what they are supposed to do and how they will go about doing it? Are they in agreement with what is to be done? (*Working agreements*)

> Are key people willing to participate? If not, how will you deal with their resistance? (*Target systems*)

These are the questions we will explore in this chapter.

ACTION SYSTEMS

From the beginning of the problem-solving process you'll be keeping your eyes open for people and resources that can help with the problem. In the preparation phase, while you were asking how people were interacting to maintain the problem, you were at the same time looking ahead to explore how they could be interacting to effect a solution.

This way of thinking is second nature to creative generalists, who look at situations with the "bias" of resources and connectedness. Can existing relationships be defined in a way that brings potential resources to life? What kind of synergistic connections can be made? What tasks are best handled by people in the informal system? How can the resources of human service organizations be brought into the picture? While such questions are in the back of your mind throughout the problem-solving process, in the design phase you'll need to make some decisions about your action system.

The people you need to involve in the solution are often suggested by the nature of the situation. Suppose you are working with an elderly client to help her to recuperate at home after a hospitalization. The woman has a daughter living in town and a next-door neighbor she is friendly with. You arrange for a visiting nurse to administer medications and change bandages when necessary. The neighbor will stop by during the day to help with small household chores, and the daughter will pitch in after work a few evenings a week and on the weekends. You make sure that both the neighbor and daughter have some backup, people they can call on at times when they are unavailable or simply need a break. Some members of the temple sisterhood the woman belongs to have also arranged to bring a hot meal during their weekly visit.

From discussions with the daughter you know that she is very concerned about how she is going to cope with the increasing infirmity of her mother. You let her know about a lecture and discussion series you have set up for adult children on care of elderly parents. In the past, this series has proven to be more than just a good source of information. It has led to the development of informal ongoing supportive relationships between some of the participants who live in the same part of town or belong to the same church or temple. By making arrangements for car pooling to the meetings and allowing plenty of time for informal discussion over coffee and refreshments, you have encouraged such relationships.

Let's take another example. Suppose you are working in a county social service department. The police have just picked up a 14-year-old kid from your caseload, who ran away from his foster home. In some ways you are not surprised that he took off. Aside from your own agency, the list of people and agencies involved with this kid include the police, the juvenile court, the guidance counselor at school, the foster parents, the natural parent, the neighborhood center and the psychologist at the mental health center. The kid's problems have been compounded by various people not knowing what the others are doing and by inter-agency hostilities (resulting in mixed messages, conflicting expectations, and working at cross purposes). And the kid is skillful at manipulating systems by playing one person against another. You decide it's time to get everyone together at a case connference in order to iron out the difficulties and come up with a coordinated plan.

A couple of final examples illustrate yet another aspect of forming action systems. Suppose a community center you work at wants to set up a task force to address a problem of vandalism in the neighborhood. There is a wide choice of people you can consider for the task force. The success of the group will depend in part on its composition. You want to involve local business people, whose support you'll need, law enforcement people who are knowledgeable about attempts to deal with the problem, and so on. You also want to be sure that the people on the task force can work together and not use it as an arena for their personal agendas.

Or, say you work at a mental health center and are forming a group for single parents whose kids have been in trouble with the law. You want to make sure that you meet at a convenient time and location and that the group is small enough for people to get to know one another. But you don't want the group so small that a few dropouts would end the group. You also want to get people who are similar enough in background that they are able to identify and feel comfortable with each other but different enough in personality to have a balanced group; too many reticent people or too many very aggressive people would not make for good interaction.

Examples such as these suggest the range of knowledge and skills required in forming actions systems.

Knowledge of Formal Resource Systems

Formal resource systems are agencies, organizations, and programs in the broad area of human services. Knowledge of such systems means more than just being able to locate them in a resource file. If I needed help in finding a lawyer, I would want to talk with someone who knew many different lawyers, the things they were good at, how well they might fit my style and the kind of service they had provided to other people. Such knowledge grows out of your experience and the experience of others in using those formal resource systems. It includes awareness of their strengths and weaknesses, eligibility requirements and intake policy, the reception different kind of clients might expect, and other information useful to a prospective user of the resource.

Skills in Linking People to Formal Resource Systems

The realization that people who are referred to a resource often either fail to get there or receive a needed service has led social workers to pay more attention to skills in making effective referrals.[1] Small gestures such as calling ahead to set up appointments for people and giving them a slip of paper with pertinent information (e.g., time and date of appointment, name and phone number of the agency, and travel directions from their home) helps ensure that they will make it to the resource. It is also important to prepare people for the referral by explaining what to expect at the other agency, by discussing any concerns they have about using the service, and by arranging for practical matters such as transportation and child care.

Effective referrals in the world of formal resource systems also depend on using the informal relationships you develop with people in that world, favors and information you trade back and forth, shortcuts and ways of stretching rules you pick up and ways of presenting information or preparing applications that increase people's chances of getting what they need.

Finally, follow-up with the person or the resource is important. It not only lets you know if the referral was successful, but also alerts you changes in the services or procedures of the resource. When people have difficulty getting a needed service, you may have to advocate in their behalf.[2]

Knowledge of Informal and Natural Helping Systems in the Community

People in trouble usually turn first to their own network of friends and relatives, natural helpers in the community, and various self-help or mutual aid groups.[3] In recent years, social work's interest in natural helping systems has been fueled by a phenomenal growth in the self-help movement, by budget cuts in the formal resource sector, and by a growing appreciation of the value of the help people receive through indigenous systems.[4]

Some people develop reputations as natural helpers by virtue of their personality and boundless energy. Neighbors seem to turn to them for advice, concrete help, or simply to catch up on neighborhood gossip. Other people, by virtue of their work as bartenders, hairdressers, waitresses or health food store owners, fill that role in some communities. Ethnic groups usually have their own cultural institutions and practitioners who provide help with personal and health problems.[5] It is as important for you to be knowledgeable about these helping systems as it is to be knowledgeable about formal resource systems. Indigenous helping systems and self-help groups have rules and norms that differ markedly from the "professional" culture we are used to operating in. It is necessary to know how to bridge those differences if you want to work with such systems.[6]

In an earlier chapter I suggested that doing circles maps of people's natural helping networks (or having them draw the map) is a good way to understand their situation and tune into potential resources in their networks. (You can also ask who they turn to for various types of help or listen for names of people they bring up. One social worker kept track of who visited a patient in the hospital to learn about the patient's personal network.) Regularly constructing such maps is one way of learning about the informal resource systems in a community.

Skills in Coordinating Resource Systems

The involvement of several organizations or services with the same client may result in duplication of efforts, lack of communication, and working at cross purposes. It is important, therefore, that someone take the responsibility for coordination (or "case management," as the current literature refers to the task).[7] Though much of the work of coordination can be done through individual meetings, phone contacts or memos, at some point it is usually desireable to hold a case conference with the key people involved in the situation.

The purpose of a case conference is to get agreement on overall goals and objectives, as well as the specific tasks and responsibilities each participant will undertake. These conferences usually begin with people introducing themselves and their interest in the situation. The coordinator's job is to facilitate interaction and decision making. He or she helps identify the common ground that serves as the basis for a plan.[8]

Another aspect of coordination is forging a partnership between the formal and informal resource systems involved. Unfortunately, relationships between both types of systems are often antagonistic. Recent studies, however, have shown that productive partnerships can be developed. Froland et al. note that these relationships must be built on principles such as sensitivity and respect for different conceptions of helping, equality of status between professional and informal caregivers, shared responsibility for care, and respect for the way individuals and local groups define their problems. The authors go on to suggest that the philosophical orientation with which the task is approached is more important than the techniques and procedures presumed by a specific program model.[9]

Knowledge of Factors Affecting Group Interaction

When you bring a group of people together, factors such as group size, composition and setting will affect the interaction in the group and the ability of the group to accomplish its purposes. Though in many circumstances you won't have any control over such factors, when you do, you can use them to your advantage.[10]

Getting People to Agree to Participate

Identifying people you would like to involve in your action system is one thing. Getting them to participate is another. Understanding their motivations and self-interests is important. I'll talk more about this in the next section on working agreements.

The knowledge and skills I've listed above could easily serve as the agenda for a course by itself. Indeed, since a large part of the business of social work involves connecting people with resources, creating new resource systems, and making resource systems responsive to people, it is important that this knowledge and skill base be built into the curriculum. The references I've cited will provide additional information in further exploring these topics.

I'd like to conclude this section by noting that an action system is another type of pattern to which our left and right mind make their contributions. In forming an action system, our rational mind looks for logical connections; given a number of possible action system members, and given our objectives, it looks for reasons for selecting a given person. As we immerse ourselves in the situation, become aware of the resources, think in terms of relatedness, our intuitive mind starts suggesting potentially useful connections. Again, it's whole-mind thinking at work.

WORKING AGREEMENTS

> *"I'll ask the community center director about the meeting room, and you be sure to call the parents who weren't here tonight and let them know about the new plans."*
>
> *"O.K., I'll do that. By the way, we never discussed getting that grant money from the Bellview Foundation."*
>
> *"You're right. Glad you reminded me. I'd better make a note to bring it up at next week's meeting. See you then."*
>
> *"Bye."*

Our day-to-day practice is filled with such exchanges, reminders to keep us on course, keep our actions aimed at getting the job done. Some are relatively simple exchanges covering only a small piece of the total picture. Others are more extensive, covering the entire design. We will refer to the latter as "working agreements." You arrive at a working agreement in the course of clarifying goals, specifying objectives, and detailing tasks. A working agreement usually contains three elements:

1. The reasons you are working together and what you hope to accomplish.

2. The tasks you and others are responsible for carrying out within a particular timeframe.

3. The necessary details of your working together, such as how often you will get together and what records will be kept.

Basically, that's it. How you elaborate or adapt these elements will depend on the particular circumstances you are working with. Also, working agreements are flexible and will change over time as things are tried out and goals and objectives are reevaluated. That is one reason for using the term *working* agreement.

Though you develop working agreements with all the people responsible for carrying out the solution, the most important one you develop is with the client. In fact, the "client system" is defined by the fact that the system has engaged your services to deal with a problem and has arrived at an agreement with you on how to proceed. Without a working agreement, you in effect don't have a client. I mentioned before that in cases where you are working with someone who doesn't want to be there (perhaps a person on probation or a man who has been abusing his wife) the client system is actually society at large, which sanctions your agency to intervene in such situations. The person you are assigned to work with is initially the target system.

Many times you will start the preparation phase with an initial or preliminary working agreement, a time limited agreement to explore a problem or set up a trial period to work on it. This initial agreement gives you and the other person(s) a chance to feel each other out, see how you'll work together, and do some further exploration before making a more long range commitment. For people who may not know what to expect from you, or who come with negative or guarded expectations, the preliminary agreement is especially helpful.

Contracts vs. Working Agreements

The term "contract" is frequently used in social work as an alternative to "working agreement." Because it is difficult to get away from the connotation of "contract" as a legal commitment, we prefer to use "working agreement." The working agreements I am discussing here are aids in the social work process. However, in practice you will come across agreements and contracts that serve other purposes.

In some agencies or organizations a written signed contract, often referred to as a service agreement, is required in all cases. A standardized contract form, with room to fill in the particulars, is provided by the organization and signed by worker and client. This contract may serve a variety of administrative purposes including providing data for quality control evaluations and satisfying policy, legal, or insurance requirements. It may also authorize the organization to obtain the client's medical or other records. If you want an agency service agreement to serve as your working agreement as well, you'll have to be sure it's not treated as just another bureaucratic form to fill out.

In certain settings, especially probation and child welfare, you may be working with people who have been through legal proceedings that have resulted in a contract with the courts. This contract usually stipulates certain conditions the person must meet (e.g., refraining from taking drugs, reporting to the worker each week, attending a parenting skills group) and spells out consequences for non-compliance (e.g., return to prison, removal of children from the home). These are not the mutually arrived at voluntary working agreements I described earlier. However, even in these situations, there is often some discretion in how the terms of the mandate are to be carried out, and room for negotiating additional terms if the person is interested. This may require that you separate your role as supervisor of the court-ordered contract (person as target system) and your role as social worker (person as potential client). "This is what you and I are required to do. Aside from that, are there some things that you are interested in my working on with you?"

Still another form of contract is a "treatment contract," often used in group homes and institutional settings that employ behavior modification techniques. Failure to comply with contract terms results in punishments like loss of privileges. Such programs, however, build in positive incentives and rewards for compliance as well.

Working Agreement as Tool

Developing and using a working agreement aids the social work process in a number of ways. Let's review some of them.

Holding information

In discussing the creative process we have stressed the importance of writing things down in order to capture ideas. Written lists, circles maps, and other visual representations of information were shown to be important aids for right-mind thinking. The working agreement evolves from all the little notes scribbled on writing pads, circles maps drawn on butcher paper, and various matrices, flow charts and other visual representations of the problem and the solution that you have constructed. Actually seeing the agreement on paper is important. It begins to create a concrete reality from ideas and visions. It holds a lot of information in a convenient form. That's why it is important to get your working agreements in written form.

Clarification

You and others may develop different views of why or how you are working together. It is easy for misunderstandings to occur, especially in an emotionally charged situation. In addition, both you and others have expectations based on previous experiences which color your communications. One of my class assignments calls for the student to ask a client or action system member with whom they are working to write down what they see as the purpose of their working together. The student does the same and compares both versions. You might want to try this yourself. You'll sometimes be surprised by the differences that appear.

In working with task forces, case conferences and staffings, one important concern is that people follow through on what is decided at the meeting. It's useful at the end of the meeting to summarize what was decided and who is expected to do what, within what time limits. You can repeat the same material in the minutes of the meeting or in a memo going out to all the parties involved. This is another means of clarifying the working agreement.

In earlier chapters we discussed the importance of tolerating ambiguity, avoiding premature closure, and allowing time for "incubation" in the problem-solving process. Remember that there is always a tension between clarity and ambiguity; you need to keep an appropriate balance between the two.

Mutuality

The give and take of developing a working agreement fosters a mutuality that facilitates the problem-solving relationship. You show your respect for people when you change and adapt your ideas and understanding to get a better "fit" with them. You set the tone for working together and give expression to an important social work value.

Credibility

One semester my field unit was approached about doing an assessment of the mental health component of a Head Start program. After two exploratory meetings between members of the field unit and the administrative staff of the program, we drew up a preliminary working agreement. The first paragraph of that agreement reads as follows:

> Due to budget cuts, many professional mental health services previously utilized by Head Start and its clients are no longer available. Head Start must develop a federally mandated mental health services plan which reflects this reality yet continues to provide for essential client needs. To creatively deal with this situation it is necessary to reconsider what constitutes a "mental health service," what are realistic goals for clients, and what resources can be utilized to attain those goals. Head Start wants to develop a plan, based on such considerations, which doesn't necessarily call for any additional paid staff resources and which minimizes any administrative restructuring of the program. Head Start views the development of the plan as an opportunity to clarify and specify the nature and structure of its mental health component and to develop quantifiable measures of the operations and outcomes of that component.

This opening paragraph was followed by a detailed statement of the objectives of the work to be done by the field unit, the methods to be formality and amount of detail in this agreement goes beyond that in most working agreements, it served an important purpose for us. Since this was the first connection we had with the Head Start program, I was interested in establishing the credibility of the field unit. The agreement demonstrated that we could quickly and accurately capture the nature of the problem they were grappling with, that we had a conceptual as well as pragmatic way to frame it, that we had specific methods for exploring the problem and estimating the amount of work involved, and clear expectations for ourselves and for them.

How you arrive at a working agreement as well as what the final product looks like provides an opportunity for you to establish your credibility with a potential client system.

Monitoring and revision

Flexibility in changing the working agreement is important. When people (including yourself) fail to carry through on agreements, we treat this as valuable *information*. Unlike formal contracts, the intent of the working agreement is not to force or induce compliance. Rather, it is a tool for getting a job done. If it doesn't work, then it means we are headed in the wrong direction or misusing the tool.

If people don't follow through, your job is to find out the reasons and see if you can remedy the situation. Perhaps the person lacks the ability to follow through. Perhaps you didn't correctly assess the person's motivation or self-interest. You can check if the goals and objectives are realistic or if they need to be revised. Perhaps the person doesn't have the resources to carry out the tasks or unexpected obstacles came up. Involving people in decision making along the way will lessen, but not eliminate, the chances of such things happening.

We should also remember that a lapse between intention and action is common to all of us.[11] A simple reminder, a little pressure, a plea as to the urgency of the situation, will often get people back on task. For some clients however, the inability to follow through on agreements and commitments may in fact be part of their problem. If you have made sure they have the resources to carry out the tasks, then pressure to hold up their end may be warranted. However, if agreements are repeatedly broken, you should question the client's desire to continue, and the original purpose of your working together should be rediscussed.[12]

I'd like to end this section on working agreements with an example. In this example Dick Becker, a former student, relates an experience while employed as the coordinator of an employee assistance program in a large company. By considering his boss as the client, Dick was able to apply ideas about working agreements to his situation. When someone requests your help with a problem, regardless of his or her formal relationship to you, it is often useful to view the person as a client.

> I was designated by management to write a policy which would prohibit smoking in company offices and facilities. The primary reason for doing this was concern for employee health in light of evidence concerning the effects of smoking. I set up a meeting with several of my "clients" (my supervisor and his boss), drawing up beforehand an understanding of what it was that I understood to be my responsibility.
>
> When we discussed the understanding, I accomplished several things. First, with regard to delineating roles and tasks, I asked whether, in addition to drawing up the policy, I was also supposed to be in charge of implementing it, and therefore needed to write a plan for implementation as well as a policy statement. The looks exchanged by my two clients told me that they hadn't thought about anything other than a policy statement. They discussed things and then decided that, yes, it would be necessary to implement as well as just write the policy and that I would be the one responsible.
>
> Next, I asked whether the policy would apply to all smoking or just cigarette smoking and whether the policy would apply in all offices or just some. Again, the look—after which they determined that what they wanted was an all-inclusive policy.
>
> The second major area involved that of establishing mutual concerns. I wanted to hear from them what kinds of concerns they had with regard to the implementation of such a policy. In fact, I asked them to

talk about why they wanted such a policy at all. This helped me understand the process they had gone through in arriving at the decision and it also helped give me some idea of what it was they wanted as the statement itself—what they wanted to communicate to employees as the reason(s) for implementing it. Were they concerned with the possible publicity they might derive from a policy? Had they considered the reaction by "militant" smoking employees? Had they thought about viewing smoking as not just a dirty habit but as an addiction and would they want to provide assistance to employees who might want to quit smoking? What kind of a timeline for implementation had they been thinking of?

I received answers for all of these questions and concerns. In addition, the whole process really made the clients think much more about exactly what it was they really wanted and intended to accomplish. They came away from the meeting having a much clearer picture of what I would do (and what *they* could expect me to do and when). For my part, I certainly had a better understanding of what my clients expected and wanted.

If I had not contracted with them, a lot of time would have been lost in a "feeling out" kind of process. I would have wasted much time perhaps writing a policy statement that would have been nowhere near what they intended. Additionally, the material I would have given them would not really have been all that they were implicitly expecting.

Also, one of the underlying concerns that I had when the project was first proposed was the welfare of the smoking employees who would be told that they could no longer do so on the job. My clients had been looking at smoking as simply a habit that people were going to be told they could not engage in anymore. When I helped them view it as an addictive habit and expressed my concern that we provide help for those interested in obtaining it, they were all for it. It was just something that they hadn't thought of before.

Finally, one of the best things on a personal level that happened was that I think my "clients" came away from the meeting feeling good about me. They appreciated the fact that I took the time to find out what the problem was, as they viewed it, that I gained an understanding of their perception of the problem, that I helped them think through the whole process to arrive at a clearer idea of what was required, and that they knew going in what they could expect as far as assistance from me and when to expect it.

PREPARING PEOPLE TO CARRY OUT TASKS

We have seen that the working agreements you develop call for people to carry out certain tasks. And the success of your solution depends in part on the ability and motivation of the people involved to do so. In designing the tasks, you took care to make them specific and feasible, within the understanding and capabilities of the people involved. In addition, a good way to help ensure the successful completion of tasks is to use the Task Implementation Sequence (TIS) proposed by William Reid.[13]

The TIS is a procedure for discussing, planning and practicing a task or responsibility before attempting to carry it out. The TIS procedure is used after a challenging task is formulated in general terms and agreed to by the other person. The TIS encompasses the following steps: (1) enhancing commitment by providing a rationale for the task, (2) planning the details of carrying out the task, (3) analyzing and planning for obstacles that may be encountered, (4) modeling and rehearsing the actions required, and (5) summarizing the task and conveying expectations that the task will be completed.

Though I have touched on some of these activities in earlier discussion it is useful to review them here as part of the TIS. This procedure can be built into the contracting process. Though the steps are presented here in a logical sequence, in practice certain steps may overlap, vary in order, or be omitted.

Enhancing Commitment

Commitment is enhanced when people understand the rationale for and expected benefits from carrying out a task or action. It is helpful to get people to state their understanding of the rationale and benefits in their own words. You can then add other positive consequences not mentioned by the person.

If you have developed a synergistic solution, people will be able to see how completing the task will be a benefit to themselves as well as others. A business that donates certain services to a community center may benefit in turn from favorable publicity. A young couple who agrees to shop for an elderly neighbor who is recovering from an illness may be establishing a relationship with someone who could do babysitting during the day.

Detailing the Task

One reason people fail to complete a task is that once they begin an activity they may realize they are not sure what they are supposed to do to complete it. When a task is time consuming, requires a lot of effort or involves actions perceived as difficult or unpleasant, the person can use the ambiguity of the task as a reason for not completing it. Detailing the plan ahead of time provides an opportunity to anticipate excuses or reasons people may have for not carrying out a task.

You can ask the person specific questions that will enable him or her to spell out what is going to be done, when it will be done, and how it will be done. You can ask questions that help the person consider alternative ways of doing the task. When a person has trouble, or you foresee difficulties, you can make suggestions or brainstorm ideas.

This way of detailing the tasks fits with the goal of teaching problem-solving skills to people. The questions you ask and ideas you share are ways of teaching the person what goes into constructing a plan. Simons and Aigner caution that these questions should not be asked in a challenging or patronizing manner.[14] However, if you really view yourself as a partner in the problem-solving process and are genuinely interested in how the task is to be carried out, that message will get conveyed to the person. You should also reciprocate by describing when and how you will be carrying out the tasks you have agreed to complete.

Analyzing Obstacles

Part of the preparation for carrying out a task is being prepared for barriers that may be encountered. You can encourage exploration of potential obstacles by questions such as, "What if the visiting nurse doesn't show up?" or, "What will you do if the teacher needs more time to make a decision?" Situational factors such as lack of transportation as well as psychological barriers such as fears associated with the task should be discussed, and plans made to meet them. The "worst case scenario" technique I discussed in Chapter 9 can be used here. If you are prepared for the worst thing that could happen, other obstacles become much easier to deal with.

Rehearsing the Task

Another aspect of preparation is practicing the part of the task that the person may have difficulty with because of lack of skills or fears associated with it. These parts often involve interaction with others (e.g., going for a job interview). Roleplaying the task is an excellent way of both getting practice and pinpointing difficulties the person may be having with the task. You can provide some examples of what the person might say or do in the situation.

Summarizing

A final review of the tasks and plans serves as a check that you are in agreement on what needs to be done. You can also use this as an opportunity to convey expectations that the task will be completed or at least every effort made to do so. Comments such as, "I look forward to seeing how things work out," not only convey your expectations but also your interest in the person's situation. It's important to restate your commitment to carry out your end of the agreement and to give a progress report at the next meeting.

TARGET SYSTEMS AND RESISTANCE

There will be times when people who are key to the problem-solving effort refuse to participate or cooperate. An agency director may not want to send a representative to a task force meeting. A person may refuse to go to marriage counseling with his or her spouse. A city council member may be opposed to voting for a certain project. Though you did your best to appeal to their self-interest or other motives, they just don't agree with your goals and objectives or your methods of achieving them. What do you do now?

First, it's useful to remember that short of physical coercion, you can't make people do something they don't want to do. You are not God. Sometimes we get so caught up in a situation that we forget this simple fact. Honestly acknowledging our limitations can help put things back in perspective.

Next, try to understand the resistance from the other person's point of view.[15] I don't mean that you have to feel sorry for the person or agree with his or her motivations. Rather, this understanding is important to finding a way of dealing with the resistance. Treat the resistance as a problem to be solved, not an annoyance to be eliminated with resistance-reducing techniques. Use your problem-solving skills. Understanding is aided by shifting your perspective. What appears to us as resistance is, from the other side, a motivation (toward a goal that is different from ours). Instead of asking why the person is resisting, you can reframe and ask what the person is motivated to do? What function does the resistance serve? What is it a solution to? This kind of questioning can help you get a handle on the problem and turn it around.

If that doesn't work, ask yourself how crucial this person is to the solution. Can someone else do the job or make the decision? Maybe the resistant person can be taken out of the design without any major damage. We sometimes get so committed to a particular idea or approach that we lose our ability to generate or consider alternatives. This is a time to challenge assumptions. Do you really need the principal's approval to start that after school group, or could you set it up under the auspices of the neighborhood center? Do you really need to start this group, or is there another way of accomplishing your goals with those kids? I'm not talking about backing out of conflict. Some conflict is inevitable. But it's just not efficient to waste a lot of energy dealing with resistance if your aims can be more easily accomplished another way.

"O.K.," you say. "I've considered all these things, but I can't find any alternatives. We have to get the building department to enforce the housing code and make the landlord repair the building whether he wants to or not." When things reach that point, and your goals are important enough, then you may indeed have to resort to power tactics such as protests, boycotts, and legal pressure. In such cases you need to make sure that you and the client have assessed the risks involved and are in agreement on the approach you are taking.

Most of the time, understanding the reasons for the resistance will lead to developing an appropriate and effective strategy for dealing with it. Let's consider a few options you might employ.

Prevention Through Involvement of Target System

A big source of resistance comes from expectations or change being thrust on people without their having a say in the changes that are made. Fear or uncertainty over what will happen also raise people's defenses. One way to deal with such resistance is to try and prevent its occurrence in the first place through involving the target system in the preparation and design process (or at a minimum, keeping them informed all along the way). This sounds reasonable—so why is it often not done? Time constraints, failure to value people's contributions, underestimating the impact of the change on them, lack of understanding of their values, or plain laziness, all play a part. The investment of time and effort you put in at the beginning with a potential target system will usually pay off down the line.

Acknowledge the Resistance

Simply acknowledging the resistance, openly discussing it, letting people express their anger, concerns, suspicions, and objections can be a first step in problem solving *with* the target system. When we have strong feelings about a proposed change, we want our opinions heard and the legitimacy of our feelings recognized. The objective is not to placate the person but to honestly exchange points of view and create an opening for finding some common ground.

Reframe to Work with the Motivation

John Enright and Ron Estep developed an interesting approach to dealing with the resistance of juvenile offenders who were referred by the courts for counseling.[16] The counseling was offered as an alternative to disciplinary action or incarceration. The program was popular with the youth who saw sitting with a counselor for a few hours as "easy time" compared to the alternative legal action in store for them. And sitting there, without saying much of anything, was about all they did—a very frustrating situation for the counselors.

In discussing the problem the staff realized that they had to find a way of connecting the motivation of the youth (to avoid legal disposition) to the activity of talking in an involved and meaningful way about their lives in a counseling session. They came up with the following procedure. In the initial interview the person was told that a minimum of six hours of counseling was required to satisfy the court. This did not have to be literally six hours; 12 half-hour sessions, 36 ten-minute sessions, or any combination totaling six hours would do. The only further requirement was that the youth interest the counselor during the time spent in the session. Whenever, in the counselor's opinion, the youth stopped talking in an interesting and involved way, the session was over and credit was given only for the actual amount of time spent in that session. The metaphor of the taxi meter, which only runs while the cab is hired, suggested the name "metered counseling" for the process. A dramatic improvement resulted from the use of this procedure.

Once you have identified a motivation, reframing the problem can help you discover ways of linking that motivation to your goals.

Using the Force of the Resistance

Similar to reframing is the martial arts strategy of actually using the force of the resistance to your advantage. Let me illustrate this with a delightful story that appeared in *The New Yorker* about Ben and Jerry's, a small Vermont ice cream company.[17] Pillsbury, the owner of Häagen-Däzs ice cream, was using various legal actions to prevent the smaller company from marketing its product in the Boston area.

Not being able to counter the massive resources of the big company, Ben and Jerry's realized they needed a different approach to the problem. Eventually they came up with the idea of starting a campaign in the Boston area with the theme, "What's the Doughboy Afraid Of?" Newspaper ads urged people to write protest letters to Pillsbury. The novelty of the idea, and the fact that Ben and Jerry's was the underdog, caught people's imagination. The campaign was much discussed and got a lot of free publicity. As a result, the more effort Pillsbury put into stopping Ben and Jerry's, the worse they looked in the public eye. The adverse publicity finally caused them to back off of their attempts to stop the smaller company.

Providing Ways of "Saving Face"

If a proposed change threatens a person's status, power or prestige, you can expect efforts to protect her or his position. Likewise, when people in an organization are singled out as targets of change, they may be concerned that it reflects badly on their competence or otherwise is damaging to their reputation. To reduce resistance from these sources you need to understand what the target system is trying to protect.

Social workers who engage in advocacy work, for example, have found that making it easier for the target to say "yes" will increase chances for success. This might mean providing people with an excuse that doesn't make them look bad to their superiors, or finding ways of giving them credit for positive results.

Make the Target Part of the Solution Rather than Part of the Problem

Sometimes resistance will come from the fact that people see no need for change, do not want to take responsibility for the problem, or blame the problem on others. When I worked with children's groups, I would often give a prestigious job (like serving refreshments or getting the basketball from the equipment closet) to the kid who was being disruptive. Recruiting the target as a helper encouraged identification with the group and resulted in improved behavior.

Another example is provided by Tough Love, a self-help group for parents of delinquent teenagers. The group doesn't blame the parents or expect them to admit to being part of the problem. Rather, by acknowledging the efforts the parents have put forth in dealing with their children, empathizing with their situation, and building on the members' desire to improve conditions at home, Tough Love encourages changes in parents' behavior that seem to help resolve their problems. Finding the motivation behind the resistance and understanding the functions that the resistance serves, will help you make the target part of the solution rather than part of the problem.

Working Through Other People

When you have been (or are likely to be) unsuccessful in dealing with a target system you might be able to work through third parties. A teacher who is respected by the principal might be able to convince him or her to endorse a certain proposal. The lawyer on the board of your agency might be able to talk with the city council member who hasn't returned your phone calls. In putting together your action system, it is helpful to be looking for connections that people have with potential target systems in the situation.

AGENCY AS TARGET: BUILDING A CLIMATE FOR GENERALIST PRACTICE

One of the most frustrating resistances to face is that of your colleagues or organization to your methods and the creative solutions you propose or try to implement. Aside from the other sources of resistance I have discussed, you may be facing a resistance to whole-mind thinking that is built into our left-mind dominated society. In the design phase, the creative generalist is not only concerned about the immediate problem at hand, but how her or his work can help build a climate conducive to generalist practice.

Lack of support can be posed as a problem for solving rather than a roadblock. We sometimes fail to see that the same methods of creative problem solving that we are teaching to clients to change aspects of their environments can be applied to the settings in which we work. Several recent books on effecting change in organizational settings written from the point of view of the line worker provide useful advice.[18] In addition, there are some strategies we can employ to create a more positive climate for generalist practice.

Picking the Right Problem

In Chapter 9, *Setting the Stage*, I talked about strategies creative generalists use to proactively engage problems that provide opportunities for expressing their vocational styles. One of the suggestions I made was to pick out problems that won't arouse the resistance of others, problems that others don't want to deal with or don't view as being within their domain (e.g., fighting on the school bus or vandalism in a neighborhood center). Every organization has continuing problems of this sort which nobody wants to deal with. These are good problems to tackle. Failure is no big deal since others have likely tried and failed in the past. But, if you do meet with success, it will get a lot of notice and help validate your approach.

Making Others Look Good

Consider the needs of others who must approve of your proposals and plans. For example, almost everybody hates paperwork, forms and reports. But administrators often depend on such paperwork to perform their jobs well. Taking the time to detail your proposals and reports, writing them in a language and style that make it easy for administrators to use in their work, and emphasizing points that make the organization look good will help you in the long run.

You may on occasion run into an administrator who likes to accept credit for successes in the organization while passing on the responsibility for failure to others. Though it can be exasperating when someone else takes credit for our idea, if the idea results in a better climate for generalist practice, it may be worth it. Creative generalists know that their security lies in their ability to generate, rather than protect, ideas. The freedom to create is the important issue.

Honey and Vinegar

You've probably heard that old adage, "you attract more flies with honey than vinegar." Your commitment, enthusiasm, optimism, and small successes will arouse people's curiosity and attract interest. Rather than asking how to overcome resistance to your ideas, you might ask what would give people a reason for wanting to learn more about what you are doing.

Build a Support System

One reason for proposing your ideas, even when acceptance seems unlikely, is that it helps you identify other people in the organization who are sympathetic to your way of thinking. A suggestion you make at a meeting may be turned down or a memo ignored, but a colleague at a coffee break may tell you what a good idea she or he thought it was. Taking the time to cultivate a support system will make your job much easier.

Timing and Ripeness

In discussing ways of prioritizing problems, I mentioned the idea of timing and ripeness. There are certain moments when a system is more open to change than others. Be aware of those moments and capitalize on them to propose new ideas or present a new way to handle an issue.

ENDING NOTE

In the past two chapters we have gone through the various steps in the design process: generating ideas, combining them into a rough solution (pattern), shaping and organizing them into a blueprint for action, and getting the solution ready for implementation. In the preparation phase I noted that we rarely achieve a complete understanding of a problem before needing to move on. The design phase continues our preparation in that the process of designing solutions generates additional information about the problem.

Likewise, there are limits to how detailed a plan we can develop, how many contingencies we can account for, before moving into the verification phase. It's not just that with more time we could develop a better solution. Once we set a solution in motion we can never fully predict what will happen. Our solution will get modified and further detailed in the process of verification.

Verification 14

After all the work that went into preparation and design, you're finally ready to verify the solution you developed. To verify literally means to make true; to prove, confirm or substantiate by demonstration or evidence.[1] And that is the essence of the last phase of the problem-solving process; you make the solution come true.

The social work literature typically treats implementation and evaluation as separate stages. "Verification" reminds us that evaluation is not just something done at the end point in the process. Solutions are evaluated throughout implementation; we continually monitor our actions, adjusting and adapting our solution as we go along.

Transforming a solution from idea to reality requires more than carrying out the tasks specified in a plan. Verification also involves confronting the unexpected, monitoring the process, evaluating outcomes, and concluding the process.

CONFRONTING THE UNEXPECTED

When a plan is set into motion, it takes on a life of its own, responding to unanticipated events (e.g., changes in the economy, a sudden illness) and producing unanticipated consequences. The planning we do in the design phase does help us deal with conditions or variables we already know or suspect to be important. Yet, unanticipated events and consequences can render our solutions ineffective, or sometimes even harmful.

In response, some authors have stressed exercising more *control* over the situation to make it and the effects of our actions more predictable. This approach, however, has the typical flaws of a control logic. It is believed that the more we are able to control everything happening in a situation, the more we will be able to determine what our actions will produce. But the *more* control we exercise, the *less* the situation resembles real life. For example, experiments designed to prove that a given intervention will result in a given effect must control for extraneous variables. The more highly controlled the setting, the more able you are to attribute the effect to the intervention. However, the more controlled the setting, the less it resembles the real-life situation in which the intervention must be carried out, diminishing the usefulness of the findings for the practitioner.

The more you attempt to control a system the more weaknesses it develops. This is as true for raising chickens in a factory-like environment (which makes them more vulnerable to illness by reducing their natural immunities) as it is for attempts to gain greater control over the human element in production through highly automated operations (like the General Motors plant at Lordstown which suffered from crippling wildcat strikes because people hated working there).[2]

All things are interrelated and have complex interconnections. When we face up to this, we recognize the impossibility of knowing in advance all the interconnections that have implications for our work and the limitations of approaches that isolate or separate elements to make them behave in predictable ways.

Rational planning is helpful only within the limits of a predictable future. To successfully navigate the implementation of an idea, we need to supplement the blueprint developed in the design phase with a readiness to respond to unanticipated events. To do this, the creative generalist must maintain a *discovery orientation* and hold a strong *vision* of intended outcomes.

Discovery Orientation

By "discovery orientation" I mean approaching verification as a process of discovering the best solution to the problem (in contrast to just following a blueprint to build the solution). Implementing an idea can be viewed as the start of a journey into unknown territory. In the preparation phase you gathered the materials and supplies for your journey. In the design phase you developed a rough map of the uncharted territory, based on the best available information at the time. You recognize the incompleteness of that map and the need to revise it as you go along and discover what is actually out there. You have a destination and an idea of which direction to move in but realize that the final point you want to reach may not be exactly where you thought it was. You also recognize that your vehicle and supplies may have to be adapted to changing conditions along the way.

A discovery orientation requires an ability to read the environment just as a seasoned guide knows how to read forest trails. In the absence of a detailed map you become sensitive to signs and signals from the environment to let you know if you are headed in the right direction. In other words, a discovery orientation depends upon *perceptual openness.*

Solutions are discovered through a continual process of action, reaction and adaptation. You have probably had an experience like buying a picture you have just the right spot for. When you get the picture home, you realize it would look better if the lamp and end table were moved to the other side of the chair. You do something to the room; it lets you know how it looks; you respond to what you see. Pretty soon the entire room has been rearranged to accommodate the new picture.

Arranging a room is a simple task compared to arranging a solution with people. Unlike the chair or picture, people in the situation will form their own interprations and attach their own meanings to the actions you take...and their responses may be incongruent with your intentions.[3]

Edward Popko's study of squatter settlements in Columbia provides an example of how such incongruities can develop. These settlements are the hodgepodge accumulation of shacks and jerrybuilt structures which poor migrants from the countyside contruct in nearly all cities in Third World nations. I'll summarize the Popko study:[4]

> In Latin America the squatter settlements were first regarded by city officials as public health hazards and illegal takeovers of land. But attempts to clear away the shacks often resulted in their surfacing in another part of town.
>
> From one point of view, the squatters had a right to the land. They were demonstrating initiative and independence in constructing their own dwellings. As new settlers entered into the economic life of the city, they gradually improved their bamboo and tarpaper shacks. The oldest parts of the settlements revealed a transition to more solidly constructed brick and cement structures equiped with utilities skillfully filched from the city's service system. The squatter settlement could be regarded as a system in which, with minimal investment of capital, the poor could engage in self-help.
>
> As this viewpoint gained currency, some public agencies lauched programs of self-help, offering squatter families access to materials, capital and technical assistance. "Sites and services" programs soon followed in which municipalities made available parcels of land that were graded and prepared for construction and supplied with basic services such as roads, water, sewage, and electricity. The task of selecting squatters, allocating construction loans, and distributing building materials was given to community associations. Individuals would construct their own dwellings. The program represented an attempt by the municipality to work with rather than against the squatters, to harness and support the squatters' initiative and skills, and to provide what the squatters were least able to supply for themselves.
>
> When Popko studied the program, he found incongruities between the intentions and assumptions of the planners and the interpretations and responses of the settlers. Public officials believed that the poorest of the poor settlers would take advantage of the program, purchase sites to house their own families, build their own homes, and use technical assistance.

In fact, what happened was that 30 percent of the settlers bought sites as investments, using the structures for commercial enterprises or for rental housing. Many settlers hired contractors to build the buildings and had no need for technical assistance. When the traditional building materials of bamboo, tarpaper and polyethylene had been cheap and readily available, settlers found it simple and cheap to build their own shacks. When these materials became scarce, it was necessary to turn to brick and concrete. Considering these materials too expensive to use in amateur self-help projects, they turned to professional contractors.

The settlers who used the projects as a source of income rather than housing were from the more affluent poor. Though they still had very little capital, this group had the enterprise and knowledge to develop sites as sources of family income. These people were investors. They hired contractors and had no need for technical assistance. Self-selected from among the urban poor, they saw the opportunity for investment, and acted accordingly.

When initially exploring a problem, you want to know how different key people are perceiving the situation. In the same way, as the solution unfolds, you need to keep tabs on the meanings others place on what is happening. You try to be aware of changing contexts (e.g., the market for building materials) which can invalidate assumptions on which your solutions are based. You try to develop "a nose for dilemmas" as Schön puts it (e.g., the families best able to manage the building of their own dwelling may not be those most in need of shelter).[5]

Holding a Vision

While a discovery orientation helps us respond to the unexpected *along* the trail, holding a vision helps us continually realign ourselves toward what it is that we see at the *end* of the trail. Our vision serves us like a "light in the window," guiding us through the storms that may come up. In the constant process of action-reaction-adaptation, you might sometimes get diverted or lose sight of your ultimate goal. ("When you're up to your armpits in alligators, it's difficult to remember that the original objective was to drain the swamp.") The ability to hold a vision, to picture the end point in our mind, to visualize an outcome, is critical to the process of getting there.

Studies of individuals who are successful in bringing about organizational change show that such individuals visualize the results they want in their work.[6] They create a clear and conscious *intention* as to desired outcomes and allow their actions to be guided by that frequently affirmed intention. In place of detailed plans, they start by creating an intensely alive mental representation of the end state which works through the individual's intuition and perceptual processes as she or he makes the multitude of everyday decisions which bring the goal ever nearer. Such leaders verbally communicate their intentions to others who could share their vision, and they communicate it daily through their actions and decisions. In due course, enough people share the vision and intention, and the dream becomes reality.[7]

Your problem may not involve changing an organization, but holding a strong vision of the end state and keeping your intentions clear will help you navigate the unknown. In Chapter 3, Mike pointed out that clarification of values in the direction of ethics prepares us for the anticipated while clarification in the direction of vision prepares us for the unanticipated. In a specific problem-solving effort, while our plan/blueprint guides us through anticipated details, our vision guides us through unanticipated events.

MONITORING THE PROCESS

A lot is happening in the verification phase. Just as sea captains or explorers needed a discovery orientation and vision, they also kept daily logs, notes...they monitored the process.

What Do You Need to Know?

To answer this question, let's look at what you are doing in the verification phase from three vantage points: you as *problem solver*, you as *researcher*, and you as *learner*.

You as problem solver

Here the emphasis is on the problem solving at hand. You want to record information relevant to the immediate problem. The working agreements you developed and various circles maps, matrices and flowcharts of the solution you constructed in the design phase help you identify tasks and activities you'll want to keep track of. I've already mentioned the need to be alert to changing conditions which affect the assumptions that your plan is based on and to keep aware of the meanings people place on your actions.

Contending with the unexpected is frustrating. Things get in the way. You need to persist with flexibility. Mike's point in Chapter 6, how writing things down helps maintain flexible persistence, is very applicable here. By jotting down the many questions and ideas that come up each day, you are keeping a left- and right-mind balance. You are helping your worrisome rationality keep a sense of order while giving your intuition room to work the questions into patterns of new understanding and action.

You as researcher

Here the emphasis is on your development as a practitioner, your increasing skill as a creative problem solver. Each cycle of problem solving is an opportunity to test tools, techniques and approaches that have utility beyond the specific problem at hand. Through your problem solving, you are producing information that can be useful to yourself and others in the future. For example, you may want to determine under what circumstances a technique (e.g., role playing) works best. By reviewing your notes from several different problem-solving efforts where role playing was used, you may come up with some useful observations about the technique. Through this kind of data gathering each practitioner acts as a researcher, contributing to the knowledge base of the profession.

You as learner

Here the emphasis is on your development as an individual, your self-discovery and growth. You are keeping track of the way in which you are learning to convert setbacks into new opportunities, your increasing ability to generate alternatives and visualize, your increasing sense of vocation and development of vocational style. You are reflecting on your uniqueness and self-expression.

Devices for Keeping Track

We can use both quantitative and qualitative devices to keep track of things. Quantitative devices are highly structured instruments, using precise predetermined categories for recording data. They are aimed at measuring or counting the amount of some "variable." Qualitative devices depend largely on the practitioner as the data-gathering instrument.[8] These devices are aimed at gathering descriptive information; meanings are established afterward. Let's look at some examples.

Quantitative measures

Goal Attainment Scaling is used to monitor progress in goal achievement.[9] This device consists of a grid in which each column represents a different goal and each row a different level of goal attainment. Five levels are specified for each goal, from "most unfavorable outcome thought likely" to "most favorable outcome thought likely" (by the follow-up date). For example, suppose one of your client's goals is to find a job. The scale you construct for this goal might look like this:

LEVEL OF PREDICTED ATTAINMENT	SCALE FOR JOB GOAL
Most unfavorable outcome thought likely	No action or discussion on finding a job
Less than expected success	Mr. X discusses job hunting but takes no action
Expected level of success	Mr. X formulates concrete plans for job search and secures at least one job lead
More than expected success	Mr. X files job application or attends job interview
Most favorable outcome thought likely	Mr. X obtains a job

Behavioral recording is another quantitative monitoring device. Here, a record is kept of the frequency of a given behavior which has been targeted for change (e.g., arguments with spouse, being late for school). The behavior can be monitored by the person involved or by the worker. Often a count will be done for a time segment prior to intervention to establish a baseline from which subsequent readings can be compared and progress noted. Various rating scales for emotional states (e.g., anxiety, depression) attitudes or interpersonal behaviors can be used in a similar way. Such monitoring devices are sometimes used to make people aware of problematic behaviors and attitudes.

Qualitative measures

Qualitative devices are aimed at determining the meaning of what is happening. You try and capture as much of the actual process as possible to provide raw data for later analysis. Guidelines developed in anthropological research for taking field notes can be useful to the practitioner.[10]

Field notes contain descriptions of what you have observed and should be written up as soon as possible after the observation. (As a practitioner, in most instances you will be a participant observer.) You should begin with the date, setting, who was present, and other pertinent background information. Field notes should be concrete and detailed, including direct quotations. They should separate judgments (e.g., Ms. X was poorly dressed, Mr. Y was assertive) from actual behaviors or things you observed.

Field notes should also contain your own feelings and reactions to the experience, the personal meanings and significance of what has occurred for you. Finally, you should record your insights, interpretations, beginning analysis and working hypotheses about what is happening in the situation.

Various formats can be used in organizing and analyzing data from such notes. For example, it is often useful to use a split page where one side contains description and the other your commentary, reactions, what you would have done differently, and so on. Other logs may have major categories for reflecting on things you are particularly paying attention to, e.g., opportunities to engage people's strengths, opportunities to promote self-reliance.

Argyris and Schön suggest using the split-page log to learn how congruent your espoused theories of action are with your actual behavior.[11] You select a challenging intervention or interaction for analysis. At the top of the page you indicate the purpose of the intervention, the setting, the people involved, and any other important characteristics. Next, you write a few paragraphs regarding your strategy—what your goals and objectives were, how you intended to achieve them, why you selected those particular goals and strategies. Then, using the split page, on the right-hand side you record a few pages of the dialogue that actually occurred (as accurately as you can remember it). On the left-hand side you write down what was going on in your mind while each person (including yourself) was talking. Finally, you describe the underlying assumptions that you think you held about effective action.

Another useful device for sorting data from field notes is the Awareness Wheel.[12] It defines five dimensions of self-awareness:

Sensing — the raw data your five senses are taking in.

Thinking — the meaning or interpretations you place on the raw data.

Feeling — the emotions your experience.

Wanting — your intentions, your immediate desires, things you want or don't want for yourself in the specific situation.

Doing — the actions your take in the situation.

I have found that use of the Awareness Wheel helps raise questions about a situation that can expand your learning. For example, you could ask about data you might have missed, other interpretations you could place on the data, what your feelings tell you about your intentions, and so on. It also helps you consider "what ifs" (e.g., what if I assumed that her behavior meant such and such; how would that have changed my feelings or intentions?).

Video, audio and other means of electronic recording are excellent ways of capturing accurate data.[13] Since reviewing the data they produce can be very time consuming, you need to plan in advance how you wish to use such information.

Monitoring the process is one form of evaluation. It is aimed at improving the problem-solving effort by producing information that can be immediately used in the process. The other form of evaluation focuses on the final outcome of the process.

EVALUATING OUTCOMES

What has resulted from the problem-solving process? Was it worth the effort? Is the situation better? Did the problem get satisfactorily resolved? Were the goals accomplished? After all the dust has settled, we owe it to ourselves and to the client to pose and answer such questions.

Further, in the past decade, accountability has become a big issue. Serious questions have been raised about the worth of our programs, services and methods of practice. Social work has been under the gun to prove its effectiveness and improve its efficiency. In turn, the social worker is urged to be a "scientific practitioner," treating each situation as a mini research study with a single-case research design. A lot of emphasis is placed on defining measurable goals.

Evaluation *is* important, too important to rely solely on quantitative research methodologies to evaluate our outcomes, too important to focus on goal achievement to the exclusion of other outcomes that inform us of our effectiveness, too important to avoid scrutinizing the criteria by which we value or determine the worth of our solutions.

Qualitative and Quantitative Research

The left and right mind each have a different way of "knowing." Ask your left mind what a flower is, and you'll get a scientific definition. Ask your right mind, and you'll get a picture or poem. Which is really the flower? Both, of course. Each answers different questions about flowers. Each answer serves different purposes.

Research is essentially an empirical (relying on experience or observation) process for finding answers to questions. Analogous to left- and right-mind thinking, there are two methods of research, quantitative and qualitative. As the names imply, quantitative methods are concerned with questions of amount, measurement, how much. Qualitative methods are concerned with essential character, the meaning of something. One is based on the research model employed in the physical sciences while the other comes out of an anthropological and enthnographic tradition. One is popularly regarded as "hard" research, the other "soft." And just as left-mind thinking has dominated the field of problem solving, quantitative methods have dominated research in the social sciences.

Because of its concern with questions of meaning, qualitative methodology stresses first-hand investigation, closeness to rather than distance from the data. It emphasizes concrete detailed descriptive information. It focuses on holistic analysis rather than component analysis. Qualitative methodologies are sometimes referred to as "naturalistic" because they are directed at studying phenomena in their natural settings and are responsive to the situation at hand rather than following a rigid predetermined design.

Quantitative and qualitative research also employ different approaches to theory building. The former operates deductively. Categories for assigning data are determined before the fact, and these categories are typically based on hypotheses logically derived from some *a priori* theory. Qualitative research operates more inductively, resulting in "grounded theory" (i.e., theory which grows out of real-world experience). Grounded hypotheses are less guesses about what is likely to be the case than directions indicated by actual data.[14]

The very terminology employed by the two forms of research reflect their different approaches. For example, ethnography is described in the literature as a process of learning from people, rather than studying people. The ethnographic term, "informant," (meaning a native speaker who is a source of information) is very different from the social science term, "subject." While the typical social science researcher is interested in testing hypotheses by studying the behavior of subjects, the ethnographer seeks to discover the cultural knowledge of informants.[15]

There is a large body of literature comparing the different assumptions underlying quantitative and qualitative research and the differences in how the two deal with methodological problems such as validity, reliability, and boundary setting. Much has also been written on methods of data collection and analysis in qualitative research.[16]

The purpose of my very brief sketch of the two forms of research was just to introduce you to the topic and the issues involved.

In recent years there has been much progress in improving the usefulness (and increasing the utilization) of evaluation results by applying qualitative methodologies to evaluation research.[17] Moreover, the stance of qualitative research (e.g., closeness to data, naturalist settings, grounded theory) is very compatible with the realities of the world in which practitioners operate.

Becoming a scientific practitioner will benefit you, the client and the profession, but only if quantitative methods are balanced with qualitative methods as required by whole-mind thinking.

Goals, Outcomes and Effectiveness

One way of determining effectiveness is to define goals in terms of quantitatively measurable variables and monitor changes in those variables. Earlier, I discussed quantitative measures such as goal attainment scales and behavioral counts. If your goal is to improve Johnny's school attendance, you can count the number of days he skips school and see if that number decreases after your intervention. This approach to determining outcomes and effectiveness is very appropriate when your goals are to affect change in discrete variables such as school attendance behavior.

However, this is just one aspect of determining outcomes and effectiveness. We can never make a move which results in only the consequences intended for it.[18] When we are looking at outcomes we have to look beyond the boundaries determined by our goals. Focusing only on goals can obscure other important changes that might have occurred.

The term "side effects" occupies a prominant place in our modern vocabulary. Whether we are talking about health, ecology, the economy, or politics, news reports continually document the unintended consequences of our solutions, negative side effects which eventually exacerbate the original problem. (Fortunately, unintended and unexpected side effects sometimes improve a situation.)

The issues involved in looking at outcomes are illustrated in a study by Lewis and Hugi of the use of inpatient and aftercare centers ("therapeutic stations") by chronically mentally ill people. [19] Statistics like readmission rates made those therapeutic stations appear ineffective. But qualitative fieldwork methods, aimed at discovering how the patients viewed and used these facilities, painted a very different picture.

The researchers found that lacking a social network, the patients used these "therapeutic stations" for social and material support such as friendship, borrowing money, getting leads on housing and so on. Though professionals regarded the stations as places that provided treatment, the patients used them to supplement the scarce personal resources at their disposal. In fact, receiving treatment was sometimes viewed as the price to pay for spending time at the station.

Lewis and Hugi conclude that the rate of readmissions may tell us more about the options available to the poor than it does about the quality of mental health care. More closely aligning the goals and programs of the therapeutic stations with the way patients actually used them would increase both their effectiveness and efficiency.

When we are trying to understand the outcome of our problem-solving effort, it helps to remember what we have often stressed in this book—a solution, like a problem, is a pattern. The same methods and dimensions we use to understand the problem (how people are perceiving the situation, how they are interacting to maintain it, and so on) can be used to understand the new pattern (the solution) and draw conclusions about it.

Values and Good Solutions

In evaluating outcomes we are not just describing or measuring the results of the problem-solving process. If you remember, to evalute means to determine the worth or value of something. To the extent that our goals reflect values we are trying to promote, their worth is implied. But we also need to explicitly consider how we value the solutions we help bring about.

What is a creative generalist's conception of a good solution? What is he or she trying to promote beyond the solution of the specific problem, and how does it get reflected in the solution? How do we distinguish good solutions (which embody desired values) from bad solutions (which are destructive of those values)? In Chapter 5, Mike identified standards for creative solutions: fit, novelty, alchemy, and elegance. How do these standards help us evaluate solutions resulting from problem solving in social work? Let's first consider the fit of a solution.

Fit

In a given problem-solving activity we usually estimate the *fit* of a solution according to how well it responds to the problem at hand. Another kind of fit, part to whole, should also be evident. Any problem-solving activity (part) should fit with an overall design or larger pattern (whole).

From experience with side effects, we know that some solutions act destructively on the larger pattern in which they are contained, much like a disease or addiction acts within the body. While they may solve a problem in the short run, they ultimately worsen the problem or cause a ramifying series of new problems. Such solutions typically solve for a single purpose or goal, such as increased production or alleviation of symptoms, and usually achieve their goal at high social, biological, ecological or psychological costs.[20] The use of pesticides will increase farm productivity in the short run but endanger the health of the land as well as the consumer in the long run. Further, the use of pesticides result in the genetic evolution of stronger strains of weeds or insects that are immune to the original pesticide. Thus a stronger pesticide must be developed, continuing this vicious cycle.

It may be more efficient to run the meeting of a neighborhood center advisory board yourself than to take the time to train the members to do so. In the long run, however, you may be creating an unhealthy dependence on you and reinforcing a sense of powerlessness in the group. Public housing projects designed to provide large amounts of inexpensive housing have often been responsible for destroying the integrity of neighborhoods.

Good solutions, creative solutions, act in harmony with the larger pattern, just as a healthy organ acts within the body. As Wendell Berry has noted, the healthy organ does not give health to the body nor is it exploited for the body's health. Rather, it is a *part* of health.[21] In the same way, good solutions are part of the health of a system, be the system an individual, a family, a group, an organization or a community.

Novelty

The novelty of a creative solution typically refers to its unusualness and originality. I'd like to propose another slant to the novelty standard. Social work itself can be considered a novel profession because of the strong *value* it places on self-reliance. Throughout the book, Mike and I have emphasized problem solving *with* people as collaborators rather than as experts *for* people. Beyond solving the immediate problem, then, our solutions must reflect the person's or group's increased ability to solve future problems without our help.

Another novel aspect of social work is our concern with both the individual and society. Social workers are committed to promoting self-reliance *and* reciprocity, self-interest *and* community interest, the dignity and uniqueness of the individual *and* a diverse yet cohesive society. Though these are sometimes posed as conflicting aims, we have seen that it is possible to develop synergistic solutions that bring them into harmony. Our solutions should reflect these dual commitments.

Alchemy

Alchemy is reflected in the manner in which ideas and resources are connected in a solution. By combining the same resources in different ways, new parts and wholes emerge; they are transformed by the new arrangement or use (e.g., trash into treasure). And when you sense diversity and redundancy in a solution, you know you will soon find alchemy.

Let's use an ecosystem analogy to look at this standard. Dan Hemenway notes that there is always a variety of pathways by which an ecosystem can proceed about its business.[22] Though each organism occupies a unique niche in an ecosystem, if one species is removed, everything it does for the whole will be accomplished by other organisms. If we lose one of our senses (e.g., sight or hearing), our other senses seem to sharpen up in compensation.

The resilience of natural systems is based on diversity and redundancy. The systems and solutions we design will likewise be strengthened if we keep these principles in mind. If one solution fails, it should not rule out other solutions. Growing food in monocultures, where everything hinges on the success of one species, is self-destructive. Growing grain should not make it impossible to pasture livestock, and having a lot of power should not make it impossible to use just a little.[23]

If your program relies on multiple sources of funds, it will be less vulnerable than if it depended on a single source. Employing homemakers at your agency should not preclude mobilizing the resources of a client's natural helping system. If a strategy to influence the vote of the city council has the potential to backfire and damage your group's reputation, a less drastic approach should be tried first. If parents are learning a new way to handle the acting out behavior of their child, they should have a contingency plan should things start to fall apart. It pays to heed the valuable design lesson that nature teaches us.

Hemenway reminds us that diversity means diversity of relations between things, not just a bunch of different structures assembled.[24]

He notes that a garden with an assortment of different plants randomly arranged will not be nearly as productive as one in which the plants are arranged as co-productive companions. The various elements of our solutions should reflect alchemy in similar connections.

Elegance

An elegant solution in a given situation is one where the solution is the simplest in proportion to the complexity of the variables (e.g., the number of interrelated problems) involved. In other words, an elegant solution is multipurpose.

Riding a bicycle to work instead of driving a car may be a solution to how to build an exercise routine into your daily life. At the same time, it also saves money, reduces air pollution and saves on road repairs.

Remember the problem I discussed in Chapter 11 concerning the geriatric patients who were wandering into the wrong room? That situation was based on an actual work experience of mine. The solution we came up with to help patients find their own rooms involved having the aides review magazines with the patients and make up a collage of pictures that represented meaningful things in the patient's life. The collage was put on the doors and helped the patients recognize their rooms. This not only solved the wandering problem but had a beneficial side effect as well. By putting the collage together with the patients and seeing what pictures held meaning for them, the aides got to know them better as individuals.

And remember the elevator problem from Chapter 12? The idea of a health club not only solved the elevator problem but opened up other possibilities for making the building more attractive to the tenants. Such solutions are elegant. They have an "economy of motion" and "powerful resolution."

The relationship of simplicity of solution to complexity of problem can also be viewed in terms of scale. An elegant solution is appropriate in scale.

Issues of scale require continuous attention to the consequences of a chosen scale. Hemenway observes that small may be beautiful, but smallest is not always optimal. He points out that some things can be done well only on a large scale (e.g., manufacturing computer disks) whereas others rapidly deteriorate with increasing scale (e.g., food preparation).[25] In determining the optimal or appropriate scale for a solution, at least two factors need to be considered in combination.

Conservation of resources is one factor. Given two solutions that are equally feasible and likely to be effective, we would choose the one that consumes the least resources (e.g., money, time, energy).

Confining the solution in the lowest system level is another useful guideline. If a neighborhood is experiencing a problem, you can look for a solution that involves only the neighborhood, rather than the city, county or state. A neighborhood babysitting exchange may prove an adequate solution to a child care problem, not requiring the involvement of other systems.

The issue here is not just using fewer resources or keeping the size of the bureaucracy under control. Solutions that rely on local resources stay on a scale that people can comprehend, implement, maintain, vary in response to circumstances and pay steady attention to. Such solutions encourage people to take personal responsibility for dealing with problems while at the same time offering a way to have direct impact on those problems. Local solutions, responsive to local conditions also result in a healthy diversity of the whole. In other words, we often find elegance in local solutions.

CONCLUDING THE PROCESS

The last aspect of the verification phase involves bringing the process to an end. In the social work literature this is often referred to as "termination." While the term may be appropriate in settings where you are unlikely to see the client again, it is less applicable to settings where some kind of ongoing contact with the client is more the norm. There, the endpoint of the process merely marks a transition from one problem-solving episode to the next.

One concern in bringing the process to an end is that positive gains not be lost after you are gone. However, this is an issue that should be addressed throughout the process. We have emphasized the need to promote self-reliance and teach problem-solving skills to the client. Further, your assessment of the situation in the preparation phase (and its subsequent updates) should alert you to elements connected to the situation which might work against the changes that have been initiated. And you should have taken these into account in your design. You can use the final sessions or meetings to review and assess the problem-solving process with the client, consolidate the learning that has occurred, and make sure she or he knows what do do if further assistance is needed.

Saying good-bye to the client is the last concern in the process. Since the worker-client relationship can develop an emotional intensity, ending the relationship is sometimes difficult. If the client's relationship to the worker is one of dependency, then indeed, the client may have fears and feelings about leaving that need to be worked through.

In a problem-solving relationship, one of collaboration, the situation is different. You may have shared an intensity around dealing with the problem. You may expereince some difficulty saying good-bye to someone with whom you worked closely. There may even be a tinge of sadness in acknowledging the importance of what you contributed to each other. But we have all experienced saying similar good-byes to neighbors, colleagues or friends. We can draw on those experiences in concluding the problem-solving process with clients, For example, you could mark the end with some kind of "ceremony," (e.g., going out to dinner with the task force members, holding a party with the neighborhood association to celebrate a victory, meeting at a coffee shop for your last session with a client). Sometimes a simple "drop me a line and let me know how you are doing" may suffice. Most of us realize, when we say such things, that it is unlikely we'll be in touch again. But it's a polite way to express your affection and say good-bye to someone who has meant something to you.

ENDING NOTE

Throughout the problem-solving process you have been implicitly integrating three roles—problem solver, researcher, learner. In the verification phase you are acting, reacting, and adapting in implementing the solution (problem solving), discovering and producing knowledge useful for others (research), and growing, acquiring skill and wisdom, and affirming your "self" as a creative generalist (learning).

We have noted that the same cultural bias in problem solving (dominance of left mind over right mind) is present in research (dominance of quantitative over qualitative methodologies). Examples of the same duality can also be found in the field of education in discussions of goals and methods of learning (filling the empty vessel vs. learning to learn). This should not be surprising since the processes of problem solving, research and learning share key elements.

The creative generalist not only appreciates the need for whole-mind thinking in all three processes, but recognizes the essential unity among the processes themselves. You can't be a good researcher without being a good problem solver, and so on. We don't have to integrate research into practice; it is already there. We just have to recognize it.

What is often posed as a conflict between research and practice is more accurately stated as a conflict between right-mind-centered practice and left-mind-centered research. When we acknowledge the need for whole-mind thinking within each of the three processes, the conflicts will dissipate and we'll reap the benefits of an integrated perspective.

THE
CREATIVE
GENERALIST

Part Four

CHALLENGE

Where do we go from here? 15

Well, here we are sitting on the front porch of the last chapter. I'm tempted to stay out here listening to the crickets for a few more hours, but let's go to the kitchen table one last time... I'll heat up some coffee and tea, you get the marking pens and butcher paper for doing a few circles.

Before you leave, I want to talk about something that I'm sure you figured out a long time back. Allen and I believe in generalist social work. We believe it can make a difference, that through it we can, individually and collectively, make the world a little better than we found it.

I know this sounds optimistic so I'm asking you to keep it under your hat. There are a lot of left-mind thinkers out there and if we start sounding too optimistic they'll say we're shallow, naive and ignoring serious problems.

Marilyn Ferguson knows what I mean. That's why she called her book The Aquarian Conspiracy. If we believe we are capable of creating a better world or (even more far-fetched) that we have already begun to create that better world; if we openly talk to each other about our efforts and optimism; if we know we are part of a growing network stretching across this country of ours...well, I guess we are, in Ferguson's use of the word, conspirators.

It's not that we are conspiring on a master plan for saving the world. Instead, we are creating an organic, evolving form that has direction for the whole while encouraging diversity and uniqueness in the parts.

As a collective we share values and beliefs about the way we would like the world to be. As individuals we contribute our unique designs for achieving that preferable future. We believe the world can change for the better and commit our effort to that change. Believing the world could become a better place and designing a personal course of action to encourage this development both involve optimism.

Creative generalists, then, are *optimistic, they share the kind of optimism introduced in the opening chapter of this book,* informed *optimism. Before considering* where we go from here, *it is important that we take another look at informed optimism and expand its meaning to fit the challenges ahead.*

INFORMED OPTIMISM

Informed optimism is an aspect of the balanced, whole-mind thinking necessary for developing a creative generalist mindset. It recognizes the way things are (left mind) *and* the way they might be (right mind).

Pessimism is grounded in mistrust of ourselves and our ability to solve problems. Informed optimists are able to appraise past successes and failures while forming patterns of future possibility. They acknowledge analytic reasons for both trust *and* mistrust and consciously *choose* to emphasize trust for the positive vision and strength it offers. They combine the most promising and positive elements of a current reality into a pattern or vision of a preferred future reality. In this way they "reserve space" ahead that they then fill and verify in daily work.

"Reserved space" is essentially a vision of possibility. Such visions serve as an integrating force in our activities. They guide us in our efforts to convert problems into opportunities. They help coalesce reason with desire for realization in concrete action.

The voice of informed optimism speaks from the intellect and the heart. All of us have heard that voice when listening to some of our most powerful leaders. They are typically recognized as having unusual intuitive skill, strongly held purposes and vision.[1]

Consider for example, the voice of someone who clearly understood the meaning of informed optimism, a person who combined strategy and dream, a political tactician who wanted legislative action representing collective acknowledgment of an individual change of heart.

He was, of course, Martin Luther King, Jr., a man who went to Washington to win passage of the Civil Rights Act but also spoke from his heart about a dream.

Remember then, if you are rightfully accused of being optimistic, you are in very good company. Throughout history there have been individuals and small groups with daring and vision on the forefront of change. They understood how to make things happen. They worked to break a collective pattern of perceptions, habits of thinking. They emphasized a dream, an optimistic vision and in their work moved that idea toward critical mass. They understood that, once an idea is planted in collective awareness and nurtured through individual acts, it will grow, develop coherence, and actualize.

In this sense there is a very practical side to informed optimism. It is an important element in our attempts to change the world we live in and has a strong influence on our daily problem-solving activity. Through it we know where to direct our *energy*.

ENERGY AND INFORMED OPTIMISM

Nearly everyone has an intuitive grasp of the importance of energy. We know what it feels like to be energetic, enthusiastic. We know when a meeting "drains" our energy. We know when we've met a "magnetic" personality. We know what it means to "lend" energy to someone in need. We speak of some people as having a lot of "drive" and others as having less. Some of us feel higher energy levels at night and others in the morning. On some days we are lethargic and on others are bursting with vitality. We hear of unusual reserves of energy tapped by people in moments of crisis (e.g., a mother lifts a car off her child).

The fundamental relationship of energy to living can also be traced through many of our theories about emotions and behavior. Ingalls, for example, tells us that Jung saw his work as parallel to that of his contemporaries in physics and frequently met with Einstein. Indeed, Jung believed every psychic content had "energy value."[2]

Psychic energy was basic to Freud's theories of psychoanalysis.[3] Lewin saw human behavior in terms of charged particles in a magnetic field and developed what he called "force-field analysis."[4]

Many Western theorists view "life force" as a psychic energy field within all of us. In Eastern culture it is similarly believed that the body is surrounded by an energy field called ki, chi or prana (meaning the life force).

Biofeedback experiments have shown individuals can learn to direct energy toward healthy growth and away from malignant growth. Acupuncture re-directs energy toward a pattern of balanced health. The self-healing capacity in all living things is a form of directed energy.

Koestler tells us that the energy in spontaneous laughter and our spontaneous "AHA!" in discovering a creative idea, come from the same wellspring.[5] It is same energy built up in creative tension when we search for a creative solution. It is the energy joyfully released when we find it. It is the energy held in the visualization of that idea which sustains us through the frustrations encountered when implementing and verifying it.

We can learn more about working with this energy by understanding its action in energy *fields*.

Energy Fields

I introduced you to energy fields in the Chapter 6, *"Tools for cultivating creativity."* There I was explaining the tool of putting an idea aside when the tension of frustrated efforts reaches a certain pitch. Let's review some of that earlier discussion to see how energy fields relate to informed optimism.

If you remember I told you about a simple demonstration of the effects of an energy field. When you sprinkle sand on the sounding box of a violin and draw the bow over the strings, the energy field produced by the sound vibrations will arrange the sand into geometric patterns. The patterns vary according to pitch, intensity and so on. The same thing happens when you pass a magnet under a surface covered with metal particles. The magnet acts on the particles, they begin to move and suddenly they spring into geometric patterns.

We then looked at that demonstration in slow motion to get a better picture of what was happening. As we move the magnet closer and closer to the metal particles, they become charged with energy. Each particle becomes a magnet in miniature and begins to attract and repel other particles just like the poles of the magnet. As the magnet comes closer we see the particles begin to move. They are in a state of accelerating tension, acting on each other as the magnetic energy increases. At a certain point a chain reaction occurs and the metal particles form harmonious patterns.

I explained that in the creative process whole-mind thinking is like that magnet. The preparation stage is like drawing the magnet of whole-mind thinking closer to the problem, question or circumstance. We begin to manipulate the mental particles. With increasing attention, the energy field builds intensity. Energy flows from this increasingly powerful *creative field* to the idea material. We experience tension in the bumping, chaotic action of the mental particles. Our analytic mind works feverishly to form those geometric patterns, but it is like moving those metal particles with a tweezers. We feel tired and confused. It is time to set the idea fragments aside (incubate them) for a while.

We turn our conscious attention elsewhere, but at another level of awareness the pattern-forming process continues. When we later return to the problem we find fresh new ideas to work with. Or, sometimes without warning, we instead sense a creative possibility coming just before it bursts into our thoughts. The earlier tension is spontaneously released into that pattern of resolution and we experience relief, AHA!

By remembering how the creative field works in forming solution patterns we can learn to accept creative tension calmly with alert, sustained attention. With each succeeding cycle of problem-solving we can learn to better sense the balance point between persisting with an idea or deliberately setting it aside for a while.

In a similar way if we remember the action of another energy field we will be more effective in our problem-solving. Optimism and pessimism are rooted in positive and negative emotions. These emotions form energy fields that interact with the creative field and influence it in important ways.[6]

Emotional Fields

You're already aware of the constant interaction of your thoughts and feelings. You know that when you have negative feelings about something your mind forms negative images of it and when you experience positive feelings your mind is picturing positive images. The intensity of those feelings and the formation of emotional fields is the focus of our attention here.

Our emotions form energy fields that interact with the mental elements in the creative field. When the emotional field is congruent with the creative field, harmonious patterns emerge. When it is discordant with the creative field, dissonance, static and continued frustration are experienced.

When we talk about the importance of valuing, vocation, mission and purpose we are talking about emotional fields. The intensity and direction of both our perceptual and emotional fields are critical in problem solving. The more intense we are about wanting to solve a problem, the more quickly we activate the creative field. Throughout the process, positive emotions continue to resonate with and strengthen the developing creative field. When negative emotions erupt and gain strength they block the pattern-forming process. In other words, the more intense our emotions the more quickly they develop into an emotional field that either enhances or impedes finding a creative solution.

When you're working on a problem that's extremely important to you, your desire for a positive solution is strong. You set your thinking and mental elements moving in that positive direction. Your emotions and perceptions mirror one another and they begin to build a creative energy field. You push for a resolution. The movement of those idea fragments within the creative field intensifies with your desire and focused manipulation of ideas. You sense the tension of this movement as frustration, fatigue or impatience. This tension is a necessary part of the work of the creative field, but how you *interpret* the felt tension can bog down the process.

We all get negative feelings and thoughts in those periods of frustration and fatigue ("you are doing it wrong," "you'll never succeed," "give it up"). The point is to understand them and acknowledge them, but not to intensify them. When negative feelings are intensified they begin to influence the search direction of the creative field. To avoid this, separate the natural tension from the often corresponding self-doubts and negative thoughts. Recognize the "I can't do it" or "I'll never be able to do this" are false conclusions. Indeed, the opposite is true. In tolerating the tension of building the creative field you *are* "doing it,"you are sensing the increasing intensities and movement within the creative field doing its work for you.

With each succeeding cycle of problem solving we are more able to notice different energy intensities and transformations at the different stages. For example, when we transform the released energy of an "AHA!" into a visualization of the solution we then sense the pressure to implement it, to *do* it in the external world. Obstacles always arise and frustrate the doing of it. Those frustrations again will trigger negative thoughts (I just knew something like this would get in my way). Our creative field will accept the obstacle as information, it will adapt to it and form an updated solution pattern, *if* we keep the "now it won't work" from intensifying into an emotional field.

The "power of positive thinking," the "placebo effect," strong values, positive visualizations and informed optimism make sense in terms of the influence of energy fields.

SO WHERE *DO* WE GO FROM HERE?

As individuals we need to begin the process of designing a course of action. Later I will identify and explore with you a few key elements helpful to this design work. But as a creative designer you already know we first need to do a little preparation. Let's start with a review of a few of the basic trends in our society.

Where Is Our Society Heading?

Our country is midway in a period of transition from the *sunset economy* of an industrial age to the *sunrise economy* of an information age.[7] We are struggling to maintain the security of our industrial power, while at the same time carving out a niche in the emerging world of high technology communications.

We are steadily losing ground as an industrial power and are finding it more and more difficult to compete in the world market. The newer equipment and facilities of Japan or West Germany, for example, are more efficient than ours, and at the same time, costs of upgrading our own industries are prohibitive. The lower labor costs of developing countries give them a competitive edge over us as well.

Robotics, computers and automation are rapidly changing the face of industry with machines taking over assembly functions and human participation shifting toward idea generation, model and procedure development, communications and invention.

Satellite communications span the globe like a giant nervous system, and the business world is changing from paper and print transactions toward computers and electronic impulse transactions. Paper money, for example, is yielding to computer transfer of funds. Every day, the equivalent of billions of dollars are moved electronically in the world market.

Traditional boundaries between where and how we *live* and what we do for *work* are fading. We are using our new communications technologies as a tool to diversify those living/working arrangements. Home and family are increasingly recognized as an economic base for small business entrepreneurs, and telecommuting from living room to a distant employer is an increasingly available option.

We are decentralizing and emphasizing local self-reliance. We are shifting from fewer and larger to more and smaller. We are diversifying our interests while coming together in a new and flexible structure, the social network

Problems in the Transition

If the increases in unemployment during our changeover from an industrial to an informational economy are anywhere near as dramatic as predicted, the attention of social work will be riveted in that direction. Certainly, helping people meet basic needs (food, clothing, shelter) will be a major activity. Corresponding increases in chemical and person abuse, mental and emotional illness and crime will further strain shrinking resources and an escalating national debt.

The majority of jobs opening in the information economy will require new technical skills and extensive retraining programs. And the "sunrise" economy isn't without its share of rain clouds.

Some are concerned about our rapid acceptance of hi-tech communications and our matter-of-fact compliance with requests for more and more extensive, personal information (mortgages, credit cards, driver's licenses, medical treatment). We are primed for increased surveillance. In a period of high unemployment and depression, how quickly would we further relinquish our right to individual privacy?

Others consider individual vulnerability to invasion of privacy less critical than the growing dependence of our major institutions on electronic information systems. They warn that our banks, national defense agencies, large and small businesses and public utilities are helpless to protect themselves from terrorists, vandals and thieves armed only with computer programming skills and easily obtainable sabotage devices.

The tension between individual freedom and security of the whole (society) will increase in the information age. The key question is, *"Who* will have access to *what* information and for *what* purpose?" And it appears we may soon have to face this question.

In 1985, Shiite terrorists hijacked a TWA jetliner of American passengers. With satellite communications the world watched the hour-by-hour unfolding of events until the hostages were freed to return home fourteen days later. After their return, the White House announced its concern that rapid media reporting of the event interfered with their diplomatic strategies. They were searching for avenues of cooperation to better coordinate reporting in such periods of emergency. This concern about worldwide communication systems in periods of national emergency will likely be accentuated in the near future.

Consider all the satellite dish TV antennas popping up on the landscape. The power and number of satellite transmitters in orbit is also increasing rapidly, and the size of dish antenna receivers needed for plugging into world communications is shrinking. We now have dish mounts that can tune in on international satellites (TV from Peru, for example), and a language translation technology waiting to be connected. Predictions are that small dish antennas will soon replace conventional rooftop TV antennas.

The 1984 Cable Communications Act made it unquestionably legal for homes to receive satellite signals. Conventional television networks are losing ground to a diverse range of new, small TV stations. In the near future we may view critical incidents such as that terrorist hijacking through the perceptions and reporting of countless news sources including those from countries other than our own.

How will political powers respond to immediate reporting from such diverse sources? How will traditional avenues of negotiation be affected by the on-camera limelight? How vulnerable will information systems be to the manipulation by political enemies? How will we piece together an understanding of events from the multiple perceptions reported?

Let's compound the issue with another growing capability. We are used to watching a TV, listening to a radio broadcast, talking and listening on a telephone. But these technologies are merging. We now speak of entertainment/communication centers that receive *and transmit* information. These integrated systems contain TV, video recorders, stereo receivers, sound recorders, home computers, printers and telephones in one multifunctional package. Laser discs and holograms merge sounds and images into three-dimensional representations of reality.

In your mind hook up this receiving/transmitting unit to a dish antenna on top of your house and aim it toward a worldwide system of orbiting communications satellites. It sounds like a science fiction movie, doesn't it? How on earth (no pun intended) will we and our current institutions respond to such communications capabilities?

What is *school* when information from any library in the world is connected to that communications center in your living room? How will our political representatives react to monitoring and quickly organized political networks among constituents? Who will decide when it's time to go to war? What is a *hot line* if the world is on one huge *party line*?

The question, "Who will have access to what information and for what purpose?" is indeed complex, and the answers we come up with will have implications for social work practice as well. Perhaps the world affairs of terrorists, politics and satellite transmitters seems remote from our everyday problem-solving activities, but consider this:

Information is the source of power in an information economy. Will the poor have access to that power? Will they have access to the technology in neighborhood centers or public libraries? Will they know how to use it?

Opportunities in the Transition

It is tempting to either love or hate, fear or desire our hi-tech inventions. We speak of them as if they are good or evil. But they are tools. Computers, satellite transmitters, stereos, TVs, video recorders, telephones, robots, laser disks, holograms...all tools. How we use them is a question of values, human values.

Take the computer for example. Many fear it. Why? Because it threatens to replace us in our jobs. Computers *are* more efficient in certain kinds of jobs. They *will* replace us in those jobs. But humans will decide what jobs. If we create robots that dance or paint portraits, will we call them artists? How long would we attend basketball games or tennis matches or broadway plays if the performers were robots?

We say computers are dehumanizing our jobs and causing unemployment. Consider the many jobs, especially in industry, that have been dehumanizing since their inception. Put the word, "employment," out of your awareness for a minute and ask yourself if we should, for example, computerize (dehumanize) the coal mining industry.

Now bring that word, "employment," back again and take a long hard look at it. Our future will challenge many of our assumptions about that word. Can you conceive of a world without that word? How about a world where only half the people fit its conventional meaning? We treat the word as if there were no alternative (except disaster). We have fashioned our lives around that word. It is imbedded in our conception of the "good life". We use it to order and arrange reality.

A person is either employed, unemployed or retired from employment; you work for someone, or you don't. If you start your own business, you are *self*-employed. To be employed you *must* work for someone even if that someone is yourself.

The words, "employment" and "unemployment," "employee" and "employer," gained special meaning in the industrial age. Will they have the same meaning in an information age? With increasing part-time work, job-sharing, diversified individual work agreements and a growing emphasis on thinking, deciding, inventing and communicating, the boundaries between working and living are dissolving. Imagine that in ten years we have a 50% employment (or unemployment) rate. What will all those people be doing if they aren't *working* for an *employer*? What will *you* be doing? Don't hurry with your answer we have time...computers are giving it to us. The questions of the future will be value questions, questions of how to best use the time and flexibility we are creating.

Computers are not only performing more of the menial, physical or dangerous work of industry. Artificial intelligence is developing to the point where it may take over many of the analytic thinking tasks of humans.

In *The Cognitive Computer*, Shank suggests we not fear this development, for he sees it as freeing us to explore and develop our human creativity and imagination. He believes we will consider the things a machine does (including certain forms of thinking) less important simply because a machine *can* do them. In his view we'll again emphasize activities that we devalued over the last fifty or so years (e.g., art, architecture, conservation and farming). We'll focus our work on the *enhancement* of human values.[8]

Are we being sold a bill of goods by Shank, Vallee, Toeffler, Naisbitt, Ferguson and others who look down the road and see a renaissance in human values? Not if we are optimistic. But creative generalists are challenged to be *informed* optimists. We must square off with the space between *here* and that *down the road* . The meaning of employment and work may be changing, but how does our advancing technology relate to the person who is unemployed *right now?*

Predictions about enhancing human values may help us develop our informed optimism on the vision end, but what about those practical day-to-day problems we face? For a beginning answer, let's take a close look at an emerging social structure, the one Vallee refers to in his book, *The Network Revolution.*[9]

A Point of Leverage and Intervention

I believe the point of leverage for participating in shaping the world of the future is also a point of intervention for the day-to-day problem solving of creative generalists in social work. It is a growing trend that would benefit from our skills and support. It has immediate potential for realizing our values and honoring our commitments...it is that phenomenon called networking.

We know of the many critical problems we are facing. The promise is not that the hi-tech information age will be problem free. Rather we will face new potentials, complexities and risks.

The promise is not in the technology but in our capacity to *use* technology as a tool for solving complex problems. The determination to face our problems openly, to tolerate the complexities and ambiguities of living, to challenge assumptions, to take charge, to combine ideas in the search for creative solutions, to persist, to test and verify ideas in concrete action...here is the promise and the place of optimism. If others are using technology to develop structures such as computer networks and if we as a profession value the direction of this development, we should actively participate in it.

Now let me tell you something. I am not infatuated with the buzz and flicker of the hi-tech age. I find no special joy in staring at a computer monitor. Video games never held any special appeal for me, either. Our black-and-white TV has a 10-inch screen, and I drive a vintage car of the rusting hulk variety as infrequently as possible. I seldom go to a movie and never wear my digital watch/mini-calculator. I have yet to experience the thrill of an automated teller. I don't own any chrome furniture, and I'll admit that, when I see all those folks walking up and down the shopping mall with musical headphones and boom boxes, I fear they are turning their minds to mush...in the eyes of the next generation I am likely a stick in the mud.

But as an individual I *did* decide to learn how to operate a home computer. I bought one and set it up on a card table in our bedroom. I *am* convinced that networking offers us a chance to increase our political participation, renovate our failing institutions and reinvigorate our sense of home, family and community. If we take the opportunity to participate in networks, if we get inside the communications technology to guide it in a direction that protects and promotes what we value, if we teach others how to use rather than fear or be exploited by this tool...I believe we will encourage the self-reliance, diversity and mutual exchange that will eventually increase the quality of life choices for everyone.

Informed optimism is rooted in the mindset of the creative generalist. It is in the *readiness* to act. It is in the awareness of vocation and creative capacity. It is in deciding to *make things happen*...and if we apply that mindset to computer networks, we will help make things happen.

To better grasp the potentials here, let's look closer at those computer networks.

Computer Networks

Computer networks combine the computer with another communications technology, usually the telephone (sometimes radio receivers), allowing users to send messages, pass on gossip and news, search through indexed data files, manage diverse businesses and keep in touch with friends.

Basically here's how it works. You dial a telephone number and set the phone receiver on a device (modem) connected to your computer. A tone or message tells you when you are "on-line." If you are entering a long-distance network you might type in a code for a cheaper rate. You then type in your name, identification number (recognized by your network) and a secret password (to keep others from entering under your identification number).

On your computer screen the network welcomes you and asks if you want to check your "mail" for any messages. After reading the mail you type in your special interest (send a message, scan the news, play a game, post an item on the bulletin board or see who's on-line talking to each other), maybe exchanging a few comments.

Perhaps you're looking for a sympathetic response in an emotional crisis or seeking ideas for a small business venture. You might be shopping in a buyers' network, voting or joining a town meeting on some local political issue.

You might be using a network for the more mundane uses of directory assistance, travel information, the weather announcement or some mail-order purchase. On the other hand you might be exchanging ideas on some scientific project with a distant co-worker, bartering through a network of neighborhoods or tracking down a financial resource for a friend.

You might be checking one of the many community bulletin board systems for want ads, greetings or general graffiti. Perhaps you have connected with an instructional network for a daily lesson in which you interact with other on-line students, or one of the franchised information centers offering conferences, writing and editing consultation, and reading materials.

ELEMENTS OF DESIGN

Tear off a sheet of that butcher paper, would you? Put it down here so we can organize some of the key points so far by drawing a few circles.

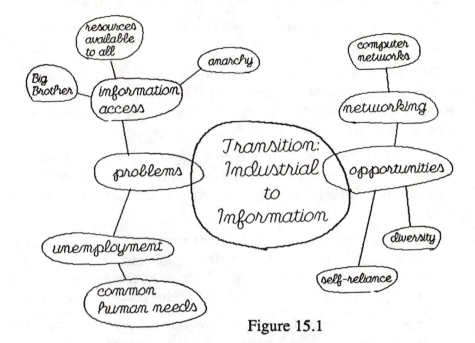

Figure 15.1

Now, I'm going to use some of the information summarized in the above circles to develop a story that should be helpful for identifying elements important to designing a personal and professional course of action. In it I am asking you to imagine you are the main character and already have a home computer.

Scene One

You've invited a friend named Mary over for dinner. While you're talking, she tells you about a special award she is going to receive at a very "uptown" banquet. She's nervous about the presentation and says she'll probably calm down if she ever manages to find the right dress for the occasion. She's checked a number of shops but hasn't found anything she really likes.

"Want to do a little shopping right now?" you ask.

"I don't think there are any stores open this late," Mary answers.

"Oh, yes, there are," you say while walking over to turn on your home computer.

With the two of you seated facing the monitor, you switch the modem on and type into a regional retail sales network. You select a few of your favorite stores, type in "evening dress" and watch as the images come on the monitor screen.

The two of you are using the computer as if you were paging through a catalog. You look through the special sale items, check on a section called "latest fashions" and proceed to "shop" a number of stores.

You explain to Mary that if she finds anything she likes, you can type in her choice and the dress will be delivered to her door by a specified time. She will even get a discount if she makes advance payment by typing in her credit card or checking account number.

The two of you are really enjoying yourselves and Mary is surprised at how quickly she is learning to work with your computer. You have another surprise in store for her. You connect into a national network, and shortly you are looking through dresses in one of the fancier shops in San Francisco.

This is one of the promised *luxuries* of the home computer, shopping from your armchair. The clothing industry will undoubtedly support this kind of retail sales network with toll-free numbers and high quality advertising displays. For them it will mean increased sales through impulse buying and saving the cost of catalog printing and mailing.

But your home computer has other potential *luxuries*. Imagine that you leave the national network and return to the regional one. You select a fabric shop and type in "evening dress patterns." On the screen a welcome message appears and you are instructed to type in descriptive information regarding the consumer (height, weight, dress size, hair style and color, etc.). An image appears approximating Mary. You are now free to use all patterns from the store supply and can rearrange design elements to suit your taste. As you make choices of bows, lace, sleeves and belts, the dress on the screen image of Mary changes accordingly. Next you are free to choose from a wide variety of fabrics suitable to whatever design you have created.

You and Mary do design a dress, but neither of you has the sewing skill necessary to complete it. You therefore exit the retail stores network and type in a community bulletin board. Here you find listings similar to classified ads in a newspaper. You don't see any ads related to tailoring/sewing so you consider listing your desire for a network relationship with someone who would sew custom designed clothing for you. In such a relationship your tailor/seamstress would have your sizes, special interests, cost range and material preferences. Through the computer you could work with your tailor-seamstress in making choices and changes.

While you're talking over this possibility with Mary, an idea strikes you. One of your clients is an elderly man named Tom. Tom has accepted responsibility for raising three of his grandchildren. You know he has sewing skill because he has been making clothes for the children for years. You have marveled at his talent in the past and believe he would do well with Mary's design. He is not employed and certainly could use the extra money. You explain this to Mary and she's willing to give it a try if you think you could arrange something with Tom.

You talk with Tom, and he is delighted with the idea. He accepts the sewing job and surprises Mary with his unusual skill and creative flair. Tom tells you how great it would be to have sewing jobs like Mary's on a regular basis, and you suggest putting an ad on the community network bulletin board. Tom is willing to try this but says he doesn't know anything about computers. You agree to help him learn and get his business started by using your computer to connect with potential customers. Tom does line up a number of other sewing jobs and is very enthusiastic. Later you find that the local community center has a public access computer available, and Tom is off and running as a budding entrepreneur.

Scene One Discussion

It might seem that you could have used a newspaper ad to get Tom's business going, so why use the computer? First, let's say Tom lives in a small rural community 40 miles from a city of potential customers. With a computer he can develop a relationship with a circle of repeat customers in which preferences, modifications, fabrics and special needs are transmitted and stored in computer memory. He can integrate accounting, design images, correspondence, tax-reporting, reminders and dates and ongoing communications with customers (designers) with the same tool.

Using the classified ad of a computer network has more potential than that of a newspaper because of the speed and flexibility it offers. Large amounts of information are immediately available for decision making.

In networking the relationships between producer and consumer are more personal and responsive than the typical retail store purchase. Currency transactions are often converted to barter and trade.

What would happen if trading, buying and selling through bulletin boards really caught on? Consider our dress-making example. How many homebound individuals have sewing skill? What if they began participating in network exchanges? What impact would this have on the mass-production clothing industry? How long would it take before we began to hear of layoffs and unemployment in the garment industry? On national news we would be told of the devastating blow to the clothing industry...and with your third ear you ask *which* clothing industry? If you were an unemployed dressmaker, how long would it take before you were contracting directly with computer network dress designers?

We hear of the many illegal aliens working in garment factories. Would such individuals be interested in network transactions? Would they continue to accept the risks of becoming illegal aliens if network marketing opportunities were available to them? Why wouldn't network transactions extend beyond national borders?

Now erase the word "dress" from this example and insert other items, products, reports or services. Consider them in terms of local, regional, national and international networks. Want ideas for building a chicken coop? renting a room in Houston? selling an antique lamp? swapping a collection of bubblegum baseball cards? getting a social work position in Toledo? Put it on a bulletin board.

Do you think those in current power positions are unaware of this potential? Do you think, for example, the garment industry has failed to recognize it?

I read that organized labor wants to make it illegal to *telecommute*. *Telecommuting* refers to employees of companies who stay and work at home using the computer to relate to their employers (as different from the entrepreneur development I was suggesting in my example). The unions warn of "electronic sweatshops," underpaid telecommuters who are denied typical benefits. They believe children in some homes would be forced to help parents fill computer-derived jobs and tell us the unions could not be expected to monitor home-based employees for such transgressions.

At a 1983 convention the AFL-CIO called for a ban on telecommuting. They want to expand a 1943 legislation that banned industrial homework in the garment and jewelry businesses and are requesting enforcement of other policies (e.g., local zoning laws that restrict home businesses) to prevent the spread of home-based industrial work.[10]

Perhaps the unions have a legitimate concern about the potential of home-based sweatshops. On the other hand, it may be that they're worried about organizing and trying to collect dues from people working out of their homes. The point here is that the potential of computers and home-based employment is already recognized.

Wouldn't you know it? Here you are trying to get an unemployed person named Tom a little extra income, and you walk right into an organized opposition. Seems as if some of the network poentials might be nipped in the bud, doesn't it? But don't underestimate the ability of computer networks to quickly organize.

Two years ago the city planners of Colorado Springs decided to tighten their city ordinance that regulates working out of the home. One person, Dave Hughes, testified against it when it came before the planning commission, and the commission tabled the matter for 30 days. Dave put the text of the ordinance onto a computer bulletin board and sent a letter to the editors of two local newspapers. In the letters he said he didn't like the ordinance, and if anybody wanted to read it, they could check the computer bulletin board. One hundred seventy-five people showed up at the next planning commission meeting. Someone had used a word processor to revise the ordinance and it wound up going back to the planners four times. Each time it went up on the bulletin board until it was resolved.[11]

Typically, organizing people for political action (meetings, phoning people) takes a lot of energy. The computer network economizes that energy tremendously by making it possible for people to mobilize electronically. In this case they only had to come together for one meeting...the actual hearing.

A final point on the Scene One example...when you know the issues and consciously decide to participate in computer networks you are making pragmatic, holistic and political decisions. Connecting Tom to a home-based, clothes-making business was pragmatic in the story. It is also holistic in its connection to national unemployment and our transition from an industrial to an information economy. It is political in its potential impact on industrial structures and regulatory policies.

Scene Two

Let's add to the Scene One example. Say you're a school social worker in a small community (e.g., 5,000 population). It's a consolidated district so you travel around quite a bit visiting families in other small towns and rural locations. You also have a lot of professional connections in a large community (200,000) about 40 miles away. Your success with helping Tom find work has stimulated your interest in looking for other possible network arrangements.

You also have a strong professional/personal interest in holistic health, exercise and nutrition and have been invited to be on a panel at a regional conference on "Holistic Health and Family Practice". Your topic is the food-health connection. Imagine yourself as that panel member. When it's your turn to speak, you present something like the following:

> We are more and more recognizing that the efficient, inexpensive, centralized, mass production of food through chemical agriculture has many hidden costs. The "bigger is better" viewpoint of the industrial age assumed a simplistic measurement of successful food production. By centralizing the growing function in giant "food factories," we believed we could maximize the ratio of money put in (petroleum-based food additives, preservatives, pesticides, herbicides and fertilizers) to the amount of food we got out of the process.

> But the food factory concept of efficiency is being rightfully challenged. Jeremy Rifkin has pointed out that when we talk about the efficiency of American agriculture and how much progress we have made, we are considering only the *quantity* of food that can be produced by one person-hour of work.

> A peasant farmer produced 10 calories of food for every calorie expended in *human* labor. An Iowa farmer produced 6000 calories of food energy for every calorie expended in *human* labor. With these measures it does seem we have made much progress in the efficient production of food.

> A different picture emerges when we consider *total* energy expenditures. To produce a can of corn containing 270 calories of energy, the Iowa farmer expends 2790 calories when you include the energy consumed in farm machinery, synthetic pesticides and fertilizers. In other words the American farmer actually uses over 10 calories of energy for every calorie of food energy produced.[12]

When we thought petroleum-based energy was a limitless resource, we didn't care about those total energy expenditures, but we now understand more about *non-renewable* energy supplies.

Our earlier measures of food production efficiency also failed to account for other important costs falling outside a simplistic energy equation. The "bigger is better" mentality overlooked the costs of destroying our farmland through chemical abuse. It failed to consider the political implications of our over-dependence on foreign oil supplies necessary to maintain chemical agriculture. It payed little attention to the rapidly disappearing family farm, the cherished values and traditions of small farm communities in America... and it failed to recognize an attribute of food as important as quantity...*quality*.

We are learning of the complex relationships between our health and the food we eat. The old adage, "you are what you eat," means more to us now than it did a few years ago. A fruit or vegetable raised with pesticides (to kill the bugs), herbicides (to kill the weeds), dyes (to color it) and preservatives (to prevent decay) "carries" those additives to our plates and bodies. We are no longer surprised to hear that toxic chemicals have been found in our ice cream, soft drinks, meats, chewing gum or the glue on our postage stamps. We are no longer surprised to hear that a food processing chemical we can't pronounce is causing a disease we didn't know existed.

We *treat* disease with counteracting chemical *medicines*, and in our struggle to maintain health we are promoting the same petro-chemical industry that controls our food production system.

The same industry that fuels farm machinery and fuels the growth of foods produced, fuels a transportation system to haul it to the supermarket and to haul us to and from that supermarket. It fuels a chemical food *problem* and fuels a chemical medicine *solution*...anybody worth his or her salt substitute should recognize that from an ecological point of view the *cost* of our food is quite high.

All of us have become more receptive to an ecological perspective. We understand more about holistic health, living in harmony with nature, healthy individuals in healthy societies. We are beginning to recognize some of our previous solutions as part of our current problems. For example, we spend billions to maintain the illusion of clean health. We spray our home environments with chemical scents. We have deodorizing, hygienic, antiseptic products for every human orifice. We wash our sinuses, floors and walls with chemicals. We scotch-guard our furniture, spray our underarms with antiperspirants and hang chemical strips to kill our bugs.

We are beginning to reconsider ideas we used to think of as strange (e.g., macrobiotics: that food grown in a certain geographical locality is healthier for humans living in that locality than food grown elsewhere.) And slowly we are finding that our problems are also our opportunities. For example, a plant carries the poisons we feed it, but it also will carry the extra nutrients we feed it. A stringbean will use certain nutrients for its own healthy growth and maturation but will also pick up extra nutrients (if available to it) and *store* them as a bonus for humans.

A knowledgeable food producer using organic growing principles can *ask* that little stringbean to pack a few extras on the trip to your plate. Of course, it takes the grower a little more time and attention to talk to that stringbean so it will *cost* more in the market (while *costing* less in terms of our health).

Our fear of disease has encouraged a very profitable insurance industry. Perhaps our desire for holistic health will help us see that little stringbean as a far less expensive insurance premium.

During open discussion following the panel-member presentations, someone comments on the difficulty of obtaining quality food as you had suggested in your presentation. Others in the audience chimed in, adding that it's especially difficult to seek alternatives to the supermarket as full-time working parents. Another asks where you are hiding all those "knowledgeable organic farmers," and everyone laughs.

Right then it hits you, and you wonder why you hadn't thought of it before. In your home community you know of a farm family struggling to sell their high quality foods. They have a beautiful place. Small, but well-designed with gardens, fields, pastures, a greenhouse, pond and stream, orchards and animal shelters. They are an excellent local source of organically produced vegatables, grains, fruits, mushrooms, herbs, poultry, milk, eggs, nuts, fish, pork, beef, honey, and other foods but have had difficulty developing a reliable form of marketing. They participate in a farmer's market, but it is seasonal and unpredictable.

You tell the audience about this farm family and pass around a sign-up sheet for anyone interested in developing some sort of producer/consumer agreement with them. The response is very enthusiastic. You agree to talk to the farm family and get back to those listed on the sign-up sheet.

Like the conference participants, the farm family is enthusiastic about developing a buy/sell agreement. After a number of organizational meetings and lot of circles mapping, a one-year trial agreement is reached.

Twenty families from the original sign-up sheet eventually participate on a regular basis. The farm family, as well as several of the "buyers group" families, have home computers that are quickly recognized as essential to the continued success of the arrangement.

The farm family continually communicates with participating families through a computer network. All have ample opportunities for face-to-face contact as well. The farm has picnic tables available during pick-your-own seasons and encourages family outings. Potluck seminars on food-related topics are often arranged. Recipes for trying new and unusually nutritious food flash back and forth across computer screens.

The relationships here are far different than what we think of in typical producer/consumer transactions. The farm family knows members of the network families personally. Special dietary needs, taste preferences and desires for experimentation are recorded in computer files.

With new knowledge, participating families learn to *design* their foods according to specific health needs. Changing needs are accommodated because of the interactive relationship between grower and consumer.

The farm family has the security of knowing what food to produce for a guaranteed market, and the network families have a secure source of healthy, high quality foods. It is a synergistic relationship that encourages continued information sharing and learning.

Scene Three

The success of both Tom's clothes-making enterprise and the family food group encourages you to experiment with other computer network arrangements during the following year. But this is the last week of school and your mind is attracted to one of the benefits of your school social work positions, summer vacations.

This year you have planned a two-month, cross-country traveling/camping tour. You have saved a long time for this and just purchased a van-sized camper rig. It has a complete dinette (sink, stove, eating area), cupboards, lights, heater, pull-out bed, closet, carpeting, curtains…the works. You even have a special area reserved for storing your computer.

Each evening you've been spending a few hours in it packing things away, sitting at the dinette table to plan your route, meals, and flexible schedule of arrivals. You're excited not only about the trip, but all the other uses you have thought of for this new camper of yours.

You think of all the short jaunts around the state you'll make throughout the year, the instant shelter and private space it provides. It's really a portable living and working space. Even those tedious periods of year-end report writing would be easier. You'll just grab a few supplies and your computer and head for a weekend of state park camping.

You begin to think about how useful this camper will be in your daily work as well. Whenever you want to meet with a working parent during the day, the noon hour is typically the best time available. Privacy is often difficult to find at the parent's workplace, so you typically end up meeting at a restaurant. This solution poses its own problems (time lost in travel and parking, expense and noisy noon-hour restaurants). Now you can have your portable home/office ready for action at a moment's notice.

You laugh to yourself when imagining the reaction of one of your favorite working mothers. She enjoys teasing you, and you know she'll have a lot of sarcastic comments to make about your "traveling dog and pony show."

While you're daydreaming, you sense another idea about to surface. You gaze at all the cupboards, the nooks and crannies you could use to store things in your little portable office. You imagine yourself at the table drawing a circles map with a client. You see yourself with her checking something out on the computer...The ideas come faster now, connecting, merging and forming an overall image, an idea worth testing.

Something that has bothered you all year long is the limited accessibility to computer networks for many individuals and families that you know would benefit a great deal from participation.

Though more and more people are buying computers, there are many others who simply cannot afford them. A few public access computers are available, but use is restricted to library or neighborhood center hours, involves travel and waiting your turn.

A computer's advantages are related, in part, to the speed of on-the-spot information gathering and decision making. Many times, when you were talking to a client, you wished you had your own computer along to pull in information on an existing service, generate ideas by scanning a bulletin board or save key points after a discussion.

Because of this, you had planned to take yours along with you on home visits starting next year but still didn't know what to do about the many contacts you have with people outside of their homes (e.g., computer on a restaurant counter?).

Now you see a pattern forming that responds to these concerns. You'll use this work and play living space of your camper as a mobile networking office. You'll collect and store all sorts of resources on disk. For example, you'll have eligibility requirements for traditional programs and services available, you could even have copies of application forms on file. You'll organize and file all the key people and informal connections you have made throughout the community over the years. You have learned many of the pathways around constraints for getting something done. Now you'll see that names, phone numbers and procedures are also available, right there in that computer file. You'll use it to keep track of incubating ideas, of community events, bits and pieces of information on little known or emerging resources.

Soon your idea develops into an image similar to what I described as a *resource peddler* in the chapter on vocational styles. Right here before your eyes is a new version of that peddler wagon. You know it will take some time to get all that information typed into your computer, but you are excited about the possibilities. You could become a community bulletin board for those who don't have access to computers at this time. You see yourself gathering ideas through an ongoing community resource inventory.

You reframe some of your ideas to fit with your school social work position and begin to envision a school/community exchange. In later proposing it to your school board you include components such as routine visitation (which the school system sees as helpful to encouraging parent participation). You can encourage economic development (your examples of Tom and the family food farm now serve you well) and keep track of employment opportunities you hear of as well.

Since you participate in a national computer network of social workers, you tell others of your project and pick up more practical ideas...

READINESS TO MAKE THINGS HAPPEN

I developed the above three-scene story to illustrate how an individual design *might* develop. In Scene Three, previous experiences and understandings combined into a form (in this case a school/community exchange program) that externalized a vocational style (resource peddler) in a flexible pattern responsive to "where things are going" and "what we might do about it."

I did not present the story as *the* answer. In each scene of the story I emphasized the kinds of things you *might* be doing in your daily living and problem solving and how these *might* develop into an ongoing activity (e.g., a project or program). It may have seemed you were simply following your nose as one or another opportunity fell into your lap. But when we step back and view the story from a different angle, we see that your ability to perceive and act upon opportunities involved a *readiness*. With the mindset and tools of the creative generalist you were *ready* to make things happen. Let's use the story to show how the mindset and tools were instrumental to this readiness.

MINDSET AND TOOLS

In the story you took advantage of events because of your readiness as a creative generalist. Your mindset and tools (values, knowledge, creativity and skills in problem solving and establishing problem-solving relationships) prepared you to act upon opportunities. It is also important that you perceived opportunities because you believed they were there and looked for them (informed optimism).

Our rational mind sizes up the activities of the story as the cause/effect result of a sequence of fortuitous events. A whole-mind perspective includes the intuitive awareness of an endless chain of holistic possibilities. The answers you found in the story may seem obvious and logical. But with a whole-mind perspective you have also connected them (as parts) to an overall pattern that incorporates making things happen at other levels of design awareness.

Martial Arts Strategy

In the story you illustrated a belief often apparent in the work of a creative generalist; you have more power to guide the course of events by moving with the flow of energy than opposing it. This is a martial arts strategy of action.

For example, you didn't argue against Mary's desire (movement, direction) for a new dress by chiding her affluence or telling her to apply the purchase price to a social good. Instead you encouraged her desire and guided it toward an arrangement that benefited both Tom *and* Mary.

You didn't tell the conference audience that the only way they could change things was to boycott or somehow protest the factory approach to food production. Instead you encouraged their desire for high quality food and connected it to a food producing family.

You didn't avoid the use of a computer in a personal stand against the abusive and exploitive potentials of this communications tool. Instead, you emphasized and developed a positive potential also existing in this technology. You aimed the strength of your energy toward encouraging the use of computer networks.

Multiple-Problem Perspectives

You were responding to immediate problems (e.g., Tom's unemployment, the farm family's marketing struggle) pragmatically. Yet holistic and political awareness were also apparent in your actions.

You helped arrange practical solutions to local problems that were at the same time *small steps* toward solving problems at a societal level (unemployment as key problem in declining industrial economy and access to information as key issue in the information economy).

The same practical solutions can be viewed as political in that they encouraged local self-reliance and the development of business entrepreneurs as an alternative to consuming the products of centralized clothing and food industries.

You encouraged mutually beneficial relationships between Tom and Mary and the farm family and the conference participants. In a small way you helped break through the conventional barriers of urban/rural, educated/uneducated and employed/unemployed.

Value Connections

Your actions in the story reflected the dual commitment of our profession to both individual and community (society). You helped solve not only a problem in time but a problem over time. The arrangements you encouraged between people helped bridge the natural tension between the individual and society (e.g., unemployment as an expected part of transition) and increased their awareness of mutual exchange (synergy).

You also helped revitalize other beliefs, values and commitments articulated earlier in the history of social work. The mindset of a creative generalist capitalizes on the powers of perception. The way we perceive history also determines its usefulness as a resource in our daily problem-solving activities. Each of us sees ourself as separate, whole, unique and alive in the present but also know we are extensions of people and events in our past. We can learn to perceive our relationships to those of the past in ways that help fortify our readiness to make things happen.

Try approaching the history of social work in the same way as many now attempt to trace their family roots. Search the material to find the roots of your *social work* family. Try to see the people behind the sentences in dusty, gray covered books. Consider their convictions with the same interest and tolerance you would have for a great, great grandmother.

Read the lines and read *between* the lines. Capture the ideas and challenge the assumption that they are old, outdated, irrelevant to the current course of events.

Grab an idea, stretch it, toy with it, energize the thoughts and emotions that went into it by *re-viewing* it in the present. Connect its intuitive direction to what you now understand.

Keep it simple; select a few individuals and a few convictions and start from there. Read them, listen to their ideas, invite them to a meeting and ask them how they might approach the problems you are facing. Draw a circles map and let them pitch in a few ideas.

Jane Adams and the Settlement House traditions were in that story with you. We are all immigrants in a new world, requiring new skills for participation. We need new decision-making models for high-speed communications. We have new potentials for participatory democracy and increased self-reliance. The computer networker in a mobile office adds new meaning to another tradition of "friendly visiting."

Edward Lindeman was a social worker and adult educator who often wrote on the power of information and ideas to change our lives. Much of what he said years ago is pertinent to our work in the information age.

As we learn to develop our capacity for creative thinking we add new meaning to that old phrase "conscious use of self."

Increasing unemployment encourages us to listen to those in our past who experienced the Depression and knew the meaning of the term "common human needs."

We find the barriers between where we live and where we work gradually disappearing. More and more of us are moving to smaller cities adn towns hoping to renew our sense of community. A social worker named Bertha Reynolds has much to tell us about the participation of our profession in this development. For example in her 1951 book, *Social Work and Social Living* she reminds us that our professional worth is tested in our living as social beings, that we must learn to use our common heritage as members of communities to bring about desired changes, that just as we are influenced by what society wants of us, our beliefs and practice will imprint upon the society of our time.[13]

Explore our history and traditions. You will find powerful alliances for making a difference in the present.

Vocational Style and Creative Talent

In the story, your experiences evolved into a project idea that fit with the "resource peddler" vocational style. Elements of the alchemist-trashpicker (transforming problems into opportunities) and the organic social worker (encouraging strengths and capacities) were tied in as well.

The story could also be restated to emphasize other vocational styles and creative talents perhaps more closely approximating your personal inclinations. For example, the mobile office could be a tool for the:

— *improvisor* (a "Johnny Appleseed" stimulator).

— *craftsperson* (a "quality cabinetmaker" who uses the computer to fit needs and resources into quality-built solutions).

— *inventor* (a "resource tinkerer" who combines old parts like the food producer and consumer in new ways like the food network).

— *innovator* (a "Robin Hood" who finds access to the riches of the information age and gives them to the poor through computer networks).

— *generator* (a "wise wizard" who might use the school/community exchange to develop new decision-making procedures, new forms of citizen participation in local politics).

Creative Problem-Solving Connection

Obviously your design, the way you incorporate vocational style and creative talent into a work form will be an expression of your creativity. The process involves perceptual openness, flexible persistence, associating/ combining ideas and judging/expressing them.

The question, "Where do we go from here?" is our *problem*, and we want our individual answers, our designs, to be creative. We want them to meet those rule-of-thumb standards we talked about in earlier chapters—*fit, novelty, alchemy* and *elegance*.

Fit

The individual designs we come up with must, of course, be responsive to the problems we attend to in daily practice. They must be open and flexible, adaptive to the variety of circumstances we encounter. At the same time they must be coherent, a point of stability to sustain us in the complexities of our work. The design you ended up with in the story, for example, was both adaptive and reliable. It helped you integrate your values, knowledge and skills in a form (resource peddler) that would continue to serve you in a variety of problem situations.

Novelty

Our design should have enough audacity of imagination to attract others and encourage imitation. It should be something recognizable in a sea of programs, projects, acronyms and legalese.

The portable office developed in the story could be adapted to project a variety of images reflecting your individuality or the needs of a specific situation (e.g., traveling medicine show, country doctor, peddler or troubleshooter). A mobile living space decorated to express your unique personality, a vast amount of information and resources at your fingertips, traditions and rituals of doing circles and brewing fresh coffee on the stove...such become your trademarks, your way of extending "at-homeness."

Alchemy

We want a design that helps us convert problems into opportunities. In the story, for example, you transformed the "office interview" into a "portable workshop," a place of resources, materials, collaboration and personality, a place where the Toms and Marys, food producers and consumers could transform their problems into opportunities.

Elegance

Finally, our design should be elegant. It should be practical enough to use in day-to-day practice yet connect to larger issues. Its arrangement should be simple, yet complex. In the story your activity was responsive to the problems at hand yet connected to the societal issues of unemployment and accessibility to information and technology. In teaching others your skills of creative problem solving, in helping others break through the mystique of computers, you are encouraging self-reliance, decentralization, diversification and mutual exchange. Your ideas were straightforward yet incorporated political, pragmatic and holistic awareness.

Nothing here needs to be earth-shaking. In the story you were just a creative generalist forming problem-solving relationships and using a common garden variety of creativity to make things happen.

SUMMARY AND ENDING COMMENT

In this final chapter I tried to show a way in which we each can go about answering the question, "Where do we go from here?" I tried as well to show how you might weave the information presented in earlier chapters into a personalized work pattern. The pattern you come up with should enhance your cultivation of creativity, your experimentation with technlogy, your sense of vocation. It should also serve as a reminder that you are not alone in this. Many of us, like you, want to participate in a profession that is adaptive, responsive and creative.

In a very real sense we are all at the starting point; we stand in the doorway to a world that could be very different. Around us social problems are increasing dramatically. Because of a debt-ridden government, we are witnessing program cutbacks as never before. The demand (problems) is increasing while the supply (financial support) is decreasing. We are pressed, justly or not, to develop local solutions to our difficulties.

As painful and depressing as this may be, the message is clear...we must change our course. But there is reason for optimism. Creative generalists in social work, like those elsewhere, are accepting the challenge and committing their energies toward creating a preferable future...it's time to go to work.

Notes

Chapter 1

1. Pincus, Allen, and Anne Minahan. *Social Work Practice: Model and Method.* Itasca, Illinois: F. E. Peacock Publishers, 1973.
2. Bodner, Joan (Ed.) *Taking Charge of Our Lives.* New York: Harper and Row, 1985; Lipnack, Jessica and Jeffrey Stamps. *Networking.* New York: Doubleday and Company, 1982; United States Office of Consumer Affairs. *People Power: What Communities Are Doing to Counter Inflation.* 1982.
3. Ferguson, Marilyn. *The Aquarian Conspiracy.* Los Angeles: J. P. Tarcher, 1980, page 16.

Chapter 2

1. Meyer, Carol H. *Clinical Social Work in the Eco-Systems Perspective.* New York: Columbia University Press, 1983, page 6.
2. Aptekar, Herbert H. Generalist practice and specialization in professional education. In D. S. Sanders, O. Kurren and J. Fischer (Eds.). *Fundamentals of Social Work Practice.* Belmont, California: Wadsworth Publishing Company, 1982, page 114.
3. Boehm, Werner W. The nature of social work. *Social Work.* April 1958, Vol. 3, pages 10-19, page 18.
4. Germain, Carel B. An ecological perspective in casework practice. *Social Casework.* June 1973, Vol. 54, page 326.
5. National Association of Social Workers. *Standards for Social Service Manpower.* Washington, D.C.: National Association of Social Workers, 1973, pages 4-5.
6. Council on Social Work Education. Curriculum Policy for the Master's Degree and Baccalaureate Degree Programs. In *Social Work Education.* New York: C.S.W.E., 1982, page 3.
7. Naisbitt, John. *Megatrends.* New York: Warner Books, 1982, page 85.
8. Irey, Karen. The social work generalist in a rural context: an ecological perspective. *Journal of Education for Social Work.* Fall 1980, Vol. 16, pages 36-37.
9. Pincus, Allen, and Anne Minahan. *Social Work Practice: Model and Method.* Itasca, Illinois: F. E. Peacock Publishers, 1973, pages 9-14.
10. Bartlett, Harriet M. *The Common Base of Social Work Practice.* New York: National Association of Social Workers, 1970, page 96.
11. Meyer, Carol H. *Clinical Social Work in the Eco-Systems Perspective.* New York: Columbia University Press, 1983, page 21.
12. Pincus and Minahan, *Social Work Practice*, page 14.

13. Schwartz, William. Private troubles and public issues: one social work job or two? *The Social Welfare Forum, 1969.* New York: Columbia University Press, 1969, page 38.

14. Pincus and Minahan, *Social Work Practice,* page 15.

15. Sarason, Seymour B., and Elizabeth Lorentz. *The Challenge of the Resource Exchange. Network* San Francisco; Jossey-Bass, 1979, page 145.

Chapter 3

1. Ornstein, Robert E. *The Psychology of Consciousness.* New York: Harcourt Brace, 1977.

2. Working definition of social work practice. Copyright 1958, National Association of Social Work. Reprinted with permission from *Social Work.* April 1958, Vol. 3, No. 2.

3. Working statement on the purpose of social work. Copyright 1981, National Association of Social Work. Reprinted with permission from *Social Work.* January, 1981, Vol. 26, No. 1, page 6.

4. NASW code of ethics. Copyright 1979, National Association of Social Work. Reprinted with permission. This code was revised and adopted by the 1979 Delegate Assembly of NASW.

5. Vigilante, Joseph L. Between values and science: education for the profession during a moral crisis or is proof truth? In Daniel S. Sanders, Oscar Kurren, Joel Fischer, *Fundamentals of Social Work Practice.* Belmont, Calif.: Wadsworth, 1982.

6. Tillich, Paul. Critique and justification of utopia. In Frank E. Manuel, *Utopias and Utopian Thought.* Boston: Beacon Press, 1971, page 302.

7. Koestler, Arthur. *Janus.* New York: Vintage Books, 1978, page 27.

8. Fuller, R. Buckminster. *Synergetics.* New York: Macmillan, 1975.

9. Benedict, Ruth. Patterns of the good culture. *Psychology Today.* 1970, Vol. 4, No. 1, pages 53-55 and 74-77.

10. Maslow, Abraham H. *The Farther Reaches of Human Nature.* New York: Viking Press, 1971.

11. Benedict, *Patterns,* pages 54-55.

12. Maslow, *The Farther Reaches,* page 203.

Chapter 4

1. Jones, Russel A. *Self-Fulfilling Prophesies.* Hillsdale, N.J.: Lawrence Erlbaum Associates, 1977, page 159.

2. Naisbitt, John. *Megatrends.* New York: Warner Books, 1982, page 201.

3. Schumacher, E.F. *Small is Beautiful.* New York: Harper & Row, 1973.

Chapter 5

1. Fabun, Don. *You and Creativity.* Beverly Hills, Calif.: Glencoe Press, 1971, page 5.

2.   Davis, Gary A. *Creativity Is Forever*. Cross Plains, Wis.: Badger Press, 1981, page 2.

3.   Noble, Daniel. Creativity and the changing environment. In *Creativity: the State of the Art*. Racine, Wis.: A pamphlet published by The Thomas Alva Edison Foundation Institute for Development of Educational Activities, Inc., and the Johnson Foundation, 1972, page 20.

4.   Raudsepp, Eugene. *Managing Creative Scientists and Engineers*. New York: MacMillan, 1963, page 4.

5.   Lenowitz, James M. The "ah ha!" experience. In *Creativity: the State of the Art*. Racine, Wis.: A pamphlet published by The Thomas Alva Edison Foundation Institute for Development of Educational Activities, Inc., and the Johnson Foundation, 1972, pages 10-11.

6.   MacKinnon, Donald W. The study of the creative person. In Jerome Kagan (Ed.). *Creativity and Learning*. Boston: Beacon Press, 1967, pages 20-35.

7.   Barron, Frank. The disposition toward originality. In Calvin Taylor and Frank Barron (Eds.). *Scientific Creativity: Its Recognition and Development*. New York: Wiley and Sons, 1963.

8.   MacKinnon, Donald W. Personality correlates of creativity. In Mary Jane Aschner and Charles E. Bish (Eds.). *Productive Thinking in Education*. Washington D.C.: National Education Association, 1965, page 160.

9.   Barron, Frank. An eye more fantastical. In Gary A. Davis and Joseph A. Scott. *Training Creative Thinking*. New York: Holt, Rinehart and Winston, 1971, pages 181-193.

10. Taylor, Irving A. *A Theory of Creative Transactualization*. Buffalo, New York: Creative Education Foundation, Occasionsional Paper Number Eight, 1972.

11. Ferguson, Marilyn. *The Aquarian Conspiracy*. Los Angeles: J.P. Tarcher, 1980. See Also. Ornstein, Robert E. *The Psychology of Consciousness*. New York: Harcourt Brace, 1977.

12. Guilford, J. Traits of creativity. In J. Anderson (Ed.). *Creativity and Its Cultivation*. New York: Harper, 1959, pages 142-161.

13. Weil, Andrew. *The Natural Mind*. Boston: Houghton, Mifflin, 1973.

14. de Bono, Edward. *Lateral Thinking*. New York: Harper, 1972.

15. Koestler, Arthur. *The Act of Creation*. New York: MacMillan,1969.

16. Ornstein, Robert E. *The Psychology of Consciousness*. New York: Harcourt Brace, 1977, page 23.

17. Torrance, E. Paul. A longitudinal examination of the fourth grade slump in creativity. *Gifted Child Quarterly*. Vol. 12, No. 4, pages 195-199.

18. Gordon, Willian J.J. *Synectics*. New York: Collier Books, 1961, page 12.

19. Fabun, Don. *You and Creativity*. Beverly Hills, Calif.: Glencoe Press, 1971, page 5.

Chapter 6

1.   Osborn, Alex F. *Applied Imagination*. (Third edition). New York: Scibners, 1963. For reporting on Osborn's deferred judgment technique see also: Arici, H. Brainstorming as a way of facilitating creative thinking. *Dissertation Abstracts*, 1965, Vol. 25, No. 11, pages 6381-6382; Brilhart, J.K., and L.M.

Jochem. Effects of different patterns on outcomes of problem-solving discussion. *Journal of Applied Psychology*.1964, Vol. 48, No. 3, pages 175-179; Dunnette, M.D., and J. Campbell, and K. Jaastad. The effect of group participation on brainstorming effectiveness for two industrial samples. *Journal of Applied Psychology*. 1963, Vol. 47, No. 1, pages 30-37; Lindgren, H.C. and F. Lindgren. Brainstorming and orneriness as facilitators of creativity. *Psychological Reports*. 1965, Vol. 16, No. 2, pages 577-583; Parnes, S.J., and A. Meadow. Development of individual creative talent. C. W. Taylor and F. Barron (Eds.).*Scientific Creativity*. New York: John Wiley & Sons, 1963.

2. Vargiu, James. Creativity. *Synthesis*. Vol. 3, No. 4, pages 17-53.

3. Koestler, Arthur. *Janus*. New York: Vintage Books, 1978, and *The Act of Creation*. New York: MacMillan, 1969.

4. Gordon, William J.J. *Synectics*. New York: Collier Books, 1961.

5. Davis, Gary A. *Creativity Is Forever*. Cross Plains, Wis.: Badger Press, 1981, page 67.

6. Gordon, *Synectics*, page 49.

7. Whiting, C. S. *Creative Thinking*. New York: Reinhold, 1958.

8. de Bono, Edward. *Lateral Thinking*. New York: Harper, 1972.

9. Crawford, Robert P. The techniques of creative thinking. In G. A. Davis and J. A. Scott (Eds.). *Training Creative Thinking*. Huntington, New York: Drieger, 1978.

10. Allen, Myron S. *Morphological Creativity*. Englewood Cliffs, N.J.: Prentice-Hall, 1962.

11. Raudsepp, Eugene with George P. Hough, Jr. *Creative Growth Games*. New York: Jove Publications, 1977.

12. Adams, James L. *Conceptual Blockbusting*. New York: N. W. Norton, 1979.

13. de Bono, *Lateral Thinking*. See Also, *New Think*. New York: Avon Books, 1971.

Chapter 7

1. Koestler, Arthur. *Janus*. New York: Vintage Books, 1978, pages 127-128.

2. Hartman, Ann. Diagramatic assessment of family relationships. *Social Casework*. October 1978, pages 465-476.

3. Rico, Gabriele Lusser. *Writing The Natural Way*. Los Angeles: J. P. Tarcher, 1983.

4. Jung, C. G. The structure and dynamics of the psyche. In Gerhard Adler, Michael Fordham, William McGuire, and Herbert Read (Eds.). *The Collected Works of C. G. Jung*. Trans. by R.F.C. Hull. Bollinger Series XX. Vol 8. Princeton, N.J.: Princeton University Press, 1969.

5. Delbecq, André and Andrew Van de Ven. A group process model for problem identification and program planning. *Journal of Applied Behavioral Science*. July-August 1971, Vol. 7, pages 466-492.

6. Hall, John T. and Roger A. Dixon. Cybernetic sessions: a technique for gathering ideas. In *The 1974 Handbook For Group Facilitators*. La Jolla, Calif.: University Associates, 1974.

7.   Osborn, Alex F. *Applied Imagination* (Third Edition). New York: Scribners, 1963.

Chapter 8

1.   Pincus, Allen, and Anne Minahan. *Social Work Practice: Model and Method.* Itasca, Illinois: F. E. Peacock Publishers, 1973, pages 53-68.
2.   Compton, Beulah R. and Burt Galaway. *Social Work Processes* (Third Edition). Homewood, Illinois: The Dorsey Press, 1984, page 223.
3.   Ibid., page 226.
4.   Bennis, Warren, Kenneth Benne and Robert Chin. *The Planning of Change* (Second Edition). New York: Holt, Rinehart and Winston, 1969, page 152.
5.   Specht, Harry. Disruptive tactics. In R. Kramer and H. Specht (Eds.). *Readings in Community Organization Practice.* Englewood Cliffs, New Jersey: Prentice Hall, 1969, pages 372-386.
6.   Minahan, Anne. Social workers and oppressed people (editorial). *Social Work.* May 1981, Vol. 26, No. 3, pages 183-184.

Chapter 9

1.   Kirk, Stuart, and James Greenley. Denying or delivering services. *Social Work.* July 1974, Vol. 19, pages 443-444.
2.   Argyris, Chris, and Donald Schön. *Theory in Practice: Increasing Professional Effectiveness.* San Francisco: Jossey-Bass, Inc., 1974, pages 149-152.
3.   Ibid., page 150.
4.   Froland, Charles, Diane Pancoast, Nancy Chapman and Priscilla Kimboko. *Helping Networks and Human Services.* Beverly Hills: Sage Publications, 1981, page 169.
5.   Jones, Russell A. *Self-Fulfilling Prophecies.* Hillsdale, New Jersey: Lawrence Erlbaum, Publishers, 1977.
6.   Anonymous. Another sleepless night: a parent's viewpoint. *Social Work.* January 1973, pages 112-114.
7.   Pincus, Allen, and Anne Minahan. *Social Work Practice: Model and Method.* Itasca, Illinois: F. E. Peacock Publishers, 1973, page 104.
8.   Compton, Beulah R. and Burt Galaway. *Social Work Processes* (Third Edition). Homewood, Illinois: The Dorsey Press, 1984, page 357.

Chapter 10

1.   Cartwright, T.J. Problems, solutions and strategies: a contribution to the theory and practice of planning. *American Institute of Planners Journal.* May 1973, pages 179-187.
2.   Ibid., page 183
3   Pincus, Allen, and Anne Minahan. *Social Work Practice: Model and Method.* Itasca, Illinois: F. E. Peacock Publishers, 1973, page 131.
4.   Ibid., page 139.

5. Jones, Russel A. *Self-Fulfilling Prophecies*. Hillsdale, New Jersey: Lawrence Erlbaum, Publishers, 1977.

6. Tice, Louis. *New Age Thinking for Achieving Your Potential*. Seattle, Washington: The Pacific Institute, 1980.

7. Simons, Ronald L. and Stephen M. Aigner. *Practice Principles: A Problem-Solving Approach to Social Work*. New York: MacMillan Publishing Company, 1985, page 58.

8. Pincus and Minahan, *Social Work Practice*, page 118.

9. Simons and Aigner, *Practice Principles*, page 49.

10. Germain, Carel B. An ecological perspective in casework practice. *Social Casework*. June 1973, Vol. 54, pages 323-330.

11. Pincus and Minahan, *Social Work Practice*, page 121.

12. Simons and Aigner, *Practice Principles*, page 59.

13. Pincus and Minahan, *Social Work Practice*, page 131.

14. Bales, R. F., S. Cohen and S. Williamson. *Symlog: A System for the Multiple Level Observation of Groups*. New York: Free Press, 1980.

15. Kutner, Saul S. and Ruth D. Kirsch. Clinical applications of symlog: a graphic system of observing relationships. *Social Work*. November-December 1985, Vol. 30, No. 6, pages 497-503.

16. Watzlawick, Paul. A structured family interview. *Family Process*. September 1966, Vol. 5, pages 256-271; Minuchin, Salvador, and Braulio Montalvo. *An Approach for Diagnosis of the Low Socio-Economic Family*. Psychiatric Research Report 20, American Psychiatric Association, February 1966, pages 163-174.

17. Minuchin and Montalvo, *An Approach for Diagonsis*.

18. Pincus and Minahan, *Social Work Practice*, page 131.

19. Ibid., page 131.

20 Ibid., page 132.

21. Ibid., page 133.

22. Ibid., page 134-138.

23. Ibid., page 139.

24. Ibid., page 134.

Chapter 11

1. Vallee, Jacques. *The Network Revolution*. Berkeley: And/Or Press, Inc., 1982, page 46.

2. de Bono, Edward. *Lateral Thinking*. New York: Harper and Row, Publishers, 1970, page 27.

3. Hartman, Ann. Diagrammatic assessment of family relationships. *Social Casework*. October, 1978, Vol. 59, 465-476.

4. Delbecq, André and Andrew Van de Ven. A group process model for problem identification and program planning. *Journal of Applied Behavioral Science*. July-August 1971, Vol. 7, pages 466-492.

5. Rickards, Tudor. *Problem-Solving Through Creative Analysis*. Epping, Essex, Great Britain: Gower Press, 1974, page 7.

6. Nadler, Gerald. *Work Systems Design: The IDEALS Concept*. Homewood, Illinois: Richard D. Irwin, Inc., 1967.

7. This problem comes from Volekma, Roger J. *An Empirical Investigation of Problem Formulation and Problem-Purpose Expansion*. Doctoral Dissertation, University of Wisconsin, Madison, 1980.

8. Watzlawick, Paul, John Weakland and Richard Fisch. *Change: Principles of Problem Formation and Problem Resolution*. New York: W. W. Norton, 1974, page 104.

9. These solutions appear in Adams, James L. *Conceptual Blockbusting* (Second Edition). New York: W.W. Norton & Co., 1979, pages 26-29

Chapter 12

1. de Bono, Edward. *PO: Beyond Yes and No*. New York: Pelican Books, 1973, page 90.

2. Koberg, Don and Bagnall, Jim. *The Universal Traveler*. Los Altos, California: William Kaufmann, Inc., 1976, page 108.

3. Ibid., page 108.

4. Simons, Ronald L. and Stephen M. Aigner. *Practice Principles: A Problem-Solving Approach to Social Work*. New York: MacMillan Publishing Company, 1985, page 72.

5. Garvin, Charles D. and Brett A. Seabury. *Interpersonal Practice in Social Work*. Englewood Cliffs, N. J.: Prentice-Hall, 1984, page 181.

Chapter 13

1. Abramson, Julie. Six steps to effective referrals. In Harold Weissman, Irwin Epstein and Andrea Savage (Eds.). *Agency-Based Social Work*. Philadelphia: Temple University Press, 1983; Weissman, Andrew. Industrial social services: linkage technology. *Social Casework*. January 1976, Vol. 57, pages 50-54.

2. Weissman, Harold, Irwin Epstein and Andrea Savage. Chapter 5, Advocate. *Agency-Based Social Work*. Philadelphia: Temple University Press, 1983.

3. Golan, Naomi. Intervention in times of transition: sources and forms of help. *Social Casework*. May 1980, Vol. 61, pages 259-266; Green, James. *Cultural Awareness in the Human Services*. Englewood Cliffs, N. J.: Prentice-Hall, 1982.

4. Collins, Alice and Diane Pancoast. *Natural Helping Systems*. Washington D.C.: National Association of Social Workers, 1976; Miller, Pamela, A. Professional use of lay resources. *Social Work*. September-October 1985, Vol. 30, No. 5, pages 409-416; Whittaker, James K. and James Garbarino. *Social Support Networks*. New York: Aldine Publishing Company, 1983.

5. Delgado, Melvin and Denise Humm-Delgado. Natural support systems. *Social Work*. January 1982, Vol. 27, pages 83-90; Green, *Cultural Awareness*.

6. Froland, Charles, Diane Pancoast, Nancy Chapman and Priscilla Kimboko. *Helping Networks and Human Services*. Beverly Hills: Sage Publications, 1981.

7. Weissman, Harold, Irwin Epstein and Andrea Savage. Chapter 3, Case Manager. *Agency-Based Social Work*. Philadelphia: Temple University Press, 1983

8. Garvin, Charles D. and Brett A. Seabury. *Interpersonal Practice in Social Work*. Englewood Cliffs, N. J.: Prentice-Hall, 1984, page 211.

9. Froland, *Helping Networks*, pages 167-168.

10. Pincus, Allen, and Anne Minahan. *Social Work Practice: Model and Method*. Itasca, Illinois: F. E. Peacock Publishers, 1973, pages 204-219.

11. Garvin and Seabury, *Interpersonal Practice*, page 179.

12. Ibid., page 180.

13. Reid, William J. Test of a task-centered approach. *Social Work*. January 1975, Vol. 20, pages 3-9.

14. Simons, Ronald L. and Stephen M. Aigner. *Practice Principles: A Problem-Solving Approach to Social Work*. New York: MacMillan Publishing Company, 1985, page 85.

15. Klein, Donald. Some notes on the dynamics of resistance to change: the defender role. In W. Bennis, K. Benne and R. Chin (Eds.). *The Planning of Change* (Fourth Edition). New York: Holt, Rinehart and Winston, 1985.

16. Enright, John and Ron Estep. Metered counseling for the reluctant client. *Psychotherapy: Theory, Research and Practice*. Winter 1973, Vol. 10, No. 4, pages 305-307.

17. Trillin, Calvin. American Chronicles. *The New Yorker*. July 8, 1985, pages 31-45.

18. Brager, George and Stephen Holloway. *Changing Human Service Organizations*. New York: The Free Press, 1978; Resnick, Herman and Rino J. Patti. *Change From Within: Humanizing Social Welfare Organizations*. Philadelphia: Temple University Press, 1980; Weissman, Epstein and Savage, *Agency-Based Social Work*.

Chapter 14

1. Verify - from the Latin *verus* (true) plus *facere* (to make).

2. Harrison, Roger. Strategies for a new age. In W. Bennis, K. Benne and R. Chin (Eds.). *The Planning of Change* (Fourth Edition). New York: Holt, Rinehart and Winston, 1985, page 133.

3. Schön, Donald. Conversational planning. In W. Bennis, K. Benne and R. Chin. *The Planning of Change* (Fourth Edition). New York: Holt Rinehart and Winston, 1985, page 250.

4. This summary is adapted from Ibid., page 250-252.

5. Ibid., page 253.

6. Harrison, Strategies for a new age, page 134.

7. Ibid, page 135.

8. Guba, Egon G. and Yvonna Lincoln. *Effective Evaluation*. San Francisco: Jossey-Bass Publishers, 1981.

9. Kiresuk, Thomas J. and Robert Sherman. Goal attainment scaling. *Community Mental Health Journal*. 1968, Vol. 4, pages 443-453.

10. This discussion of field notes is based on Patton, Michael Quinn. *Qualitative Evaluation Methods*. Beverly Hills: Sage Publications, 1980, page 163.

11. Argyris, Chris, and Donald Schön. *Theory in Practice: Increasing Professional Effectiveness*. San Francisco: Jossey-Bass, Inc., 1974, page 41.

12. Miller, Sherod, Elam W. Nunnally and Daniel B. Wackman. *Alive and Aware*. Minneapolis: Interpersonal Communication Programs, Inc., 1975.

13. Dabbs, James M., Jr. Making things visible. In John Van Maanen, James Dabbs, Jr. and Robert Faulkner, *Varieties of Qualitative Research*. Beverly Hills: Sage Publications, 1982.

14. Guba and Lincoln, *Effective Evaluation*, page 101.

15. Spradley, James P. *The Ethnographic Interview*. New York: Holt, Rinehart and Winston, 1979, page 28-32.

16. See, for example, Guba and Lincoln, *Effective Evaluation*; Miles, Matthew B., and Michael A. Huberman. *Qualitative Data Analysis: A Sourcebook of New Methods*. Beverly Hills: Sage Publications, 1984; Patton, *Qualitative Evaluation Methods*; Patton, Michael Quinn. *Utilization Focused Evaluation*. Beverly Hills: Sage Publications, 1978; Spradley, *The Ethnographic Interview*.

17. Guba and Lincoln, *Effective Evaluation*; Patton, *Qualitative Evaluation Methods*; Patton, *Utilization Focused Evaluation*.

18. Schön, *Conversational Planning*, page 249.

19. Hugi, Rob and Dan A. Lewis. Therapeutic stations and the chronically treated mentally ill. *Social Service Review*. June 1981, Vol. 55, No. 2, pages 206-219.

20. Berry, Wendell. Solving for pattern: standards for a durable agriculture. *The New Farm*. January 1981, page 71.

21. Ibid., page 71.

22. Hemenway, Dan. Four pairs. *Whole Earth Review*. Fall 1985, No.48, pages 72-73.

23. Berry, Solving for pattern, page 72.

24. Hemenway, Four pairs, page 73.

25. Ibid., page 73.

Chapter 15

1. Harrison, Roger. Strategies for a new age. In Warren Bennis, Kenneth Benne an Robert Chin (Eds.). *The Planning of Change*(Fourth Edition). New York: Holt, Rinehart & Winston, 1985.

2. Ingalls, John D. *Human Energy*. Reading, Mass.: Addison-Wesley, 1976.

3. Freud, Sigmund, *A General Introduction to Psychoanalysis*. Garden City, New York: Permabooks, 1953.

4. Lewin, Kurt. *Resolving Social Conflicts: Selected Papers on Group Dynamics*. New York: Harper & Row, 1948.

5. Koestler, Arthur. *Janus*. New York: Vintage Books, 1978, pages 127-128.

6. Vargiu, James. Creativity. *Synthesis*. Vol. 3, No. 4, pages 17-53.

7. Naisbitt, John. *Megatrends*. New York: Warner Books, 1982.

8. Shank, Rober B. *The Cognitive Computer*. Reading, Mass.: Addison-Wesley, 1984, page 237.

9. Vallee, Jacques. *The Network Revolution*. Berkeley, Calif.: And/Or Press, 1982.

10. Stewart, Doug. Whatever happened to the electronic cottage? *Popular Computing*, July 1985, Vol. 4, No. 9, pages 65-67 and 132-135.

11. Hughes, Dave. The neighborhood ROM. *Whole Earth Review*. March 1985, No. 45, page 89.

12. Rifkin, Jeremy. *Entropy: A New World View*. New York: Bantam, 1981, page 139.

13. Reynolds, Bertha Capen. *Social Work and Social Living*. Washington D.C.: NASW, 1975, in forward, page viii.

References

Abramson, Julie. Six steps to effective referrals. In Harold Weissman, Irwin Epstein and Andrea Savage (Eds.). *Agency-Based Social Work*. Philadelphia: Temple University Press, 1983.

Adams, James L. *Conceptual Blockbusting* (Second Edition). New York: W.W. Norton & Co., 1979.

Allen, Myron S. *Morphological Creativity*. Englewood Cliffs, N.J.: Prentice-Hall, 1962.

Anonymous. Another sleepless night: a parent's viewpoint. *Social Work*. January 1973, pages 112-114.

Aptekar, Herbert H. Generalist practice and specialization in professional education. In D. S. Sanders, O. Kurren and J. Fischer (Eds.). *Fundamentals of Social Work Practice*. Belmont, California: Wadsworth Publishing Company, 1982.

Argyris, Chris, and Donald Schön. *Theory in Practice: Increasing Professional Effectiveness*. San Francisco: Jossey-Bass, 1974.

Bales, R. F., S. Cohen and S. Williamson. *Symlog: A System for the Multiple Level Observation of Groups*. New York: Free Press, 1980.

Barron, Frank. An eye more fantastical. In Gary A. Davis and Joseph A. Scott. *Training Creative Thinking*. New York: Holt, Rinehart and Winston, 1971, pages 181-193.

Barron, Frank. The disposition toward originality. In Calvin Taylor and Frank Barron (Eds.). *Scientific Creativity: Its Recognition and Development*. New York: Wiley and Sons, 1963.

Bartlett, Harriet M. *The Common Base of Social Work Practice*. New York: National Association of Social Workers, 1970.

Benedict, Ruth. Patterns of the good culture. *Psychology Today*. 1970, Vol. 4, No. 1, pages 53-55 and 74-77.

Bennis, Warren, Kenneth Benne and Robert Chin. *The Planning of Change* (Second Edition). New York: Holt, Rinehart and Winston, 1969.

Berry, Wendell. Solving for pattern: standards for a durable agriculture. *The New Farm*. January 1981, pages 70-72.

Bodner, Joan (Ed.). *Taking Charge of Our Lives*. New York: Harper and Row, 1985).

Boehm, Werner W. The nature of social work. *Social Work*. April 1958, Vol. 3, pages 10-19.

Brager, George and Stephen Holloway. *Changing Human Service Organizations*. New York: The Free Press, 1978.

Cartwright, T.J. Problems, solutions and strategies: a contribution to the theory and practice of planning. *American Institute of Planners Journal*. May 1973, pages 179-187.

Collins, Alice and Diane Pancoast. *Natural Helping Systems*. Washington D.C.: National Association of Social Workers, 1976.

Compton, Beulah R. and Burt Galaway. *Social Work Processes* (Third Edition). Homewood, Illinois: The Dorsey Press, 1984.

Council on Social Work Education. Curriculum Policy for the Master's Degree and Baccalaureate Degree Programs. In *Social Work Education*. New York: C.S.W.E., 1982.

Crawford, Robert P. The techniques of creative thinking. In G. A. Davis and J. A. Scott (Eds.). *Training Creative Thinking*. Huntington, New York: Drieger, 1978.

Dabbs, James M., Jr. Making things visible. In John Van Maanen, James M. Dabbs, Jr. and Robert Faulkner, *Varieties of Qualitative Research*. Beverly Hills: Sage Publications, 1982.

Davis, Gary A. *Creativity Is Forever*. Cross Plains, Wis.: Badger Press, 1981.

de Bono, Edward. *Lateral Thinking*. New York: Harper and Row, Publishers, 1970.

de Bono, Edward. *PO: Beyond Yes and No*. New York: Pelican Books, 1973.

Delbecq, André and Andrew Van de Ven. A group process model for problem identification and program planning. *Journal of Applied Behavioral Science*. July-August 1971, Vol. 7, pages 466-492.

Delgado, Melvin and Denise Humm-Delgado. Natural support systems. *Social Work*. January 1982, Vol. 27, pages 83-90.

Enright, John and Ron Estep. Metered counseling for the reluctant client. *Psychotherapy: Theory, Research and Practice*. Winter 1973, Vol. 10, No. 4, pages 305-307.

Fabun, Don. *You and Creativity*. Beverly Hills, Calif.: Glencoe Press, 1971.

Ferguson, Marilyn. *The Aquarian Conspiracy*. Los Angeles: J. P. Tarcher, 1980.

Freud, Sigmund, *A General Introduction to Psychoanalysis*. Garden City, New York: Permabooks, 1953.

Froland, Charles, Diane Pancoast, Nancy Chapman and Priscilla Kimboko. *Helping Networks and Human Services*. Beverly Hills: Sage Publications, 1981.

Fuller, R. Buckminster. *Synergetics*. New York: Macmillan, 1975.

Garvin, Charles D. and Brett A. Seabury. *Interpersonal Practice in Social Work*. Englewood Cliffs, N. J.: Prentice-Hall, 1984.

Germain, Carel B. An ecological perspective in casework practice. *Social Casework*. June 1973, Vol. 54, pages 323-330.

Golan, Naomi. Intervention in times of transition: sources and forms of help. *Social Casework*. May 1980, Vol. 61, pages 259-266.

Gordon, Willian J.J. *Synectics*. New York: Collier Books, 1961.

Green, James. *Cultural Awareness in the Human Services*. Englewood Cliffs, N. J.: Prentice-Hall, 1982.

Guba, Egon G. and Yvonna Lincoln. *Effective Evaluation*. San Francisco: Jossey-Bass Publishers, 1981.

Guilford, J. Traits of creativity. In J. Anderson (Ed.). *Creativity and Its Cultivation*. New York: Harper, 1959, pages 142-161.

Hall, John T. and Roger A. Dixon. Cybernetic sessions: a technique for gathering ideas. In *The 1974 Handbook For Group Facilitators*. La Jolla, Calif.: University Associates, 1974.

Harrison, Roger. Strategies for a new age. In W. Bennis, K. Benne and R. Chin (Eds.). *The Planning of Change* (Fourth Edition). New York: Holt, Rinehart and Winston, 1985.

Hartman, Ann. Diagrammatic assessment of family relationships. *Social Casework.* October 1978, Vol. 59, pages 465-476.

Hemenway, Dan. Four pairs. *Whole Earth Review.* Fall 1985, No.48, pages 72-73.

Hughes, Dave. The neighborhood ROM. *Whole Earth Review.* March 1985, No 45, page 89.

Hugi, Rob and Dan A. Lewis. Therapeutic stations and the chronically treated mentally ill. *Social Service Review.* June 1981, Vol. 55, No. 2, pages 206-219.

Ingalls, John D. *Human Energy.* Reading, Mass.: Addison-Wesley, 1976.

Irey, Karen. The social work generalist in a rural context: an ecological perspective. *Journal of Education for Social Work.* Fall 1980, Vol. 16, pages 36-42.

Jones, Russel A. *Self-Fulfilling Prophecies.* Hillsdale, New Jersey: Lawrence Erlbaum, Publishers, 1977.

Jung, C. G. The structure and dynamics of the psyche. In Gerhard Adler, Michael Fordham, William McGuire, and Herbert Read (Eds.). *The Collected Works of C. G. Jung.* Trans. by R.F.C. Hull. Bollinger Series XX. Vol. 8. Princeton, N.J.: Princeton University Press, 1969.

Kiresuk, Thomas J. and Robert Sherman. Goal attainment scaling. *Community Mental Health Journal.* 1968, Vol. 4, pages 443-453.

Kirk, Stuart, and James Greenley. Denying or delivering services. *Social Work.* July 1974, Vol. 19, pages 439-447.

Klein, Donald. Some notes on the dynamics of resistance to change: the defender role. In W. Bennis, K. Benne and R. Chin (Eds.). *The Planning of Change* (Fourth Edition). New York: Holt, Rinehart and Winston, 1985.

Koberg, Don and Bagnall, Jim. *The Universal Traveler.* Los Altos, California: William Kaufmann, Inc., 1976.

Koestler, Arthur. *Janus.* New York: Vintage Books, 1978.

Koestler, Arthur. *The Act of Creation.* New York: MacMillan, 1969.

Kutner, Saul S. and Ruth D. Kirsch. Clinical applications of symlog: a graphic system of observing relationships. *Social Work.* November-December 1985, Vol. 30, No. 6, pages 497-503.

Lenowitz, James M. The "ah ha!" experience. In *Creativity: the State of the Art.* Racine, Wis.: A pamphlet published by The Thomas Alva Edison Foundation Institute for Development of Educational Activities, Inc., and the Johnson Foundation, 1972, pages 10-11.

Lewin, Kurt. *Resolving Social Conflicts: Selected Papers on Group Dynamics.* New York: Harper & Row, 1948.

Lipnack, Jessica and Jeffrey Stamps. *Networking.* New York: Doubleday and Company, Inc., 1982.

MacKinnon, Donald W. Personality correlates of creativity. In Mary Jane Aschner and Charles E. Bish (Eds.). *Productive Thinking in Education.* Washington D.C.: National Education Association, 1965.

MacKinnon, Donald W. The study of the creative person. In Jerome Kagan (Ed.). *Creativity and Learning.* Boston: Beacon Press, 1967, pages 20-35.

Maslow, Abraham H. *The Farther Reaches of Human Nature*. New York: Viking Press, 1971.

Meyer, Carol H. *Clinical Social Work in the Eco-Systems Perspective*. New York: Columbia University Press, 1983.

Miles, Matthew B., and Michael A. Huberman. *Qualitative Data Analysis: A Sourcebook of New Methods*. Beverly Hills: Sage Publications, 1984.

Miller, Pamela, A. Professional use of lay resources. *Social Work*. September-October 1985, Vol. 30, No. 5, pages 409-416.

Miller, Sherod, Elam W. Nunnally and Daniel B. Wackman. *Alive and Aware*. Minneapolis: Interpersonal Communication Programs, Inc., 1975.

Minahan, Anne. Social workers and oppressed people (editorial). *Social Work*. May 1981, Vol. 26, No.3, page 183.

Minuchin, Salvador, and Braulio Montalvo. *An Approach for Diagnosis of the Low Socio-Economic Family*. Psychiatric Research Report 20, American Psychiatric Association, February 1966, pages 163-174.

Nadler, Gerald. *Work Systems Design: The IDEALS Concept*. Homewood, Illinois: Richard D. Irwin, Inc., 1967.

Naisbitt, John. *Megatrends*. New York: Warner Books, 1982.

National Association of Social Work. Working definition of social work practice. *Social Work*. April 1958, Vol. 3, No. 2.

National Association of Social Work. Working statement on the purpose of social work. *Social Work*. January, 1981, Vol. 26, No. 1, page 6.

National Association of Social Workers. *Standards for Social Service Manpower*. Washington, D.C.: National Association of Social Workers, 1973.

Noble, Daniel. Creativity and the changing environment. In *Creativity: the State of the Art*. Racine, Wis.: A pamphlet published by The Thomas Alva Edison Foundation Institute for Development of Educational Activities, Inc., and the Johnson Foundation, 1972.

Ornstein, Robert E. *The Psychology of Consciousness*. New York: Harcourt Brace, 1977.

Osborn, Alex F. *Applied Imagination*. (Third edition). New York: Scibners, 1963.

Patton, Michael Quinn. *Utilization Focused Evaluation*. Beverly Hills: Sage Publications, 1978.

Patton, Michael Quinn. *Qualitative Evaluation Methods*. Beverly Hills: Sage Publications, 1980.

Pincus, Allen, and Anne Minahan. *Social Work Practice: Model and Method*. Itasca, Illinois: F. E. Peacock Publishers, 1973.

Raudsepp, Eugene with George P. Hough, Jr. *Creative Growth Games*. New York: Jove Publications, 1977.

Raudsepp, Eugene. *Managing Creative Scientists and Engineers*. New York: MacMillan, 1963.

Reid, William J. Test of a task-centered approach. *Social Work*. January 1975, Vol. 20, No. 1, pages 3-9.

Resnick, Herman and Rino J. Patti. *Change From Within: Humanizing Social Welfare Organizations*. Philadelphia: Temple University Press, 1980.

Reynolds, Bertha Capen. *Social Work and Social Living*. Washington D.C.: NASW, 1975.

Rico, Gabriele Lusser. *Writing The Natural Way*. Los Angeles: J. P. Tarcher, 1983.

Rickards, Tudor. *Problem-Solving Through Creative Analysis*. Epping, Essex, Great Britain: Gower Press, 1974.

Rifkin, Jeremy. *Entropy: A New World View*. New York: Bantam, 1981.

Sarason, Seymour B., and Elizabeth Lorentz. *The Challange of the Resource Exchange Network*. San Francisco: Jossey-Bass Publishing, 1979.

Schön, Donald. Conversational planning. In W. Bennis, K. Benne and R. Chin. *The Planning of Change* (Fourth Edition). New York: Holt, Rinehart and Winston, 1985.

Schumacher, E.F. *Small is Beautiful*. New York: Harper & Row, 1973.

Schwartz, William. Private troubles and public issues: one social work job or two? *The Social Welfare Forum, 1969*. New York: Columbia University Press, 1969.

Shank, Roger B. *The Cognitive Computer*. Reading, Mass.: Addison-Wesley, 1984.

Simons, Ronald L. and Stephen M. Aigner. *Practice Principles: A Problem-Solving Approach to Social Work*. New York: MacMillan Publishing Company, 1985.

Specht, Harry. Disruptive tactics. In R. Kramer and H. Specht (Eds.). *Readings in Community Organization Practice*. Englewood Cliffs, New Jersey: Prentice Hall, 1969, pages 372-386.

Spradley, James P. *The Ethnographic Interview*. New York: Holt, Rinehart and Winston, 1979.

Stewart, Doug. Whatever happened to the electronic cottage? *Popular Computing*. July 1985, Vol. 4, No. 9, pages 65-67 and 132-135.

Taylor, Irving A. *A Theory of Creative Transactualization*. Buffalo, New York: Creative Education Foundation, Occasional Paper Number Eight, 1972.

Tice, Louis. *New Age Thinking for Achieving Your Potential*. Seattle, Washington: The Pacific Institute, 1980.

Tillich, Paul. Critique and justification of utopia. In Frank E. Manuel, *Utopias and Utopian Thought*. Boston: Beacon Press, 1971.

Torrance, E. Paul. A longitudinal examination of the fourth grade slump in creativity. *Gifted Child Quarterly*. Vol. 12, No. 4, pages 195-199.

Trillin, Calvin. American Chronicles. *The New Yorker*. July 8, 1985, pages 31-45.

United States Office of Consumer Affairs. *People Power: What Communities Are Doing to Counter Inflation*. 1982.

Vallee, Jacques. *The Network Revolution*. Berkeley: And/Or Press, Inc., 1982.

Vargiu, James. Creativity. *Synthesis*. Vol. 3, No. 4, pages 17-53.

Vigilante, Joseph L. Between values and science: education for the profession during a moral crisis or is proof truth? In Daniel S. Sanders, Oscar Kurren, Joel Fischer, *Fundamentals of Social Work Practice*. Belmont, Calif.: Wadsworth, 1982.

Volekma, Roger J. *An Empiracal Investigation of Problem Formulation and Problem-Purpose Expansion*. Doctoral Dissertation, University of Wisconsin, Madison, 1980.

Watzlawick, Paul. A structured family interview. *Family Process*. September 1966, Vol. 5, pages 256-271.

Watzlawick, Paul, John Weakland and Richard Fisch. *Change: Principles of Problem Formulation and Problem Resolution.* New York: W. W. Norton, 1974.

Weil, Andrew. *The Natural Mind.* Boston: Houghton, Mifflin, 1973.

Weissman, Andrew. Industrial social services: linkage technology. *Social Casework.* January 1976, Vol. 57, pages 50-54.

Weissman, Harold, Irwin Epstein and Andrea Savage. *Agency-Based Social Work.* Philadelphia: Temple University Press, 1983.

Whiting, C. S. *Creative Thinking.* New York: Reinhold, 1958.

Whittaker, James K. and James Garbarino. *Social Support Networks.* New York: Aldine Publishing Company, 1983.

Index

Book Production Notes

Composition: Text and graphics by IBM Personal Computer and Apple Macintosh.

Camera copy: Apple LaserWriter.

Type & Size: Times Roman, 12 pt. on 14.

Paper: Text, 50# Lakewood White, 428 P.P.I.
Cover, 12 pt., C1S.

Ink: Text, standard black.
Cover, 2 color PMS with Duro Sheen.

Printing: Cameron belt press, BookCrafters, Inc., Chelsea, Michigan.
Account executive, Stacy Hosler.

Binding: Perfect (adhesive).

Micamar Publishing is owned and operated by Michael Heus and Allen Pincus.

We have more materials in the works. First on the list is tentatively titled, *The Creative Generalist: A Guide to Resources*. If you would like to be on our mailing list for notices on this and other developments, please write to us at:

Micamar Publishing
P. O. Box 56
Barneveld, WI 53507

Please include the following information. (You may copy this form if you'd rather leave the book intact.)

Please put me on the creative generalist mailing list:

Name: _____

Address: _____

City: _____ State: _____ Zip: _____

Include any comments on the book, your needs, interests, and so on: